Education for Wicked Problems and the Reconciliation of Opposites

The recognition and reconciliation of 'opposites' lies at the heart of our most personal and global problems and is arguably one of the most neglected developmental tasks of Western education. Such problems are 'wicked' in the sense that they involve real-life decisions that have to be made in rapidly changing contexts involving irreducible tensions and paradoxes. By exploring our human tendency to bifurcate the universe, *Education for Wicked Problems and the Reconciliation of Opposites* proposes a way to recognise and (re)solve some of our most wicked problems.

Applying an original theory of bi-relational development to wicked problems, Adam proposes that our everyday ways of knowing and being can be powerfully located and understood in terms of the *creation, emergence, opposition, convergence, collapse* and *transposition* of dyadic constituents such as nature/culture, conservative/liberal and spirit/matter. He uses this approach to frame key debates in and across domains of knowledge and to offer new perspectives on three of the most profound and related problems of the twenty-first century: globalisation, sustainability and secularisation.

This book is a comprehensive study of dyads and dyadic relationships and provides a multidisciplinary and original approach to human development in the face of wicked problems. It will be of great interest to students and academics in education and psychosocial development as well as professionals across a range of fields looking for new ways to recognise and (re)solve the wicked problems that characterise their professions.

Raoul J. Adam is an Adjunct Senior Lecturer in the College of Arts, Society and Education at James Cook University, Australia. He gained a PhD in Cultural-Cognitive Development from the University of Queensland in 2008 and has since lectured and researched on the cognitive-epistemic dimension of complex social problems. His lecturing was recognised by a National Citation for Teaching and Learning in 2010 and his research was supported by a fellowship with The Cairns Institute in 2014. *Education for Wicked Problems and the Reconciliation of Opposites* is his first book.

Education for Wicked Problems and the Reconciliation of Opposites

A theory of bi-relational development

Raoul J. Adam

LONDON AND NEW YORK

First published 2016
by Routledge
2 Park Square, Milton Park, Abingdon, Oxon OX14 4RN

and by Routledge
711 Third Avenue, New York, NY 10017

Routledge is an imprint of the Taylor & Francis Group, an informa business

© 2016 Raoul J. Adam

The right of Raoul J. Adam to be identified as author of this work
has been asserted by him/her in accordance with sections 77 and
78 of the Copyright, Designs and Patents Act 1988.

All rights reserved. No part of this book may be reprinted or
reproduced or utilised in any form or by any electronic, mechanical,
or other means, now known or hereafter invented, including
photocopying and recording, or in any information storage or
retrieval system, without permission in writing from the publishers.

Product or corporate names may be trademarks or registered
trademarks, and are used only for identification and explanation
without intent to infringe.

Trademark notice: Product or corporate names may be trademarks
or registered trademarks, and are used only for identification and
explanation without intent to infringe.

British Library Cataloguing in Publication Data
A catalogue record for this book is available from the British
Library

Library of Congress Cataloging in Publication Data
Names: Adam, Raoul J., author. Title: Education for wicked
problems and the reconciliation of opposites: a theory of
bi-relational development/Raoul J. Adam. Description:
Abingdon, Oxon; New York, NY: Routledge is an imprint
of the Taylor & Francis Group, an Informa Business, [2016]
Identifiers: LCCN 2015037002 | ISBN 9781138962859 |
ISBN 9781315659152 Subjects: LCSH: Opposition, Theory of. |
Polarity (Philosophy) | Dialectic. | Reconciliation. | Cognition.
Classification: LCC BF455.A34 2016 | DDC 153.4/3–dc23LC
record available at http://lccn.loc.gov/2015037002

ISBN: 978-1-138-96285-9 (hbk)
ISBN: 978-1-315-65915-2 (ebk)

Typeset in Bembo
by Sunrise Setting Ltd, Paignton, UK

For my teachers who are students and my students who are teachers

Life hangs in the balance but rarely in the middle.

Contents

List of illustrations	viii
Acknowledgements	ix
Credits	x

PART I
Theory — 1

1	Wicked problems and the reconciliation of opposites	3
2	Wicked problems and the recognition of opposites	20
3	The origins and classification of dyads	55
4	A theoretical background to bi-relational development	80
5	A theory of Bi-relational Development (BirD)	116

PART 2
Illustrations — 151

6	Illustrations of bi-relational development in life narratives	153
7	Bi-relational development and wicked socio-cultural problems	184
8	Bi-relational development and wicked socio-ecological problems	198
9	Bi-relational development and wicked socio-religious problems	214

PART 3
Applications — 231

10	General applications of bi-relational development in education	233
11	Narrative explorations of bi-relational development in education	250
12	Conclusion and final reflections on bi-relational development	275

Index	281

Illustrations

Figures

3.1	Visual representation of orthogonal and isomorphic dyads	67
3.2	Development of dyadic constituents retrospectively perceived	70
3.3	Bi-relational interactions between individual and group dispositions	72
5.1	A visual representation of Bi-relational Development (BirD)	117
5.2	A representation of bi-relational positions over time	138
5.3	The brightness illusion	145
5.4	Rabbit or duck?	147
10.1	The Cartesian See-saw (CSS)	242

Tables

1.1	Illustrative list of dyads	5
3.1	Domain-specific and domain-general dyads	76
4.1	A general comparison of BirD and related theories	101
5.1	Symbolic representation of Bi-relational Development (BirD)	119
8.1	Examples of dyads in socio-ecological literature	201
9.1	A symbolic representation of the relationship between faith (F) and reason (R)	218

Acknowledgements

No author is an island. The expression of gratitude to those who have personally encouraged and influenced the writing of this book seems especially important given its explorations of the deep entanglement between self and other. Therefore, in no particular order, I would like to acknowledge my colleagues, mainly fellow teachers and academics, who over the past two decades have willingly discussed and debated the ideas that I present in the following pages. To Eric Wilson and Professor Colin Lankshear – who mentored a young academic to appreciate the school of life and the life of a school. To Dr Cliff Jackson, Dr Philemon Chigeza, Miriam Torzillo, Dr Snowy Evans, Associate Professor Hilary Whitehouse, Dr Pauline Taylor, Dr Paul Kebble and Peter Bachelor – for our lunchtimes together spent playing down the rabbit hole – arguably, such serious humour kept me sane. To our inimitable receptionist, Wendy Cahill, for not letting us stay down the rabbit hole for too long. To Professors Bob Stevenson, Komla Tsey and Neil Anderson – for your encouragement and guidance in related projects. To my postgraduate students, Ellen Field, Jen Nicholls, Melanie Miller, Mary Williams, Aimee Watkins, Leo Pearman, Jennifer Yin Foo, Jacqueline Rooks and Rudolf Kotsch – for many supervisory meetings that informed my own ideas as much as your own. To the many undergraduate students who participated in research and robustly discussed some of the key concepts in lectures and tutorials – this lecturer learned a lot from you. And to the generous participants in the studies that have informed this book – I hope to have valued your experiences and reflected deeply on your insights. Also to Omid Haj Hashemi and Gill Cowden for their administrative support. Collectively, these individuals have confirmed, challenged and changed my ways of thinking about and communicating the ideas in this book.

I have also been blessed with a loving and insightful wife whose practical encouragement speaks louder than words and whose words always have the quality of wisdom. Also to my mother, who has patiently followed my journey into *two* and whose own scholarly journey, while different to my own, has better shown the past, present and future possibilities of my own ways of knowing and being. Finally, to my two young children, whose frequent visits to Daddy's office for 'merry-go-round-office-chair-rides' have made for a book more slowly written but, for me at least, more worth the writing.

Credits

Parts of this book have appeared previously, in considerably altered form, in the following publications: *Crossroads: An Interdisciplinary Journal for the Study of History, Philosophy, Religion, and Classics* ('Towards a synthesis of cultural and cognitive perspectives on fundamentalism', *1*(2), 2007); *Archive for the Psychology of Religion / Archiv für Religionpsychologie* ('Relating faith development and religious styles: Reflections in light of apostasy from religious fundamentalism', *30*(1), 2008); *Spirituality in Australia: Directions and applications* ('Losing my religion: Religious development and the dynamics of apostasy', *2*, 2009); *The International Journal for the Study of Spirituality and Society* ('An epistemic analysis of religious fundamentalism', *1*(1), 2011); *Journal of Learning Design* ('Bi-relational design: A brief introduction and illustration', *8*(1), 2015); and *Australian Teacher Educators Association (ATEA) annual conference proceedings* ('Engaging the epistemic dimension of preservice teachers' identity: A pedagogical tool', 2011).

Part I

Theory

Chapter 1

Wicked problems and the reconciliation of opposites

The recognition and reconciliation of 'opposites' lies at the heart of our most personal and global wicked problems and is perhaps the most neglected developmental task of Western education. Somewhere on this planet, at this very moment, there is an expectant couple contemplating how best to bring a child into the world (traditional/alternative), to raise it (permissive/authoritarian) and to educate it (learner-centred/teacher-centred). There is a physician considering how to treat a young woman with debilitating anxiety (mind/body). There is a businessman waiting for a train near a beggar with an outstretched hand wondering whether charity is part of the solution or part of the problem of poverty (dependence/independence). There is a young man in a prison cell reflecting on the cause of his crime (nature/nurture) and a judge deciding his sentence (punishment/rehabilitation). There is a conservative politician campaigning for war and a liberal politician campaigning for peace (war/peace, conservative/liberal). There is a group of loggers preparing to clear a forest and a group of activists who have chained themselves to its trees (develop/conserve). There is a cleric who is lamenting a faithless world and a scientist who is celebrating it (faith/reason; spirit/matter). Almost by definition, life's wickedest problems and solutions involve the expression and reconciliation of 'opposites'.

Many readers will be familiar with such pairings (i.e. *dyads*) and polarities. Rightly so, some readers will question the implicit stereotypes. Could not the scientist lament a godless world and the cleric appeal to reason? Could not the physician heal the body through the mind? Could not the conservative politician advocate for peace and the liberal politician advocate for a just war? Could not a young man's nature be his ancestors' nurture and his punishment his rehabilitation? Why associate the masculine with criminality and the feminine with anxiety? My premise is that the ways we know and live in relation to such dyads is profoundly important to the way we recognise and (re)solve wicked problems. Our ability to reconcile opposites is a developmental task that demands serious attention, especially from educators. Of course, the task is nothing new. However, the recognition and reconciliation of apparent opposites in the modern world (e.g. unity/diversity; faith/reason; develop/conserve) is more globally consequential and communicable than ever before.

4 Theory

Accordingly, this book introduces a bi-relational (i.e. *relations between two*) approach to wicked problems that I have, with pun on wings intended, called BirD (i.e. **Bi-r**elational **D**evelopment). BirD is an attempt to map out some of our archetypal ways of knowing and being in relation to the dyads that identify our most pressing concerns. It is a representation of human development that spans from our first divisions of knowledge, through its binary oppositions, and on to our final attempts to put it back together. Such developments have much to do with the ways we recognise and (re)solve wicked problems.

A 'wicked problem' (Rittel and Webber, 1973) has no definitive formulation, no immediate or ultimate test of solution, no clear contextual delineation and is open only to (re)solving rather than final objective solutions. The concept is sometimes used interchangeably with 'ill-structured problems' (King and Kitchener, 2002; Mitroff *et al.*, 2004), 'messes' (Ackoff, 1993), and 'social messes' (Horn, 2004). King and Kitchener (2002) describe 'ill-structured problems' as those about which 'reasonable people reasonably disagree' (p. 37). The type of wicked problems I hope to identify in this book could be known more specifically as *entangled problems*, which arise at the interface of interdependent polarities. They are 'wicked' in the sense that this interface is contextually dynamic and problems must be (re)solved in context rather than solved once and for all. Such problems are perplexing; they involve paradox, dialectic and necessary tensions. There are hints and traces of the reconciliation of opposites in the literature on wicked problems. For example, in *Tackling Wicked Problems through the Transdisciplinary Imagination* Brown *et al.* (2010) write: 'In traditional research, a paradox is treated as a pair of opposites. In an open inquiry, the pairs of opposites are treated as complementary and provide a useful indicator of the heart of an issue' (p. 63). However, I am unaware of any comprehensive treatments that explore the development of such bi-relational logics in the approach to wicked problems.

The bi-relational ways we know and live in relation to wicked problems are not just academic concerns. The sample dyads in Table 1.1 relate to everyday struggles in real-world contexts. Our attempt to coordinate them is what makes us collectively human and individually and culturally diverse.

The ways we recognise and navigate between dyadic poles can see us deeply divided over the ways to raise our children (attachment/independence) and to educate them (teacher-centred/learner-centred), the ways to improve our health (natural/synthetic), run our economies (capitalist/communist), manage the planet (conservation/development), engage with nature (nature/culture), understand our histories (mythos/logos), organise our cultures (local/global), make our ultimate meanings (matter/spirit) and conceptualise our existence (birth/death). Of course, the act of living means that 'we have to draw the line somewhere' amid the wicked problems we face. The educative rationale for a bi-relational approach to wicked problems is simply that these lines can be drawn more effectively with a deeper understanding of what it is they divide.

Table 1.1 Illustrative list of dyads

Subjective/Objective	Sacred/Profane	Science/Art
Relative/Absolute	Attraction/Repulsion	Produce/Consume
Empirical/Rational	Theory/Practice	Common/Rare
Change/Stability	Complex/Simple	Formal/Casual
A posteriori/A priori	Nature/Nurture (Culture)	Explicit/Implicit
Faith/Reason	Progressive/Conventional	Cognitive/Affective
Mind/Body	Heteronymous/Homogenous	Create/Destroy
Collective/Individual	Intrinsic/Extrinsic	Innovate/Replicate
Intuitive/Rational	Descriptive/Prescriptive	Rich/Poor
Everything/Nothing	Freedom/Control	Competitive/Collaborative
Perception/Reality	Holistic/Reductive	Give/Take
Symbolic/Literal	Future/Past	General/Particular
Mythos/Logos	Chaos/Order	Love/Hate
Spirit/Matter	Justice/Mercy	Success/Failure
Synthetic/Analytic	Quality/Quantity	Pleasure/Pain
Autonomous/Dependent	Passive/Active	Defend/Attack
Immanent/Transcendent	Theism/Atheism	Agree/Oppose
Isolated/Integrated	Hierarchical/Egalitarian	Hope/Despair
Divergent/Convergent	Teach/Learn	Positive/Negative
Expansive/Reductive	Deficit/Surplus	Conflict/Peace
Abstract/Concrete	Supply/Demand	Left/Right
Self/Other	Certainty/Doubt	Natural/Synthetic
Liberal/Conservative	Similar/Different	Capitalist/Communist
Birth/Death	Masculine/Feminine	Local/Global

The preceding list is illustrative rather than exhaustive and contains structurally different types of dyads that I discuss in Chapter 3. The list is not static and fixed; rather, it is an illustrative representation of dyads from a range of contexts and domains of knowledge. The meanings of these dyads shift and change over time and in different contexts but I argue that there is currently and cross-contextually enough stability and familiarity to make them worthy topics for discussion. Accordingly, this book explores dyadic structures and relationships as they appear in the context of wicked problems. It offers an analytical framework (i.e. BirD) to map the dyads, dyadic relationships, developments and dynamics that give structure and content to our most wicked problems. And this, so that we may be more masters over, rather than mastered by, our ability to bifurcate the *uni*verse.

Dyads and dyadic relationships

In some ways, the possibly dense analysis that follows is but a complex elaboration of the simple insight that socio-cultural dyads require the same coordination and development of dexterity in the (re)solution of wicked problems as hands, eyes and feet in the resolution of physical problems. I argue that some

6 Theory

aspect of our minds is as symmetrically bifurcated as our hands, eyes and feet. This is not necessarily an optimal adaptation. Indeed, we have had a little less evolutionary time to coordinate our bifurcated minds or to evolve out of them altogether than we have had to coordinate our hands, eyes and feet, which at least are more immediately apparent than their cognitive-epistemic equivalents. However, I am purposefully slower than others have been to dismiss the bifurcation of the mind as *just* child's play. Rather, like hands, feet and eyes the bifurcated mind can enable dexterous navigation of wickedly complex mental terrains. The mental coordination of dyadic constituents or the 'reconciliation of opposites', like the physical coordination of hands, eyes and feet, is a definitive task of human development.

The ubiquity of such dyads (e.g. conservative/liberal) and dyadic relationships (e.g. binary oppositional, complementary and unitary) across almost all domains of knowledge (e.g. politics, philosophy and science) makes for a topic worthy of attention. As C. G. Jung (1991) surmised, 'The idea of the pairs of opposites is as old as the world' (p. 72). These dyads and dyadic relationships are not *just* abstract or metaphysical concerns and constructions; rather, they have concrete expressions in everyday lives. Dyads or polarities allow us to orientate ourselves – to move, to act, to choose, to know and to *be* – within the most mundane and profound domains of life. We can be taller or shorter, faster or slower, happier or sadder, for better or worse. Dyads allow us to locate our ways of knowing (i.e. epistemologies) and being (i.e. ontologies) in relation to the knowing and being of others. Dyads allow us *to be* and *to belong* in relation to the being and belonging of others. We can be apart or together, in love or in hate, included or excluded, conservative or liberal and structured or spontaneous. Dyads are enablers of difference and decision that make *knowing* powerful and *being* meaningful. We can give or take, create or destroy, analyse or synthesise and let go or hold on. Finally, we can relate dyadic constituents through opposition, complement, dialectic, negation, union and paradox. These *dyadic relationships* both create and reflect the worlds we live in, the meanings and values we make and the wicked problems and challenges we face. Dyadic relationships provide a structure for understanding the problems and challenges that give meaning to our individual and social ways of being and knowing – what I term *onto-epistemological developments*. Accordingly, my elaborative project is to sketch out some bi-relational locations and dynamics – much like a cartographer plots lines of longitude and latitude between poles – to help identify and navigate some of our most complex human terrains and wicked problems.

Of course, one cannot talk meaningfully about *two* (i.e. a dyad) without locating it among discussions of zero, one, three and infinity. Accordingly, the aim of this book is to explicate and engage an existential riddle at the core of human development:

> *What becomes one*
> *Which then becomes two*

Which then becomes something
That is often thought of
And may well be fought of
As Zero
Or One
Or Two
Or Three
Or even by some
As In-fin-ity?

(Note that I have used capitalisation to emphasise a more deleveoped or encompassing way of knowing a concept, e.g. *One* rather than *one*.) Riddle-solving is, of course, a ridiculously serious business, and I think it is fair to say that nihilists, monists, dualists, triadists, multiplists and infinitarians have contested their solutions to this wicked problem as much with the sword as with the stylus since knowing and being began. Indeed, such contestations are as modern as they are ancient.

Twenty-two centuries ago the Eastern philosopher Lao Tzu grappled with the number of reality:

One produces two
Two produce three
Three produce myriad things

(2006, Ch. 42)

In the fifteenth century, German philosopher Nicholas Cusa examined the coincidence of opposites, which he coined *coincidentia oppositorum*. In the last century, Jung appropriated the same term and observed, 'One is not a number; the first number is two, and with it multiplicity and reality begin' (1970, p. 462). Early in our own century, neuroscientists examined the neurobiological correlates of the experience of 'oneness' and posited the existence of a 'binary operator' in the left inferior parietal lobe of the human brain (Newberg *et al.*, 2001). And, physicists, mathematicians and cosmologists continue to speculate on the nature of *nothing* (Battersby, 2013; Greene, 2004; Stewart, 2013). Thus, in the present as in the past, we recognise and grapple with the bifurcations and binary oppositions that characterise our ways of knowing and influence our ways of being. And, in the present as in the past, we occasionally glimpse the *oneness* that makes this *twoness* possible. But how are we to understand and relate such numerical metaphors in the context of human development and everyday wicked problems?

Dyads are ubiquitous. They permeate our vocabularies and discourses and frame the worlds we know and live in. For example, we orientate ourselves with dyads in our most mundane encounters with the spatial (left/right) and temporal worlds (past/future) and in our most intimate human relationships (love/hate; trust/caution). We orientate ourselves with dyads in relation to law (anarchy/order; justice/mercy), cultural policy (inclusion/exclusion; unity/diversity)

8 Theory

and political persuasion (conservative/liberal; freedom/control; autocracy/democracy). We orientate ourselves with dyads in professions such as medicine (mind/body; therapeutic/pharmacological), psychology (subjective/objective) and education (transmission/discovery). In philosophical encounters we orientate and identify ourselves with dyads (freewill/determinism; a posteriori/a priori; relative/absolute) and in theological and existential encounters, too (mythos/logos; faith/reason). Then there are the dyads that perhaps most define us in the twenty-first century (global/local; ecological/technological; nature/culture; natural/artificial; spirit/matter; conservation/development). And, through all of these mundane encounters with information and sophisticated pursuits of knowledge and wisdom, we continue to orientate ourselves with perennial dyads that give us place and purpose in the universe (birth/death; good/evil; hope/despair).

Likewise, dyadic *relationships* are ubiquitous. They appear in our dialogues as complements and in our diatribes as binary oppositions. In a plain sense, dyadic relationships appear as aphorisms, such as 'thinking in black and white', seeing the 'shades of grey', being 'one-eyed', 'sitting on the fence', 'having a foot in both camps', 'having a bet both ways', 'hanging in the balance' and 'walking a fine line'. We find relationships between dyadic constituents like general/particular expressed through aphorisms like 'can't see the wood for the trees' and 'the truth is in the detail'. The individual/collective dyad is expressed through aphorisms like 'too many cooks spoil the broth' and 'many hands make light work'. The unity/diversity dyad is expressed through aphorisms like 'divide and conquer', 'all for one and one for all' and 'unity in diversity'. Some of these relationships call us to separate and value one *against* the other. These relationships are binary oppositional. Others call us to synthesise one *with* the other. These relationships are dialectical. Still others call us to value the one *and* the other, even in opposition or apparent contradiction. These relationships are paradoxical.

Some commentators see the human predilection for dyadic thought, especially in its binary oppositional form, as being the source of much wickedness more literally understood. Exclusively *binary* oppositions between male and female, black and white, rich and poor and young and old have riven lives and societies from antiquity. Likewise, exclusively binary oppositions between nature and culture and matter and spirit have alienated many of us from our own planet and the possibility of purposeful existence. The onto-epistemological challenge is to identify and conceptualise life's wicked problems in a way that does not exacerbate them by forcing them into exclusively binary oppositional solutions or neglecting them altogether on the grounds that they have no solutions or (re)solvability at all. Exclusively binary oppositional relationships (i.e. either/or) can constrain and contain us, causing opposition, enmity and conflict, blinding us rather than binding us to the unity and continuity of the very thing we have divided. When infinite shades are forced into black or white, when acute degrees of difference are lost between poles or set to right angles and when infinity is squashed between an immoveable beginning and end,

The reconciliation of opposites 9

we can destroy the very truths we first sought to reveal. And yet without beginnings and endings and blacks and whites we may struggle to know or be anything at all.

My premise is that the way we perceive and describe (r)eality (e.g. as one, two, three ...) affects the construction and recognition of our most wicked problems and challenges: from how to raise our children to how *not* to destroy the planet. My thesis is simply that the study of common dyads offers a powerful insight into our everyday ways of knowing and being. My original approach to bi-relational development (i.e. BirD), to be explicated in Chapter 5 and illustrated and applied in subsequent chapters, is that our everyday ways of knowing and being can be powerfully located and understood in terms of the *creation, emergence, opposition, convergence, collapse* and *trans-positioning* of dyadic constituents. These bi-relational positions or dyadic relationships and dynamics offer some explanations for the complex challenges and wicked problems that arise in many different domains of knowledge and life.

Different dyads expose our most mundane and profound human concerns. And the changing nature of dyadic relationships during our lives and epochs reveals our deepest onto-epistemological questions: *how* do we know and *how* do we live? As a number of researchers in epistemological development appreciate, the ways we know are deeply and concretely linked to the ways we relate, love and hate. As Hofer (2002) notes, 'In our most mundane encounters with new information and in our most sophisticated pursuits of knowledge, we are influenced by the beliefs we hold about knowledge and knowing' (p. 3). Bawden (2010) concurs: 'The ability to act systemically in the world, with an acute appreciation of "wholeness", "interconnectedness" and "emergence", is a function of particular intellectual and value assumptions concerning the nature of reality, the nature of knowledge and of knowing, the nature of human nature' (p. 90). Reich, perhaps one of the most direct advocates for epistemological development beyond binary oppositional thinking towards relational and contextual reasoning, writes:

> My claim is that, were they to use RCR, they would better their chances for improving personal relationships, tackling complex social problems such as getting people to follow good health habits, and dealing more effectively with social and political situations in strife-torn areas such as Northern Ireland, the Balkans, the Middle East, and elsewhere.
>
> (2002, p. 6)

Kamerling and Gustavson describe similarly high stakes for exclusively binary oppositional approaches to wicked problems that require more relational and contextual (re)solutions:

> Opposites collide in a battle between universal polarities where all peoples and culture reside. Two cultures project degrading and disparaging images

10   Theory

on one another. The west is seen as morally corrupt, socially degenerate, non-intellectual, untrustworthy, passive, ungodless, soulless, and materialistic. The Islamic world is viewed as fanatical, religious, backward, primitive, and aggressive. Issues clash, contradicting, locked in conviction, differing in position, struggling for dominance, unwilling to reconcile. Democracy versus theocracy, Feminism versus antifeminism, modernization versus traditionalism, secularism versus spirituality, and globalization versus anti-globalization, all creating a tension of exploding forces that are enacted on the current world stage.

(2012, p. 32)

The clash of civilisations has an equivalent, and perhaps even its seed, in the clash of opposites in our individual lives. I share the general hope of these authors that there are ways of knowing and being (i.e. *onto-epistemologies*) that can facilitate better ways of identifying and (re)solving wicked problems.

Bi-relational development (BirD)

To reiterate, my primary purpose is to identify archetypal dyads and dyadic relationships that characterise wicked problems. If there are different dyadic relationships (e.g. binary oppositional, dialectical, complementary) that reflect and affect our ways of knowing and being, as I propose, are there also developments between them? And, if so, to re-invoke Howard Gruber's (1986) perennial question of development: 'Which way is up?'.

There is a picture book of opposites on my young son's bookshelf. Each illustrated page is dedicated to simple dyads like *happy/sad*, *hot/cold*, *short/tall* and *big/small*. Understandably, these are some of the dyads that first occupy a child's mind. Perhaps the most obvious and accessible dyadic relationship is *binary* and then *binary oppositional*. In early childhood at least, the mind seems relatively preconscious of degrees of difference between hot-*ter* and cold-*er*, the relativity of big-*ger* and small-*er*, the mytho-poetic and merismetic relationship between heaven and hell or the semantic interdependence between happy and sad. There is a refreshing immediacy and simplicity in the child's egocentric transposition between binary perceptions and reality. However, this simplicity is perhaps necessarily complicated by the discovery of other minds, which seems to relativise knowing (e.g. hot to you but cold to me), and/or technologies, which seem to objectivise knowing (e.g. thermometers). Here we find the seeds of opposition. I remember my first encounter with this particular opposition in a Year 8 science exam that asked, 'Is human skin a good judge of temperature? Yes or No?'. I briefly thought, 'compared with what?', wrote 'yes' and was marked wrong. The semantics and structure of such questions and their broader implications still interest me. My point is that there seems to be a cognitive-epistemic development that allows for progressive dexterity in the relation of dyadic constituents. To extend the physical metaphor, the coordination of

The reconciliation of opposites 11

mental bifurcations, like the coordination of limbs, means that we tend to crawl before we can walk and walk before we can run. The trouble with development in the mental domain is that its bifurcations are harder to see than their physical analogues. It is easier to observe the physical transitions from crawling to walking to running than the transitions from pre-dyadic to pro-dyadic to post-dyadic knowing.

On my own bookshelf there is a copy of Albert Camus' (2005) philosophical treatise *The Myth of Sisyphus*, Nikolai Grozni's (2008) metaphysical odyssey *Turtle Feet*, Douglas Hofstadter's (1999) opus, *Godel, Escher, Bach* and a collection of Escher's illusive etchings (Ernst, 1995). In his early pages, Camus (2005) writes of the beginning and end of knowing: 'Beginning to think is beginning to be undermined' (p. 3). In his last pages, Grozni (2008) describes the end of his epistemological journey into Tibetan dialectics: 'Existence was nonexistence was existence was nonexistence. Right was wrong was right was wrong. The past was the present was the future was the past. Here was there was here and there' (pp. 317–18). Like many ancients before him and contemporaries with him, especially the masters of Zen, Grozni is struck by the seemingly absurd union and negation of opposites. The two become nought and one. Similarly, Hofstadter (1999) is profoundly affected by this strange loop that seems to simultaneously destroy and create consciousness, describing it as 'an interaction between levels in which the top level reaches back down towards the bottom level and influences it, while at the same time being itself determined by the bottom level' (p. 709). The two are entangled in one. I imagine, too, that Escher's similar realisation prompted many of his paradoxical self-referencing sketches and his observation that:

> Anyone who plunges into infinity, in both time and space, further and further without stopping, needs fixed points, mileposts, for otherwise his movement is indistinguishable from standing still. There must be stars past which he shoots, beacons from which he can measure the distance he has traversed.
>
> (Escher and Brigam, 1971, p. 40)

Here, *one* is a number that helps us to stand and *two* (i.e. fixed points, mileposts, beacons) is a number that helps us to measure and move between the otherwise un-navigable darkness between zero and infinity; or in existential terms, between nothing and everything. I have emphasised the most literal and esoteric ways to relate dyadic constituents early and late in life to suggest that there are developments, or at least different positions and dispositions for relating dyads, that have loose chronological affinities.

Perhaps these literary anecdotes contain generalisable truths about the development of knowledge and knowing from infancy to adulthood, both in individuals and cultures. This book is a small contribution and perhaps a continuance of this act of generalisation that can be found in many different

12 Theory

domains of knowing and being. Thus, I acknowledge my affinity with the general dyadic explorations of such literati and others closer to my own domain of knowing (i.e. educational psychology), such as Piaget (1970), Perry (1970) and Reich (2002). For example, Perry (1970) pioneered a theory of epistemological development and described the realisation of relativity after the stability of absolutism as the silent and most violent revolution of adult knowing. Similarly, I hope to show that there are bi-relational locations on the journey of knowing between infancy and old age, and that they are revealed in almost all modes of human expression, aspects of being and fields of knowledge. However, I also hope to problematise linear and teleological trajectories of development by identifying cyclical and chaotic dynamics of knowing and being.

Onto-epistemological development

Perhaps prematurely, I have used the term *onto-epistemological* to describe the type of human development with which I am most concerned. I use the term to express the inseparability and complementarity of our ways of knowing and being, and to focus an examination on the intersection between them. I owe the specific term to Karen Barad (2007), who uses it in recognition of the necessary entanglement of structure and content, and being and knowing in descriptions of individual and social 'reality/ies'. Wicked problems arise from the meeting of these individual and social realities, and I use the term to acknowledge the need for a paradigm that expresses the epistemological and ontological nature of such meetings. The term is defined elsewhere in compatible ways. Diversi and Moreira defend their *onto-epistemological stance* in a way that captures my own intention to recognise unity in separation, and to approach knowledge and theory 'in the flesh' of human experience:

> We see the apparent dichotomies of mind and body, physical and metaphysical, object and subject, theory and method, as differentiations of one, all-encompassing, system: Being ... The mind and its interpretations of reality and being are not separate from the flesh but part of it – one perceives the world before any reflection takes place ...We are claiming that the dominant discourse in academia is still colonized by the ontological dualism of logical-positivism (that is, idealism versus materialism, mind versus body, fact versus fiction, science versus arts).
>
> (2009, pp. 31–3)

DePryck's analysis acknowledges a similar entanglement between ontology and epistemology:

> Ontological and epistemological questions cannot be dealt with independently from one another. Understanding the world, regardless of the

extent of our knowledge, implies an understanding of its structures and relations. These structures and relations in turn determine to what extent they can access themselves and thus also to what extent they can reflect upon themselves.

(1993, p. 19)

Likewise, Geerts and van der Tuin (2013) use *onto-epistemological* in the context of women's studies to acknowledge that 'being and knowing are always already entangled' (p. 171). Accordingly, this book is an attempt to co-develop the abstract theory and concrete lived experiences of BirD.

As a brief illustrative aside, my own journey towards the term *onto-epistemological* can itself be seen as a bi-relational development. While no book has an absolute beginning, this book 'began' almost 15 years ago, with a structural-cognitive analysis of religious fundamentalism, the topic of a masters thesis (Adam, 2003). To reflect on my own onto-epistemological development, it is fair to say that I was so deeply impressed with the explanatory power of structural developmental theories (e.g. Fowler, 1981; Reich, 2002) that I forgot to fully acknowledge the ontological events that gave rise to these epistemological explanations. Indeed, it was perhaps not until late into my doctoral thesis (Adam, 2008) that I was deeply struck by my neglect of the ontological dimension of my cognitive-epistemic analyses. I then found the clearest expression of this 'awakening from dogmatic slumbers' in Streib's (2001) complaint that structural developmental theories view cognitive-epistemic structures as the motor of human development and put the cart before the horse.

Thus, it is not without a sense of irony that I recognise my own onto-epistemological development towards the (re)union of *knowing* and *being* in the description of human development. This dyadic description contains the seed of this book's primary concern: that dyads and dyadic relationships offer powerful ways of understanding diverse trajectories of human knowing and being. Accordingly, I hope to offer an approach to wicked problems that acknowledges the entanglement between epistemology and ontology, though without 'mixing them up' completely.

Caveats

There are several caveats that are important to express at the outset of this book. First, I am well aware, and it may already be apparent, that an onto-epistemological project of this sort cannot escape the strange loops and dyadic structures it seeks to describe. As Lovejoy reflects in *The Revolt against Dualism*:

Man, in short, is by nature an epistemological animal ... he will necessarily wish to know himself as knower, and therefore to understand the seeming mystery and challenging paradox of knowledge – the possibility which it implies of going abroad while keeping at home, the knower's apparent

14   Theory

> transcendence of the existential limits within which he must yet, at every
> moment of his knowing, confess himself to be contained.
>
> (1930, p. 12)

I will often be inescapably contained by the very dyadic structures I seek to step outside of to describe. My only defence, my only rationale, is that there is a peculiar type of freedom that lies as much in accepting one's inevitable constraints as it does in trying to escape them.

While there are innumerable poetic, mythic, artistic and esoteric treatments of dyadic relationships, there are few attempts to explore dyadic relationships with a reflexive awareness of the tensions, dualisms, paradoxes, complements and oppositions that govern that very exploration. For example, some explorations tend towards a spiritual-esoteric symmetry that is arguably unmindful or at least too disentangled from the material complexity, asymmetry and entropy revealed by the natural sciences. Conversely, other explorations tend towards a naturalistic asymmetry that is similarly unmindful or disentangled from the relative simplicity, symmetry and teleology revealed by the cosmological sciences. A book about dyads is always going to have a disciplinary identity crisis, though it is a crisis I intend to at least acknowledge and explore. Accordingly, the onto-epistemological task is not to destroy the dyadic construct altogether; rather, it is to expand the repertoire of relationships between polarities beyond mere opposition so that we may first grasp and then work on wicked problems with two hands working as one. Thus, the reader will find herein a combination of prosaic and poetic, mythic and literal, pure and applied and concrete and abstract attempts to communicate the dyads and dyadic relationships that reflect and construct wicked problems. However, I recognise that in the finite pages of a book this division of focus may somewhat weaken two parts to strengthen a whole.

While there are many more limitations that I intend to acknowledge throughout this book, perhaps the limitation I feel most obliged to acknowledge at the outset is the level of generalisation that there is in introductions – not just an introductory chapter but a whole book as an introduction to a particular approach. No doubt, further and finer analyses will find that I have assumed too much structural similarity between some dissimilar dyads and too much symmetry between some asymmetrical developments. Nonetheless, I hope to have done enough thinking, living and researching to show that more can be done, and more is worth doing, in understanding the bi-relational dimension of wicked problems.

Overview of chapters

In summary, this book has three premises. The first is that the common appearance of dyads in a particular domain of knowledge can help us to recognise its definitive wicked problems. For example, the educator will wrestle with nature and nurture, the physician with mind and body, the politician with liberal and conservative, the architect with pragmatics and aesthetics, the philosopher with a priori and a posteriori, the psychologist with subjective and objective, the physicist with relative and universal, the theologian with immanent and transcendent, the scientist with data and interpretation and the civilisation with order and chaos. Of course, there is also a sense in which every one of us will wrestle with them all.

The second premise is that dyadic relationships and dynamics provide a powerful framework for understanding how wicked problems can be approached and exacerbated in different ways. For example, one educator may leave students to their nature and disregard their nurture; another may nurture their students without regarding their nature. One physician may seek to heal the mind with pharmacological treatments; another may seek to heal the body only through the mind. At one time they may oppose each other; at other times they may unite.

The third premise is that epistemologies (i.e. ways of knowing) and ontologies (i.e. ways of being), as all dyads, are entangled like chicken and egg in the production of wicked problems. I hope to reflect this entanglement by infusing epistemological theory with lived experiences, especially in the second part of this book. Theories are neat and human experiences are messy, but they are nonetheless inextricably linked.

This book is structured using three parts that respectively offer a theory, illustrations and educational applications of BirD. Specifically, Part 1 provides a general introduction to key concepts, a theoretical background and detailed description of BirD. Part 2 provides illustrations of BirD across a wide range of dyads representing different wicked problems. And Part 3 offers some general and specific applications of BirD as a bi-relational approach to understanding wicked problems in the context of formal education. The following paragraphs provide more detail on the individual chapters within these parts.

Part 1: theory

So far, this chapter has sought to introduce the book's overarching concepts, including *dyads* and *dyadic relationships, wicked problems, onto-epistemology* and *BirD*. The aim of Chapter 2 is to establish the ubiquity of dyads and dyadic relationships apparent in everyday wicked problems. Accordingly, Chapter 2 provides an illustrative review of dyads and dyadic relationships in literature from different domains of knowledge.

Having identified the structure of dyads in context in Chapter 2, Chapter 3 discusses the origins of dyads and the classification of different types of dyads. The related discussion further reveals why BirD and the reconciliation of opposites is central to the recognition and (re)solution of wicked problems and a worthy topic of attention in formal education.

Chapter 4 prepares the way for a bi-relational theory of development (i.e. BirD) as part extension, rejection and integration of some existing theories of

16 Theory

development. Specifically, the chapter positions BirD in relation to a selection of closely related theories, including: Piaget's (1970) stages of intellectual development, Perry's (1970) stages of epistemological development, King and Kitchener's (1994) reflective judgement model, Baxter Magolda's (1992) epistemological reflection model; Kuhn and Weinstock's (2002) levels of epistemological understanding, Basseches' (1984) and Riegel's (1979) dialectical thinking and Reich's (2002) levels of relational and contextual reasoning. The chapter concludes with a general discussion of the nature of a bi-relational theory as preparation for a more detailed description of the book's specific bi-relational theory (i.e. BirD) in Chapter 5.

Chapter 5 offers an introductory description of BirD as an approach to recognising and (re)solving wicked problems. BirD is not so much an attempt to defend dyadic structure (i.e. the division of reality into two) as it is an attempt to describe such divisions, their effects, developments, intra-relations and interrelations with non-dyadic positions. The chapter offers visual and symbolic representations of BirD's archetypal regions, positions, trajectories and dynamics. It also provides brief illustrations and some general metaphors to illuminate BirD as a theory that crosses boundaries between formal and postformal logics, linear and non-linear understandings of development and divided and united notions of *self*. The chapter then provides descriptions of BirD's key relational dynamics that describe and create diverse trajectories of knowing and being. Together with BirD's archetypal positions, regions and trajectories, these dynamics provide an interpretive framework for understanding the illustrations and applications of Parts 2 and 3 respectively.

Part 2: illustrations

The purpose of Part 2 is to illustrate the theory in relation to wicked problems. These illustrations use BirD's archetypal positions and dynamics to understand wicked problems as they are manifested in individual lives and on global stages. To this end, Chapter 6 offers an illustrative analysis of a collection of short dyadic narratives written in response to a semi-structured questionnaire. The narratives summarise participants' epistemological beliefs, reflections and related life experiences in relation to a dyad that they find most salient. For example, the analysis uses participant extracts to illustrate onto-epistemological trajectories in relation to dyads such as despair/hope, stability/change, feeling/thinking, future/past, teaching/learning, mind/body and faith/reason. Accordingly, the chapter also illustrates the ubiquity of dyadic constructs in everyday wicked problems.

Chapters 7, 8 and 9 provide general discussions of three interrelated wicked problems. Chapter 7 presents a bi-relational discussion of socio-cultural problems in relation to dyads such as global/local and traditional/modern. Chapter 8 presents a bi-relational discussion of socio-ecological problems in relation to the nature/culture dyad. Chapter 9 presents a bi-relational approach to socio-religious problems in relation to the spiritual/material and faith/reason dyads. In plain terms, the interrelated problems presented in these chapters reflect human-to-human relationships, human-to-earth relationships and human-to-cosmos relationships. Collectively, these chapters provide a platform for considering the role of bi-relational education in the identification and (re) solution of wicked problems.

Part 3: applications

Part 3 considers some practical applications of a bi-relational approach in the context of formal education. Chapter 10 offers a general discussion of the pedagogical and educational applications of BirD, along with a series of specific bi-relational strategies for use in formal educational contexts.

Chapter 11 provides bi-relational analyses of two teachers' narratives to illustrate wicked pedagogical problems in formal education. The first explores a dance teacher's understanding of the mind/body dyad in relation to her ways of teaching. The second explores a mathematics teacher's understanding of the concrete/abstract dyad in relation to his ways of teaching. Together, these explorations highlight the reality of bi-relational development and its implicit influence in formal education.

Finally, Chapter 12 offers a condensed summary of the book and a discussion of future directions for its bi-relational approach to onto-epistemological development and wicked problems. Its final section revisits the 'serious riddle' posed at the beginning of the book to once more affirm the bi-relational nature of human development and need to reconcile opposites in the (re)solution of wicked problems.

References

Ackoff, R. L. (1993). The art and science of mess management. In C. Mabey and B. Mayon-White (Eds.), *Managing change* (pp. 47–54). London: PCP.

Adam, R. J. (2003). *Fundamentalism and structural development: A conceptual synthesis and discussion of implications for religious education.* Masters (research) thesis. James Cook University. QLD, Australia. Retrieved from http://researchonline.jcu.edu.au/13/

Adam, R. J. (2008). Relating faith development and religious styles: Reflections in light of apostasy from religious fundamentalism. *Archive for the Psychology of Religion/Archiv für Religionpsychologie*, 30(1), 201–31. doi: 10.1163/157361208X317204.

Barad, K. (2007). *Meeting the universe halfway: Quantum physics and the entanglement of matter and meaning.* Durham, NC: Duke University Press.

Basseches, M. (1984). *Dialectical thinking and adult development.* Norwood, NJ: Ablex Publishing.

Battersby, S. (2013). Pathways to cosmic oblivion. In J. Webb (Ed.), *Nothing: From absolute zero to cosmic oblivion – amazing insights into nothingness* (pp. 216–29). London: New Scientist.

Bawden, R. (2010). Messy issues, worldviews and systemic competencies. In C. Blackmore (Ed.), *Social learning systems and communities of practice* (pp. 89–101). London: Springer.

18 Theory

Baxter Magolda, M. B. (1992). *Knowing and reasoning in college: Gender-related patterns in students' intellectual development*. San Francisco, CA: Jossey-Bass.

Brown, V. A., Harris, J. A. and Russell, J. Y. (2010). *Tackling wicked problems through the transdisciplinary imagination*. London: Earthscan Publishers.

Camus, A. (2005). *The myth of Sisyphus* (J. O'Brien, Trans.). London, UK: Penguin Books. (Original work published 1942.)

DePryck, K. (1993). *Knowledge, evolution and paradox: The ontology of language*. Albany, NY: State University of New York Press.

Diversi, M., and Moreira, C. (2009). *Betweener talk: Decolonizing knowledge production, pedagogy, and praxis*. Walnut Creek, CA: Left Coast Press.

Ernst, B. (1995). *The magic mirror of M. C. Escher*. New York: Taschen America LLC.

Escher, M. C., and Brigham, J. E. (1971). *The graphic work of M. C. Escher*. New York: Ballantine Books.

Fowler, J. W. (1981). *Stages of faith: The psychology of human development and the quest for meaning*. San Francisco, CA: Harper and Row.

Geerts, E., and van der Tuin, I. (2013). From intersectionality to interference: Feminist onto-epistemological reflections on the politics of representation. *Women's Studies International Forum, 41, Part 3*(0), 171–8. doi: http://dx.doi.org/10.1016/j.wsif.2013.07.013.

Greene, B. (2004). *The fabric of the cosmos*. London: Penguin.

Grozni, A. (2008). *Turtle feet*. New York: Riverhead Books.

Gruber, H. E. (1986). Which way is up? A developmental question. In R. A. Mines and K. S. Kitchener (Eds.), *Adult cognitive development: Methods and models* (pp. 112–33). New York: Praeger Publications.

Hofer, B. K. (2002). Personal epistemology as a psychological and educational construct: An introduction. In B. K. Hofer and P. R. Pintrich (Eds.), *Personal epistemology: The psychology of beliefs about knowledge and knowing* (pp. 3–14). Mahwah, NJ: Lawrence Erlbaum Associates, Inc.

Hofstadter, D. R. (1999). *Godel, Escher, Bach: An eternal golden braid*. London: Penguin Books.

Horn, R. E. (2004). To think bigger thoughts: Why the human cognome project requires visual language tools to address social messes. *Annals of the New York Academy of Sciences,* 1013(1), 212–20. doi: 10.1196/annals.1305.015

Jung, C. G. (1970). *Myseterium coniunctionis: An inquiry into the separation and synthesis of psychic opposites in alchemy (The collected works of C. G. Jung, Vol. 14)* (G. Adler and R. F. C. Hull, Trans.). Princeton, NJ: Princeton University Press. (Original work published 1955.)

Jung, C. G. (1991). *Analytical psychology: Notes of the seminar given in 1925* (W. McGuire, Ed.). Princeton, NJ: Princeton University Press.

Kamerling, J., and Gustavson, F. (2012). *Lifting the veil*. Carmel, CA: Fisher King Press.

King, P. M., and Kitchener, K. S. (2002). The reflective judgment model: Twenty years of research on epistemic cognition. In B. K. Hofer and P. R. Pintrich (Eds.), *Personal epistemology: The psychology of beliefs about knowledge and knowing* (pp. 37–61). Mahway, NJ: Lawrence Erlbaum.

King, P. M., and Kitchener, K. S. (1994). *Developing reflective judgment*. San Francisco: Jossey-Bass.

Kuhn, D., and Weinstock, M. (2002). What is epistemological thinking and why does it matter? In B. K. Hofer and P. R. Pintrich (Eds.), *Personal epistemology: The psychology of beliefs about knowledge and knowing* (pp. 121–44). Mahwah, NJ: Erlbaum.

Lovejoy, A. O. (1930). *The revolt against dualism: An inquiry concerning the existence of ideas.* Chicago: Open Court.

Mitroff, I. I., Alpaslan, M. C., and Green, S. E. (2004). Crises as ill-structured messes. *International Studies Review*, 6(1), 165–94. doi: 10.1111/j.1521-9488.2004.393_3.x.

Newberg, A., D'Aquili, E., and Rause, V. (2001). *Why God won't go away: Brain science and the biology of belief.* New York: The Ballantine Publishing Group.

Perry, W. G. (1970). *Forms of ethical and intellectual development in the college years: A scheme.* New York: Holt, Rinehart and Winston.

Piaget, J. (1970). *Structuralism* (C. Maschler, Trans.). New York: Basic Books.

Reich, K. H. (2002). *Developing the horizons of the mind: Relational and contextual reasoning and the resolution of cognitive conflict.* Cambridge, UK: Cambridge University Press.

Riegel, K. F. (1979). *Foundations of dialectical psychology.* New York: Academic Press Inc.

Rittel, H. W. J., and Webber, M. M. (1973). Dilemmas in a general theory of planning. *Policy Sciences*, 4(2), 155–69. doi: 10.1007/BF01405730.

Stewart, I. (2013). Zero, zip, zilch. In J. Webb (Ed.), *Nothing: From absolute zero to cosmic oblivion – amazing insights into nothingness* (pp. 118–25). London: New Scientist.

Streib, H. (2001). Faith development theory revisited: The religious styles perspective. *The International Journal for the Psychology of Religion*, 11(3), 143–58. doi: 10.1207/S15327582IJPR1103_02.

Tzu, L. (2006). *Tao Te Ching: Annotated & Explained* (D. Lin, Trans.). Skylight Paths. Retrieved from http://www.taoism.net/ttc/complete.htm

Chapter 2

Wicked problems and the recognition of opposites

To reiterate, this book proposes a bi-relational approach to wicked problems that explores the development of our ways of knowing and being in relation to dyads. It does so in order to contribute to an understanding of the wicked problems that define much of what it means to be human. For example, there is a relationship between our bi-relational conceptualisations of *nature* and *culture* and the ways we live in our ecological environments; *male* and *female* and the ways we live in intimate relationships; *local* and *global* and the ways we live in, and among, different cultures; and *spirit* and *matter* and the ways we experience life and death and understand science and religion. The purpose of this chapter is to recognise the ubiquity of dyads and dyadic relationships across different domains of human knowledge in order to establish the relevance of a bi-relational approach to wicked problems. More specifically, this chapter (a) illustrates the ubiquity of dyads across many domains of knowledge in which wicked problems arise and (b) illustrates the ubiquity of dyadic relationships across different domains of knowledge. This establishment of dyads and dyadic relationships as a ubiquitous heuristic lays a foundation for the book's original theory of bi-relational development (i.e. BirD). BirD is then grounded in the theory of Chapter 4, explicated in Chapter 5 and illustrated and applied in subsequent chapters.

The ubiquitous dyad

As introduced in the previous chapter, the ubiquitous dyad finds expression in the depth and breadth of human experience. C. G. Jung (1970) noted, 'The opposites and their symbols are so common in the texts that it is superfluous to cite evidence from the sources' (p. 4). Indeed, there is a sense in which this ubiquity makes the dyadic structure blindingly obvious. We discover and create dyads in our natural habitats with the *ebb* and *flow* of the tide, *wax and wane* of the moon and the *rise* and *set* of the sun in *day* and *night*, *light* and *dark* and *dawn* and *dusk*. We allegorise the *ups* and *downs* of hills and valleys, the *peaks* and *troughs* of waves and the *hot* and *cold* and *wet* and *dry* of seasons. We discover and create dyads, too, in the symmetries and polarities of our physical forms as *birth*

The recognition of opposites 21

and *death*, *young* and *old*, *male* and *female*, *short* and *tall* and *big* and *small*. And we discover and create dyadic structures in our most mundane synthetic objects, such as the seesaw sprung *up* and *down*, the pendulum swung *left* and *right*, the scale tipped *heavy* and *light*, the rope pulled *to* and *fro* and the hourglass tipped from *top* to *bottom*.

Dyads give structure and meaning to the most childish and sagacious mythologies and the most simple and complex physical and mathematical descriptions. In Western mythology, Goldilocks takes her place between *hot* and *cold*; hare and tortoise pit fast and fleeting against slow and steady; Sisyphus bears his boulder *up* and *down* a mountain for eternity, symbolising the perpetuity of the human struggle; and Christ is crucified between *heaven* and *hell*, symbolising an eternal hope within the human struggle. In Eastern mythology, Krishna and Arjuna stand between two seething armies contemplating *peace* and *war*, the choosing of sides and *life* and *death*. Even the physicist evokes dyads and dyadic structures such as *wave* and *particle*, *position* and *momentum* and *electro* and *magnetic* to describe the universe, while the mathematician sees dualities in *complex* and *simplectic* geometries. Whether in mythopoetic or more literal forms, the dyad is perhaps the most pervasive, persistent and yet elusive construct of human knowing and being. The pervasiveness of dyads is evident in the familiarity and number of dyadic metaphors and symbols. The elusiveness of dyads is evident in the rarity of our reflexivity about their pervasiveness in life's wicked problems.

The dyadic structure helps to capture the essence of problems – not just problems about which 'reasonable people reasonably disagree', but problems that may well put one in 'two minds'. This is the dimension of wicked problems that I hope to illustrate and explore. Of course, wicked problems are usually demonstrated in relation to grand issues such as poverty, sustainability and globalisation, all of which deserve attention. However, I would argue that the basic structures of these grand problems are played out on smaller scales in everyday lives. This is the smaller scale of the time-constrained doctor who struggles with the dominance of pharmaceutical treatments for complex illnesses; the resource-constrained teacher who struggles with the dominance of inclusive and differentiated pedagogies in diverse classrooms; the burdened judge weighing heavily the defendant's heinous crime with his horrific childhood; and the troubled parent knowing if, how and when to comfort their crying infant. Indeed, it may just be the accumulation of these smaller scales, which are no less wicked for being so, that makes for grander problems. The problems of a single life are the problems of the village and the problems of a village are the problems of the planet. The smaller scales can help us to appreciate the messy situatedness of problems that is sometimes lost in grand epistemological narratives. To recall, I have appropriated Barad's (2007) technical term *onto-epistemological* to acknowledge the human contexts and situatedness of dyadic structures and wicked problems. Accordingly, throughout this book I hope to represent the scale of wicked problems from small to grand, individual to universal.

22 Theory

Illustrative dyads and dyadic relationships in context

Dyads are a ubiquitous construct because they reflect something fundamental, not just about the way we organise knowledge but about the nature of knowing itself. As a way of understanding the nature of knowledge one could also expect that contestations and reflections over dyadic relationships (e.g. binary oppositional, complementary, dialectical) be ever present in different domains of human knowledge. It is not surprising, then, that the dyadic structure and reflections on its nature are to be found in almost all domains of life and knowledge. I offer brief glimpses into a range of domains (e.g. politics, psychology, medicine, theology, physics) in order to illustrate the ubiquity of dyads and the wicked problems that imply them.

It is often the psychoanalysts and the mythologists who are most cognisant of this ubiquity. Indeed, some of the most explicit analyses of dyads and dyadic relationships are found in literary and descriptive studies of human culture and mythology. Freilich *et al.* identify dyads that define the 'human dilemma' and structure mythologies that both express and engage that dilemma:

> The human dilemma around which so many myths weave their questions and answers now shows itself in great clarity: survival or sanity; pragmatism or aesthetics; law or justice; function or meaning; nature or culture (Levi-Strauss); space or time (Bergson); control or purpose (Rapoport); signs, which look outward, i.e., to space, or symbols, which focus inward, i.e., to time (Frye); living-in-nature or living-in-history (Whitehead); sphere of life or sphere of mind (Teilhard de Chardin); and the smart or the proper.
>
> (1975, p. 237)

Freilich *et al.*'s (1975) 'human dilemmas' are expressed in the wicked problems of all domains of knowledge and life. For this very reason, to *know* ourselves we must recognise the bi-relational or dyadic structures through which we know. The structures *create* and *reflect* our ways of knowing and being.

However, my claim is that the dyadic structure is found not just in explicit literary analyses but everywhere that knowledge exists, even in unlikely places. For example, Cloke and Johnston name and address the dyads that define the nature and study of geography:

> But geography itself has subdivisions – many of them binary: physical and human; for example; or qualitative and quantitative; or economic and cultural ... A clear distinction between practices on either side of the human–physical binary divide within geography reflects the nature of their subject matter and scientific approaches.
>
> (2005, pp. 7–8)

The recognition of opposites 23

This quote appropriates a particular bi-relational stance to its dyads (i.e. *binary*). Accordingly, the following sections offer wide-ranging illustrations of the ubiquity of dyadic structures and relationships in many domains of knowledge where wicked problems appear.

Politics

One of the most blindingly obvious dyadic allusions relates to the liberal and conservative, or left and right, wings of political discourse. As Jacoby (1988) observes, 'The liberal-conservative continuum provides a convenient mechanism for citizens to structure their beliefs about political parties, candidates, and issues. After all, the political world itself seems to be organised along these lines' (p. 316). Jacoby goes even further to suggest that the dyadic conceptualisation is actually an indicator of 'political sophistication' because it demonstrates a high level of abstraction. Semantically, the left is most associated with egalitarianism, collectivism, movement and progress, whereas the right is most associated with hierarchy, competition, stability and tradition.

Historically, the relationship between position and politics had its origins in the French Revolution of 1789, when advocates for the Republic and the Monarchy sat to the *left* and the *right* respectively of the Estates General. Most recently, this dyadic structure has been implicitly reaffirmed by the movement of 'the third way' in Western democracies such as the US, UK and Australia. Proponents of the third way generally seek to synthesise the humanitarian concerns of the traditional left with the free markets of the traditional right. For example, in *Beyond Left and Right*, Anthony Giddens (1994) proposes the future of radical politics as 'one of reconciling autonomy and independence in the various spheres of social life, including the economic domain' (p. 13). He sees this reconciliation as necessary, perhaps inevitable, given the inversion of labels and meanings over time: 'the right here has turned radical, while the left seeks mainly to conserve' (p. 9). Giddens' analysis implies the significance of the bi-relational approach herein: that is, to make explicit the ways we relate dyadic constituents that define wicked problems. In order to expand our onto-epistemological repertoire, our ways of knowing and being political, we must move beyond exclusively or excessively binary oppositional politics (i.e. conservative vs. liberal) while recognising and managing the role and place of opposing perspectives.

So powerful and pervasive is the left/right dyad in politics that it was used to structure an online 'vote compass' for public awareness in the lead-up to the 2013 Federal election in Australia (ABC, 2013). This particular tool helps voters to see their dyadic affinities with political parties in relation to wicked election issues (e.g. immigration, welfare, multiculturalism). Similarly, Jacoby offers a fascinating analysis of the dyadic structure in US politics with the suggestion that the left/right dyad is used as a structuring principle in correlation with

24 Theory

educational attainment. That is, relative lack of educational attainment may serve *against* left/right reasoning:

> Education is expected to influence ideological thinking because formal schooling provides individuals with exposure to information, and training in the use of conceptual knowledge. Both of these factors should facilitate the application of general abstract principles like the liberal-conservative continuum, to specific events, people, and situations. In contrast, the lack of education may denote relatively impermeable cognitive limitations which serve as barriers against ideological reasoning.
>
> (1988, p. 318)

These findings are not so simple as to suggest that the abstractions of higher education necessarily lead to accurate judgements. That is, the ability to generate an abstract dyadic continuum (i.e. left–right) can actually work against correspondence with political reality. As Jacoby notes, 'Several studies have demonstrated that people often distort their perceptions in order to make them more schema-consistent (Taylor and Crocker, 1981; Lodge and Hamill, 1986)' (1988, p. 320). This is an important point that relates to my later discussion of dyads as creating and/or reflecting reality. Whether in politics, law, medicine, science or religion, we need to coordinate our abstractions with the concrete realities they presume to describe. While concrete political judgements may precede abstract political judgements in developmental order (i.e. concrete > abstract), it is important to reconcile the two in context (i.e. concrete <=> abstract), rather than merely reverse the order of a binary opposition (i.e. concrete < abstract).

Needless to say, the treatment of this political dyadic relationship (i.e. left/right, liberal/conservative) and the location or position that has political power at any time is of great significance to the type of societies that operate within any nation and the relations between nations. Illustratively, Tangerås offers a dyadic game-theory analysis of democratic and autocratic regimes as a predictor of international conflict:

> Democratic leaders can credibly be punished for bad conflict outcomes, whereas autocratic leaders cannot. Due to the fear of being thrown out of office, democratic leaders are (i) more selective about the wars they initiate and (ii) on average win more of the wars they start. Foreign policy behaviour is found to display strategic complementarities. Therefore, the likelihood of interstate war is lowest in the democratic dyad (pair), highest in the autocratic dyad with the mixed dyad in between.
>
> (2009, p. 99)

Arguably, the dyadic structure of wicked international conflicts can be similarly applied to inter-individual and even intra-individual conflicts between egalitarian and hierarchical ways of structuring reality. Collectively, these sources illustrate the ubiquity of dyadic structures and relationships in and beyond the domain of political knowledge.

Medicine

Dyads and dyadic relationships also relate to how medical professionals treat their patients and society conceptualises health and well-being. For example, Segal recognises 'a well-established set of dyads in medicine: body/mind; physical/mental; objective/subjective' (p. 238) and continues:

> The standard dyads structure many of the things physicians say to patients: 'your disease is all in your head' (meaning, 'your mind has imagined the suffering of your body') or 'your symptoms are just the result of stress' (meaning, 'your mind is to blame for your body') or 'you are clinically depressed' (meaning, 'your body is to blame for your mind').
>
> (2007, p. 238)

These dyads relate to systematic divisions between traditional and alternative medicine that some are trying to integrate into more effective and encompassing practice. As Rakel writes in the introduction to *Integrative Medicine*:

> The philosophy of integrative medicine is not new. It has been talked about for ages across many disciplines. It has simply been overlooked as the pendulum of accepted medical care swings from one extreme to the other. We are currently experiencing the beginning of a shift towards recognizing the benefits of combining the external, physical, and technologic successes of curing with the internal, non-physical exploration of healing.
>
> (2013, p. 2)

Similarly, Graham-Pole identifies a modern resurgence of complementary and alternative medicine (CAM), noting:

> Many terms have been coined to describe the emergence (or re-emergence) of a system of health care not generally recognized as part of mainstream medical practice. They include alternative, complementary, unconventional, non-allopathic, integrative, holistic, healing arts, non-traditional, and even traditional.
>
> (2001, p. 662)

His article identifies and implies common dyads such as art/science, traditional/ alternative and mainstream/holistic and calls for better understanding and coordination of these spectra in medical training.

26 Theory

Grace offers a context for understanding and critiquing the dualities of medical discourse and argues that they reflect gendered ontologies and epistemologies:

> In my own case, the first encounter with problems of dualism resulted from interviewing women about their use of the health services for chronic pelvic pain, and discovering how their experiential discourse was traversed, constrained and shaped by the medical duality of pain being due to either somatic or psychological causes (Grace, 1995, 1998); if it's not one, it must be the other, a choice that is a clear example of the body/mind dualism in medicine. I thus approach the problematic of dualism in the workings of the life sciences and the practice of medicine from the point of view of a concern with how this science constructs, shapes, interacts with, and co-produces socio-cultural forms of embodiment; this concern is particularly important in the field of gender studies.
>
> (2007, p. 1)

Here *dualism* is used to mean *binary opposition* and to show how problems arise in medical practice that is defined, either knowingly or unknowingly, by exclusively oppositional and separative practices. Such sources reveal the onto-epistemological relationship between specific dyads (e.g. mind/body; traditional/alternative) and wicked problems, such as the conceptualisation and treatment of pain and illness.

Collectively, these sources pose more general questions: for example, what is the dyadic disposition of any doctor, nurse, field of medicine, or health system in relation to mind/body questions? Is one doctor more likely to take a pharmacological (i.e. body) approach than a therapeutic (i.e. mind) approach to any illness? Perhaps one hospital is known for its quality of care (decency), while another is known for its quantity of care (efficiency). Similarly, how do our healthcare systems weigh quality and quantity of life? McNeil *et al.* (1981) examine trade-offs between quality and quantity of life in relation to treatment for laryngeal cancer, concluding 'that treatment choices should be made on the basis of patients' attitudes toward the quality as well as the quantity of survival' (p. 982). And Struber (2003) reflects on the dilemma that physiotherapy faces in the context of modern health: 'Practitioners desiring evidence-based practice would traditionally concentrate on biomedically styled "gold standard" quantitative research, yet this must be melded with systematic 'humanistic' qualitative research to establish a basis of patient-centred care' (p. 3). Struber invokes dyads such as biomechanical/humanistic, quantitative/qualitative, paternalistic/maternalistic and traditional/modern to describe modern physiotherapy's identity crisis.

Approaches to health and medicine also relate to individual/social and psychological/sociological dyads. For example, Bandura (2004) describes an integrative social cognitive approach to health that moves beyond simple dichotomies. He proposes an approach to 'health promotion and disease prevention from the perspective of social cognitive theory', suggests that 'Human health is a social matter, not just an individual one' and emphasises that 'a comprehensive approach to health promotion also requires changing the practices of social systems that have widespread effects on human health' (p. 143). Such social changes further implicate the cultural dimension of approaches to health and medicine.

Some dyads offer a structural basis for understanding cross-cultural differences in approaches to health and medicine. Kaptchuk identifies a secondary dyad (i.e. Western/Eastern medicine) as constituted by primary dyads such as isolating/integrating, mechanistic/holistic and analytic/synthetic. He suggests:

> The difference between the two medicines, however, is greater than that between their descriptive language. The actual logical structure underlying the methodology, the habitual mental operations that guide the physician's clinical insight and critical judgment, differs radically in the two traditions.
>
> (1983, p. 3)

Kaptchuk takes a complementary approach to these two logics and traditions:

> Chinese medicine considers important certain aspects of the human body that are not significant to Western medicine. At the same time, Western medicine observes and can describe aspects of the human body that are insignificant or not perceptible to Chinese medicine.
>
> (1983, p. 2)

There are also dyadic constructs underlying the nature of specialisations within healthcare. For instance, Northoff (1992) identifies 'structure/function' and 'localisation/holism' as dyads that define the tension between neurology and psychiatry and argues that these dyads need to be bridged for successful treatment of some syndromes and disorders.

Clearly, in the discourse of medicine we find dyads and dyadic relationships that may help us to understand, if not to (re)solve, some of the wicked problems affecting human health. What dyadic trade-offs does each hospital make and what broader social effects do whole healthcare systems have if they take a polarised approach to the dyadic constructs that define them? The answers to such questions reflect our health systems from the onto-epistemological dispositions of individual health professionals (e.g. doctors) and health institutions (e.g. hospitals) to national healthcare systems and even international approaches to disease, disorder and death.

Law

Dyads and dyadic relationships relate to the justice system of any society. In the context of law, Spader (1995) explicitly identifies dyads such as privacy/publicity.

28 Theory

In *The Paradoxes of Legal Science*, Cardozo (2000) identifies change/conservation as the primary dyad affecting law, and comments 'if life feels the tug of these opposing tendencies, so also must the law which prescribes the rule of life' (p. 7). The justice systems of any society can be compared and contrasted with the ways they relate the constituents of dyads such as retribution/rehabilitation, responsibility/clemency, free-will/determinism and freedom/control.

Gray summarises criminology's wicked problem:

> The key issue in modern criminology may be summarized in one brief question: is punishment or treatment of criminals the wiser social policy? A grasp of the essentials involved in this particular question provides a general understanding of the field of criminology as a whole.
>
> (1963, p. 160)

Gray (1963) goes on to suggest that advocates for punitive criminology are 'a distinct minority' and that 'by far the dominant voice emphasises both the desirability and the need for rehabilitation of the criminal element' (p. 160). Thus, Gray's approach emphasises the rehabilitative function of criminal law. Conversely, Alschuler (2003) traces the historical shifts between retributive and rehabilitative approaches to criminal law in the US during the twentieth century, concluding that 'Retribution, the purpose of punishment most disparaged from the beginning of the century through the end, merits recognition as the criminal law's central objective' (p. 1). This perennial struggle between these two interpretations is illustrated in the oldest traditions of law in matters of *justice* and *mercy*.

In the context of Jewish law, Levine (2006) takes a more complementary approach to justice and mercy. He suggests 'looking beyond the mercy/justice dichotomy' and advocates for the 'complementary roles of mercy and justice' (p. 455) as a general principle for human societies. Thus, while some systems of law and enforcement emphasise harshness of punishment as the most effective path to quality and quantity of life and others emphasise rehabilitation, still others emphasise complementary approaches.

Aron (2005) expands the domain of law to engage even more broadly with the axiology of good and evil in Judeo-Christian mythology. He analyses different exegeses of the story of the Garden of Eden and the tree of knowledge as profoundly affecting ways of knowing and being at individual and cultural levels. Aron appreciates the dyadic nature of wicked problems and their profound implications, which have inspired my own project:

> The controversy, which has profound implications, reflects differences in worldviews concerning the good life, autonomy and relatedness, assertion and submission, will and surrender, obedience and rebellion, independence and interdependence, subjectivity and intersubjectivity.
>
> (2005, p. 681)

The recognition of opposites   29

Thus, in law and criminology as in all fields of knowledge, domain-specific dyads (e.g. punishment/rehabilitation) are entangled with domain-general dyads (e.g. subjective/objective; good/evil). The ways we relate such dyadic constituents, through opposition and/or complement, both reflects and creates the societies we live in and the wicked problems that define them.

Psychology

Psychology represents a domain of knowledge with diverse and often contested ways of knowing. Indeed, psychology's *identity crisis* has been well documented and clearly articulated for nearly a century (e.g. Buhler, 1929; Henriques, 2004; Staats, 1983; Stam, 2000, 2003). For example, one of the more persistent tensions that defines, divides and sometimes unites the domain of psychology in higher education is between *objective* and *subjective* representations of knowledge. This dyadic construct has strong conceptual affinities with positivist/constructivist, universalist/relativist, individual/social, reductive/holistic and empirical/phenomenological approaches to knowledge. This particular epistemic tension and its persistence is illustrated in Costin's early attempts to characterise psychology as an objective science:

> The common goal of the first course in psychology is for students to acquire specific information concerning the scientific and professional characteristics of psychology. Usually this knowledge includes the meaning of 'science' as related to psychology, techniques of describing and explaining psychological phenomena, scientific and professional areas of specialization, and the relationship of these areas to other scientific and professional fields. Practically all elementary psychology text books present these topics, while most instructors of the introductory course discuss and examine their students' understanding of this kind of information. As a rule, instructors regard the gaining of such knowledge as part of a broader goal – the development of more objective ways of observing and interpreting behavior.
>
> (1964, p. 458)

However, this approach to psychology is challenged by other commentators as lacking epistemic reflexivity and overstating the strength of the positivist stance:

> The relationship between epistemology and method is rarely articulated through our formal coursework education either at undergraduate or post-graduate level; certainly this is true in many psychology programmes ... I begin by outlining the constructionist view and differentiating this from the positivist stance. I do this for two reasons; first, to demonstrate the dominance of the positivist perspective in psychology students' education and second, because I personally subscribe to a constructionist worldview.
>
> (Darlaston-Jones, 2007, pp. 19–20)

30 Theory

The tension between objectivist and subjectivist, and positivist and constructivist epistemologies has some affinity with traditional psychology's tendency to isolate individual cognition from the fluid and formative social contexts emphasised by social constructivists.

Darlaston-Jones' stance has some affinity with Buss' (1979) earlier dialectical critique of traditional psychology: 'The individual-society dialectic has been obliterated and ignored for too long by psychologists. The social, historical, and developmental dimensions of psychological ideas should not, and indeed cannot, be separated. Psychological ideas are part of a larger totality' (p. ix). Similarly, Riegel's (1979) dialectical critique of psychology, published in the same year, claimed to reject 'the preference for stable traits, abilities, and competencies deeply rooted in Western psychological thinking' (p. 1). However, Riegel also rejected the biases towards equality and balance that began to accompany the rise of relativism. Just five years later, Basseches (1984) contextualised his dialectical approach to psychology against a dominance of relativist epistemologies in popular psychology, claiming 'the greatest threat to the process of knowledge-building comes from a voice which portrays people as not pursuing truth at all' (p. 14). Here we see the affinity between dyads such as subjective/objective and relative/universal in the way a field of knowledge is conceptualised. These dyadic contestations represent wicked problems inasmuch as they play out in socially complex and dynamic contexts (e.g. psychology courses and professional organisations) and involve sweepingly significant conceptualisations of, and approaches to, mental health and well-being.

The task of engaging epistemological diversity within psychology, as within any discipline, is itself an onto-epistemological task. The appreciation of psychology as relationally and contextually objective *and* subjective, positivist *and* constructivist, fixed *and* fluid, unified *and* diverse is a complex epistemological task. Indeed, one of several relatively recent commentaries on the diversity of psychology within higher education argues:

> Calls for unification, no matter how well articulated, will likely fall on deaf ears since there are already deeply entrenched positions in the discipline that are supported by the implicit unity of method and framework ... the current state of psychological theory and its attendant features is neither fixed nor entirely fluid.
>
> (Stam, 2004, p. 1262)

This is not to discount either a positivist or relativist approach to psychology: it is to appreciate the necessary tensions *and* potential syntheses between such dyads, in context. In the concrete, the dyads frame useful and necessary dichotomies that facilitate choices in context. In the abstract, the dyads serve as interdependent polarities containing a spectrum of possibilities and degrees of difference. Disciplinary identity problems arise when (a) the spectrum of positions between polarities is ignored such that the polarities are pruned into mutually exclusive binaries or (b) the polarities are seen as fixed rather than relational and contextual. As Ivic comments in relation to division between soft sciences, hard sciences and the humanities:

> This argument is based on the idea about the fundamental difference between natural sciences and humanities and their methods. It implies binary oppositions: objective/subjective, nature/culture, repeatable/unique, true/constructed, natural/mental etc, where the first term designates natural sciences, while the second designates humanities.
>
> (2008, p. 29)

Psychology is one of the disciplines often caught between these binary oppositional labels. As the internal struggle suggests, the line between subjective and objective paradoxically blurs and comes into focus when we examine ourselves. Accordingly, the explicit presence of dyadic constructs in the quest to define psychology as a domain of knowledge serves once again to illustrate their ubiquity.

Design and design thinking

As a relatively recent movement in design-related fields (e.g. architecture), design thinking has grappled with wicked problems in implicitly dyadic terms. More current models of design thinking tend to encompass, rather than choose between, traditional design dichotomies such as user/producer, analysis/intuition, natural/synthetic and concrete/abstract. As such, there is an increasing amount of research beginning to explore the cognitive-epistemic nature of design thinking. For example, Brown (2008) reflects on integrative thinking as valuing analytical processes but also 'the ability to see all of the salient – and sometimes contradictory – aspects of a confounding problem and create novel solutions that go beyond and dramatically improve on existing alternatives' (p. 3). Martin (2010) identifies a three-phase design process, where, 'As understanding moves from mystery to heuristic to algorithm, extraneous information is pared away; [and] the complexities of the world are mastered through simplification' (p. 39). Beckman and Barry (2007) identify a four-phase cycle – Observations (contexts), Frameworks (insights), Imperatives (ideas) and Solutions (experiences) – and draw on Kolb's (1984) theory of experiential learning to show how these phases cross-cut dichotomies between concrete/abstract and analysis/synthesis. Ritchey (1991) and Owen (1997, 1998) move beyond traditional oppositions between analytic and synthetic epistemologies in their approaches to science, systems thinking and design thinking. Martin (2010) expresses this dialogic way of thinking succinctly: 'Neither analysis nor intuition alone is enough. In the future, the most successful businesses will balance analytical mastery and intuitive originality in a dynamic interplay that I call "design thinking"' (p. 38). Collectively, such discussions reveal the salience of dyadic structures in the recognition and (re)solution of the wicked problems of design.

32 Theory

Business

While modern consumer societies continue to ponder resource limitations, the businesses that compete for market share within consumer economies also have their characteristic dyadic concerns. In the context of business, O'Driscoll (2008) identifies dyads as 'values-in-tension', including cognition/emotion (buyer behaviour), commoditisation/differentiation (buyer value), mass/one-on-one (communication), acquisition/retention (customers), deliberate/emergent (market planning), specialist/generalist (organisation), globalisation/localisation (marketing), wasteful/sustainable (marketing) and theory/practice (business theory). In a study of 46,000 managers from over 40 countries, Hampden-Turner et al. (2000) identify dyads that appear in managerial conflicts, including universalism/particularism, individualism/communitarianism, specificity/diffusion, achieved status/ascribed status, inner-direction/outer-direction and sequential time/synchronous time. Such dyads provide powerful ways to conceptualise the wicked problems and opportunities that global markets present. What are the long-term trade-offs of any economic system, managerial style or approach to business? Furthermore, how do these trade-offs work in new knowledge markets such as higher education?

The reconciliation of dyadic constituents poses many wicked problems that play out in the domain of higher education in a *neoliberal* (i.e. market-driven) milieu. Some commentators have associated neoliberalism with positivist epistemology (e.g. Hunter, 2002) and the commodification and marketisation of knowledge (e.g. Caffentzis, 2004). The marketisation and commodification of knowledge can marginalise some domains of academia that identify with epistemologies that are not easily or readily branded, quantified or able to compete with more mass-marketable 'products'. For instance, Hunter's (2002) position is that 'neo-liberal understandings of positivism and the institutional power that perpetuates them are to be criticised in favour of epistemological diversity in the academy' (p. 119). So even at the nexus of business and education we find domain-general dyads such as positivist/relativist used to identify and contest distributions of power.

Education

Education has always been a contested space at the intersection of disciplines and value systems. The dyadic constituents most valued in a particular education system powerfully reflect its society's onto-epistemological dispositions. The stakes are high and the practiced relationships between dyadic constituents such as teacher-centred/learner-centred, transmission/discovery, constructivism/behaviourism and direct instruction/inquiry-based learning are important. Formal education's wicked problems and challenges relate to learner diversity and conflicting perspectives on the purpose and value of education (e.g. emancipatory/citizenship). Likewise, the proliferation of 'gogies' in the modern era also reflects

The recognition of opposites   33

changing understandings of identities and power relationships between teacher and learner. *Pedagogy*, which traditionally connoted a hierarchical power relationship between teacher and learner, is being differentiated from new terms like *andragogy* (Knowles, 1980), *heutagogy* (Hase and Kenyon, 2007), *peerogogy* (Rheingold, 2012) and *cybergogy* (Wang, 2008), which emphasise lifelong learning, self-determined learning, peer-to-peer learning and learning through online social networks respectively. Collectively, these neologisms signal a socio-cultural shift in the dyadic relationship between teaching and learning.

The ubiquity of dyads and dyadic relationships in education is widely recognised. Illustratively, Pearson (2011) proposes three sources of dyads in his analysis of Indigenous education. These include (1) a 'spiritual, mystical or metaphysical source', (2) 'nature', and (3) 'human perceptions and interpretations of reality' (pp. 101–2). Not only does he explicitly use dyadic structures in his polemic against 'leftist' educators, he recognises the need to consider the origins of dyadic structures to invoke them for the purpose of counterbalancing in education.

One of the most common secondary dyads in education is teacher-centred/student-centred. The primary dyad here is teaching/learning. Teacher-centred and student-centred approaches to learning reflect an interest in the ownership and control of curriculum knowledge and pedagogy. Student-centred approaches tend to adopt a facilitation model of pedagogy that foregrounds student ownership over the selection and delivery of curriculum knowledge and student empowerment to self-discover and construct knowledge that is relevant to them. Of teacher-centred approaches, Churchill *et al.* note:

> The focus on the teacher is associated with a repertoire of activities and actions that have been central to the collective images of teaching for the last 150 years: the teacher standing at the front, talking, writing on the board, and controlling (at least in intent) virtually everything that takes place within the classroom.
>
> (2011, p. 51)

Teacher-centred and student-centred approaches are often contrasted and represented in a developmental relationship. Arguably, the dominant relationship reflected in recent Western progressive education posits a development from teacher-centred approaches to student-centred approaches as the most desirable form of pedagogy. This progression is implicit in Churchill *et al.*'s (2011) lament concerning the 'overwhelming power of this taken-for-granted [teacher-centred] view of teaching' (p. 51). In epistemological studies of pedagogical views, Richardson (2005) and Wideen *et al.* (1998) claim that preservice teachers and beginning teachers are more likely to have a teacher-centred view.

The secondary student-centred/teacher-centred dyad and its primary teaching/learning dyad have strong affinities to other dyads in education. For example, Slavich and Zimbardo identify a pedagogical affinity between active learning,

34 Theory

student-centred learning, collaborative learning, experiential learning and problem-based learning, and argue:

> At the deepest conceptual level is the fact that these approaches share similar theoretical roots. At the heart of all types of active and student centered learning, for example, is the constructivist notion that students generate knowledge and meaning best when they have experiences that lead them to realize how new information conflicts with their prevailing understanding of a concept or idea.
>
> (2012, p. 6)

They contrast these collective approaches with 'a lecture-based approach, in which instructors assume the role of "sage on the stage" and dictate information to students, who have little role in shaping the experience' (p. 3). These contested educational values are sometimes most obvious at cultural interfaces. Wong (2007) notes that the teacher-centred approach to mathematics is a culturally dominant model in Hong Kong, grounded in the belief that it can help students to move between the concrete and the abstract. Herein lies the 'wickedness' of the problem of comparing and choosing educational systems and outcomes in a rapidly globalising world.

These dyadic approaches to pedagogy find expression in sub-disciplines within education, and competition between dyadic constituents can manifest as disciplinary 'wars'. For instance, Thomas (2011) laments that 'divisions in the [Australian mathematics] community that arose in the 1990s have taken a terrible toll', yet notes of the US math wars, 'while it may have been destructive at the time, it has led to much greater cooperation between the various bodies' (p. 137). Similarly, Izmirli (2011) writes of an approach to dyadic relationships in the context of mathematics: 'The proposed epistemological revision would ameliorate our synthesis of the seemingly dichotomous categories such as teaching and learning, theory and application, logic and intuition by demonstrating the unity of practical (concrete) mathematical knowledge and its theoretical (abstract) counterpart' (p. 28). Some educators (e.g. Butterfield, 1994) imply abstract/tactile and isolated/holistic dyads to argue for more culturally sensitive pedagogies that recognise different epistemologies in mathematics and science. Butterfield (1994) engages dyadic structures in the context of Indigenous education, arguing that 'practices most consistent with how Native students learn mathematics and science best include (a) simultaneous processing (seeing the whole picture) instead of successive processing (analysing information sequentially)' (pp. 4–5). Needless to say, in the meeting of cultures across borders and within mathematics' staffrooms and classrooms, there are epistemic conflicts, as there are in any other domain of life and study. Dyadic structures and relationships help us to recognise and possibly (re)solve such conflicts and wicked problems in the domains of formal education, and in education writ large.

The recognition of opposites   35

In the context of cross-cultural education, Battiste argues for a synthesis or balance between Western and Indigenous ways of knowing that moves beyond simple oppositional binary relationships:

> Indigenous scholars discovered that Indigenous knowledge is far more than the binary opposite of western knowledge ... Indigenous knowledge fills the ethical and knowledge gaps in Eurocentric education, research, and scholarship. By animating the voices and experiences of the cognitive 'other' and integrating them into educational processes, it creates a new, balanced centre and a fresh vantage point from which to analyse Euro-centric education and its pedagogies.
>
> (2002, p. 5)

However, in the context of Australian literacy and numeracy for Indigenous students, Noel Pearson provides an example of an epistemic-pedagogic approach that argues for a deliberate developmental school-based imbalance in the context of a broader balance between the skills and knowledge/creativity and critique dyad:

> Creativity will not be killed by giving priority to basic skills ... All diver-sions and impediments – every excuse, every suggestion that harm will come from such a focus, every appeal to 'balanced' approaches to basic skills mastery – have to be removed.
>
> (2011, p. 108)

Pearson is fiercely combative when it comes to the pedagogies of the progressive left and argues for a need to 'sail on an uneven keel' to *right* the historical wrongs of the left. For Pearson, the left is characterised by its focus on students' self-esteem, feelings and a resistance to testing: 'Seen in terms of the Old Left, this kind of critical pedagogy is just the teaching of false conscious-ness, powered by moral vanity' (p. 110). The right is characterised by 'basic skills mastery ... practice makes perfect ... and a solid grounding in knowledge' (pp. 108–9). Pearson's 'uneven keel' analogy illustrates yet another approach to dyadic relationships in contested spaces.

These few examples powerfully illustrate the semantic affinities between different dyads in and beyond the domain of education (e.g. left, traditional, teacher-centred, content vs. right, progressive, student-centred, creativity). I have often wondered at the extent of these affinities and our conscious sen-sitivity to them. A single throwaway line in a conversation or a subtle aspect of physical appearance can signal a complex web of ideological and attitudinal affinities that operate in the classroom, the lecture theatre and the theatre of life.

A second dyad that relates to education but is relevant to all domains of knowledge and existence is nature/nurture. Teachers who emphasise nature

36 Theory

tend to view their students' behaviour, learning ability, intelligence and personality as inherited and fixed. Teachers who emphasise nurture tend to view their students' behaviour, learning ability, intelligence and personality as constructed and malleable. Walker and Plomin (2005) argue that a nurture-based bias can be found in Western educational psychology and teacher-training programmes. However, their survey of 667 primary teachers revealed 'that teachers and parents appear to have moved beyond the nature versus nurture debate, and hold the more balanced viewpoint that both genes and the environment are important' (p. 515). Arguably, a teacher's view of the relative influence of nature and nurture in a particular domain (e.g. intelligence) can have a powerful impact on their engagement or disengagement with some students. For instance, a nature-biased teacher may offer less support to a student who scores lowly on an IQ test to improve their performance than to a student who scores highly on an IQ test to apply their performance. A nature–nurture bias is as likely to affect teacher identity as it is to affect learner identity. Henderson and Dweck (cited in Fives and Buehl, 2010) found that learners with nature-based beliefs about intelligence attribute poor performance to uncontrollable factors, whereas learners with nurture-based beliefs about intelligence tend to attribute poor performance to laziness or external influences (p. 492). Needless to say, a teacher's relational disposition to the nature/nurture dyad can have a profound influence on their students' ways of knowing and being.

Another educational dyad identifies approaches to teaching that emphasise inclusive or exclusive approaches to student learning. Inclusive approaches tend to emphasise the student's 'right to participate and the school's duty to accept the child' (Churchill *et al.*, 2011, p. 138). Exclusive approaches tend to detach 'groups and individuals from social relations and institutions and prevent them from full participation in society' (p. 138). Arguably, the modern Western educational milieu is characterised by an historical and pedagogical shift towards inclusion. For example, in an Australian context, this shift is similarly reflected in Education Queensland's continuum of practice for inclusivity. Here development from novice to expert teacher is described as follows:

> (1) No activities recognise the varied learning needs of students from diverse backgrounds. (2) Several activities recognise the varied learning needs of students from diverse backgrounds. (3) Activities recognise the varied learning needs of students from diverse backgrounds for all, or nearly all, of the lesson.
>
> (2002, p. 16)

The relational trade-offs between inclusion and exclusion influence schooling and the societies within which schools function. For example, attitudes towards students with special needs, co-educational and single-sex schooling and streaming for intellectual and physical ability all relate to the nature of relations we understand between exclusion and inclusion.

A significant dyad in educational psychology involves intrinsic/extrinsic approaches to student motivation. Intrinsic approaches tend to value and foster motivation that arises from a sense of achievement and efficacy within the individual learner. Extrinsic approaches tend to value and utilise motivations from external incentives (i.e. punishments or rewards). Extrinsic and intrinsic approaches are sometimes aligned to behaviourist and humanist approaches respectively. Accordingly, it seems fair to suggest that the Western educational milieu reflects an historical shift from the privileging of extrinsically motivating pedagogies to the foregrounding of intrinsically motivating pedagogies. The centrality of the dyad in teaching and the historical shift between poles is evident in modern textbooks. For example, 'it is apparent that educators interested in promoting meaningful and engaging learning experiences must also be prepared to prime an individual's motivation to learn – and arguably do so on a level beyond extrinsic rewards' (Churchill *et al.*, 2011, p. 118). A related dyad that has recently influenced educational practice concerning motivation is Dweck's (1999, 2006) fixed/growth mindset. Dweck argues that students and teachers who view ability as innate or fixed limit opportunities for growth and improvement.

Another educational dyad identifies permissive/authoritarian approaches to behaviour management as a key consideration in teacher identity. Authoritarian approaches tend to emphasise a teacher's non-negotiable control and responsibility as creator and enforcer of rules. Permissive approaches tend to emphasise student agency in the establishment and organisation of rules or, more extremely, the abolition of rules and organisational structure altogether. The latter is seen as a way to engage students in the intrinsic construction of their own evolvable boundaries and guidelines. The current and dominant milieu of Western education reflects an historical and pedagogical development from 'control' to 'engagement' in behaviour management. Churchill *et al.* (2011) reflect: 'While the "control" approach is dominant in schools and popular culture, it is the "engagement" approach, broadly speaking, that has come to be dominant in the normative research and policy discourses of education' (p. 56). This shift is further reflected in the language shift from 'classroom discipline' to 'behaviour support' and 'safe, supportive environment', endorsed in modern policy documents (e.g. QCT, 2006). The construct of behaviour management has also been used in studies of epistemic identity. Fives and Buehl (2010) identify classroom management as one of five central themes related to teachers' beliefs about knowledge and teaching. Thus, in education, too, dyads and dyadic relationships help us to recognise the wicked problems of everyday classrooms and (re)solve them relationally and contextually, rather than making them worse by trying to solve them once and for all with a single approach.

In summary, how we teach and learn (teaching/learning; transmission/inquiry), motivate (intrinsic/extrinsic), manage behaviour (permissive/authoritarian), organise and value ability and culture (exclusion/inclusion) and attribute ability (nature/nurture; fixed/growth) can all be expressed in dyadic forms. The ways we conceptualise such dyads and relate their constituents profoundly affect and reflect our educational systems, institutions and the individuals who teach and

38 Theory

learn (or fail to learn) within them. Formal education is a particularly fertile environment for wicked problems as it is perhaps the most powerful means by which positions are passed from one generation or group to another. As teachers are well aware, the classroom and lecture theatre are interfaces for different and often competing perspectives across all domains of knowledge. For this reason I have chosen to discuss and illustrate the applications of bi-relational pedagogy in Part III of this book. My rationale, to be explicated in later chapters, is that teachers have a significant influence on the formation of learners' onto-epistemological dispositions, much of which concerns the recognition of dyads and the coordination of dyadic constituents.

Gender studies

One of the most enduring and ubiquitous dyads is male/female. Butler ponders the tyranny of this and other dyads in the form of binary oppositions that, by their very formation, render powerless the spectrum of realities that lie between them, or perhaps the reality beyond them that cannot even be mapped onto spectra or continua with their implied values:

> Power seemed more than an exchange between subjects or a relation of constant inversion between a subject and an Other; indeed, power appeared to operate in the production of that very binary frame for thinking about gender. I asked what configuration of power constructs the subject and the Other, that binary relation between 'men' and 'women', and the internal stability of those terms? What restriction is here at work? Are these terms untroubling only to the extent that they conform to the heterosexual matrix for conceptualizing gender and desire? What happens to the subject and to the stability of gender categories when the epistemic regime of presumptive heterosexuality is unmasked as that which produces and reifies these ostensible categories of ontology.
>
> (cited in Leitch *et al.*, 2001, p. 2489)

We see here a critique of the way that binary formulations of gender normalise and prescribe some ways of being and exclude others. Such critiques highlight not just the ubiquity of the male/female dyad but the epistemic power that its formulation has on the perpetuation of the realities it expresses, affirms or denies.

Binary oppositional ways of relating gender have been the subject of most criticism in feminist writings. However, authors have disagreed as to how best to subvert or redress these imbalances. For example, Helen Cixious' work reflects a paradoxical way of reconciling masculine and feminine oppositions by refusing to participate in them:

> The real scandal of Cixious's work lay in her insistence on its two incompatible logics. On the one, she claimed that ecriture feminine was characterized

by the explicitly female body parts that had been repressed by traditional discourse and were being expressed by the woman writer...Yet on the other hand she claimed that both men and women could write ecriture feminine. How can both claims be true at the same time?

The binary logic that structures the opposition between 'male' and 'female' is set up as a relation not between 'A' and 'B' but between 'A' and 'not A'...One half of the opposition is essentially destroyed for the other half to make 'sense'...That is why Cixious declares 'I am not a feminist'. Feminism, for her, participates in the same logic of opposition as traditional logocentrism or its companion, phallocentrism (the description of sexual difference as a difference between having and lacking the phallus.

(Leitch, 2001, pp. 2037–8)

Here, the binary opposition between male and female is most powerful when one or the other is present only as an absence.

Some commentators seek to move the gender discourse beyond binary oppositional divisions by disrupting the traditional designations of who or what is male or female:

Again, it is curious that the loudest voices calling for such holistic approaches have been those of women, but Midgely does not believe this opens the door to a view of philosophy as essentially gendered because, as she says, 'I want to say that we are all both. I do think very profoundly that we are all male and female, that these are elements in all of us, that there should not be and isn't warfare ...'

(Baggini and Strangroom, 2003, p. 129)

This sort of destruction or subversion of binary oppositions is central to the process of *deconstruction*, which involves an inversion of power in binary oppositions that momentarily collapses the whole idea of opposition. Possibly, the centrality of the male/female dyad accounts for the depth of dyadic explorations that concern it.

Perhaps more than any other domain of knowledge, gender studies has scrutinised and questioned the politics, not just of binary oppositions like male/female but of all dyadic structures. Singer writes in *Androgyny*:

The polarities are expressed in a variety of ways; for example – light and dark, positive and negative, eternal and temporal, hot and cold, spirit and matter, mind and body, art and science, war and peace. One pair, male and female, serves as the symbolic expression of the energetic power behind all of the other polarities.

(2000, p. 5)

40   Theory

Needless to say, these dyads are contested because of the significant realities they reflect and construct. Numerous wicked problems, such as domestic violence, body image disorders (e.g. anorexia bulimia and anorexia nervosa), gay marriage, the ordination of women priests, abortion and contraception have a gendered dimension that is inextricably linked to dyadic ways of knowing and being masculine and/or/nor feminine.

Literature and literary criticism

The feminist project has much in common with the broader aims of critical theory, which concerned itself with the deconstruction of the binary oppositions that enabled the power imbalances of modernity. For some literary theorists, like Paul de Man, the true destruction of binary oppositions must go beyond 'playful reversals':

> The polarities of inside and outside have been reversed, but they are still the same polarities that are at play: internal meaning has become outside reference, and the outer form has become the intrinsic structure. A new version of reductiveness at once follows this reversal ... The recurrent debate opposing intrinsic to extrinsic criticism stands under the aegis of an inside/outside metaphor that is never seriously being questioned ... I merely wish to speculate on a different set of terms, perhaps less simple in their differential relationships than the strictly polar, binary opposition between inside and outside and therefore less likely to enter into the easy play of chiasmic reversals.
>
> (1973, pp. 27–8)

Destructions of dyadic structures and playful dyadic reversals both reflect epistemological locations, perhaps *developments*, beyond simplistic binary oppositions. As I shall explore later, one of these trajectories of development is the negation and destruction of duality altogether.

Johnson (1980) offers a particularly nuanced analysis of the destruction of binary oppositions, including masculine/feminine, literature/criticism, prose/poetry, reference/self-reference, clarity/obscurity, science/literature, syntax/semantics and naïve/ironic. Her claim is that 'the differences *between* entities ... are shown to be based on a repression of differences *within* entities' (p. x) and that 'the "deconstruction" of a binary opposition is thus not an annihilation of all values or differences; it is an attempt to follow the subtle, powerful effects of differences already at work within the illusion of a binary opposition' (p. xi). The claim suggests, and I concur, that binary oppositions all tend to fail under critical examination, but 'that perpetual error we call life' (p. xii) is somehow made meaningful by the differences they create. Johnson's (1980) work serves to illustrate the presence of dyads and a particular dyadic relationship. The sophistication of this dyadic relationship represents a characteristic onto-epistemological development, the type of which I hope to represent in Chapter 5's original approach to bi-relational development (i.e. BirD).

Some of the clearest dyads and most sophisticated explorations of dyadic relationships are found in literature. From the works of Shakespeare to the works of Dr Seuss and D. H. Lawrence, dyads provide almost universal narrative structures. Lawrence (1954) explores the human predicament in his essay *Life*: 'We are balanced like a flame between the two darknesses, the darkness of the beginning and the darkness of the end. For us, the beginning is not the end; the two are not one' (n.p.). Dr Seuss' (1990) verse characterises life as 'a great balancing act' to be walked with a well coordinated left and right foot. Poets such as Coleridge and Poe had well developed dyadic philosophies that they expressed in verse. As Ramey (1978) notes, 'The most fundamental aspect of both Coleridge's and Poe's view of the world and poetry is the recognition of two forces' (p. 2). Sometimes, the diverse ways of relating dyadic constituents inspire literary-epistemic conflicts. William Blake seeks to reconcile opposites in the aptly titled *The Marriage of Heaven and Hell*, as highlighted in the following lines:

> Without Contraries is no progression. Attraction and Repulsion,
> Reason and Energy, Love and Hate, are necessary to Human existence.
> From these contraries spring what the religious call Good and Evil.
> Good is the passive that obeys Reason. Evil is the active springing from energy.
> Good is heaven. Evil is Hell.
>
> (2014)

C.S Lewis' (1945) book *The Great Divorce* offers a response to Blake's marriage of opposites that seeks to counter its proceeding relativism and return a sense of absolute identity to the division between good and evil. While much populist literature is structured using binary oppositional archetypes, much classical literature and literary theory plays with, subverts or reconceptualises these oppositions. While the examples are almost inexhaustible in this domain, my aim here is to briefly illustrate the presence of dyads and dyadic relationships that belie the wicked problems within and beyond yet another domain of knowledge.

Theology

Much theological comment on the nature and existence of God concerns the number and gender of 'His' nature. Is there one all powerful God (i.e. monotheism), two equally powerful opposing gods (one of good and one of evil (i.e. dualism)), one God with two natures, one God in three (i.e. Trinitarianism) or a pantheon of gods? The answers divide ways of knowing and being within and across religions. For example, Pauline Christianity takes a different approach

42 Theory

to Manichaeism and Gnosticism as to the unity and duality of God. In Hinduism, the Vedic scriptures seem to indicate a pantheon of gods, whereas the later Upanishads indicate a God beyond these gods (i.e. *Brahman*). While Buddhism is commonly portrayed as non-theistic, some Mahayana traditions worship the Buddha in a way that is very similar to the omnipotent supernatural God of some Judeo-Christian traditions. In some Zen traditions, the Dharmakaya is conceptualised in a way that is similar to Tillich's (1951, 1957) transtheistic Ground of Being from a Christian tradition. It is unsurprising that the existential riddle I posed at the beginning of this book finds its clearest and most abstract manifestations in the number of God(s). That the answers to this riddle are contested within and across religions and secular philosophies suggests the universal *and* provincial nature of the quest to define reality in relation to two.

A conceptually similar question concerns the gender of God: is God masculine and/or feminine? In one sense, the answer splits traditional Abrahamic monotheisms, where God is commonly referred to as 'He' and 'Father', from neo-pagan religions, which are often characterised by worship of a Goddess referred to as 'She' and 'Mother'. As Singer contends:

> This cataclysmic separation of the masculine and feminine can be understood psychologically as the creation of a duality that was the inevitable though long-delayed consequence of the disintegration of the primordial androgyny ... The history of the Aries era provides a background for the myth of male superiority in the countless legends of the patriarchy of men under the fatherhood of God.
>
> (2000, p. 52)

However, different onto-epistemological dispositions within these cultures challenge the binary opposition, as even the God of Abrahamic monotheism can be seen to transcend gender or embrace both masculine and feminine characteristics; and the neo-pagan appropriation of the Goddess can also be seen as ironic, counterbalancing and contextual in the presence of dominant male images. Thus, dyads and dyadic relationships (e.g. masculine/feminine) are implicated in our answers to ultimate theological questions, and perhaps even to the generation of the questions themselves. The historically violent contestations over the *noneness*, oneness, twoness, threeness, multiplicity, masculinity, femininity and/or androgeny of (G)od/s are well documented. Again, the fact that these contestations have occurred as much within traditions as between them suggests to me that there is an onto-epistemological dimension to the wicked problems of religion that is as transcendent in form as it is immanent in expression.

Perhaps one of the most significant theologians of the twentieth century, Paul Tillich, used dyadic structures such as human/divine, subject/object and sacred/profane to communicate profound theological understandings that often arise from the reconciliation of opposites. In *Systematic Theology*, Tillich writes:

> Theology formulates the questions implied in human existence, and theology formulates the answers implied in divine self-manifestation under the guidance of the questions implied in human existence. This is a circle which drives man to a point where question and answer are not separated. This point, however, is not a moment in time.
>
> (1951, p. 61)

This circular driving together and collapsing of dyadic constituents is at the heart of Tillich's trans-theism, where God cannot be understood in terms of subject/object, being/non-being dichotomies. For Tillich, God is the *Ground of Being*, beyond all subject/object distinctions. My claim is that such theological explanations can be understood as epistemic locations and developments that are qualitatively different from binary oppositional ways of knowing. My intention, especially in Chapter 5, is to systematically represent such locations in order to understand their origins and everyday manifestations.

C. G. Jung's life work represents another direct attempt to use the dyadic structure to unlock the meaning of religion and the nature of God/god. For example, in *Mysterium Conjunctionis*, Jung reflects on the nature and number of God in relation to dyads such as male/female, spiritual/corporeal, and heaven/earth:

> Mercurious, however, is not just the medium of conjunction but also that which is to be united, since he is the essence or 'seminal matter' of both man and woman. *Mercurius masculinus* and *Mercurius foemineus* are united in and through *Mercurius menstrualis*, which is the 'aqua'. Dorn gives the 'philosophical explanation' of this in his 'Physica Trismegisti': In the beginning God created one world (unus mundus). This he divided into two —heaven and earth. Beneath this spiritual and corporeal binarius lieth hid a third thing, which is the bond of holy matrimony . . .
>
> (1970, p. 462, section 659)

For Jung, unlike Nietzsche (1962, 1967) and Freud (1989), Christ crucified was the most powerful symbol/reality that gave meaning to the mysterious union and division of opposites found in most religious traditions. Sanford offers a Jungian interpretation of the Genesis stories that draws attention to the opposites they create and the hermeneutical possibilities for their reconciliation:

> The problem of the opposites in the Bible begins as soon as man makes his appearance. First it is suggested in the contrast between the two creation stories. The first creation story describes man as made in the image of God . . . But the second creation story says: '. . . then the Lord God formed man of dust from the ground . . . .' This is not a contradiction but a paradox.

44 Theory

> Man is torn between his divine image and his lowly earthy substance ... The story of the origin of the opposites is told even more graphically in the second creation story's tale of the first man and the first woman. Adam and Eve live in innocent bliss in the beautiful Paradise of Eden.
>
> Everything is permitted them, save one thing: they must not eat of the tree of the knowledge of good and evil. Unfortunately there is one flaw in the Garden of Eden – the snake. It tempts Eve, appealing to her desire for power and knowledge, 'to be like God, knowing good and evil,' and she in turn tempts Adam. Man and woman eat the forbidden fruit. As they do so their eyes are opened, they experience shame, and in the realization of their opposite sexuality, they make themselves aprons of fig leaves. Their bliss is shattered because now they know the opposites. With this knowledge, guilt, shame and fear have entered into human existence.
>
> (1989, p. 128)

Sanford's analysis illustrates the presence of dyads (e.g. male/female, human/ divine, good/evil) and the exegetical importance of different dyadic relationships (e.g. oppositional, paradoxical) in the (re)solution of wicked problems. Theologies of binary opposition, theologies of paradox and theologies that reconcile even opposition and paradox can represent vastly different ways of knowing and being, even, and perhaps especially, when they occur in the 'same' religious tradition. Far from being just abstract and esoteric concerns, the wicked dyadic problems of religion are powerfully connected to everyday life decisions and socio-political policies concerning everything from the use of contraception to the mitigation of climate change (Fien, 2002; Hildén, 2011; Mortreux and Barnett, 2009; Wardekker et al., 2009).

For Eastern traditions, the union or negation of opposites is found in the experience of *satori* (Zen Buddhism), *nirvana* (Buddhism) and *moksha* (Hinduism). All of these represent a moment or state of clarity and release from a captivating illusion (i.e. *maya*) where *two* are made *none* in the becoming of *One*. In many religious traditions, this release from the oppositional tensions of everyday consciousness is purported to offer calm and clarity. For example, the Bhagavad-Gita records Krishna's reflection: 'That serene one absorbed in the Atman masters his will, he knows no disquiet in heat or in cold, in pain or pleasure, in honour or dishonour'. At this stage, my immediate purpose is merely to illustrate, rather than interrogate, these dyadic structures and relationships. Much of theology, like much of modern physics, is an attempt to understand the nature of God or Reality through the separation, negation or reconciliation of apparent opposites.

Physics

Modern physics, especially cosmology, is seen by some as the domain in which the truest knowledge of the nature of knowing and being will be found. Unsurprisingly, modern cosmology seeks and expresses its most profound discoveries and conundrums in dyadic terms. CERN is one of the centres of this expectant universe, and many wait expectantly for quantum collisions to reveal everything and/or nothing about ourselves. Indeed, there is much ado about this particular dyad (i.e. everything/nothing) in modern physics. Mathematician Ian Stewart (2013) begins his chapter *Zero, zip, zilch* in New Scientist's *Nothing: From Absolute Zero to Cosmic Oblivion – Amazing Insights into Nothingness* with the lines: 'Nothing is more interesting that nothing, nothing is more puzzling than nothing, and nothing is more important than nothing' (p. 119). Battersby (2013) concludes the same book with some speculations on quantum resurrection: 'Even if we face a future in which the cosmological constant reduces us all to a set of isolated particles, there is some hope ... [of] restarting the cosmic cycle of life and death' (p. 229). The more cosmologists progress, the more similar the dyads (e.g. life/death, hope/despair, everything/nothing, relative/absolute) and dyadic relationships they invoke (e.g. pendulum swings, unions, cosmic cycles) seem to be to other disciplines. Greene reflects on the 'full circle development' of space-time's long story:

> We followed the pendulum of opinion as it swung between relationalist and absolutist positions on space, time and space-time ... I believe that an experimentally confirmed, background independent union between general relativity and quantum mechanics would reveal a gratifying resolution to this issue.
>
> (2004, p. 491)

Similarly, Atiyah writes in *Duality in Mathematics and Physics*:

> But the evidence is there, it is very spectacular, and large parts of mathematics have been swept up by this kind of band-wagon of duality ... We have seen how it [duality] relates to many things that everyone is familiar with in mathematics (group theory, topology, analysis, Fourier theory), and so it is not surprising that it also arises in physics, where one can use the same sort of ideas.
>
> (2007, p. 90)

One wonders how far this interdisciplinary similarity can spread. What symmetries lie between the mental odysseys of the arts and the physical explorations of science that may offer a glimpse into the collapse of the science/arts dichotomy?

Some modern physicists also see a unity between explorations of the mental and the physical. For example, Kaku writes:

> The infinite chain of observers each one viewing the previous observer, ultimately leads to a cosmic observer, perhaps God himself. In this picture,

46 Theory

the universe exists because there is a deity to observe it. And if Wheeler's interpretation is correct, then the entire universe is dominated by consciousness and information. In this picture, consciousness is the dominant force that determines the nature of existence ... Wigner's interpretation puts the question of consciousness at the very center of the foundation of physics. He echoes the words of the great astronomer James Jeans, who once wrote, 'Fifty years ago, the universe was generally looked on as a machine ... When we pass to extremes of size in either direction – whether to the cosmos as a whole, or to the inner recesses of the atom – the mechanical interpretation of Nature fails. We come to entities and phenomena, which are in no sense mechanical. To me they seem less suggestive of mechanical than of mental processes; the universe seems to be nearer to a great thought than to a great machine'.

(2005, p. 368)

Similarly, Reich (2002), a former engineer-physicist at CERN turned developmental psychologist of religion, draws on wave-particle complementarity as a metaphor for his model of the cognitive-epistemic development of relational and contextual reasoning. The professional lives and writings of such individuals highlight the importance of dyads and dyadic structures in and across domains of knowledge.

I have so far illustrated some of the dyads that characterise and often crosscut the wicked problems and descriptive dilemmas of different domains of knowledge. The bi-relational dilemma (i.e. how to reconcile apparent opposites) presents itself in so many shapes and forms that it is worth making more explicit in the discussion of wicked problems and how to (re)solve them. I intend in the remaining section to illustrate the ubiquity and importance of dyadic relationships.

Illustrative dyadic relationships

Bi-relational development implies different types of connections (e.g. binary opposition, interdependence and complementarity) between dyadic constituents. A key premise of my specific approach to bi-relational development (i.e. BirD) is that ways of knowing are powerfully revealed by dyads and dyadic relationships, and that these relationships influence, and are influenced by, human *being* in the most mundane and profound ways. This section briefly illustrates dyadic relationships in context as a prelude to Chapter 5's introduction to BirD, which is a systemic organisation and representation of different dyadic relationships and dynamics.

So far, I have sought to illustrate the ubiquity of dyadic structures: that is, the presence of *two* across domains of knowledge. However, it is almost impossible to illustrate the presence of dyadic structures without implicitly illustrating the presence of different dyadic relationships. Working backwards through the previous paragraphs, Reich (2002) invokes 'complementarity' for the relationship between wave and particle; Kaku (2005) reconciles mechanism and mind at different levels of abstraction; Greene (2004) writes of unity between relationalist and absolutist cosmologies; Atiyah (2007) affirms the descriptive power of duality; Battersby (2013) invokes cosmic cycles between life and death; Sanford (1989) advocates for paradoxical understanding of the two Genesis stories; C. G. Jung (1970) invokes the marriage of two as a third thing; likewise, Blake (2014) marries the opposites of heaven and hell together, while C. S. Lewis (1945) seeks to maintain their sense of divorce; Johnson (1980) acknowledges the illusion and reality of binary oppositions; Tillich (1951) invites the destruction of two for the understanding of One; Paul de Man (1973) questions all polarities; Singer (2000) seeks to androgenise binary oppositions between male and female; Cixious (in Leitch *et al.*, 2001) invokes 'two incompatible logics' to move both through and beyond dualism; Pearson (2011) calls for a time to sail on 'an uneven keel' to counterbalance and 'right' the wrongs of the left; Grace (2007) attacks the implicit mind/body dualisms of diagnostic medicine and Rakel (2013) calls for integration between traditional and alternative medicine; Giddens (1994) observes a radical inversion of political opposites that informs a third way; and Buss (1979) maintains tensions and dialectic as part of a larger totality. Thus, in establishing the ubiquity of two, I have already begun to reveal the diversity of dyadic relationships.

Perhaps some of the clearest expressions of dyadic relationships are visual symbols that abstract and distil meaning. The act of abstraction that defines a symbol implies meaning across space and time. The longevity and reiterations of some symbols illustrate the different types and the general ubiquity of dyadic relationships.

The Chinese yin–yang symbol is one of the most commonly recognised representations of unity, duality and the reconciliation of opposites. Yin (i.e. black) represents the soft, passive, feminine aspect, while yang (i.e. white) is the hard, active, masculine aspect. The transformative seed of each 'side' is found in its complementary opposite and both are parts of a single whole. The expression and deep exploration of such dyadic relationships is powerfully evident in core Taoist texts such as the *Tao Te Ching* (Tzu, 2006), which explores dyadic relationships beyond mere opposition:

> Thus being and non-being produce each other
> Difficult and easy bring about each other
> Long and short reveal each other
> High and low support each other
> Music and voice harmonize each other
> Front and back follow each other

(Ch. 2)

Likewise, the *Sri Yanta* like a *mandala* is a contemplative geometrical symbol for cosmological origins and balance. The symmetries and polarities of the cosmos

48 Theory

emanate from a central inexpressible point, or *bindu* (i.e. one or zero), that can be rediscovered through the contemplation of symmetries (i.e. two) present in division.

The widespread symbol of a winged serpent or dragon is a union of opposites between sky (bird) and earth (snake). The mercurial dragon of alchemy is 'light and dark, poison and *medicina*. Yet the toxic vapors at the beginning of the work have the potential to become the healing "sublimates" through which one eventually glimpses the pearl of wisdom' (Martin, 2010, p. 704). Here, we see a paradoxical union (i.e. One) of opposites (i.e. two) that defines the discovery of wisdom.

A related symbol, the *ouroboros*, commonly depicts a snake or serpent consuming its own tail. This ubiquitous symbol is found in many contexts, including ancient Egyptian funerary texts from 1400 BCE, Platonic and Gnostic imagery, Eastern esotericism and pre-modern alchemy. The ouroboros can symbolise the cycle of life and death or the illusory division of two (i.e. separateness) that is revealed at the point of self-consumption (i.e. Oneness or nothingness). In many mythologies, the snake or serpent itself is a dualistic symbol for positive and negative, creator and destroyer, light and dark, good and evil. Here again, we see the attempt to express the paradoxical reconciliation of opposites.

Woven with a snake, the Rod of Asclepius, god of healing for the ancient Greeks, also expresses serpentine dualities. The rod represents a duality between sickness and health, poison and medicine, wherein 'psychologically, painful insights that hit the mark, internal conflict actively engaged, corrosive sadness, bitterness or remorse both sicken and heal' (Martin, 2010, p. 740). The persistence of duality is found, too, in the symbolic appropriation of modern discoveries such as the structure of the double helix (e.g. Pope, 2001) and wave/particle dualities (e.g. Reich, 2002).

One of the most intriguing symbols of duality in Western mythology is the cross. It is intriguing because the battle over linear and cyclic cosmologies is apparent in its variations and appropriations. For example, its variations on the Latin cross most associated with Christianity include the x-shaped *saltire*, or St Andrew's cross, and the inverted cross of St Peter. While the cross is one of the most polysemous of symbols, its juncture has been regarded in many traditions as the meeting of opposites: the place for the reconciliation of one and many. This junction of opposites can be seen as a place of pain and death at the realisation of opposites and as a place of resurrection into the realisation of life beyond these dualisms:

> The symbolic equivalent to the reality of crucifixion could only be the most drastic, excruciating forms of psychic tension, where harrowing dualities and oppositions rend body and soul ... Here, the suffered crucifying tension between opposites becomes the vessel in which one is liberated *from* the opposites.
>
> (Martin, 2010, p. 744)

The recognition of opposites   49

There is an interesting symbolic difference in the presentation of the cross *with* and *without* the crucified Jesus of Christian mythology. Many Protestant denominations tend to display a cross without the crucified Christ, emphasising life through the resurrection as the overcoming of death. Alternatively, many Catholic traditions display the cross with the crucified Christ, emphasising the experience of suffering and death that precedes the resurrection.

Like the cross, the pentagram is a profound representation of the interpretation of duality, opposition and unity in human history and consciousness, for the orientation of the pentagram represents the triumph or primacy of good or evil. In most early representations, the orientation of the pentagram, with the single point above, symbolised the primacy of the spirit: the ultimate good of the heavenly realm to which earthly elements led. However, the inverted pentagram, or *Baphomet*, symbol of modern Satanism, represents the finality of duality piercing the heavens with the horns of a goat and subordinating the three points of the holy trinity:

> A reversed pentagram, with two points projecting upwards, is a symbol of evil and attracts sinister forces because it overturns the proper order of things and demonstrates the triumph of matter over spirit. It is the goat of lust attacking the heavens with its horns.
>
> (Eliphas, 1999)

Such inversions highlight one of the ultimate contestations of philosophy, that of dualism and non-dualism. Is reality one (One) or two (Two)? If reality is two (or zero or infinity) then it seems there is no ultimate triumph of Truth and Reality, for it is divided, negated or multiplied beyond recognition. If it is One then the possibility of ultimate Truth and Reality remain. The bi-relational approach I elaborate in later chapters aims to locate such onto-epistemological positions in relation to each other. This approach maintains the integrity of each position while raising the possibility that *One* can only be glimpsed and experienced through the division of parts and *Two* can only be understood in relation to the unification of parts.

The labyrinth too draws the perceiver into the paradoxical reconciliation of opposites. For example, the labyrinth of the Cathedral of Notre Dame draws the seeker into the realisation of symmetries contained within the circular whole in order to come to a point of intersection at the origin of the cross: 'The essentially dual, paradoxical nature of the labyrinth is both circular and linear, simple and complex, historical and temporal ... Thus the labyrinth simultaneously incorporates confusion and clarity, multiplicity and unity, imprisonment and liberation, chaos and order' (Martin, 2010, p. 714). In some Christian theologies, such symbols belie an ineffable third thing (e.g. Tillich's (1957) Ground of Being) that meaningfully sustains this otherwise purely dualistic process.

Collectively, these symbols and the sources I have reviewed reveal dyadic relationships that seem at least deeply entrenched in the human psyche, if not in the whole fabric of reality. Whether to extricate our modern minds from

50 Theory

obsolescent ancient bifurcations or to see these bifurcations more clearly and translate their significance in facing modern wicked problems, dyadic structures and relationships demand our attention.

References

ABC. (2013). Vote Compass project. Retrieved from http://www.abc.net.au/votecompass/

Alschuler, A. W. (2003). The changing purposes of criminal punishment: A retrospective on the past century and some thoughts about the next. *The University of Chicago Law Review*, 70(1), 1–22. doi: 10.2307/1600541.

Aron, L. (2005). The tree of knowledge: Good and evil: Conflicting interpretations. *Psychoanalytic Dialogues*, 15(5), 681–707. doi: 10.1080/10481881509348859.

Atiyah, M. F. (2007). Duality in mathematics and physics. *Lecture notes from the Institut de Matematica de la Universitat de Barcelona (IMUB)*, 69–91. http://www.fme.upc.edu/arxius/butlleti-digital/riemann/071218_conferencia_atiyah-d_article.pdf.

Baggini, J., and Strangroom, J. (2003). *What philosophers think*. London: Continuum.

Bandura, A. (2004). Health promotion by social cognitive means. *Health Education & Behavior*, 31(2), 143–64. doi: 10.1177/1090198104263660.

Barad, K. (2007). *Meeting the universe halfway: Quantum physics and the entanglement of matter and meaning*. Durham, NC: Duke University Press.

Basseches, M. (1984). *Dialectical thinking and adult development*. Norwood, NJ: Ablex Publishing.

Battersby, S. (2013). Pathways to cosmic oblivion. In J. Webb (Ed.), *Nothing: From absolute zero to cosmic oblivion – amazing insights into nothingness* (pp. 216–29). London: New Scientist.

Battiste, M. (2002). *Indigenous knowledge and pedagogy in first nations education: A literature review with recommendations*. National Working Group in Education, Canada.

Beckman, S. L., and Barry, M. (2007). Innovation as a learning process: Embedding design thinking. *California Management Review*, 50(1), 24–56.

Blake, W. (2014). The marriage of heaven and hell. *Bartleby*. (Original work published 1793.) Retrieved from http://www.bartleby.com/235/253.html

Brown, T. (2008). Design thinking. *Harvard Business Review*, June, 1–9.

Buhler, K. (1929). *Die Krise der Psychologie [The crisis of psychology]*. Jena: Gustav Fischer.

Buss, A. R. (1979). *A dialectical psychology*. New York: Irvington Publishers Inc.

Butterfield, R. A. (1994). Blueprints for Indian education: Improving mainstream schooling. ERIC Digest. *ERIC*.

Caffentzis, G. (2004). *Attacks on academic freedom, free speech, and free press (sponsored by the Association of Concerned Africa Scholars)*. Paper presented at the African Studies Association Meetings, New Orleans. https://webspace.utexas.edu/hcleaver/www/330T/350kPEECaffentzisAcademicFreedom.htm

Cardozo, B. (2000). *The paradoxes of legal science*. New York: Columbia University Press. (Original work published 1930.)

Churchill, R., Ferguson, P., Godhino, S., Johnson, N., Keddie, A. M., Letts, W., and Vick, M. (2011). *Teaching: Making a difference*. Milton, Australia: John Wiley and Sons.

Cloke, P., and Johnston, R. (2005). Deconstructing human geography's binaries. In P. Cloke and R. Johnston (Eds.), *Spaces of geographical thought: Deconstructing human geography's binaries* (pp. 1–20). London: Sage.

Costin, F. (1964). The effects of an introductory psychology course on students' perceptions of psychology and psychologists. *The Journal of Educational Research*, 57(9), 458–63. doi: 10.2307/27531456.

Darlaston-Jones, D. (2007). Making connections: The relationship between epistemology and research methods. *The Australian Community Psychologist*, 19(1), 19–27.

De Man, P. (1973). Semiology and rhetoric. *Diacritics*, 3(3), 27–33. doi: 10.2307/464524.

Dweck, C. S. (1999). *Self-theories: Their role in motivation, personality and development.* Philadelphia: Psychology Press.

Dweck, C. S. (2006). *Mindset: The new psychology of success.* New York: Random House.

Education Queensland. (2002). *A guide to productive pedagogies: Classroom reflection manual.* QLD, Australia: QLD Government. Retrieved from http://education.qld.gov.au/public_media/reports/curriculum-framework/productive-pedagogies/pdfs/prodped.pdf.

Eliphas, L. (1999). *Transcendental magic, its doctrine and ritual [Dogme et rituel de la haute magie]* (A. E. Waite, Trans.). York Beach, ME: Weiser.

Fien, J. (2002). Synthesis: A cross-cultural reflection. In J. Fien, D. Yencken and H. Sykes (Eds.), *Young people and the environment: An Asia-Pacific perspective* (pp. 151–71). Dordrecht, The Netherlands: Kluwer Academic Publishers.

Fives, H., and Buehl, M. M. (2010). Teachers' articulation of beliefs about teaching knowledge: Conceptualizing a belief framework. In L. D. Bendixen and F. C. Feucht (Eds.), *Personal epistemology in the classroom* (pp. 470–515). New York: Cambridge University Press.

Freilich, M., Jong, P. E., Fischer, J. L., Littleton, C. S., Amnon, O., Tokarev, S. A., and Voigt, W. J. (1975). Myth, method, and madness [and comments and replies]. *Current Anthropology*, 16(2), 207–26. doi: 10.2307/2741121.

Freud, S. (1989). *The future of an illusion.* London: W. W. Norton & Company. (Original work published 1927.)

Giddens, A. (1994). *Beyond left and right: The future of radical politics.* Cambridge: Polity.

Grace, V. (2007). Beyond dualism in the life sciences: Implications for a feminist critique of gender-specific medicine. *Journal of Interdisciplinary Feminist Thought*, 2(1), 1–18.

Graham-Pole, J. (2001). "Physician, Heal Thyself": How teaching holistic medicine differs from teaching CAM. *Academic Medicine*, 76(6), 662–4.

Gray, D. J. (1963). Criminology: The treatment–punishment controversy. *William and Mary Law Review*, 4(2), 160–8.

Greene, B. (2004). *The fabric of the cosmos.* London: Penguin.

Hampden-Turner, C., Trompenaars, F., and Lewis, D. (2000). *Building cross-cultural competence: How to create wealth from conflicting values.* Chichester: John Wiley & Sons.

Hase, S., and Kenyon, C. (2007). Heutagogy: A child of complexity theory. *Complicity: An International Journal of Complexity and Education*, 4(1), 111–18.

Henriques, G. R. (2004). Psychology defined. *Journal of Clinical Psychology*, 60(12), 1207–21. doi: 10.1002/jclp.20061.

Hildén, M. (2011). The evolution of climate policies – the role of learning and evaluations. *Journal of Cleaner Production*, 19(16), 1798–1811. doi: 10.1016/j.jclepro.2011.05.004

Hunter, M. (2002). Rethinking epistemology, methodology, and racism: Or, is white sociology really dead? *Race and Society*, 5(2), 119–38. doi: http://dx.doi.org/10.1016/j.racsoc.2004.01.002

Ivic, S. (2008). Explanation and understanding in the history of philosophy from hermeneutics to Ricoeur. *Crossroads: An Interdisciplinary Journal for the Study of History, Philosophy, Religion, and Classics*, 3(1), 26–34.

52 Theory

Izmirli, I. M. (2011). Pedagogy on the ethnomathematics–epistemology nexus: A manifesto. *Journal of Humanistic Mathematics*, 2(1), 27–50. doi:10.5642/jhummath.201102.04.

Jacoby, W. G. (1988). The sources of liberal-conservative thinking: Education and conceptualization. *Political Behavior*, 10(4), 316–32. doi: 10.1007/BF00990806

Johnson, B. (1980). *The critical difference: Essays in the contemporary rhetoric of reading*. Baltimore: John Hopkins University Press.

Jung, C. G. (1970). *Myseterium coniunctionis: An inquiry into the separation and synthesis of psychic opposites in alchemy (The collected works of C. G. Jung)* (G. Adler and R. F. C. Hull, Trans., Vol. 14). Princeton, NJ: Princeton University Press. (Original work published 1955.)

Kaku, M. (2005). *Parallel worlds: A journey through creation, higher dimensions, and the future of the cosmos*. New York: Doubleday.

Kaptchuk, T. (1983). *The web that has no weaver: Understanding Chinese medicine*. New York: McGraw-Hill.

Knowles, M. (1980). *The modern practice of adult education: From pedagogy to andragogy*. Wilton, CT: Association Press.

Kolb, D. A. (1984). *Experiential learning: Experience as the source of learning and development*. Englewood Cliffs, NJ: Prentice-Hall.

Lawrence, D. H. (1954). *Life*. St. Ives: Ark Press.

Leitch, V. B., Leith, V. B., Cain, W. E., Finke, L. A., Johnson, B. E., McGowan, J. and Williams, J. J. (Eds.). (2001). *The Norton anthology of theory and criticism*. New York: W.W. Norton & Co.

Levine, S. J. (2006). Looking beyond the mercy/justice dichotomy: Reflection on the complementary roles of mercy and justice in Jewish law and tradition. *Journal of Catholic Legal Studies*, 45(2), 455–71.

Lewis, C. S. (1945). *The great divorce*. London: Geoffrey Bles.

Martin, M. (Ed.). (2010). *The book of symbols: Reflections on archetypal images*. Cologne: Taschen.

Martin, R. (2010). Design thinking: achieving insights via the 'knowledge funnel'. *Strategy and Leadership*, 38(2) 37–41. doi: http://dx.doi.org/10.1108/10878571011029046.

McNeil, B. J., Weichselbaum, R., and Pauker, S. G. (1981). Speech and survival: Tradeoffs between quality and quantity of life in laryngeal cancer. *The New England Journal of Medicine*, 305(17), 982–7. doi: 10.1056/NEJM198110223051704.

Mortreux, C., and Barnett, J. (2009). Climate change, migration and adaptation in Funafuti, Tuvalu. *Global Environmental Change*, 19(1), 105–12. doi:10.1016/j.gloenvcha.2008.09.006

Nietzsche, F. (1962). *Philosophy in the tragic age of the Greeks* (M. Cowen, Trans.). Washington, DC: Henry Regnery Company. (Original work written in 1873.)

Nietzsche, F. (1967). *The birth of tragedy* (R. J. Hollingdale, Trans.). Cambridge: Cambridge University Press. (Original work published 1872.)

Northoff, G. (1992). Approaches to neuropsychiatry as a transition in the separation of neurology and psychiatry. *Schweizer Archiv fur Neurologie und Psychiatrie*, 143(1), 27–38.

O'Driscoll, A. (2008). Exploring paradox in marketing strategy: Managing ambiguity towards synthesis. *Journal of Business and Industrial Marketing*, 23(2), 95–104.

Owen, C. L. (1997). Understanding design research: Toward an achievement of balance. *Journal of the Japanese Society for the Science of Design*, 5(2), 36–45.

Owen, C. L. (1998). Design research: building the knowledge base. *Design Studies*, 19(1), 9–20. doi: 10.1016/S0142-694X(97)00030-6.

Pearson, N. (2011). *Radical hope: Education and equality in Australia.* Collingwood, Australia: Black Inc.

Pope, C. (2001). A twisted history: The double helix of DNA and Genesis. Retrieved from http://dwij.org/forum/future_link/future1.html.

QCT. (2006). Professional standard seven: Safe and supportive environment. Retrieved from http://www.qct.edu.au/pdf/standards/standard7.pdf.

Rakel, D. (2013). *Integrative medicine.* (3rd ed.). Philadelphia: Elsevier.

Ramey, S. L. (1978). *The reconciliation of opposites in the poetry of Coleridge and Poe* [Masters dissertation]. Texas Tech University. Retrieved from repositories.tdl.org.

Reich, K. H. (2002). *Developing the horizons of the mind: Relational and contextual reasoning and the resolution of cognitive conflict.* Cambridge: Cambridge University Press.

Rheingold, H. (2012). Peerogogy: A learning handbook. Retrieved from http://peeragogy.org/

Richardson, J. T. E. (2005). Students' approaches to learning and teachers' approaches to teaching in higher education. *Educational Psychology*, 25(6), 673–80. doi: 10.1080/01443410500344720.

Riegel, K. F. (1979). *Foundations of dialectical psychology.* New York: Academic Press Inc.

Ritchey, T. (1991). Analysis and synthesis: On scientific method – based on a study by Bernhard Riemann. *Systems Research*, 8(4), 21–41. doi: 10.1002/sres.3850080402.

Sanford, J. A. (1989). *Dreams: God's forgotten language.* New York: Harper & Collins.

Segal, J. Z. (2007). Illness as argumentation: A prolegomenon to the rhetorical study of contestable complaints. *Health: An Interdisciplinary Journal for the Social Study of Health, Illness and Medicine*, 11(2), 227–44. doi: 10.1177/1363459307074695.

Seuss, D. (1990). *Oh, the places you'll go!* New York: Random House.

Singer, J. (2000). *Androgyny.* York Beach, ME: Nicolas-Hays.

Slavich, G. M., and Zimbardo, P. G. (2012). Transformational teaching: Theoretical underpinnings, basic principles, and core methods. *Educational Psychology Review*, 24(4), 569–608. doi: 10.1007/s10648-012-9199-6.

Spader, D. J. (1995). Conflicting values and laws: Understanding the paradox of the privacy act and the freedom of information act. *Legal Studies Forum*, XIX(1), 21–42.

Staats, A. W. (1983). *Psychology's crisis of disunity: Philosophy and method for a unified science.* New York: Praeger Publishers.

Stam, H. J. (2000). Theoretical psychology. In K. Pawlik and M. R. Rosenzweig (Eds.), *International Handbook of Psychology* (pp. 551–69). London: Sage.

Stam, H. J. (2003). *Is there a place for theory in psychology?* Paper presented at the Annual meeting of the Canadian Psychological Association, Hamilton, Ontario.

Stam, H. J. (2004). Unifying psychology: Epistemological act or disciplinary maneuver? *Journal of Clinical Psychology*, 60(12), 1259–62. doi: 10.1002/jclp.20069.

Stewart, I. (2013). Zero, zip, zilch. In J. Webb (Ed.), *Nothing: From absolute zero to cosmic oblivion – amazing insights into nothingness* (pp. 118–25). London: New Scientist.

Struber, J. C. (2003). Physiotherapy in Australia – Where to now? *The Internet Journal of Allied Health Sciences and Practice*, 1(2), Article 5, 1–5.

Tangerås, T. (2009). Democracy, autocracy and the likelihood of international conflict. *Economics of Governance*, 10(2), 99–117. doi: 10.1007/s10101-008-0055-6.

Thomas, J. (2011). Maths matters: Mathematics education in Australia, 1980–2011. *The Australian Mathematical Society Gazette*, 38(3), 131–8.

Tillich, P. (1957). *Dynamics of faith.* New York: Harper and Brothers Publishers.

Tillich, P. (1951). *Systematic theology* (Vol. 1). Chicago, IL: University of Chicago Press.

54 Theory

Tzu, L. (n.d./2006). *Tao Te Ching: Annotated and explained* (D. Lin, Trans.). Skylight Paths. Retrieved from http://www.taoism.net/ttc/complete.htm.

Walker, S. O., and Plomin, R. (2005). The nature–nurture question: Teachers' perceptions of how genes and the environment influence educationally relevant behaviour. *Educational Psychology*, 25(5), 509–16. doi: 10.1080/01443410500046697.

Wang, M. J. (2008). Cybergogy for engaged learning. *Journal of Open and Distance Education in China*, 14(2), 14–22.

Wardekker, J. A., Petersen, A. C., and van der Sluijs, J. P. (2009). Ethics and public perception of climate change: Exploring the Christian voices in the US public debate. *Global Environmental Change*, 19(4), 512–21. doi: 10.1016/j.gloenvcha.2009.07.008.

Wideen, M., Mayer-Smith, J., and Moon, B. (1998). A critical analysis of the research on learning to teach: Making the case for an ecological perspective on inquiry. *Review of Educational Research*, 68(2), 130–78. doi: 10.3102/00346543068002130.

Wong, N.-Y. (2007). Hong Kong teachers' views of effective mathematics teaching and learning. *ZDM Mathematics Education*, 39(4), 301–14. doi: 10.1007/s11858-007-0033-4.

Chapter 3

The origins and classification of dyads

Where do dyads come from? Why are they so pervasive? What purpose do they serve? And, do they have any grounding in *reality*? As Gould notes with some lament:

> The human mind seems to work as a categorising device (perhaps even, as many French structuralists argue, as a dichotomizing machine, constantly partitioning the world into dualities of raw and cooked [nature vs. culture], male and female, material and spiritual, and so forth).
>
> (1997, p. 39)

The origin of dyads has been pondered in many different domains and I am well aware that the two epistemes that most characterise recent occidental thought (i.e. empiricism and postmodernism) are somewhat based on the destruction of epistemology with its infuriatingly subversive dualisms. However, 'Duality is an old topic, but it is still very much alive and kicking' (Atiyah, 2007, p. 90). For some empiricists, the natural world, though real and accessible, is many and multiple, resisting simple dyadic categorisations and requiring detailed descriptions. For the postmodernists, the 'real' world is similarly diverse and complex, but is relationally constructed and therefore susceptible to binary oppositional politicking and power plays.

For many philosophers and scientists, the end of epistemology was a triumph against a particularly disruptive period of philosophical history that gave voice to Cartesian dualism. As Lovejoy (1930) describes in *The Revolt against Dualism*, 'the thing above all others needful for philosophy in our time has appeared to many acute intelligences to be to get rid of this "bi-furcation of nature"' (p. 3). Objective science, then, was the progressive overcoming of subjective ignorance. Dualism and the bifurcation of reality were defeated. The project now was to declare the good news that science had won and the subjective–objective duality was defeated. And yet, in a strange turn of events, no sooner had the death of duality been proclaimed than the new physics of relativity with its quantum uncertainties resurrected its descriptive power: 'The dualism of subjective appearance and objective reality is "a passed mode, an outworn theme"; the

56 Theory

same dualism is the corner-stone of the new physics' (Lovejoy, 1930, p. 5). My approach to dyadic structures is similar to Lovejoy's approach to dualism. Dyads cannot be entirely dismissed as passed modes, outworn themes or brief disruptions of history. They are more ubiquitous and persistent than that:

> [T]he way of thinking so named by philosophers [i.e. *dualism*] is no accidental or artificial product of seventeenth-century metaphysics, no sophistication of speculative minds; it is simply the account which man, grown capable of holding a number of facts together in a single view and drawing what seem plain inferences from them, will normally give of the situation in which he finds himself when he is engaged in what he calls 'knowing'. From these roots the same conclusions would, in all probability grow again, though Descartes were not only dethroned but forgotten.
>
> (Lovejoy, 1930, p. 24)

Lovejoy's point is perhaps supported by the continuance of dyadic contestations over consciousness in modern philosophy and science, particularly neuropsychology. Proponents of monism (i.e. one), like Daniel Dennett (1991), Paul Churchland (1989, 1995) and Patricia Churchland (1986), maintain the total biophysical origins of consciousness. Proponents of dualism (i.e. *two*) maintain a separation of the substance of mind and body. Some dualists still observe the interactions between these two, while noting the general supremacy of one or the other. Proponents of trialism (i.e. *three*), like John Carew Eccles and Karl Popper (1977), similarly approach the mind–body problem by separating physical properties from subjective and objective states, while acknowledging their interactions. My own bi-relational position is similar to Gopnik's (2013), 'The really curious thing about minds and brains is that the truth about them lies not somewhere in the middle but simultaneously on both extremes' (p. 7). My claim is that these contestations over the mind–body problem (i.e. one vs two vs three) are structurally similar to the relational contestations over many other dyads such as nature/nurture, subjective/objective, mythos/logos, conservative/liberal and holism/reductivism. We can increase our repertoire of dyadic relationships to more dexterously (re)solve wicked problems, but we cannot destroy the orientations that these dyads provide and live in the resultant vacuum for any length of time.

Of course, dyadic structures in the cognitive-epistemic world, like the bi-lateral symmetries in the biological world, are not the only adaptive ways to manage wicked problems in uncertain terrains. Possibly, there are cognitive-epistemic equivalents of radial symmetries (e.g. jellyfish), spherical symmetries (e.g. apples) and even rare asymmetries (e.g. sponges) that represent fit ways to know and live in complex environments. However, I suspect that our cognitive-epistemic evolution is not as recent and thus not as adaptively refined or bi-laterally dexterous as the evolution of our physical limbs. We too are in transition – solving problems adequately but not optimally – like transitional forms of flatfish awaiting

The origins and classification of dyads 57

the migration and coordination of a second eye. Our cognitive-epistemic anophthalmia (i.e. an absent or dysfunctional eye) leaves us susceptible to binary oppositional ways of engaging complex problems. To briefly extend the metaphor, even with two eyes open we can fail to rotate and coordinate them (i.e. strabismus) to focus on the infinite degrees of difference within a field of vision. Illustratively, Rose identifies binary oppositional relationships as:

> a conceptual shorthand for wrapping our minds around things, making a point in the flow of conversation, and moving on. But like all dichotomies, they also reduce complexity, seduce our understanding, and cut off deeper, more nuanced analysis. And that's why we need to seriously rethink them.
>
> (2008, p. 31)

For some, the paradox of dualism is an important element in the resolution of conflict. For example, Cameron and Quinn (1988) argue that the notion of paradox can offer powerful ways to resolve conflict and conceptualise disruptions. Likewise, Hampden-Turner (1990) argues for a movement beyond binary opposition which values 'the capacity of acknowledging those dilemmas which arise from competing and contrasting claims and of combining both ... in a resolution which enhances all values in contention' (p. 10). Boisot et al. (1997) argue for a complementary logic that 'takes us beyond the disjunctive logic that requires us to choose between A or B and moves us towards the conjunctive logic of choosing A and B' (p. 79). However, for others, the notion of paradox clouds concrete judgements. As O'Driscoll (2008) argues in a different context: 'Either-or dilemmas represent an idea of paradox that is unhelpfully exclusive, totalizing, and ultimately of limited value in addressing management and marketing problems. It is symptomatic of a hypothetico-deductive worldview and a dominant modernist logic of scientific realism' (p. 95). The point is well made, that the imposition of dyadic symmetry can paralyse real decision making in the face of real-world problems – all sides are paradoxically right so we had better stay still or at least not mind which way we lean. Ironically, O'Driscoll's complaint can be understood dyadically as a legitimate response to the dominance of hypothetical, abstract, reasoned formulations and their disconnection from real-world problems where decisions with real consequences have to be made. Arguably, dyadic formulations can help to identify the domains, parametres and possibilities from which decisions concerning wicked problems can be made in context.

Another criticism of dyadic formulations is expressed in Lloyd's (1966) argument that 'certain manifest natural oppositions, such as day and night, male and female, and perhaps especially right and left, are often taken as the symbols or embodiments of fundamental religious or spiritual antitheses ("pure and impure", "blessed and cursed")' (p. 38). The dangerous disposition of binary oppositional thinking is that it reifies the value of one side (e.g. female) by associating it with a more malevolent natural opposition (e.g. night). The emancipating disposition

58 Theory

of paradoxical or complementary thinking is that it exposes the contextuality and provincialism of such associations. However, the dangerous disposition in-between oppositional and complementary thinking is a tendency towards multiplicity and paralysing balance in context, which simply replaces the tyranny of left or right with the tyranny of equality or the inert middle. In an anthropological context, Herzfeld highlights this dynamic when he criticises post-structuralism's paradoxically oppositional attacks on binary oppositions:

> It is fashionable in this post-structuralist era, to attack any binary code as evidence of the imposition of a foreign system on indigenous values ... But it does not automatically follow that oppositions such as those between male and female will not be salient for local actors. What must be resisted is the temptation to credit them with coercive power over those actors; for it is the *actors* who use *them*.
>
> (1989, p. 113)

The point is significant; relational and contextual approaches to dyads must encompass binary oppositions in a complementary way, or at least maintain some reflexivity as to the ways in which oppositional thinking is sometimes *oppositionally* dismissed.

The opposition/paradox dyad forces us to consider most deeply what lies beyond the binary opposition. My thesis is that the *One* beyond dyadic oppositions must be held *and* opposed in context for both physical and psychic survival. Perhaps one of the clearest expressions of this elusive concept that I have come across provides an appropriate bridge to my original elaborations on bi-relational development: 'the human mind must overlook unity once we begin thinking at all ... we must re-discover it if we continue thinking clearly enough and long enough' (Wilson in Scarfalloto, 2003, p. xiii). The conceptual framework elaborated in Chapter 5 (i.e. BirD) is one way of representing onto-epistemic journeys and figure–ground or figure–figure shifts between this necessary division and return to unity. BirD represents an attempt at onto-epistemological cartography that is self-conscious of its own constructedness. That is, it is an attempt to map ways of knowing and being in relation to wicked problems, while acknowledging that mapping itself, is an onto-epistemological act.

I am well aware that any book, and especially a book on dyads, will reflect a particular set of authorial choices and be read from range of different epistemological perspectives. Indeed, some of the choices I have made will mean that this book is closed shortly after opening or never picked up in relation to the onto-epistemological stances of some potential readers. Understandably, some more positivistic readers are likely to be uncomfortable with the inclusion of mythopoetic imagery and quantum allusions (i.e. entanglement and singularity). The more relativistic readers are likely to be uncomfortable with the structural and developmental dimensions of BirD, seeing a grand narrative that is too neat

The origins and classification of dyads   59

to reflect the glorious messiness of multiple realities. And, paradoxically, this book may seem too agnostic for the spiritual reader and the secular reader alike. There is a sense in which all of these readers would be right. But given the existence of their antipodean critics, there's also sense in which they would all be wrong. Already, I am evoking a particular approach to dyads: a complementary/ oppositional way of relating their constituent parts that can inform an understanding of their origin and function.

The natural origins of dyads

Are dyads (a) neurophysiological constructions that originate from the simplest bifurcations of neural networks and the efficiency of functional simplicity and/ or (b) cultural constructions that originate and spread mimetically through histories, symbols, rituals and myths? Neither of these attributions sheds much light on whether dyads reflect an empirical reality or a cognitive illusion, though many commentators tend to believe that cultural constructions of dyads, like nature/culture, traceable as they are in the mythologies of antiquity, necessarily reflect poor pre-scientific thinking. For example, Jelinski claims:

> 'Balance' highlights nature as a beneficent, stable and holistic force whereas 'imbalance' emphasizes notions of disequilibria, chaos and hence unpredictability ... the 'balance of nature' metaphor expresses an ancient cultural concept, not a conception derived from empirical evidence, though the metaphor implies that nature is an essentially static, orderly system being integral to the economy of nature ... The dichotomization of nature and culture gave license to mastery over the natural world.
>
> (2005, pp. 272–5)

The metaphor of balance and its associations with harmony, equality and holism are seemingly ubiquitous across cultures and fields (Egerton, 1973; Frazer, 1993). Jelinski rightly attacks the tyranny of balance that reflects only one way of relating dyadic constituents (e.g. nature/culture). The more nuanced point is that the broadest scales and abstractions that give the appearance of balance must be held in paradoxical tension, rather than balance, with relatively small-scale imbalances, randomness, impermanence, disproportion, flux and instability. Arguably, Jelinski does not take seriously enough the semantic relationality of these terms (e.g. flux is meaningful only *in relation to* stability) and the scales and levels of analysis that make empirical comparisons between balance and imbalance possible. To argue that nature is exclusively and actually imbalanced and random is to make the same mistake as to argue that nature is exclusively balanced and ordered. For balance and imbalance, order and entropy make sense only in relation to each other.

Jelinski (2005) argues critically that cosmologies of ultimate stability and balance are historically linked to notions of harmony as a mark of a wise and

60 Theory

benevolent creator. He notes the persistence of such cosmologies in modern science and supports Elton's (1930) early attack on notions of balance in nature:

> The balance of nature does not exist, and perhaps, has never existed. The numbers of wild animals are constantly varying to a greater or lesser extent, and the variations are irregular in period and always irregular in amplitude.
>
> (Jelinski, 2005, p. 280)

Jelinski attacks the balance of nature linked to notions of 'stability, equilibrium, holism, homeostasis and orderly neatness' and defends the reality of nature (and arguably the nature of reality) as 'characterised by non-steady position dynamics', 'destabilizing', in 'flux', 'thermodynamically open', 'random' and 'heterogeneous' (pp. 277–83). My claim is that the truer conceptual balance or designation of polarities creates *in toto* dyads, such as random/ordered, whole/part, heterogenous/homogenous and fixed/fluid, from which to identify and communicate relational degrees of difference *in situ*. Accordingly, this is not a book endorsing balance as a form of fence-sitting or an equal celebration of every life trajectory, not unless balance is also conceptualised as the simultaneous and/or contextual valuing of paradox and opposition, balance and imbalance. I suspect that Jelinski ultimately has a similar position and is critiquing a naïve form of balance still found in the ecological sciences. His affirming reference to 'discordant harmonies' and his plea for conservationists 'to accept that many of nature's algorithms are decidedly beyond full comprehension' (p. 285) could be described as an attempt to counterbalance the positivistic symmetry of many appeals to 'Mother Nature' with the relatively indeterministic and asymmetrical nature of many complex ecological systems. In a way, Jelinski's rejection of balance can be understood as a form of counterbalance.

One could also explore the physical correlates of dyadic constructs, as if a neurological substrate is the most legitimate place to search for origins. For example, Newberg *et al.* identify a *binary operator* as a neurological mechanism that 'enables the mind to make fundamental sense of things by reducing the most complicated relationships of space and time to simple pairs of opposites – up versus down, in versus out, left versus right, before versus after, and so on' (p. 50). Their thesis is that the same binary operator that evolved for the efficiencies of physical survival was naturally recruited to organise our responses to the existential crises of metaphysical survival:

> So, when the cognitive imperative, driven by some existential fear, directs the binary operator to make sense of the metaphysical landscape, it obliges by ... rearranging it into the pairs of irreconcilable opposites that become the key elements of myth: heaven and hell; good and evil; celebration and tragedy; birth, death and rebirth; isolation and unity.
>
> (2001, p. 64)

So perhaps the dyadic construct is a product of a configuration of neural networks that evolved to help us manage complexity through rough and simplistic

The origins and classification of dyads 61

but generally efficient approximations. In chronological sequence at least, Newberg *et al.*'s (2001) thesis, that the physical efficiencies of the binary operator gave rise to the cultural-mythological efficiencies of the binary operator, makes sense. Notwithstanding their nuanced analyses, other neurological explorations of cognition reflect a privileging of the critical attitude – an attitude that assumes that a biophysical explanation of dyadic thought warrants its total characterisation as an outdated pre-scientific way of thinking. Here, dyadic structures are 'mere' or 'just' artefacts of neural architecture that do not capture 'reality'. While I think this is true in a sense, I think there is a second naïveté or postformal sense in which duality reappears as a significant and sophisticated concern.

A somewhat more playful recognition of this phenomenon is found in Gopnik's analysis of the neuropsychology of consciousness for *The New Yorker*:

> Neuro-enthusiasts are always declaring that an MRI of the brain in action demonstrates that some mental state is not just happening but is really, truly, is-so happening ... Yet asserting that an emotion is really real because you can somehow see it happening in the brain adds nothing to our understanding.
>
> (2013, p. 3)

Gopnik suggests that neurological explanations of phenomena need Spocks (rational and analytic) and Kirks (intuitive and holistic) to 'preserve the twoness' of the emerging enterprise. In agreement, I would suggest that while 'natural' neurological inquiries cannot assume the 'nature of the natural', they can counter some of the persistent past and present errors made by mytho-enthusiasts who somewhat precociously replace the natural with the mythical, or Spocks with Kirks.

Perhaps one of the more ironic and illustrative debates involving the origin of dyads and dyadic relationships concerns biosymmetry. Is there a fundamental principle of dyadic or bilateral symmetry in the biological world, and if so, why is it there? It is not too difficult to find evidence of bilateral zoological symmetry in the form of hands, eyes, ears, nostrils, fins and feet, and botanical bilateral symmetry in the forms of leaves, petals and the distribution of limbs and roots. Arguably, natural bilateral symmetries have adaptive advantages in asymmetrical environments. It may be easier to coordinate symmetrical feet in the act of fleeing or fighting in asymmetrical terrain than to coordinate asymmetrical feet or stand on one leg. Such natural symmetries can seem to lend weight to the metaphysical claim that life evolves towards the deep underlying symmetries and balances that Jelinski (2005) critiques. However, there are asymmetries in nature too. The beaks of the wrybill and crossbill, eyes of flatfish and tusk of the narwhal seem to represent functional asymmetries. And these are the select few of a hoard of dysfunctional asymmetries that made brief appearances before encountering a selective occasion. Cognitive-epistemic symmetries may also have adaptive advantages, enabling more dexterous problem solving and perception in complex socio-cultural environments. However, this is not to discount the possibility of problems that are better solved by the wrybills and crossbills amoungst us.

62 Theory

The debate over biosymmetry is often contested in relation to the structure of the human brain. Is the brain divided into two hemispheres? Are these hemispheres responsible for different functions? And are these functions oppositional or complementary? Popular educational psychology tends to represent the brain in dyadic terms related to hemispheric function (e.g. reductive/holistic, logical/intuitive, masculine/feminine, linear/cyclic, reason/imagination, structure/spontaneity), implicating the left and right hemispheres respectively. For example, Edwards' (1979) popular *Drawing on the Right Side of the Brain* championed the rise of creative and holistic thinkers, who have been dominated by systems that favour left-brained analytical styles. Such representations are popular enough to have gained critical attention in books such as Lilienfeld *et al.*'s *50 Great Myths of Modern Psychology*:

> The urge on the part of pop psychologists to assign all mental abilities to unique left and right compartments probably owes more to politics, social values, and commercial interests than to science. Its detractors have dubbed this extreme view 'dichotomania' because of pop psychologists' tendency to dichotomize the hemispheres' functions.
>
> (2009, p. 27)

On one hand, the popularisation of dichotomised hemispheric function *does* represent a gross over-simplification of neural processes. Hemispheric exchange involves complex communications via the corpus collosum; neuro-plasticity and hemispherectomy at a young age reveal that both hemispheres can be adapted to serve similar functions; and some hemisphericity relates more to the speed of task assignment than to neurophysiological ability to perform a task. Nuanced empirical studies tend to highlight the relative differences between hemispheres, while affirming that 'the two hemispheres are much more similar than different in their functions' (Lilienfeld *et al.*, 2009, p. 27). On the other hand, while science should remain ever vigilant against over-simplistic dichotomisations and exploitations of its findings, I have some time for the phenomenology of this particular popularisation as *not just* driven by charlatans and snake-oil sellers.

The 'tendency to dichotomise the hemispheres' functions' can result from ignorance or exploitative intent; however, it can also represent a much more complex and ironic appropriation of *science as metaphor* to expose significant but otherwise intangible binary oppositions in society writ large. Thus, functional hemisphericity becomes almost a literary device to interrogate the onto-epistemological dominance of *relatively* logico-mathematical, analytical and reductive ways of knowing that *do* find expression in the values of social, political and educational institutions (e.g. formal schooling, status of professions). The irony is that science, as the dominant way of speaking knowledge in Western culture, will have its findings simplified, jingoised and appropriated in order to make points that may otherwise remain unheard. Thus, the phenomenological point of much dichotomising hemisphericity is actually *to challenge or counterbalance*

The origins and classification of dyads   63

the more insidious and simplistic binary oppositions that *do* operate in dominant Western culture (e.g. analysis > synthesis, atomism > holism, reason > intuition, knowledge > imagination). Perhaps the development beyond binary oppositional ways of knowing is precipitated by the temporary reversal of a dominant opposition as a transition to see that the reality lies not at one pole or the other, but simultaneously at both extremes and all in-betweens. Just as neuroscience helps to reveal the complexity of connectivity between hemispheres, a bi-relational approach can help us to appreciate the complex connectivity, symmetry and degrees of difference between many polarities.

The cultural origins of dyads

I earlier abbreviated one of Jung's (1991) quotes to read: 'The idea of the pairs of opposites is as old as the world'. The quote continues: 'and if we treated it properly, then we should have to go back to the earliest sources of Chinese philosophy' (p. 72). I would add, 'and perhaps further and broader, still'. In this section, I briefly explore some of the cultural origins of dyads to add weight to the claim that the construct is pervasive and persistent in human knowledge and knowing. For twentieth-century scholars of mythology like Eliade (1961), Campbell (1988), Levi-Strauss (1970) and Jung (with Franz, 1964) the diverse mythologies of the world's cultures (ancient and modern) were united by a common dyadic structure.

One of the most lucid accounts of the cultural origins of dyadic structure comes from mythologist Mircia Eliade:

> [I]t was lunar symbolism that enabled man to relate and connect such heterogeneous things as: birth, becoming, death, and resurrection; the waters, plants, woman, fecundity, and immortality; the cosmic darkness, prenatal existence, and life after death, followed by a rebirth of lunar type ('light coming out of darkness'); weaving, the symbol of the 'thread of life,' fate, temporality, and death; and yet others. In general most of the ideas of cycle, dualism, polarity, opposition, conflict, but also of reconciliation of contraries, of *coincidentia oppositorum*, were either discovered or clarified by virtue of lunar symbolism. We may even speak of a metaphysics of the moon, in the sense of a consistent system of 'truths' relating to the mode of being peculiar to living creatures, to everything in the cosmos that shares in life, that is, in becoming, growth and waning, death and resurrection. For we must not forget that what the moon reveals to religious man is not only that death is indissolubly linked with life but also, and above all, that death is not final, that it is always followed by a new birth.
>
> (1961 pp. 156–7)

Eliade's insight is implicitly unitary in that the cultural origins of dyadic structures cannot be separated from their natural origins, for the two are inextricably linked. Of course, this still leaves the question of development: is dyadic thought

64 Theory

developed beyond or returned to as a mark of maturity? BirD is an attempt to represent such positions and engage such questions.

Another popular appropriation of dyads from antiquity is Nietzsche's (1967) reference to Apollonian and Dionysian opposites. Both sons of Zeus in Greek mythology, Nietzsche uses Apollonius to represent the rational and logical polarity of a dyadic construct and Dionysus to represent the instinctual and creative polarity. Nietzsche (cited in Robinson, 1987) invokes, too, the union of opposites found in the Greek philosopher Heraclitus' ancient aphorisms:

> A road, uphill, downhill, one and the same (Fragment 60)
> Beginning is together with end (Fragment 103)
> Into rivers, the same ones, on those who step in, different waters flow (Fragment 12)

The dyadic construct also appears in ancient Egyptian mythology in the opposition between the gods Set, representing disorder and death, and Osiris, representing order and life. Similarly, in fifth-century-BCE Zoroastrianism, we find a similar dualism between Ahura Mazda (the spirit of goodness) and Ahriman (the spirit of evil). And in neopagan Wiccan mythology, the dyadic construct is apparent in the relationship between the Oak King and Holly King, which invokes oppositions between summer/winter, light/dark and night/day.

Some commentators see a functional value in the mytho-cultural expression of dyadic oppositions. Freilich *et al.* see myth as a cathartic 'tension-reduction' tool in the presence of binary oppositions that reflect the real nature of human beings:

> Humans, halfway creatures with one foot in nature and one in culture, live in two worlds. Human life, therefore, is of necessity filled with conflict. The pressure from nature is 'adapt or die – life must be maintained at any cost.' The pressure from culture is 'be proper or suffer psychically – dignity must be maintained at any cost.' With contradictory forces constantly impinging on them, humans seek catharsis either in active (wars, etc.) or passive (drama, ritual, myth) involvement with conflict. Myth, in short, is a tension-reduction tool, a vital system for the maintenance of human sanity.
>
> (1975, p. 209)

Hermann Hesse's psychoanalytic novel *Steppenwolf* explores the possibility of a release from such culturally and cognitively imposed dyads and polarities:

> Harry is not made up of two characters, but of hundreds, of thousands. His life, like that of every human being, does not oscillate between two poles only – say between the body and the mind or spirit, between the saint and the profligate – but between thousands, between innumerable polar opposites.
>
> (2012, p. 61)

The origins and classification of dyads 65

Here, the dyads and polarities of our human narratives are not cathartic; rather, they entrap us into the painful experience of contradictions that do not actually exist.

Neither natural nor cultural explanations for the origins of dyads warrant the status of first cause. And yet each explanation adds something important to our understanding of where dyadic structures come from and why they persist. It makes no sense to choose between them or to give one ultimate primacy over the other; rather, each offers a level of analysis necessary for understanding a whole. In a way, this is what I want to say about the whole business of relating the dyadic constituents of wicked problems. It is relatively easy to see the adaptive advantage of bilateral hands, left and right, recruited in all manner of combinations to perform the most complicated tasks. There is no a priori primacy between left and right. They are opposite but potentially equal. They are *functionally opposite*. In context, we may well see that one needs be more dominant in a task than the other, or that both are needed in equal measure. We may in a place and for a time hygienically designate one hand to work lower than the other so that we are less likely to mix the wiping of our brows and bottoms, but should the environments that threaten our hygiene change, the persistence of a once valuable tradition can be seen as no more than foolish superstition. Needless to say, the persistence of corporal punishments for left-handedness in some recent histories highlights the need for vigilant attention to the flux of environments and the ultimate bilateral value of left and right.

Types of dyad

So far, I have tacitly assumed, rather than explicitly addressed, the definition of a dyad as it applies to bi-relational theory. This section provides some guidelines for the identification of dyads as they are used here. Some dyadic types are more relevant than others to the dynamics explored by BirD. Indeed, much confusion can arise over the nature of relationships between dyads when types of dyad are not first qualified. Without such differentiation it is too easy to fall prey to semantic oversights, sweeping generalisations and false dichotomies. There are important categorical differences between cat/dog, happy/sad, science/religion, apples/oranges and absolute/relative. The main distinctions I wish to make here are between (a) primary and secondary dyads, (b) weak and strong dyads, (c) isomorphic and orthogonal dyads, (d) positive, negative and neutral dyads and (e) transitional dyads.

Primary and secondary dyads

Primary dyads have a pure or abstract form that has been derived from applied or concrete observations (i.e. they are essences). Secondary dyads are based on these primary forms but have additional dressings (i.e. they are forms). For example, *cats and dogs* is a secondary dyad that is loosely based on more primary dyads such as solitary/social, cautious/trusting and recalcitrant/obedient. *Men and women* is a secondary dyad that is often linked to primary psychosocial dyads such as reason/emotion, logic/intuition and justice/compassion. Likewise, *science and religion* is a secondary dyad that is related to primary dyads such as reason/emotion, description/interpretation, matter/spirit, is/ought, logic/intuition, hope/despair, fact/myth, subjective/objective and analysis/synthesis.

The primary/secondary distinction is important because secondary forms are relatively dynamic and complex, while primary essences are relatively fixed and simple. Treating secondary dyads as primary dyads can cause much confusion due to the complexity of parts or the evolution of forms. For example, many cats can be obedient and many dogs can be recalcitrant; many men can be compassion-orientated and many women can be justice-orientated; some aspects of science can be intuitive (e.g. hypothesis formation) and some aspects of religion can appeal to logic. It is important to recognise relatively stable primary dyads manifesting in relatively complex and dynamic forms.

Weak and strong dyads

A second important distinction is between strong dyads and weak dyads. Strong dyads are interdependent or co-definitive. Weak dyads are disconnected and mutually exclusive: the constituent parts do not have a strong enough relationship to warrant a direct comparison or interdependence. For example, *pleasure and pain* is a strong dyad because of the codependence and symmetry of parts. *Apple and oranges* is a weak dyad in that the constituent parts are not codependent: that is, apples do not define oranges, which do not define apples. Weak dyads help to define strong dyads by showing what they are not.

Isomorphic and orthogonal dyads

A third important distinction is between isomorphic and orthogonal dyads (Figure 3.1). Isomorphic dyads represent polarities on a continuum or spectrum where both polarities relate directly to the same phenomenon or concept. For example, *hot/cold* is a strong isomorphic dyad because the constituents both relate directly to degrees of temperature. Orthogonal dyads represent different but interdependent dimensions or aspects of a phenomenon. For example, *quality/quantity* is a strong orthogonal dyad because while measuring different dimensions of a phenomenon (e.g. production), these dimensions are quite interdependent. These different dyads can be represented on a Cartesian plane. Orthogonal dyads can be represented by the intersecting lines of a Cartesian plane. Isomorphic dyads are represented on a single line or axis.

This is an important distinction for understanding relationships between dyadic constituents such as science and religion as they are doubly complicated as secondary and orthogonal dyads but share an important interdependence.

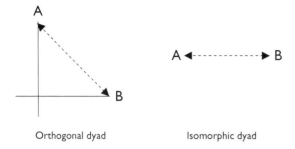

Figure 3.1 Visual representation of orthogonal and isomorphic dyads.

The strongest and most simple dyads are isomorphic, in that there is a clear continuous relationship between A and B. The relationships between constituents of orthogonal dyads are more difficult to see but are still entangled. To extend the geometrical metaphor, imagine that the orthogonal A–B line is of fixed length. Point B of the isomorphic line cannot be moved further along the horizontal axis without Point A being proportionately moved lower on the vertical axis. Point A or B can never reach zero without the whole notion of an axis disappearing. This applies to all strong dyads. For example, consider *quality and quantity*. One constituent measures number (i.e. quantity), the other is a measure of excellence (i.e. quality). However, there is a symmetry or interdependence to the relationship. That is, there is a relationship between the quality of a thing and its quantity. All things being equal, the quantity of apples a farmer can produce is proportionate to the quality of the apples produced. This does not mean that farmer Bob cannot produce more or less apples than farmer Joe, given the quality of the different soils or the number of workers they have access to (or any other number of variables): it means that all things being equal, the quality of apples will remain proportional to the quantity of apples.

In this example, (i.e. quality and quantity of apples) we see that there seems to be no ultimate winner: that is, we simply reduce quality if we have quantity, and quantity if we have quality. So why does balance count for anything at all? The geometrical metaphor represents my answer, for the measurement that matters most is not the distance between A and B, which can extend infinitely; rather, it is the sum of points at which A and B are found or the area of the triangle that the line from A to B forms with its respective axes. Any change in the angle of this line by any fraction of a degree, such that one point is of greater or lesser value than the other, and the sum of both is reduced. My claim is that this basic dynamic applies to all true dyads and has explanatory power for many everyday situations and wicked problems. Life is defined by trade-offs in the context of a dynamic equilibrium. By analogy, any attempt in life to claim ground for one or the other constituent of a dyad – for example, to lessen pain

68 Theory

through the pursuit of pleasure, to pursue happiness through the extinction of suffering, to nurture while disregarding nature, to pursue freedom without control, to pursue success without holding failure in high regard, to revel in misery without acknowledging its connection to happiness or to proclaim meaning without a respect for absurdity – lessens the experience of life, the sum of it all. Thus, the equation of balance is always greater than the sum of an imbalance and yet it is the act of balancing that gives meaning to life. This geometrical metaphor highlights an important consideration for the life–world implications of dyads and the imperative struggle for dynamic equilibrium or balance through sustainable and complementary 'opposition'.

Positive and negative dyads

Another important distinction relates to positive, neutral and negative dyadic forms. Positive dyadic forms are value-laden with an affirmative bias. Negative forms are value-laden with a critical bias. Neutral forms are face-value or literal meanings that are relatively free of negative or positive connotations or meanings. For example, consider the relatively neutral dyad *conservative/liberal*. A positive conservative bias could represent this dyad as *responsible/liberal* or negatively as *conservative/irresponsible*. A positive liberal bias could represent this dyad as *conservative/humanitarian* or negatively as *fundamentalist/liberal*. In both cases, a neutral term has been replaced with a positive or negative one. This concept is quite important for understanding the dynamics of binary oppositions in everyday discourse. Socio-cultural discourses can entrench binary oppositional thinking in language by removing relatively neutral dyadic forms. Impetus for development often requires exposure to relatively neutral forms so that oppositions can be located and contextualised within broader paradigms of balance or equilibrium. Inasmuch as it is possible, BirD attempts to present each constituent of a dyad in its neutral form, while examining the relationship between value-laden forms, the perpetuity of conflict and the reconciliation of opposites.

Transitional dyads, or triads

Transitional dyads, or triads, occur when a dyadic opposition creates a third position which then splits to form two new oppositions. For example, the opposition between the poles of a secondary dyad such as 'science/religion' can form a synthesis such as 'spirituality'. However, the synthesis can then split in relation to the poles such that 'religion/spirituality' and 'spirituality/science' form new oppositions that coexist or compete with the original dyad (e.g. science/religion). Further examples include past/present/future, male/transgender/female, thesis/synthesis/antithesis and black/grey/white. Such transitional dyads or triads significantly reveal the dynamic process of bi-relational developments. They also give some insight into the particular developments and wicked problems that an individual or culture is experiencing at a given time. For example, the prevalence of terms such as 'bi-sexual', 'transgender', 'spirituality' and public expressions of 'grey areas' can reveal a significant stage in the reconciliation of opposites.

Summary

Dyads and dyadic relationships are ubiquitous structures that find expression in our most wicked problems. Arguably, much of this wickedness is to do with confusions between different types of dyad, such that we discuss secondary dyads as if they were primary dyads, orthogonal dyads as if they were isomorphic or even unrelated, negative dyads as if they were neutral dyads, weak dyads as if they were strong dyads and transitional dyads isolated from their synthetic origins. The dyads that are of most concern in the book are relational, interdependent and mutually definitive. It is impossible to describe one of the pair without either implicit or explicit reference to the other. One part of the dyad cannot subsume the other without being subsumable by the other. So *pleasure* makes little sense without *pain*, *subject* without *object*, *natural* without *cultural*, *male* without *female* and so on. The parts of the dyad may be seen as ends of the same spectrum. That is, it is almost possible to understand degrees of *darkness* (least to most) that descriptively exclude *light*, while understanding degrees of light (least to most) that descriptively exclude darkness. Herein, darkness or light is the totality of the spectrum, such that there is a sense in which *darkness is light is darkness*. If everything is *physical*, then the *metaphysical* is *physical*. If everything is *metaphysical* then the *physical* is *metaphysical*. The danger here is to see the equivalence of language (e.g. light is dark is light) and disregard it as sophistry or absurdity while failing to see the intended figure–ground shift and unity it represents. The former sees contradiction where the latter sees paradox.

Furthermore, the dyads I deal with herein are generally strong primary dyads that must be distilled from weak secondary dyads before useful comparisons and contrasts can be made. The dyads are also related in context. However, the accumulation of evidence from actual contexts and the possibility of infinite contexts seem to create/reflect dyads that imply balanced interdependence. Thus, the question of whether A or B (e.g. nature or nurture) is superior is akin to inquiring as to the length of no specific piece of string. For a thing to be evaluated as light or dark or left or right the thing must be relatively isolated then compared and contrasted. The evaluation relies on the simultaneous disconnection of the thing from all other instances to form a judgement that relies on its relation to all previous likenesses of the thing. Finally, as much as is possible, I seek to frame and understand dyads in relatively neutral terms in order to appreciate the negative and positive connotations that produce and describe dyadic divisions and oppositions. The following sub-sections offer a more abstract discussion of the relations between dyads and dyadic constituents as a prelude to the introduction of the more specific theory of BirD in Chapter 5.

Dyadic relationships and development

Development of dyadic constituents

There may be a developmental logic to the order of dyadic constituents that most reflect our ways of knowing and being at different ages and stages of life. In other words, a disposition towards one constituent may develop before a disposition towards the other and a reconciliation of both. For example, consider Kuhn and Weinstock's developmental exploration of the relationship between *subjective* and *objective* dimensions of reality:

> Initially, the objective dimension dominates to the exclusion of subjectivity. Subsequently, in a radical shift, the subjective dimension assumes an ascendant position and the objective is abandoned. Finally, the two are coordinated, with a balance achieved in which neither overpowers the other.
>
> (2002, p. 123)

It is possible that this developmental logic extends to many other dyads, as represented in Figure 3.2.

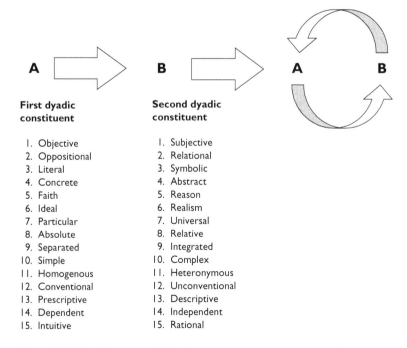

Figure 3.2 Development of dyadic constituents retrospectively perceived.

The origins and classification of dyads 71

If this developmental sequence exists then it raises important questions about interrelations between positions. For example, educative attempts to reverse the order-in-context may confuse and complicate development if it is not done with sensitivity to the natural order of development. For example, if there is a developmental logic that children first experience concrete play as a means to develop and internalise abstract thinking, it may not serve the complex coordination of both (i.e. concrete/abstract) to merely introduce externalised abstract thinking as a substitution for concrete play in early childhood. Nor would it be useful to assume that concrete play is alone sufficient for the development of abstract thought through later ages. In teaching and in parenting there is wisdom in the observation that 'one must learn to walk before one can run' and perhaps that running and walking both serve different purposes later in life, even if one develops before the other.

The main premise of this book is that there are different ways of relating dyadic constituents (e.g. binary oppositional, complementary, dialectical) in the engagement of wicked problems and that there may be a loose developmental progression to these relationships. I suspect that some dyadic relationships are more cognitively accessible than others, such that they appear earlier in development. For example, binary oppositional thinking may precede relational and contextual thinking as a movement from simple to complex. These developing relationships are implicit in Figure 3.2, where a focus on one dyadic constituent (i.e. binary opposition) precedes the reconciliation of opposites (i.e. complementarity). Chapter 5 introduces a more comprehensive model of these dyadic locations and relations (i.e. BirD) as the basis for exploring individual and social developments.

Interactions between individual and group developments

Much attention has been given to the entanglement and interactions between individual development and social development (Figure 3.3). The field poses questions such as: can a culture or social group reflect a particular way of structuring (i.e. knowing) the world? And, what happens when an individual with one onto-epistemological disposition encounters a group or culture with a different disposition, either as an insider or an outsider? The same questions relate to inter-individual and intercultural interactions. For example, what happens when an individual with a domain-specific disposition to perceive problems with a binary-oppositional approach encounters an individual with a disposition to engage problems with a relational and contextual approach, or an individual with a similar binary oppositional approach who supports the opposing dyadic constituent?

To give a dyadic example, what interactions occur (e.g. conflict, synthesis, complementarity) when an individual with a complementary approach to optimism and pessimism engages a culture with a binary oppositional sense of optimism? In metaphorical terms, what interactions can occur when an individual who sees the glass as half empty engages with a group who sees the

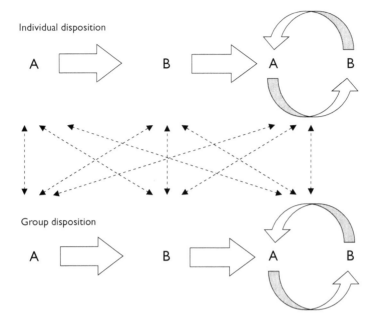

Figure 3.3 Bi-relational interactions between individual and group dispositions.

glass as half full? My broader claim is that many wicked problems arise or are exacerbated at the interface of different onto-epistemological dispositions that creates dissonance or even outright conflict between individual and group, cognitive and social.

Doise and Mugny (1984) identify the social interaction of different cognitive-epistemic dispositions as significant in the production of *sociocognitive conflict*. A sociocognitive conflict is an internalised struggle between social and emotional influences and the need to maintain cognitive-epistemic consistency and integrity. They observed the conflict between social context and cognitive development in experiments with groups of children at different levels engaging in Piagetian tasks and concluded, 'Conflict may exist … for an isolated individual when the operations he [sic] seeks to apply to a particular situation are contradicted by the existence of various social norms governing this situation' (p. 154). Their later elaboration of the concept is worth quoting in detail:

> sociocognitive conflict is a source of disequilibrium. It is disequilibrium that is at once both social and cognitive. It is cognitive disequilibrium in that the cognitive system is unable to integrate simultaneously its own responses and those of others within a single coherent whole. It cannot account for others and itself at the same time. It is social disequilibrium

since this is not simply cognitive disagreement. It involves relations between individuals for which this conflict poses a social problem.

(1984, p. 160)

They further suggest that a gap exists in studies that implicitly or explicitly recognise the interactivity between an individual's cognitive-epistemic dispositions and their socio-cultural influences: 'Nevertheless, at the level of empirical investigations, the issue of a possible feedback effect of the social on the cognitive is not considered; research goes no further than ascertaining the existence of correlations between the two domains' (1984, p. 7). Accordingly, I have sought to integrate ontological and epistemological approaches to development without assuming the primacy of one or the other a priori.

Scholars of religious development have also observed the interactivity between cognitive-epistemic and socio-cultural influences noted by Doise and Mugny. James Fowler, author of *Stages of Faith: The Psychology of Human Development and the Quest for Meaning*, contends:

The formal structural characteristics of faith stages can be employed ... to test the normative structuring tendencies of a given content tradition. They can also be employed to evaluate a given faith community's *particular* appropriation of the content-structural vision of its tradition.

(1981, p. 302)

Streib's ontological approach challenges the primacy of Fowler's cognitive-epistemic approach to development:

the faith development paradigm, with its focus on religious cognition and its almost unquestioned adoption of the structural-developmental 'logic of development,' needs to be qualified in order to account for the rich and deep life-world-related dimensions of religion – but also of fundamentalist turns.

(2001, pp. 143–4)

Similarly, Reich (2002) acknowledges the presence of social factors on cognitive development and notes his own lack of systematic attention to the relationship: 'Also, cognitive performance and development are not independent of the social context ... While acknowledging this fact, social context is hardly dealt with here in any systematic fashion as far as discussing relational and contextual reasoning proper is concerned' (p. 12). Arguably, cognitive/social is a dyad of the type that is subject to bi-relational developments. I hope to offer at least some balance, integration and unification of the two approaches in my illustrations of bi-relational development. At the very least, their reconcilability and codependence are assumed in BirD.

While Piaget acknowledged the importance of socio-cultural influences on cognitive-epistemic development, there are few neo-Piagetian studies that actively

74 Theory

integrate these influences (Brainerd, 1983, 1987). Arguably, this lack of attention has given rise to some deficiencies in cognitive-epistemological approaches to human development. As Fowler notes, there is a gap in research that takes seriously the structuring power of contents:

> It is true, however, that in trying to construct these empirically founded descriptions of structural stages in faith I and my associates neglected, until very recently, any effort at a theoretical account of the interplay of structure and content in the life of faith.
>
> (1981, p. 273)

Other psychologists of religion also acknowledge the integrative gap between epistemological and ontological approaches. In *The Psychology of Religion: An Empirical Approach*, Spilka *et al.* (1985) claim: 'Little is known about the environmental factors that influence the stage of religious cognitive development' (p. 75). So there is a neglected half in theory espousing structure and content. This neglected half has to do with culture and its contents. Again, in Fowler's terms:

> The other half has to do with the contents of faith – the symbols, narratives, practices and communities – and the emotional and imaginal responses to life conditions and experiences that exert powerful existential shaping influences on person's patterns of interpretation, habit, mind, and action.
>
> (2004, p. 164)

Oser and Gmünder's (1991) studies of religious development also highlight the interaction and potential conflict between the individual and the social, the epistemological and the ontological: 'Different chronological ages lead people to make different religious judgments ... persons at different points of their religious development interpret significant questions of life (theodicy, creation, suffering and death, chance and fortune, the religious texts they read) differently' (pp. 9–10). They later acknowledge 'it becomes necessary to do theology decisively from the perspective of structural development, even if the distinction between phylogenetics and ontogenetics ... must be clarified further with new and progressive research' (1991, p. 153). Much broader than theology, I would suggest that any exploration of human development, bi-relational or otherwise, must acknowledge the entanglement between ontology and epistemology, and ontogeny and phylogeny.

Reich's work on the development of relational and contextual reasoning further acknowledges this point:

> As a rule, a person is 'embedded' in the current developmental stage ... the person *is* the stage. When moving to the next stage, the structure of the previous stage becomes the content of the (structurally enlarged) new

stage: the person is presently aware of the lower stage characteristics and therefore can *have* it, that is deal with it, differentiate its characteristics.

(2002, p. 12)

He recognises a dynamic between individual and societal development that possibly relates to the production of wicked problems when individual dispositions (i.e. ways of relating dyadic constituents) conflict with societal dispositions:

Has an individual only those characteristics or patterns of behaviour, A, that were generic to the group to which he or she had been assigned ... ? Or, B, could an individual develop outside that range according to his or her own dynamic of inner abilities and outer stimuli?

(2002, p. 150)

These questions highlight the interaction between the cognitive-epistemic and socio-cultural dimensions and the epistemological and ontological dimensions of development.

Similarly, Barnes' (2000) seminal *Stages of Thought: The Coevolution of Religious Thought and Science* uses a Piagetian framework to trace cultural development. He suggests, 'A culture may maintain a simpler easier style of thought as its dominant style for many centuries or even millennia, even if some individuals go beyond the culture's general achievement' (p. 17). Still, relatively recent texts in this emerging cross-disciplinary field acknowledge that 'The field of culture and cognition is far from being widely recognised and still lacks meaningful integration of the different approaches' (Ross, 2004, p. 2). Accordingly, I hope to have adopted a complementary approach to the interactions between culture and cognition, and ontology and epistemology in my analyses of individual dyadic narratives and the dyadic dimensions of global wicked problems in Part II of this book. I intend to use a bi-relational or dyadic structure as a novel means of exploring human development, while assuming that these structures have no more causal primacy than the inextricable socio-cultural influences that reflect as well as create them.

Domain-specific and domain-general dyads

Bi-relational developments can be understood in domain-specific and domain-general terms. Domain-specific dyads express the polarities that characterise a particular context or domain of life and knowledge. Domain-general dyads relate to many different domains and contexts. Arguably, there is a logical trajectory of development from (1) awareness of dyads and dyadic dexterity in a specific domain through (2) awareness of more general dyads applicable to a specific domain and awareness of the more general applicability of specific dyads to (3) a conscious coordination of general and specific dyads. For example, Table 3.1 loosely organises dyads into specific domains of knowledge but can

76 Theory

Table 3.1 Domain-specific and domain-general dyads

Cosmology	Epistemology	Ontology	Axiology
Finite/Infinite	A priori/A	Subjective/	Good/Evil
Universe/	posteriori	Objective	Right/Wrong
Multiverse	Relative/Absolute	Mind/Body	Fair/Unjust
Order/Chaos	Analytical/	Self/Other	Peace/Conflict
Reality/Perception	Synthetic	Unity/Diversity	
	Deductive/		
	Inductive		
Physics	**Psychology**	**Sociology**	**Politics**
Space/Time	Conscious/	Individual/Social	Conservative/
Wave/Particle	Subconscious	Isolated/	Liberal
Digital/Analogue	Qualitative/	Integrated	Autocracy/
Attract/Repulse	Quantitative	Compete/	Democracy
	Internalise/	Collaborate	War/Peace
	Externalise	Egalitarian/	Freedom/Control
	Nature/Nurture	Hierarchical	
Chemistry	**Cognition**	**Economics**	**Ecology**
Acidic/Alkaline	Structure/	Rich/Poor	Wet/Dry
Natural/Synthetic	Content	Supply/Demand	Hot/Cold
Stable/Volatile	Accommodate/	Spend/Save	Hard/Soft
Positive/Negative	Assimilate	Produce/	Dense/Sparse
	Convergent/	Consume	
	Divergent		
	Concrete/Abstract		
Biology	**Emotion**	**Physiology**	**Personality**
Birth/Death	Hope/Despair	Heavy/Light	Extrovert/Introvert
Growth/Decay	Anger/Calm	Fast/Slow	Thinking/Feeling
Attack/Defend	Fear/Courage	Tall/Short	Optimist/Pessimist
Male/Female	Pleasure/Pain	Weak/Strong	Passive/Active

also be seen to have a general degree of applicability across domains of knowledge and an underlying affinity.

Even a cursory glance at this table should reveal affinities between dyads in different domains. The most profound abstract dyads found in universal cosmology, epistemology, ontology and axiology are inextricably linked to the most concrete and mundane dyads that concern individual identity from infancy. Thus, a culture's collective response to ultimate dyads (e.g. relative/absolute, good/evil, self/other, order/chaos) can affect the way it nurtures individuals from infancy and vice-versa. Onto-epistemological development tends to create domains of knowledge, define them against each other, realise their profound entanglement and then coordinate them in more relational and contextual ways. This is an important developmental sequence given the multidisciplinary nature of wicked problems, the ways of knowing that exacerbate them and the ways of knowing that (re)solve them.

The origins and classification of dyads 77

I further suspect that we have cognitive mastery over the principles of some dyads before we are able to generalise these same principles for other dyads, such that development has some domain-specificity, which gives the appearance of *decalage*, or uneven development. Thus, it may be possible, and I would argue probable, that an adult can demonstrate a binary oppositional disposition towards a dyad in one domain but a relational and contextual disposition to a different dyad in another domain. For example, a manager may be acutely aware of the orthogonal entanglement and complementarity between quality and quantity but still approach dyads like teaching/learning and freedom/control in binary oppositional ways. Thus, our dyadic development cannot be separated from our immediate contexts and formative life experiences in particular domains of knowledge. However, the appreciation of the domain-generality of bi-relational ways of knowing and being can be born out of almost any particular domain.

Dyadic affinities

It stands to reason, given the relationality of language, that there are affinities between different dyads and dyadic constituents. For example, I would hypothesise the existence of a semantic-empirical relationship between *liberal*/conservative, *left*/right, *mercy*/justice, *feminine*/masculine, *freedom*/control, *collaborative*/competitive, *creativity*/replication, *diversity*/conformity and *progressive*/traditional, where the first dyadic constituents are related to each other and the second dyadic constituents are related to each other. I further suspect that there are different expressions of similar dyads across different domains of knowledge that reflect these affinities. For example, there may be a dyadic affinity between simple dyads like active/passive and create/receive, and complex secondary dyads like constructivism/behaviourism in educational psychology. Such affinities are important because they suggest that there may be 'parent dyads' (e.g. left/right) or at least constellations of dyads or dyadic webs that structure our worldviews and cultural sensitivities. While I have generally assumed this dyadic affinity throughout this book, it is a topic that warrants much closer attention and differentiation to see what affinities exist and how they are formed in cultural contexts. For example, is there a cognitive-epistemic reason as well as a socio-cultural reason why conservative and liberal values cross-cut such a wide range of issues?

Conclusion

My subsuming claim is that the ways of producing, relating and collapsing dyads collectively provide a powerful explanatory framework for many human experiences, including experiences of wicked problems. In this chapter I have attempted to discuss the origins of dyads, introduce some basic types of dyads and highlight some important considerations related to bi-relational development and wicked problems (e.g. order of development, sociocognitive conflict, domain-specificity). These early explorations provide a starting point for the

78 Theory

book's original approach to BirD. The task of Chapter 4, before I present this approach in detail in Chapter 5, is to acknowledge the theories and theorists that have most contributed to BirD's development.

References

Atiyah, M. F. (2007). Duality in mathematics and physics. *Lecture notes from the Institut de Matematica de la Universitat de Barcelona (IMUB)*, 69–91. http://www.fme.upc.edu/arxius/butlleti-digital/riemann/071218_conferencia_atiyah-d_article.pdf

Barnes, M. H. (2000). *Stages of thought: The co-evolution of religious thought and science.* New York: Oxford University Press.

Boisot, M., Griffiths, D., and Moles, V. (1997). The dilemma of competence: Differentiation versus integration in the pursuit of learning. In R. Sanchez and A. Heene (Eds.), *Strategic Learning and Knowledge Management* (pp. 65–82). Chichester: John Wiley and Son.

Brainerd, C. J. (1983). The modifiability of cognitive development. In S. Meadows (Ed.), *Childhood cognitive development* (pp. 26–66). London: Methuen.

Brainerd, C. J. (1987). Structural measurement theory and cognitive development. In J. Bisanz, C. J. Brainerd and R. Kail (Eds.), *Formal methods in developmental psychology* (pp. 1–37). New York: Springer-Verlag.

Cameron, K., and Quinn, R. (1988). Organizational paradox and transformation. In R. Quinn and K. Cameron (Eds.), *Paradox and transformation: Toward a theory of change in organization and management* (pp. 1–18). Cambridge, MA: Ballinger.

Campbell, J. (1988). *The power of myth.* New York: Doubleday.

Churchland, P. M. (1989). *A neurocomputational perspective: The nature of mind and the structure of science.* Cambridge, MA: MIT Press.

Churchland, P. M. (1995). *The engine of reason, the seat of the soul: A philosophical journey into the brain.* Cambridge, MA: MIT Press.

Churchland, P. S. (1986). *Neurophilosophy: Toward a unified science of the mind-brain.* Cambridge, MA: MIT Press.

Dennett, D. C. (1991). *Consciousness explained.* Boston: Little, Brown.

Doise, W., and Mugny, G. (1984). *The social development of the intellect* (A. S. James-Emler and N. Emler, Trans., Vol. 10). Oxford: Pergamon Press.

Eccles, J. C., and Popper, K. (1977). *The self and its brain.* Berlin: Springer.

Edwards, B. (1979). *Drawing on the right side of the brain.* Los Angeles: Tarcher.

Egerton, F. N. (1973). Changing concepts of the balance of nature. *The Quarterly Review of Biology*, 48(2), 322–50. doi: 10.2307/2820544.

Eliade, M. (1961). *The sacred and the profane: The nature of religion* (W. R. Trask, Trans.). New York: Harper Torchbooks.

Elton, C. (1930). *Animal ecology and evolution.* New York: Methuen.

Fowler, J. W. (1981). *Stages of faith: The psychology of human development and the quest for meaning.* San Francisco: Harper and Row.

Fowler, J. W. (2004). Faith development at 30: Naming the challenges of faith in a new millennium. *Religious Education*, 99, 405–21.

Frazer, J. G. (1993). *The golden bough.* London: Wordsworth.

Freilich, M., Jong, P. E. d. J. d., Fischer, J. L., Littleton, C. S., Amnon, O., Tokarev, S. A., and Voigt, W. J. (1975). Myth, method, and madness [and comments and replies]. *Current Anthropology,* 16(2), 207–26. doi: 10.2307/2741121.

The origins and classification of dyads   79

Gopnik, A. (2013). Mindless: The new neuro-skeptics. *The New Yorker*, 9 September. Retrieved from: www.newyorker.com/magazine/2013/09/09/mindless

Gould, S. J. (1997). The late birth of a flat earth. In *Dinosaur in a Haystack: Reflections in Natural History* (pp. 38–50). New York: Three Rivers Press.

Hampden-Turner, C. (1990). *Charting the corporate mind: From dilemma to strategy*. Oxford: Basil Blackwell.

Herzfeld, M. (1989). *Anthropology through the looking-glass: Critical ethnography in the margins*. Cambridge: Cambridge University Press.

Hesse, H. (2012). *Steppenwolf*. (D. Horrocks, Trans.). Kindle edition. Retrieved from Amazon.com. (Original work published 1927.)

Jelinski, D. E. (2005). There is no mother nature – there is no balance of nature: Culture, ecology and conservation. *Human Ecology*, 33(2), 271–88. doi: 10.1007/s10745-005-2435-7.

Jung, C. G. (1991). *Analytical psychology: Notes of the seminar given in 1925* (W. McGuire, Ed.). Princeton, NJ: Princeton University Press.

Jung, C. G., and Franz, M. L. (1964). *Man and his symbols*. Garden City, NY: Doubleday.

Kuhn, D., and Weinstock, M. (2002). What is epistemological thinking and why does it matter?. In B. K. Hofer and P. R. Pintrich (Eds.), *Personal epistemology: The psychology of beliefs about knowledge and knowing* (pp. 121–44). Mahwah, NJ: Erlbaum.

Levi-Strauss, C. (1970). *The raw and the cooked: Introduction to a science of mythology* (J. Weightman and D. Weightman, Trans., Vol. 1). London: Jonathan Cape.

Lilienfeld, S. O., Lynn, S. J., Ruscio, J., and Beyerstein, B. L. (2009). *50 great myths of popular psychology: Shattering widespread misconceptions about human behaviour*. Malden, MA: Wiley-Blackwell.

Lloyd, G. E. R. (1966). *Polarity and analogy: Two types of argumentation in early Greek thought*. Cambridge: Cambridge University Press.

Lovejoy, A. O. (1930). *The revolt against dualism: An inquiry concerning the existence of ideas*. Chicago: Open Court.

Newberg, A., D'Aquili, E., and Rause, V. (2001). *Why God won't go away: Brain science and the biology of belief*. New York: The Ballantine Publishing Group.

Nietzsche, F. (1967). *The birth of tragedy* (R. J. Hollingdale, Trans.). Cambridge: Cambridge University Press. (Original work published 1872.)

O'Driscoll, A. (2008). Exploring paradox in marketing strategy: Managing ambiguity towards synthesis. *Journal of Business and Industrial Marketing*, 23(2), 95–104.

Oser, F. K., and Gmünder, P. (1991). *Religious judgment: A developmental approach*. Birmingham, AL: Religious Education Press.

Reich, K. H. (2002). *Developing the horizons of the mind: Relational and contextual reasoning and the resolution of cognitive conflict*. Cambridge: Cambridge University Press.

Robinson, T. M. (1987). *Heraclitus: Fragments*. Toronto: University of Toronto Press.

Rose, M. (2008). The binary ties that bind: Why our descriptions of our work sell us short. *About Campus*, 13(4), 30–2. doi: 10.1002/abc.263

Ross, N. (2004). *Culture and cognition: Implications of theory and practice*. Thousand Oaks, CA: Sage.

Scarfalloto, R. (2003). *The alchemy of opposites* (2nd ed.). Lincoln, NE: Writer's Showcase.

Spilka, B., Hood, R. W., and Gorsuch, R. L. (1985). *The psychology of religion: An empirical approach* (1st ed.). Englewood Cliffs, NJ: Prentice-Hall.

Streib, H. (2001). Faith development theory revisited: The religious styles perspective. *The International Journal for the Psychology of Religion*, 11(3), 143–58. doi: 10.1207/S15327582IJPR1103_02

Chapter 4

A theoretical background to bi-relational development

This chapter offers critical summaries of the theories that have most directly influenced the development of BirD. Bird is a bi-relational approach to onto-epistemological development that is particularly relevant to the recognition and (re)solution of wicked problems. As such, it has a strong lineage of traditional developmental theories, while being defined by some significant points of departure, especially in the domain of epistemological development. Specifically, I hope to position BirD as an approach that coordinates, rather than chooses between: epistemological and ontological approaches to human identity; empirical and phenomenological approaches to knowledge; linear and cyclic approaches to development; ordered and random trajectories of development; domain-general and domain-specific approaches to development; and individual and social influences on development. BirD is an approach to onto-epistemological development that is self-consistent with its claim that there are ways of knowing and being beyond exclusively binary oppositional dispositions.

While I hope to highlight some of the theories most relevant to BirD, there is an inseparable relationship between a theory or approach and an author's life world (i.e. *Lebenswelt*). So, my selection of theories is by no means exhaustive; rather, it reflects the theories that have had the most formative influence on my own life trajectories and my thinking about human development. I have already alluded to some of the theoretical influences on my bi-relational approach to development (e.g., Fowler, 1981; Reich, 2002) in previous chapters. I recognised these theories some years after I had formed a basic appreciation for the ubiquity and salience of dyadic relationships. Specifically, my appreciation for the descriptive and interpretive value of dyadic structures and relationships grew intuitively out of my own experiences and my observations of others' experiences with the particularly powerful binary oppositions that characterise religious fundamentalisms. For several years, I discarded all dyadic and dualistic thought as influential but infantile cognitive constraints. I should note, too, that throughout these years I simply referred to *binaries* as synonymous with *binary oppositions*. However, I later came to appreciate that I had perhaps discarded more than I needed to and that binary oppositions represent one type of relationship between two things. The more I explored fundamentalistic and

A background to bi-relational development 81

post-fundamentalistic thought, the more I came to realise that dyadic relationships, even in their dissolution or collapse, provide a powerful locus for understanding onto-epistemological differences and developments. Beyond exclusively binary oppositional forms, dyadic relationships can help to broaden the horizons of knowledge in order to inform selectively narrow and contextualised choices in the face of wicked problems.

Given that intuition is never far from rational inquiry, I came to appreciate the developmental theories of Piaget (1970a, 1970b, 1971a, 1971b) and, more domain-specifically, those of Perry (1970), Fowler (1981), Oser and Gmünder (1991) and Reich (2002), to name a few. However, I also began to question some of the traditional assumptions of these approaches and appreciate the shortcomings and limitations of positivistic, linear and teleological theories of development. These questions led me to the work of theorists like Streib (2001), Broughton (1987a, 1987b), Sternberg (1990), Basseches (1984) and Riegel (1979). Retrospectively, I was experiencing some dyadic dissonance of my own as I considered the cognitive-epistemic approach of Piagetian theory alongside phenomenological (e.g., Merleau-Ponty, 2010) and socio-cultural approaches (e.g. Vygotsky, 1978, 1986). Broughton's expression of my own ill formed concerns helped to clarify and consolidate these concerns:

> Developmental psychology sets goals and formulates ideals for human development and provides the means of realizing them. Rather than simply observing development, it develops us. By observing and speaking about the most intimate parts of our life history and personality, it enters into the realm of the private, participating in our formation of subjects as well as objects . . . This description of developmental psychology is not the received view.
>
> (1987a, p. 2)

I eventually came to reconcile epistemology with ontology in the context of development, rather than discard one or the other approach. To me, the truth lies not in the middle, but simultaneously at both extremes. I hope that BirD reflects this approach.

My readings in developmental psychology and epistemology were also complemented by some particularly formative literary explorations into Camus (2005), then psycho-philosophical forays into Jung (1970), Nietzsche (1961, 1967, 1996), Freud (1989), Frazer (1993), Schopenhauer (1969) and later Hofstadter (1999). In different ways, some of these theorists problematised the positivism and linear teleology that accompanies much traditional developmental theory. Accordingly, I describe and explain BirD as a linear/cyclic approach to development. My concurrent studies in the psychology of religion led to a prolonged interest in the 'four horsemen' of *neo-atheism*, Dawkins (2006), Dennett (2006), Harris (2005) and Hitchens (2007); and to their intellectual opponents, Barrett (2004), Craig (2008) and McGrath (2007a, 2007b).

82 Theory

Seeing how fundamentalists and former fundamentalists in my research engaged with these authors, and indeed how the authors engaged with each other, crystallised my understanding of the significance of bi-relational development and dynamics beyond mere binary oppositional thought. After exploring the dynamics of these oppositions and reflecting on many deconversion narratives from religious fundamentalisms, I began to rediscover and take seriously the more esoteric ideas of philosophers like Lao Tzu and theologians like Tillich (1957) as they seemed to resonate most deeply with my own ways of knowing and being both *in* and *in-between* two 'opposing' camps. Needful to say, the affinities and aversions I have had with different parts of the books that have influenced BirD have more to do with much less citable and containable life experiences than appear here.

Overall, as an approach to ways of knowing and being, BirD expresses my emerging sense that there is some contextual integrity and interdependence in all of the onto-epistemological positions I have experienced over the last two decades of study, as contradictory as they may first appear. The clash of contradictory positions, while inevitable, can also be understood in paradoxically complementary terms. I have finally come to appreciate the peculiar logic of a comment made by one of my PhD participants – a former fundamentalist. In response to a question on Fowler's (1981) locus of logic, he offered the general view that 'there are no contradictions'. I can now understand that the statement is not as absurd as I initially thought and the ways of knowing that produce such statements need to be taken as more than madness or stupidity, and relationally understood. The participant's response resonates a little with the Nietzschean (1996) view that there are no opposites except in metaphysical imaginations. BirD is a framework for mapping such positions and relations, but it was not conceived in a theoretical vacuum. The following sections selectively review some of the developmental theories and approaches that have informed my own. I hope that this review offers a prelude to the main explication of BirD in the following chapter.

Piaget's stages of cognitive development

The emergence of empirical study into different ways of knowing is generally associated with the work of Swiss psychologist Jean Piaget. Piaget's (1970a) *genetic epistemology* offered a method and rationale for explorations of the nature and development of intellectual operations applied in real-world contexts. In Piaget's (1970a) terms, 'Genetic epistemology attempts to explain knowledge, and in particular scientific knowledge, on the basis of its history, its sociogenesis, and especially the psychological origins of the notions and operations on which it is based' (p. 1). Within a similar paradigm, I attempt to explore bi-relational developments in the context of real-world wicked problems. Many of Piaget's constructs, including *adaptation, interactionism, accommodation, assimilation, structure, schema, stage, equilibrium, disequilibrium* and *cognitive operations*, are relevant for

A background to bi-relational development   83

describing the mechanisms of cognitive and epistemological change implicit in bi-relational development.

In Piagetian theory (e.g. 1970b, 1971a, 1971b; Piaget and Inhelder, 1958), development proceeds sequentially and incrementally through the *sensory motor, pre-operational, concrete operational* and *formal operational stages*. This development is characterised by the increasing availability and abstract applicability of complex logical operations. Piaget's general sequence of operations has found much empirical support (e.g. Brainerd, 1978; De Lemos, 1969; Diamond, 1991), while his age-stage relationships, emphasis on an overarching logico-mathematical structure, early assumptions on the uniformity of development and adult attainment of formal operations have been empirically criticised (Case, 1992; Kuhn, 1988; Ormrod, 2003; Pascual-Leone, 1987; Siegler, 1996). Piaget (1971b) emphasised development as a teleological process in which cognitive operations unfold towards increasingly logical ends that are increasingly adaptive.

While Piaget's theory focused primarily on the development of cognitive operations from infancy to early adulthood, BirD has an additional primary focus on postformal developments. A postformal approach:

> ...allows a person to solve problems even in situations where conflicted formal operational belief systems, and priorities overlap ... The postformal thinker knows she/he is helping create the eventual *truth* of a social interaction by being a participant in it and choosing to hold a certain view of its truth.
>
> (Sinnott, 1996, pp. 362–3)

This approach is essential for identifying and (re)solving wicked problems which require an expanding appreciation of context and complexity and a paradoxical understanding of the need to commit to a subjective reality. As Sinnott further claims, 'the developmental approach leads us across the boundaries of the "objective" and the "subjective"' (1996, p. 358). Piaget's approach to development helps to explain why we are so susceptible to binary oppositional thinking, and why it is actually useful and warranted in many contexts, but Sinnott's (1981, 1984, 1996) postformal approach reminds us that formal logic, as it is traditionally understood, does not always help us to appreciate the interdependence of opposites in a socially constructed and subjectively experienced world. In bi-relational terms, it could be said that the development of increasingly complex formal operations eventually enables the postformal synthesis, or collapsing, of dyadic constituents. Thus, BirD identifies formal *and* postformal ways of knowing and (re)solving wicked problems.

As an onto-epistemological approach to development, BirD represents changes and differences within our ways of knowing about the world. *Genetic epistemology* describes the development or emergence of ways of knowing (Flavell, 1985; Flavell and Ross, 1981). *Genetic* may be more simply understood as meaning *innate* (Miller, 1993, p. 35). *Epistemology* may be understood as 'the relation between the thinking, acting subject and the objects of his (sic) experience'

84 Theory

(Piaget, 1971b, p. 245). Piaget wanted to challenge the notion that knowing is static and immutable: 'Scientific thought, then, is not momentary; it is not a static instance; it is a process' (p. 2). Thus, he proposed that knowledge is constructed – knowing changes, emerges and develops in context. Of course, these verbs (i.e. change, emerge, develop) are all relationally understood within a context that emphasised science, knowledge and learning as static facts and truths. Accordingly, I position BirD as an approach to development that acknowledges the relative stability *and* change of knowledge and knowing. It is possible, perhaps even necessary, to abstract seemingly stable and general developmental archetypes, sequences, milestones and structures, but these abstractions must always be held in tension with fluid, dynamic and concrete contexts. The development of knowledge assumes an impetus for change. Piaget's fundamental premise was that the evolution of epistemology helps the organism *adapt* to its environment. *Adaptation* is an important concept in the onto-epistemological engagement of wicked problems.

Adaptation is the goal of any organism seeking to fit a particular environment. In a neo-Piagetian sense, it is the 'adjustment of a system to its environment' (Shulman *et al.,* 1985, p. xvii). For Piaget, adaptation was the motivation for development. Humans developed more complex cognitive operations through their inevitably increasing interaction with the environment and the accumulation of experience. Developed cognitive operations enable us to interact more effectively and independently within our environment. They help us to adapt quickly to new environments. BirD assumes this general adaptive impetus for onto-epistemological development as a rationale for expanding beyond binary oppositional ways of knowing and being.

The process of development depends on *interaction* between internal mechanisms and external stimuli. While perhaps unfairly characterised as ignoring the effects of socialisation, Piaget (1981, 1995a, 1995b, 1995c) argued that *both* nature and nurture interact to produce ways of knowing, or epistemologies: 'There is no longer any need to choose between the primacy of the social or that of the intellect: collective intellect is the social equilibrium resulting from the interplay of the operations that enter into all cooperation' (Piaget, 1970a, p. 114). Piaget's interactionism is embraced by modern developmental cognitive neuroscience, which accepts 'that the mental abilities of adults are the result of complex interactions between genes and environment' (Johnson, 2005, p. 3). Developmentalists describe these influences of nature and nurture in terms of maturation, physical experience, logico-mathematical experience, social transmission and equilibration (Phillips, 1975, pp. 17–19). The interaction between these influences is expressed by the developmentalist cliché: 'Development is not simply the unfolding of a pattern dictated by the genes, nor is it simply the importation of structures from the physical and social environment' (Campbell, 2006, para. 71). BirD presupposes the interdependence and interactivity between nature and nurture, the psychological and the social, the epistemological and the ontological.

A background to bi-relational development 85

Piaget described the interaction between innate mechanisms and external influences in terms of *accommodation* and *assimilation*. While these processes may be defined separately, they can be understood complementarily. *Assimilation* refers to the organisation of new sensory input into existing knowledge structures. *Accommodation* refers to adjustments in existing knowledge structures in light of new sensory input. Assimilation and accommodation work together as processes for continual adaptation to the environment. In BirD, accommodation and assimilation represent a classic dyad that is useful to describe the ways in which new knowledge and experiences are encountered by individuals and groups. Hyper-accommodation can fragment the stability of the self that is needed to make practised decisions and recognise familiar situations. However, hyper-assimilation can so rigidify the self that its default decisions and responses fail to address new environmental challenges (e.g. wicked problems).

The term *structure* has been mentioned several times already. Structure refers to the 'systemic properties of an event' (Phillips, 1975, p. 9). A structure could be seen as an organising pattern of contents. Piaget often used the term schemata (singular = schema) when referring to the organisational patterns of children. A particular schema could involve grasping or shaking an object. Structure underlies the 'apparent diversity of the content' (Miller, 1993, p. 37). According to developmentalists, these structures undergo fundamental changes over time. The milestones of these fundamental changes are often described as *stages*. Stages are most akin to the regions or positions in BirD (e.g. pre-dyadic, pro-dyadic, post-dyadic). Like assimilation/accommodation, structure/content is another dyad assumed in BirD's application to wicked problems which must be engaged with a dual appreciation for the particular contents of a problem and the structures that perceive them.

A *stage* is a period when knowledge is consistently organised by the same mental operations. It is a structured whole in a state of equilibrium (Miller, 1993, p. 38). Piaget argued that there is an invariant sequence of identifiable stages through which cognition develops. Cognitive developmentalists also tend to argue that stages are universal and incremental. However, this conceptualisation has been criticised as being too prescriptive and artificially delineated (Carey, 1985; Sternberg, 1990). The invariant sequence assumed in neo-Piagetian frameworks has also been challenged by recent research in religious styles:

> I therefore do not agree, without qualifications, with Fowler's (1996, p. 57) statement that the faith stages could still be 'held to be invariant, sequential, and hierarchical'; and I doubt especially that a stage is a 'structural whole'.
> (Streib, 2003, p. 5)

In acceptance of such criticisms it is useful to echo Wilber's understanding of stage, as embraced in BirD:

> These stages or levels of development are not the rigid, linear, rungs-in-a-ladder phenomenon portrayed by their critics, but rather appear to be fluid,

86 Theory

flowing overlapping waves ... These developmental stages seem to be more like concentric spheres of increasing embrace, inclusion, and holistic capacity.

(2000, pp. 146–7)

BirD takes this fluidity a step further by suggesting that stage cohesion is a probabilistic generalisation that sometimes hides the fragmented, compartmentalised and discontinuous nature of the knowing self or group. BirD claims that different positions can latently coexist in the same individual at the same time but that we *know* individual and group dispositions *in-context* by their relatively consistent and continuous display.

A related debate in developmental literature concerns the question of uneven development, which Piaget seemed to acknowledge but de-emphasise as *décalage*. Again, in the context of religious development, Streib (2003) challenges this lack of emphasis and proposes a religious-styles model that normalises *décalage*:

> The Piagetian and, even more, the neo-Piagetian understanding of *décalage* indicates an awareness of non-synchronicity of cognitive development, but it explains only a delay of an assumed developmental progression and neither Piaget, nor Piagetian scholars have explicated a 'theory of *décalage*' ... even though there is an assumption among some neo-Piagetian developmentalists, 'that horizontal *décalage* is the rule in development rather than the exception' (Canfield and Ceci, 1992, p. 289).
>
> (2003, pp. 2–3)

Wilber affirms this challenge and implies a notion of domain-specific development that is assumed in BirD:

> It further appears that, in any given person, some of these lines can be highly developed, some poorly (or even pathologically) developed, and some not developed at all. Overall development, in short, is a very uneven affair! ... According to this body of developmental research, a person can be at a relatively high level of development in some lines (such as cognition), medium in others (such as morals), and low in still others (such as spirituality). *Thus there is nothing linear about overall development.*
>
> (2000, p. 149)

BirD allows the possibility that there is at least something *linear* about overall development, but that what is linear should not be assumed a priori and should be understood in semantic relation to its non-linear antonym. Accordingly, BirD engages these debates through a complementary approach to dyads such as linear/cyclic, fixed/fluid and sequential/discontinuous. This is significant for bi-relational development as an educative project in the context of wicked problems. Domain-general developments need to be fostered and facilitated from domain-specific developments with innovative pedagogies. Similarly, wicked

A background to bi-relational development 87

problems tend to involve multiple dyads intersecting across different domains. Consequently, they require multidisciplinary collaborations to (re)solve them.

A bi-relational approach is primarily concerned with relations between two concepts. Binary oppositional ways of knowing tend to assert the primacy of one concept over another, regardless of context. Other ways of knowing tend to recognise a necessary tension or complementarity between concepts. BirD recognises that these ways of knowing or relating dyadic constituents may change and indeed develop over time and in-context. For Piaget, development is characterised by an impetus for equilibrium in an ever changing world, where this equilibrium is constantly upset. The adaptive drive to maintain equilibrium forces the knower into increasingly sophisticated stages of development as life's tasks and problems become more complex.

Equilibrium or equilibration refers to the tendency for an epistemological system to seek a harmonious balance between accommodation and assimilation, environment and internal structure. Thus, development is motivated by a constant quest for equilibrium:

> For Piaget, equilibration is the grand process that puts together all of the elements of development. Equilibration integrates and regulates, the other three main factors of development: physical maturation, experience with the physical environment, and the influence of the social environment.
>
> (Miller, 1993, p. 72)

One assumption of cognitive-epistemic development is that organisms have a natural tendency towards achieving this state of balance or self-regulation. *Disequilibrium* occurs when a set of operations is no longer sufficient for equilibrating accommodation and assimilation. Disequilibrium is a state of imbalance, cognitive conflict or dissonance between accommodation and assimilation. Disequilibrium can motivate the development of new cognitive operations and structures to address the imbalance and achieve a more adapted understanding. The state occurs when the internal structure is no longer able to assimilate or accommodate new information using available cognitive operations. Disequilibrium is related to Festinger's (1957) concept of cognitive dissonance, where resolution of disequilibrium involves either the distortion or repression of the new information to maintain equilibrium, or a change in the set of underlying operations, leading to a new equilibrium at a different stage. Conceptualised in this way, wicked problems are in essence perturbations or disequilibria that can be spread across different domains of knowledge. Binary oppositional solutions will merely exacerbate such problems by distorting or repressing them, while relational and contextual (re)solutions better reflect the nature of the problems.

The increasing repertoire of dyadic relationships and their dextrous use requires more basic *cognitive operations*. An *operation* is a cognitive ability. For example, the operation *reversibility* refers to the cognitive ability to mentally reverse a series of events or steps of procedure. *Classification* is an operation that

88 Theory

enables the identification of objects according to similar characteristics. *Decentration* is an operation enabling the coordination of multiple variables to solve a problem. And *differentiation* is an operation that enables increasingly complex discrimination of information. These operations are related. Neo-Piagetians argue that the consistent application of such operations changes as the individual develops. For example, centration on one variable can eventually lead to binary oppositional thinking about a problem, but decentration and differentiation allow for the consideration of multiple variables and degrees of difference implicated in a problem. For Piaget, stage development in operations is prompted by a temporary disequilibrium that is a natural cause of cognitive-epistemological development. All of these operations are necessary to identify and coordinate the polarities that define many wicked problems.

Piaget's scheme of cognitive development informs many later schemes of epistemological development. BirD builds on the basic structuralist and constructivist claims of Piaget's genetic epistemology – that ways of knowing are gradually constructed as individuals and groups adapt to their physical and social environments. I add *groups* to acknowledge the importance of the socio-cultural and historical dimension of individual developments. While Piaget's relative lack of engagement with the socio-cultural dimension of cognitive development is often unfairly critiqued as an omission, I acknowledge Vygotsky's (1978) primacy in establishing the importance of the social dimension of cognitive development.

In summary, it was probably my early encounters with Piagetian and neo-Piagetian theory that first resonated with my sense that there are different epistemological positions and important dynamics, processes and developments between these positions. BirD assumes the basic conceptual underpinnings of Piagetian theory, including *adaptation, accommodation, assimilation* and *equilibration*. However, it also problematises dominantly linear, teleological, cognitive and domain-general approaches to development.

Perry's stages of epistemological development

Perhaps the theorist most associated with a comprehensive psychological theory of epistemological development is William Perry. Perry's (1970) theory of epistemological development built on Piaget's genetic epistemology, focused on post-adolescent ages, and laid a foundation for many subsequent theories of development: 'We do depend heavily on his [Piaget's] particular concepts of assimilation ... and of accommodation ... Somewhat more broadly, too, we make similar assumptions about the emergent, interactional ontogenesis of intelligence' (p. 228). While not explicitly using dyadic relationships as a basis for a theory of development, Perry does recognise dualistic thinking (i.e. binary oppositions) as an important stage of development. Accordingly, there is some correlation between Perry's positions and BirD's locations.

Perry (1970) describes nine positions of intellectual development, including *strict dualism, early multiplicity, late multiplicity, relational knowing, anticipation of*

A background to bi-relational development   89

commitment, initial commitment, multiple commitments and *resolve.* These positions can be grouped into three sets: (1) the modifying of dualism, (2) the realising of relativism and (3) the evolution of commitments.

The epistemological realisation of contextual relativism represents 'a real revolution of structures' (Perry, 1970, p. 68) and 'a drastic revolution' (p. 121). The revolution that realises relativism is 'precipitated by the failure of a dualistic framework to assimilate the expanding generalisation of Relativism' (p. 122). Perry further describes the revolution as 'both the most violent accommodation of structure in the entire development, and at the same time the most quiet' (p. 123). In bi-relational terms, the epistemic revolution is the realisation that the value of A or B in a binary construct depends largely on context, that contexts are arbitrarily constructed rather than absolutely constrained and that A and B are interdependent. BirD represents this revolution as a post-dyadic development in terms of the relationship between relative and absolute, and subjective and objective. It does this to show that a form of relativism can be held in absolute ways, otherwise there is a danger of misinterpretation when giving semantic primacy to relativism in a sequence of development. While 'commitment' implies a sense of 'absoluteness', I suggest that the dyadic structure (i.e. relative/absolute) better captures the reconciliation and interdependence of the two in later developments. And while a disposition to absolute ways of knowing may sequentially precede relativistic ways of knowing, they are ultimately reunited in a cycle of meaning. Thus, BirD emphasises the sense in which the relative only makes sense in relation to the absolute.

In essence, Perry's theory maps a journey of knowing from dualism to relativism and beyond. BirD maps a similar development, but reconceptualises Perry's linear representation as linear-cyclic. The cyclic representation of development addresses the discomfort felt by many critics of traditional developmental theory's implicit teleology because it recognises the breakdown of teleological metaphors. Furthermore, the cyclic representation addresses the discomfort felt by Perry's own judges at the conceptualisation of post-relativist positions as 'growth':

> The judges found themselves in far more agreement about the Position that expressed the structure of a student's world than about the tonality that expressed his involvement in growth. They even expressed a reluctance to make these latter judgments at all. They complained that the values built into the entire scheme put them into a moral bind.
>
> (1970, p. 198)

To Perry's credit, he addressed the dilemma with a clear reflexive awareness of his own position:

> We acknowledged the reality of this dilemma ... Someone might look on a life of what we called 'alienation' as a triumph – we could disagree

90 Theory

> passionately, but we could not, as the students would say, call him wrong 'in any absolute sense'.
>
> (1970, pp. 198–9)

BirD attempts to (re)solve rather than solve this developmental dilemma with the claim that development and growth lead to a more sustained, but still fragile, reconciliation of apparent opposites (e.g. relative/absolute).

Perry's legacy has included the consolidation and application of these stages in diverse contexts and domains of knowledge. As I have attempted to illustrate in Chapter 2, a bi-relational approach can focus such contextual analyses by identifying domain-specific dyads and examining significant dyadic relationships. Dyadic relationships can actually help to clarify onto-epistemological positions, even those that define development beyond *two*.

Modern theories of cognitive-epistemological development

Perry (1970) and Piaget's (1971b) work in cognitive-epistemological development has been adapted and extended by many subsequent theories. My encounters with these theories during the last decade have reinforced my view of the general accuracy of Piaget and Perry's shared thesis: that the ways we know change and develop in discernible ways. However, the empirical applications of these newer theories have also reinforced my belief in the need for (a) more emphasis on socio-cultural interactions with cognitive-epistemic developments and (b) more emphasis on the non-linear and multi-linear nature of development. The following paragraphs provide a brief outline of some of these theories in light of their influence on BirD.

Kegan's (1982) approach to the evolving self draws strongly on Piaget's genetic epistemology and posits a development between *incorporative, impulsive, imperial, interpersonal, institutional* and *interindividual* ways of balancing subject and object or self and other. He frames his project within a sort of *metapsychology* that sees a development 'from entity to process, from static to dynamic, from dichotomous to dialectical' (p. 13) across almost all modes of knowledge. I share this general project while exploring development across a range of different dyads and engaging cyclic complements to linear trajectories of knowing and being in relation to wicked problems.

King and Kitchener's (1994, 2002) reflective judgment model (RJM) outlines a sequence of developmental stages for the construct *epistemic cognition* (Kitchener, 1983). The model has seven archetypal stages that can be loosely divided into three periods: pre-reflective (stages 1–3), quasi-reflective (stages 4–5) and reflective (stages 6–7). In the pre-reflective period, people tend to 'believe that knowledge is gained through the word of an authority figure or through first-hand observation' (2002, p. 39). The period is characterised by certainty and the treatment of all problems as if they are 'well-structured'. During the quasi-reflective period, people recognise some element of uncertainty in problems but attribute this to 'missing information or to methods of obtaining the

A background to bi-relational development   91

evidence' (p. 40). During the reflective period, people 'accept that knowledge claims cannot be made with certainty, but are not immobilized by it; rather they make judgments that are "most reasonable"' (p. 40). King and Kitchener's approach highlights the significance of reasoning about the dimension of wicked problems that this book addresses. Their developmental approach is generally compatible with the defining regions of BirD (i.e. pre-dyadic, pro-dyadic, post-dyadic and trans-positional) in reflecting a movement from binary oppositional certainty to an evaluativistic approach to knowledge that acknowledges the uncertainty of certainty and the certainty of uncertainty.

Similarly, Baxter Magolda's (1992) epistemological reflection model (ERM) identifies four periods of knowing: absolute knowing, transitional knowing, independent knowing and contextual knowing. She (2004) consolidates these stages in the context of approaches to learning and observes a development between (1) following external formulas, (2) crossroads and (3) self-authorship. Again, the general progression of these ways of knowing and learning is compatible with BirD's transitions between binary oppositional knowing in the pro-dyadic region and relational and contextual knowing in the trans-positions. However, relative to RJM and ERM, BirD does tend to emphasise a total collapse of dyads (e.g. union and/or negation) that perhaps allows more understanding of the source of ways of knowing (e.g. esotericism, mysticism, absurdism, existentialism, phenomenology) that are not easily accommodated by the psycho-developmental models most accepted in Western academia.

Kuhn and Weinstock's (2002) posit four levels of epistemological understanding: realist, absolutist, multiplist and evaluativist. These levels correspond with assertions about reality and truth that are seen as *copies*, *facts*, *opinions* and *judgements*. Again, this general progression is compatible with BirD's locations. However, BirD problematises Kuhn and Weinstock's (2002) characterisation of knowledge of higher stages as 'generated by human minds' and reality as 'not directly knowable' (p. 124) by suggesting that these characterisations are themselves relational to prior ways of knowing that emphasise certainty and external reality. BirD's bi-relational approach emphasises the relationality of dyadic constituents such as certain and uncertain, internal and external, reality and perception and subjective and objective that characterises trans-positional ways of knowing. To recall and reiterate, Kuhn and Weinstock take this position in relation to the subjective/objective dyad:

> Initially, the objective dimension dominates to the exclusion of subjectivity. Subsequently, in a radical shift, the subjective dimension assumes an ascendant position and the objective is abandoned. Finally, the two are coordinated, with a balance achieved in which neither overpowers the other.
>
> (2002, p. 123)

Arguably, though, this position could also be taken in relation to the characterisation of knowledge as direct or indirect and internally constructed or externally described.

92 Theory

Tabak and Weinstock highlight the pendulum swings that can occur in approaches to epistemological development. For example, the shift from traditional behaviourist models of learning to constructivist models has represented a pendulum swing rather than a rebalancing in some systems of Western education:

> Perhaps as a backlash to critiques of authoritarian transmission models, teachers now tend to emphasize giving students opportunities for self expression and to communicating the validity of multiple solutions and perspectives ... However, recognizing that there is "no one right answer" does not necessarily imply that one answer cannot be better than the other.
>
> (2008, p. 186)

As cited in Chapter 2, there is an implicit dyadic structure to this claim that suggests a reconciliation of opposites represents a more sophisticated development than horizontal pendulum swings within binary oppositions. BirD offers an explicit account of such bi-relational developments.

Schraw and Olafson (2008) also use a two-dimensional approach to epistemological and ontological development. They posit 'a continuum that ranges from realist to relativist endpoints' (p. 31). The use of a dyadic continuum is similar to BirD's bi-relational approach. However, while Schraw and Olafson assume that 'relativist teachers conduct a more constructivist orientated classroom that is more likely to engage students and promote deeper learning' (p. 40), BirD adopts a more relational approach to dyadic constituents (e.g. realist/relativist) that problematises the a priori primacy of one over the other. This is consistent with Tabak and Weinstock's (2008) observation concerning the peril of pendulum swings to constructivist and relativist pedagogies.

Furthermore, Schraw and Olafson's (2008) appreciation of the complex interaction between epistemology and ontology relates to BirD's use of 'onto-epistemology' as a central construct. They suggest that 'previous research has focused exclusively on epistemological beliefs without also considering what we refer to henceforth as ontological beliefs' (p. 30). They define the two terms as follows: 'Epistemology is the study of what can be counted as knowledge, where knowledge is located, and how knowledge increases ... Ontology is the study of beliefs about the nature of reality' (p. 33). This dual focus reflects my own attempt to reintegrate epistemology and ontology in BirD through its onto-epistemological focus.

Collectively, these 'neo-Perrian' models of epistemological development have influenced the development of BirD, which reflects their general consensus of growth beyond binary oppositional ways of knowing. However, I also hope to have emphasised that BirD uses a uniquely explicit bi-relational approach, problematises linear and teleological assumptions and exclusively constructivistic conceptualisations of knowledge and knowing and co-emphasises the domain-specificity and domain-generality of knowledge as well as the epistemological and ontological dimensions of human development.

Riegel and Basseches' dialectical thinking

Riegel (1979) and Basseches' (1984) approaches to dialectical thinking resonated with my intuitive discomfort at rigid and encompassing stages and the disconnection between individual/social and relative/universal in traditional psychology. Their work also reinforced my thinking about the structural usefulness of dyads in conceptualising and (re)solving wicked problems.

Riegel's dialectical psychology

Meacham's preface to Riegel's *Foundations of Dialectical Psychology* offers a concise summary of the dialectical project:

> Dialectical psychology makes clear the need to overcome polarized barriers to understanding within traditional psychology – between mind and body, between individual and society, between quality and quantity, between concrete content and abstract form, between psychologists and the objects of their research, between diagnosis and therapy, between biology and the social environment, and between subject and object.
>
> (1979, p. xi)

For Riegel, these 'polarized barriers' were reinforced by the reification, decontextualisation and abstraction of concepts like *intelligence*. Riegel criticised an overemphasis on stability and objectivity at the expense of flux and subjectivity in Piaget's theory of development:

> Piaget considers only the child's interactive operations with objects, but he does not consider that some of these objects may be other subjects who, like the child, operate actively on objects and, in particular, upon other subjects. Piaget has paid little attention to the outer or social dialectics of interacting individuals.
>
> (1979, p. 5)

These criticisms expressed concerns that had arisen from my own experience with Piagetian theory, first as a postgraduate student and later as lecturer in educational psychology. I observed that many of my first-year students conducting Piagetian tasks with children seemed to be oblivious to the social dimension of their participants' cognitive performance. Many ascribed and totalised a stage of logical operations to a child without adequately considering the social context of the clinical interview with its power dynamics (e.g. adult–child), linguistic nuances (e.g. vocabulary) and cultural bias (e.g. aspect of conservation or content of theory of mind tasks). Similarly, their analyses tended to assume the primacy of cognition as the motor of development. For example, an adolescent could not perform a task *because* they had not yet biologically developed the internal mental operations required to perceive the problem. Few appreciated the tautological dimension of the claim or considered the correlation between or co-development of neurobiological mechanisms *and* socio-cultural experiences. Thus, inasmuch as Riegel's approach has influenced BirD, it has reinforced my desire to frame a theory that is sensitive to the co-relationality of the cognitive and the social, the epistemological and the ontological, and the fixed and the fluid. I do not wish to replace the stability of Piagetian stages with flux and fluidity, the cognitive with the socio-cultural or the epistemological with the ontological – I hope to coordinate them in a more complementary approach to wicked problems.

Another significant aspect of Riegel's work that brought some clarity to my own ill defined discomforts relates to the role of crisis and contradiction in the paradigm of development. In some traditional models, and much conventional thinking, development is defined by long periods of structural stability precipitated by short bursts of crisis and dissonance. My discomfort at such characterisations was their tendency to marginalise the role of crisis and contradiction, and in some cases to interpret them in purely pathological terms. However, Riegel (1979) challenges this notion of crisis and redefines its place and status in human development. He proposes 'an alternative interpretation of crises', where 'Contradictions, doubts, and inner dialogues represent the very basis of individuals' thoughts and actions. Their social development likewise is founded upon conflicts, disagreements, and debates' (p. 131). For Riegel, the true crisis in its darkest form is premature stabilisation that refuses to engage in the necessary conflicts, doubts, disagreements and contradictions of dialectic that promote growth. This stability through denial is truly a 'pathological deviation from normal development' (p. 131). This is a direct challenge to Piaget's notion of *equilibration* as a period of stability that is the goal of all cognition. For Riegel, 'the mature individual does not necessarily equilibrate these conflicts but is ready to live with these contradictions; stronger yet, the individual accepts these contradictions as a basic property of thought and creativity' (p. 53). The (re)solution of wicked problems elicits such ways of knowing. The presence of wicked problems in human life is not just inconvenient, it is life-giving.

I appreciate Riegel's claim that contradiction is a fundamental property of thought that a mature individual accepts, while noting that this way of knowing could itself be described in terms of equilibration between the flux of 'life as contradiction' and the stability of knowing that 'such is life'. Understood on his own terms, Riegel may be described as counterbalancing (an act of equilibration) the relatively polarised stability of Piaget's structuralist project that largely defined Riegel's own socio-historical milieu. It is worth noting that Basseches (1984) similarly characterises dialectical thinking as 'a level of equilibrium', and argues that 'dialectical thinking allows the recognition of something as remaining constant amidst a far broader range of changes than formal reasoning can equilibrate' (p. 58). My hope is that BirD can represent the contradiction *and* complementarity of dyads like stability/flux and crisis/resolution.

Basseches' dialectical thinking

Basseches (1984) introduces dialectical thinking 'as an important psychological phenomenon and ... an epistemologically important psychological attribute' (p. 30). His developmental theory of dialectical thinking provides a complementary theory for the ways of knowing that characterise the later positions described in BirD. These post-dyadic positions describe ways of knowing that replace the earlier emphasis on the opposition and separation of dyads with more integrative and complementary forms. Basseches defines dialectical thinking as follows:

> I view the dialectical perspective as comprising a family of world-outlooks, or views of the nature of existence (ontology) and knowledge (epistemology) ... Dialectic defined as follows, ties together the concepts of change, wholeness, and internal relations ... Dialectic is developmental transformation (i.e. developmental movement through forms) which occurs via constitutive and interactive relationships.
>
> (1984, pp. 21–2)

For example, dialectical thinking describes the dynamic interplay and interdependence between relational oppositions such as *relative* and *universal*.

I further hope that my framing of BirD is dialectical in that I attempt to locate it as a theory that is sensitive to dyadic tensions in developmental psychology, such as linear/cyclic, relative/universal, epistemological/ontological and concrete/abstract. Basseches' own reflexivity on one of these dyads is instructive:

> I recognize that in allying my work with the Piagetian project, I may inadvertently lend support to the universalistic formal voice in genetic epistemology ... I hope it can be seen as an instance of siding with the underdog in the hegemonic struggle between relativism and universalism.
>
> (1984, p. 14)

No doubt, critics will find dyadic sidings in my presentation of BirD that I would either readily acknowledge or have inadvertently overlooked. Like Basseches, I acknowledge the subjective, socio-historical locatedness of the very theory I offer as somehow objectively descriptive and generalisable.

There is a sense in which BirD is a dialectical theory because, at face value, it ascribes equal value to the constituents of the dyads it uses to explore real-world contents and wicked problems. However, BirD also represents positions that problematise dialectical thinking by collapsing dyadic thought altogether. I appreciate Basseches' honesty in an age that is too strongly characterised by rewards for developmental theories that promise, albeit superficially, stability and peace of mind over honest descriptions of the bitter-sweet human condition.

96 Theory

> To think dialectically, is, in a certain sense, to trade off a degree of intellectual security for a freedom from intellectually imposing limitations on oneself or other people. If the primary value which guided this book were one of individual psychological well-being, it would not be at all obvious whether to advocate this trade-off or not.
>
> (1984, p. 29)

Admittedly, it is sometimes much easier to retreat into or attack from an exclusively relative or universal position, but the very developmental and dyadic nature of BirD brings such positions into deeper relationships beyond mere binary oppositions to facilitate the recognition and (re)solution of wicked problems.

Reich's relational and contextual reasoning

Though several theories of cognitive and epistemological development imply the development of increasingly sophisticated dyadic relationships, Reich's (1989, 1990, 1995, 2000a, 2000b, 2002, 2003, 2005) theory of relational and contextual reasoning (RCR) is perhaps the closest relation to BirD. RCR is essentially a theory concerning the development of ways of resolving cognitive conflict between seemingly competing explanations that are often positioned as 'opposites'. In Reich's terms, 'the issue is to "coordinate" two or more "rivalling" descriptions, explanations, models, theories or interpretations' (2002, p. 15). Reich (2002, p. 52) outlines five levels of relational and contextual reasoning (RCR) that progress from either/or relationships between different *explanada* (Reich's term for explanations of phenomenon) to complementary, relational and contextual relationships between multiple explanada. More specifically, the *intra* level sees A and B related as alternatives where one is right. The *inter* level enables the possibility that both A and B could be right. The *trans-intra* level assumes that A and B are both needed for any adequate explanation of a problem. The *trans-inter* level reveals the interrelationship between A and B as codependent explanations. The *trans-trans* level adds a level of contextual awareness to the previous appreciation of the interdependence of explanations. Thus relational and contextual reasoning (RCR) is literally the description given to the highest level of resolution of a cognitive conflict:

> RCR does not arrive fully operative at a person's birth but, given the right circumstances, develops from level I to level V ... into young adulthood and beyond. It starts functioning in earnest at level III, reached from about 11 years onward (if at all).
>
> (Reich, 2003, p. 462)

It is revealing that Reich formerly used the label 'thinking in terms of complementarity' for RCR (2002, p. 3).

A, B and C represent competing explanations, descriptions models, interpretations or theories of the same entity, phenomenon or coherent whole

A background to bi-relational development 97

(Reich, 2002, p. 13). Reich refers to the coherent whole as the *explanandum*. The 'relational' in RCR refers to the relation between A, B and C and the relations between A, B and C and the explanandum. The 'contextual' in RCR refers to the time, place, and circumstances in which the relations between A, B and C and the explanandum are considered. Finally, the 'reasoning' in RCR refers to the active coordination of A, B and C through the application of a set of rules specific to the problem. Thus, reasoning develops from binary opposition to complex contextual coordination. While focusing on the development of dyads (e.g. A/B) from their inception to their collapse, BirD's interim positions are compatible with RCR's general developmental sequence.

Reich characterises RCR as a postformal theory describing levels that move beyond the limitations of formal binary logic. He explains: 'Aware that we are all trapped in partial subjectivity, post-formal thinkers are said to make a decision about the rules of the game (nature of truth), then act on the basis of those rules' (2002, p. 20). However, Reich overtly recognises the value and applications of other thought forms. After comparing RCR with other thought forms, he writes: 'Development of RCR implies corresponding levels of Piagetian thinking, cognitively complex thought, and putatively of dialectical and analogical thought as well as at least a "feel" for, and minimal use of different types of logic' (2002, p. 74). Similarly, BirD attempts to represent both formal and postformal ways of knowing, though only in relation to domain-specific and/or domain-general dyads. BirD also represents the unification and negation of dyads in order to represent some of the more esoteric and nihilistic ways of knowing that are sometimes marginalised or sanitised in traditional theories of development.

The developing logic of RCR is perhaps best illustrated by Reich's geometrical example of ambiguous figure shift that sees two possible solutions to the number of cubes (i.e. 6 or 7) in a single picture. Reich uses this ambiguous figure to demonstrate a trivalent logic (i.e. compatible, incompatible and non-compatible) underlying RCR. He explains the trivalent logic as follows:

> To see simultaneously three faces of a given cube is compatible; the wish to see simultaneously (without mirrors) more than three faces is incompatible with reality. The meaning of non-compatible can be illustrated by answering the question 'How many full three-dimensional cubes are there?'.
>
> (2002, p. 44)

The answer to this question distinguishes Aristotelian binary logic from RCR:

> Most people will answer 'six', and, when the figure is turned on its head, 'seven.' The figure having stayed the same, applying formal binary (Aristotelian) logic would conclude that one of the answers must be wrong, and proceed to determine which one. In contrast, RCR logic will confirm that 'six' is correct in one context, and 'seven' in another context.
>
> (2002, p. 44)

98 Theory

The example underlies Reich's claim that relational contextual issues are sometimes perpetuated as problems through the exclusive use of binary logic. Teske comments on RCR as an alternative logic rather than a dominant logic:

> Moreover, RCR, while potentially inclusive of binary or context-independent logics, does present a potential alternative to the necessarily context-independent cognitive representations of the currently dominant computational synthesis.
>
> (2003, p. 444)

It is important to note that RCR is only relevant to certain types of problems and cognitive conflicts. It is not useful for solving problems that prescribe a single clear-cut answer (e.g. simple arithmetic). Similarly, BirD represents a cumulative development that reconciles oppositional relationships with complementary relationships depending on the problem and context. Just as exclusively binary oppositional approaches can exacerbate wicked problems, exclusively complementary or dialectical approaches are unlikely to be useful in solving problems with absolute solutions.

It is enlightening to examine one of Reich's examples of RCR. He demonstrates complementarity using the theory of light and quantum mechanics, likening pre-RCR binary thinking to the competition between particle and wave theories of light that were only resolved by a new thought form that gave rise to quantum mechanics:

> Thus quantum mechanics is a wonderful example of how with the development of knowledge our idea of what counts even as a *possible* knowledge claim, our idea of what counts as even a *possible* object, and our ideas of what counts even as a *possible* property are all subjects to change.
>
> (Putnam in Reich, 2002, p. 24)

In one of several biographical applications of RCR, Reich quotes Niels Bohr:

> The very nature of the quantum theory thus forces us to regard the space-time coordination and the claim of causality, the union of which characterizes the classical theories, as complementary but exclusive features of the description, symbolizing the idealization of observation and definition respectively.
>
> (2002, pp. 141–2)

It is this contextual and complementary coordination of explanations that Reich finds indicative of developing thought forms. The wave action of an electron is theory A. The particle action of an electron is theory B. Both A and B are correct in different contexts relative to the observer. Thus, the most powerful explanandum coordinates both A and B without excluding or reducing either. This is RCR.

Reich's contention is that RCR is as relevant to resolving social conflicts as it is to resolving problems of physics. Writing on the application of RCR, Teske notes:

> Perhaps some of the answers lie in that most basic of empirical understandings having to do with our shared human experience and the possibilities of openly and respectfully, even lovingly, listening to each other despite our differences, understanding that a broader concept of rationality need not deny the possibility of dissensus, and of the differentiated understanding that allows us to agree to disagree even as we work toward more integrated understandings.
>
> (2003, p. 448)

Similarly, my hope is that BirD offers some structural insights into wicked problems and social messes, while remaining sensitive to the domain-specific and contextualised ontologies and *life worlds* of human development.

One criticism of Reich's methodology raises the difficulty of identifying explananda that may be overly context dependent or inextricably linked to a particular system of belief:

> Unfortunately, in many cases of conflicts or incommensurabilities between belief systems, many differences crop up in decisions about what constitutes the explanandum, especially where the referents are theory-tied or entirely defined in terms of the belief system (sin, grace, and soul come readily to mind) . . . For conflict resolution, agreeing on an explanandum that is not so dependent may be a good way to begin.
>
> (Teske, 2003, p. 443)

Accordingly, I frame dyadic structures as 'a good way to begin' understanding what can appear to be the 'conflicts or incommensurabilities' that characterise wicked problems. In order to minimise, but not eradicate, contextual ambiguity between explananda, BirD works on the identification of dyadic explananda that are evident in context, interdependent and structurally related. Thus, it may be easier to identify an individual's onto-epistemological disposition using a domain-general structure (e.g. the dyad) within domain-specific contents (e.g. nature/nurture in the context of intelligence) than it would using only domain-general structures in context or domain-specific contents that are difficult to generalise.

In summary, BirD shares the general sequence with RCR as a development from binary oppositional to complementary ways of knowing. However, BirD is distinguished by its relative emphases on: (a) dyadic structures and relationships, (b) the identification of domain-specific dyads, (c) the onto-epistemological dimension of development and (d) the negation and unification of dyads and their expressions in nihilistic and esoteric ways of knowing and being.

100   Theory

Summary of theoretical influences

So far I have introduced and briefly described some of the developmental theories and approaches that have influenced my bi-relational approach to onto-epistemological development (i.e. BirD). Table 4.1 provides a general comparative summary of these influences. Not all spatial alignments of stages, styles and phases are accurate. Some stages and phases are not completely compatible due to differences in domain constructs (e.g. *faith* and *epistemology*). Nonetheless, my claim is that these diverse models do reflect a useful abstraction of what it means to develop, though this abstraction is lived and departed from in many different ways.

To reiterate, while BirD shares the developmental nature and sequence of most of these approaches it is differentiated by its: bi-relational focus; focus on domain-general and domain-specific dyads; direct application to wicked problems; sensitivity to more esoteric and nihilistic ways of knowing and being represented at the point of collapse; emphasis on the interdependence of epistemological and ontological dimensions; and sensitivity to continuous and/or discontinuous development across different dyads and in different contexts.

Finally, any theory is subject to its own propositions and assumptions. This is especially true for a theory or approach that explores positions, developments and trajectories of knowing and being. Accordingly, the final section of the chapter offers a self-critical and reflexive look at the nature of BirD. Collectively, the theories I have discussed so far have had a significant influence on BirD. The purpose of the following section is to consolidate these influences into some general dyadic descriptions of the nature of BirD. Specifically, I identify BirD as a domain-general *and* domain-specific, linear *and* cyclic, abstract *and* concrete, dyadic *and* monadic approach to onto-epistemological development. These descriptions position the approach for a more detailed explication of its bi-relational positions, relationships and dynamics in the following chapter.

The nature of a theory of Bi-relational Development (i.e. BirD)

The remaining section of this chapter draws together and summarises the most general insights from the theoretical frameworks that inform the intended nature of BirD. I have spent some time in university libraries and public bookshops reflecting on where I hope a future book of this nature would be shelved. It struck me that the categorisation of many books and the patronage of different browsers can also be understood in relation to some common dyads. Perhaps the first dyad that underlies the dilemma is related to whether or not a book found in a university library should also be found in a popular bookshop. I suspect that the various positions on this problem have something to do with primary dyads such as high/low culture, analytic/synthetic, reductive/holistic, empirical/phenomenological and particular/general, with the left dyadic

Table 4.1 A general comparison of BirD and related theories

Theory	Stages/Styles/Regions					
Bi-relational Development (BirD)	Creation	Pre-dyadic (Emergence)	Pro-dyadic (Opposition)	Post-dyadic (Convergence)	Collapse	Trans-positions
Cognitive Development (Piaget, 1971b)	Sensorimotor	Pre-operational	Concrete Operational	Formal Operational		
Epistemological Development (Perry, 1970)			Dualism	Multiplicity	Relativism	Commitment in Relativism
Subject–object Development (Kegan, 1982)	Incorporative	Impulsive	Imperial	Interpersonal	Institutional	Interindividual
Reflective Judgment (King and Kitchener, 1994)		Pre-reflective Reasoning	Quasi-reflective reasoning		Reflective Reasoning	
Epistemological Understanding (Kuhn and Weinstock, 2002)	Realist		Absolutist	Multiplist		Evaluativist
Epistemological Reflection (Baxter Magolda, 1992)			Absolute Knowing	Transitional Knowing	Independent Knowing	Contextual Knowing
Relational and Contextual Reasoning (Reich, 2002)			Intra Inter	Trans-intra Trans-inter		Trans-trans

102 Theory

constituents characterising academic libraries and the right characterising popular bookshops. Certainly, there should be room for books that bridge the divide, but they are no more valuable for doing so than those that rest on shelves on either side. A word, then, concerning the way I intend to position this book.

I do not see this book in the genre of scientific knowledge *or* esoteric knowledge – though I hope it has the seeds of both. In a positive sense, I hope to sow the seeds of some worthy hypotheses for more empirical testing and formulation. However, I also hope to acknowledge the seed of the great traditions of human wisdom, for their collective symmetries are evidence enough for me that modern science, perhaps beginning with cosmology, will find some of its more generalizable findings deeply reflected in ancient human ontologies. This is no appeal to the supernatural, more literally understood. It is a reasoned proposition that the theory of everything will have 'naturally' already found expression in *some* things. We should not be too surprised if we find glimpses of the profound truths of tomorrow's physics in today's psychology and yesterday's mythology.

I have as much empathy for the phenomenological sense of ancient wisdom and the counter-revolutionary origins of their neo-advocates as I do scepticism for their tendency to sacrifice empirical details for grand spiritual or esoteric narratives. So, I do not intend this book as an exposition that reveals hidden ancient truths, metaphysical symmetries or mysterious quantum psychologies. I fear that this genre is sometimes too one-sidedly symmetrical, occultic, esoteric, transcendent, sacred, holistic and metaphysical for an exploration of dyadic relationships with correspondingly asymmetrical, plain, mundane, immanent, profane, reductive and material concerns. In practical terms, as Abraham (1993) notes, 'If a person becomes exceedingly mystic and other-worldly-minded, and if he/she negates intellectual and personality development, then an imbalance of ineffectiveness occurs' (p. 40).

However, it is also not my intention to write a book that would fit easily into any genre of Western science, even the so-called *softer* sciences. I fear that this genre is sometimes too insensitive to the transience, ambiguity and fragility of words, too dismissive of the whole for the part, too blind to the phenomenological truths of alternative voices, too quick to leap the gap between 'is and ought', too rationally descriptive at the expense of the creative and imaginative and too willing to reduce the ineffable to the literal and material. And yet I have great respect for the scholarship of science that is relatively reductive, analytical, particular, quantifying, objectifying and unapologetically empirical, where the context, subject and stage of inquiry allows it. Indeed, I hope to gradually extend the empirical analyses of my bi-relational approach in different contexts. I could readily expand a particular conceptualisation of science as the only true epistemology and, therefore, the final word on epistemology, but I fear such an expansion would sacrifice its practical meaning and necessary differentiations from other ways of knowing. Positivistic descriptions of science as objective knowledge and objectifying procedures related to empirical observation and experimentation may need to be distinguished from relativistic descriptions of science as socially constructed, subjective and rhetorical demarcations of true knowledge; but if either of these conceptualisations of science is used to cast a net over all knowing and being, it will invoke counter-reactions and expansive activity from its designated 'opposition'. As for the nature of BirD, I share Taylor's (1996) approach that 'The interpenetration of the cultural and scientific is hardly something we must guard against; by recognising the contingency of such a barrier, we can work toward the edification of both' (p. 18). If there is a shelf or library that houses books under this definition, then I would be happy to find this book there. BirD represents dyadic developments that build bridges between genres and disciplines, while respecting the relatively necessary and interdependent divisions *between* them and the unity *within* them. No doubt, while I hope to bridge the best of both worlds, for some, I will seem to have built a feeble bridge to the worst of both worlds.

Domain-general/domain-specific

BirD offers an approach to wicked problems that reconciles oppositions between domain-specific and domain-general ways of knowing. Much recent research into psychological development, especially epistemological development, is sensitive to contextuality and domain specificity. This is perhaps due to an imbalance of research and methodologies that accommodate both the general and the specific. Tellingly, Hofer frames several pressing questions that inform how and where epistemological trajectories are mapped:

> How do we integrate the disciplinary views with the more global approaches to epistemology? How do individuals coordinate these beliefs? Is there an underlying framework or epistemology that provides a mental platform for these disciplinary beliefs or are these unrelated?
>
> (2002, p. 13)

BirD offers a way of crossing the divide in the examination of domain-general and domain-specific epistemologies. It utilises domain-general constructs (i.e. dyads and dyadic relationships) and domain-specific dyads (e.g. nature/culture). The use of a construct that is as domain-general as dyads avoids many of the pitfalls associated with semantically denser epistemological survey or questionnaire items. However, the use of dyads that are relevant to a particular domain, culture or individual serves the examination of structural development *in context*. This conceptualisation is consistent with an emerging appreciation for the domain-general and domain-specific nature of knowledge and knowing (e.g. Buehl *et al.*, 2002; Hofer, 2002).

Linear/cyclic

BirD offers an approach to wicked problems that reconciles oppositions between linear and cyclic approaches to human development. In Chapter 5, I represent BirD's dyadic positions as geometrically distributed on an ambiguous surface to

104 Theory

suggest the paradoxically linear and cyclic nature of onto-epistemological development. Traditional theories of human development appropriate the metaphors of lines, spirals, ladders and stairs arranged hierarchically, sequentially and incrementally with rungs, levels, stages, styles, streams and layers. The more fluid the metaphors, the more recently *developed* the theories tend to be. Indeed, some critics would have developmental theory become so fluid that it ceases to be a development in any meaningfully directional sense. BirD accommodates such criticism as a counterbalancing 'development' that arises from the dominance of fixed-stage linear theories. While many developmental frameworks assume a sequential approach to relatively fixed stages, BirD proposes a paradoxically linear and cyclic 'development' of relations between positions that involves the *inception, emergence, opposition, convergence* and *collapse* of dyads. While this linear sequence is intended to represent a domain-general logic of development, it is not prescriptive of domain-specific developments, which may be much more fragmented and multi-positional than the general abstraction would allow. As such, BirD's archetypal positions can be used to relationally describe, rather than absolutely prescribe, onto-epistemological trajectories. This approach certainly does not jettison developmental possibilities. For example, even the collapse or paradoxical rejection of binary oppositions that characterises postmodernism can still be understood as a development *in relation to* dyads. As Hebdige explains:

> [T]he idea of depthlessness as a marker of postmodernism accompanied as it is by a rejection of the vocabulary of intellectual 'penetration' and the binary structures on which post-Socratic thought is reckoned to be based (for example, reality v. appearance, real relations v. phenomenal forms, science v. false consciousness, consciousness v. the unconscious, inside v. outside, subject v. object, etc.) can be understood in this context as another step away from the old explanatory models and certainties.
>
> (1996, p. 184)

A postmodern step away from 'binary structures' can be seen as a step forward, or a development, even if that step is off a line and into a circle. In BirD, the post-dyadic step away is a step away only in relation to certainty and absolutism. However, if the postmodern step is taken too far, it will either require a step back, or it will ironically step forward in a cyclic sense into an overextended certainty of its own uncertainties, becoming the very way of knowing it sought to reject.

In order to address the linear/cyclic tension in theories of epistemological development, BirD collects and analyses data using spectra as well as continua. For example, there is no a priori primacy or developmental value given to either subjective or objective, nature or nurture. This is not to preclude developmental trajectories from one dyadic constituent to the other (e.g. objective to subjective); rather, it is not to assume them in the collection of data. My developmental assumption is that dichotomising and absolutising epistemologies are constructed from experiences where either the left or the right binary is contextually dominant. Like tossing a coin, it is generally more likely that a bias for heads or tails be constructed with one toss and challenged with many tosses. More developed epistemologies tend to account for the objective equality of the left and right binary, while acknowledging the subjective and contextual need to choose one or the other. So, in relation to traditional theories of development, BirD is lateral *and* hierarchical, spectral *and* continual, linear *and* cyclic. Its linear arrangement – that there is a general developmental sequence between the creation and collapse of dyads – is a hypothesis that can be tested through application. Its cyclic arrangement allows for the phases of development to be reconceptualised as positions or locations such that any developmental patterns can emerge from, rather than pre-constrain, the data. This allows the theory to represent order and randomness, connection and disconnection, across different domains that exist within and between individuals. For example, BirD can be used to examine multiple dyads and dyadic relationships in the same individual, possibly revealing discontinuities and domain specificities in onto-epistemological trajectories.

If developmental theories have any explanatory grip on reality, then theories of development are themselves the progeny of a development. Naïve rigidity, over-compartmentalised stages and strong teleological assumptions lend themselves to simple linear metaphors of development. The simple theory of development confidently draws a concrete line between the only two points it can see and claims to account for everything. The complex theory of development cautiously traces a hypothetical curve to show the average route between the thousands of points it can see, with the full knowledge of the possibility that the average route may never have been travelled by any individual. My contention is that the realisation of the former inadequacies of developmental theories is itself a development towards post-directional approaches, where linear teleology, purposeful abstraction and optimistic modernity must be reconciled with relative kinds of cyclic, divergent, random, messy and dynamic trajectories. This post-directional approach to development reflexively engages the meaning of 'development', which may now be seen in linear or cyclic terms. Metaphorically, there is a fine line between the well travelled and the lost, the directional and the directionless. BirD uses the geometrical metaphor to capture the paradox between linear and cyclic, and teleological and directionless representations of development. BirD maps linear development to a point of convergence and collapse, but then traces a 'developmental return'. The paradox is that continuing development tends to retrace its steps, but with a renewed dexterity and appreciation for contextuality.

The linear/cyclic nature of BirD also relates to the organisation of dyadic constituents (e.g. subjective/objective). It is tempting and common to represent ascending development from one dyadic constituent to another; for example, to represent conservatism and liberalism, absolutism and relativism, subjective and objective as lower and higher phases of development respectively. BirD is unique in that it organises the 'left and right' dyad on a spectrum intersected by

106 Theory

a continuum along which 'up and down' development occurs. It also represents a dependent relationship between spectrum and continuum (i.e. between 'up and down' and 'left and right') that is mapped onto an ambiguous surface. Thus, trajectories that go 'up' also tend to move 'left or right' towards equilibration. I have found this line/cycle dynamic to be articulated in surprising places, such as Lerman's exploration of polarities in dance:

> [F]ind something to respect at the opposite pole. And if for a moment you take this continuum and bend it into a circle, you will see that the two ends lie close, like next-door neighbours ... The respect has to be authentic, but it doesn't have to be uncritical.
>
> (2011, p. xvi)

This linear/cyclic paradox finds expression as the 'reconciliation of opposites' from Heraclitus to Hegel and Bakhtin. In *Studies of Polarity*, Hocks (1976) reflects that 'the reconciliation of opposites is as fundamental to Eliot as it was to Heraclitus', and calls for more attendance to the unification of literary works that is hinted at through the presence 'of lines that exhibit paradox and opposition' (p. 92). Likewise, Bakhtin's (1981) *Dialogic Imagination* describes a perennial and relational tension and complementarity between poles that paradoxically sustains and (re)solves the form–content dichotomy through unification and separation. Perhaps the most explicit treatment of philosophical dyads is Hegel's (1991) dialectic, which describes the iterative generation and synthesis of opposites. Hegal uses the term *Aufhebung* to describe the paradoxical overcoming and maintenance of contradiction. Accordingly, BirD maps developments between dyadic constituents without dictating a particular order or primacy, a priori. The representation of spectrum and continuum on a continuous surface also resolves the tension in onto-epistemological theories that represent linear development between 'absolute and relative' without representing the possibility of a post-linear reconnection of the absolute and relative. BirD provides descriptive and visual metaphors for this recapitulation, rejoining and return in onto-epistemological journeys.

Abstract/concrete

BirD offers an approach to wicked problems that reconciles oppositions between abstract and concrete ways of engaging wicked problems. The second visual metaphor that illustrates the dyadic nature of BirD relates to the symmetrical grid overlaying the finer shades of grey. The grid represents the relatively fixed, generalised and abstracted theoretical framework, while the finer shades of grey represent the relatively fluid, particular and concrete lived realities. While I believe that there is a powerful relationship between BirD as a theoretical abstraction and the messier everyday reality it seeks to describe, I acknowledge the inevitable and varying degrees of separation between the two (i.e. abstract representation and concrete reality) for any reader or perceiver, especially given the semantic density and diversity of the subject matter (i.e. wicked problems). The illustrations and applications in later chapters may go some way to bridging this gap. Some readers will inevitably experience more degrees of separation between BirD's abstract representations and their concrete realities than others. Though if many readers have this experience and have alternative explanations for their dyadic positions, then the approach will need revision.

The perceived disjuncture between theory and experience is a point of criticism for traditional developmental theory. Broughton (1986) reflects in his chapter *The Political Psychology of Faith Development Theory* that 'it is a sad consequence of the idealism in cognitive-developmental theory that it has ceased to be interested in actual experiences, actions, beliefs, or existence' (p. 93). BirD maintains the explanatory power of developmental theory while respecting the complexity, diversity, and relativity of real-life trajectories. It does not seek to choose between theory and experience; it recognises the interactive relationship between the two and admits its own status as an evolving observation that is, in a sense, inseparable from the observed. BirD is theoretically prescriptive in that it designates boundaries, locations and dynamics of development. However, these boundaries and locations are relative and emergent gridlines. They are archetypes, abstractions and generalisations from the collective of particular trajectories in real-life contexts. BirD is also experientially descriptive in that diverse onto-epistemological trajectories can be mapped onto these locations, as illustrated in Part II of this book.

Developmental theories also face the problem of intra-individual and inter-individual continuity and coherence, and domain-specific and domain-general applicability. For example, does an individual have a general and continuous onto-epistemological identity and/or a fragmented and dynamic identity? Is individual identity an illusory line drawn between otherwise random dots? The problem is the same whether it is posed of an individual or a group. Again, BirD is sensitive to the general/specific, continuous/dynamic, single/multiple dyads that relate to the study of identities. It does not assume that onto-epistemological identities are a priori fixed or fluid, single or multiple, continuous or dynamic, domain-general or domain-specific. It recognises the relative interdependence and applicability of these categories *in context*. Thus, identities and developments can only ever be seen as fixed or general *in relation to* fluid or specific characterisations.

BirD maps formative onto-epistemological positions and trajectories in time that characterise individual or group ways of knowing and being in relation to wicked problems. 'Development' is one type of movement between these locations. It is perhaps the most predictable and generalisable type of movement, though not the only type of movement. It may be difficult to conceptualise an individual's movement between locations as 'development' because the construct of *individual* is itself a generalisation that often fails to capture the contradictory, disjointed, fragmented and contextual nature of *a* person. Furthermore, it is

108 Theory

possible for one individual to feel for a fleeting moment what another spends a lifetime to know and be. Individual and group, continuity and randomness, connection and disconnection, part and whole are all dyads with a point of collapse. Thus, the act of theorising about individual and group trajectories of development and the relationship between them is only meaningful in relation and context.

United/diverse

BirD is a bi-relational approach in that it uses dyads and dyadic relationships as the core construct with which to describe and explore everyday realities and experiences. I have used *two* as an organising theme because it facilitates analysis of unity and multiplicity: 'No one can draw a line that is not a boundary line; every line splits a singularity into a plurality' (Escher and Brigham, 1971, p. 40). BirD is an attempt to represent how a spectrum between polarities can be understood as zero, one, two, three or a multitude of things. It represents the development and dynamics of such understandings in relation to wicked problems. For example, how does a person characterised by a well developed onto-epistemological disposition towards *Oneness* interact with another person characterised by a poorly developed onto-epistemological disposition towards binary oppositional ways of knowing and being in relation to a nature/culture or spirit/matter dyad? Or how does the 'same' person experience both dispositions within a single lifetime or even across different domains of experience? BirD acknowledges the reality *and* constructedness of dyads and represents both positions (i.e. unity and diversity) in order to explore such questions. I have called BirD a 'bi-relational approach' in recognition that everyday life tends to be lived and known in dyadic terms. However, I could have as easily acknowledged the unitary or multiple nature of BirD by naming the same approach *uni*-relational or *multi*-relational, though neither of these serve my avian acronym and metaphor (i.e. BirD) particularly well; nor do they capture the most common dyadic expression of these dynamics in everyday discourse.

Symmetrical/asymmetrical

Perhaps the most important comment on the nature of BirD relates to the concept of *balance*. I have used many metaphors that, at first glance and face value, seem to reflect the concept of balance as a premise of BirD. However, I would like to encourage a second glance for a truer insight into the nature of BirD. At first glance, the use of dyads seems to imply equality of constituent parts (e.g. left/right); reference to a spectrum seems to imply an equality of poles at both ends; and the cyclic symmetries and equidistant scaffolds of the visual representation in Chapter 5 seem to imply the embrace of a conceptual *balance*. However, the metaphor of balance I employ is relational: that is, I use it to suggest that the two sides of a thing are irreducibly significant, like the two

A background to bi-relational development   109

sides of the same coin. However, I acknowledge that even like the two sides of a coin there may well be subtle differences between weighting and contour that *do* skew the probability to one side or another in different contexts. Thus, I use the concept of balance to emphasise the interdependence of dyadic constituents (e.g. hot/cold) and their *relatively* equal importance in communicating a concept (e.g. temperature) or problem (e.g. the [water] temperature in which to bathe a baby). *Balance* is an important concept in the resolution of wicked problems, especially when the problem is exacerbated by binary oppositional approaches that repress one side, either through passive neglect or actively. To extend the previous metaphor, some of us try to control the temperature of the bathwater, either unaware that there are two taps or without the dexterity to use both effectively. BirD represents and problematises a naïve form of balance that attempts to regulate temperature for all occasions by turning two taps to the same amount at the same time. Needless to say, this approach is ineffectual for all but the most desirably 'luke-warm' occasions.

BirD recognises and locates two types of balance: a naïve form and a sophisticated form. Naïve forms of balance are prone to the balance fallacy, which is a tendency to attribute equal value a priori to multiple a posteriori claims, regardless of rational or empirical merit. For example, should geocentric models of the solar system be presented equally in science classrooms with heliocentric models because both models have adherents? Apart from the curriculum being impossibly crowded, what would be the criteria for truth, or the ultimate reason for teaching anything at all? This form of naïve balance unknowingly reduces a posteriori judgements to a priori judgements. BirD conceptualises an abstract balance between polarities in order to facilitate more informed concrete choices.

Sophisticated or postformal notions of balance maintain a priori or *in toto* (i.e. in total) tensions between abstractions (e.g. subjective/objective) rather than a posteriori or *in situ* (i.e. in context) claims about concrete truths (e.g. earth is flat/earth is round). For example, in the competition for explanatory theories about the physical structure of the solar system, a geocentric/heliocentric dyadic balance is a naïve presentation of balance. However, such false dyads often disguise more significant *in toto* tensions between subjective/objective, hope/despair and purpose/meaninglessness. Ironically, many absurd and irrational claims about physical truth (e.g. young Earthism, geocentricism, flat Earthism) may be sustained due to a false conflation with more metaphysical concerns. For example, physical geocentricism is conflated with metaphysical hope and purpose. By proxy, the heliocentric challenge is seen or perhaps 'felt' and fought as a form of despair and meaninglessness. An important bi-relational dynamic to be explored later is that, somewhat ironically, the more that physical science (e.g. heliocentrism) *is* conflated and communicated with a cold celebration of despair and meaninglessness (Latour, 2002), the more it will be challenged with inaccurate physical theories that protect a sense of existential purpose. Arguably, this inverse conflation actually sustains its opposition's absurdity and irrationality, and the

110 Theory

two become locked in a cycle of conflict. I believe this conflational dynamic to be at the heart of many wicked problems, including some of the most violent, vitriolic and divisive wars between science and religion. The dynamic illustrates the need for a careful separation of authentic and illusory dyads in the understanding of balance.

The conflation between abstract or *in toto* dyads and concrete or *in situ* dyads is understandable given their connection to human lives and survival concerns. For example, there is a physical-spatial difference between a bedroom that is abstractly described as messy and chaotic and a bedroom where the distribution of objects can be described as neat and orderly. Arguably, in particular contexts there is a survival advantage to being relatively neat and ordered. Perhaps things are easier to find, clean and maintain. Thus, the abstraction, *order,* may be attributed value derived from a concrete real-world context. However, imagine that over time the particular physical-spatial order of the bedroom no longer suits the needs of the inhabitant and a period of relative disorder or chaos is needed to appreciate and address the deficiencies of the present order. In this context, the merits of disorder and chaos may be known and valued. The abstraction of these merits (order/chaos) across changing contexts (inhabitants' changing needs) leads to the notion of balance. Naïve balancing dispositions seek to apply order and disorder in equal measure in every future situation. Naïve binary oppositional dispositions may commit to *order* simply because 'it has worked in a particular situation in the past'. Both naïve balance and naïve oppositions are maladaptive dispositions, though perhaps developmental precedents for a postformal form of balance that paradoxically represents tensions between balance/imbalance, paradox/opposition and abstract/concrete.

The semantic ambiguity of *balance* should also be acknowledged. In most everyday contexts, the word *balance* is used to point at the need to consider the range on a spectrum, or the attention given to items or domains that are important. Here, balance is not solely used to mean a strictly 50/50 numerically exact division. For example, an individual seeking to 'find more of a work/life balance' is not necessarily intending to divide time allocation and energy expenditure into daily 2x12-hour lots, for 'work' and 'life' are ambiguous constructs that are not easily or equally weighed by time and energy. Thus, balance should be able to be understood phenomenologically and contextually, as well as logically and abstractly, if we are to understand the meaning and value of polarities and dyads.

Perhaps the final word on balance concerns its use *in toto* and *in situ*. In situ, *balance* is rarely an objectively (i.e. 50/50) appropriate description of interactions (e.g. work/life balance). However, in toto – that is, over time and across contexts – balance may signify a deeper appreciation for the stability, interdependence and equal ubiquity of seemingly opposing forces. Whether or not such forces are mathematically balanced (i.e. 50/50) cannot really be known, inasmuch as contexts or boundaries around reality are perhaps infinitely expandable and contractable. There is a sense in which *in toto* is not really humanly knowable and makes sense only in relation to the part. Reciprocally, the part or imbalance also only makes sense in relation to this *in toto* understanding. Thus, balance and imbalance, equilibrium and dis-equilibrium, like all other primary dyads identified in BirD, are co-definitive.

I acknowledge that *balance* is a useful concept, especially in relation to primary dyads (e.g. subjective/objective); however, I reserve judgement as to whether or not an ultimate or universal balance exists as a fundamental basis for reality. Daoists tend to affirm such a balance; theists tend to err on the side of order and purpose; nihilists tend to err on the side of randomness and purposelessness. For me, randomness and order, and purpose and purposelessness are co-definitive concepts: one only makes sense in relation to the other. To conclude the ultimate randomness of the universe is as meaningful and meaningless as to conclude its order. Each conclusion is an act of faith, a commitment to a particular vision of a possible ambiguous figure that BirD can represent in relation to other positions, but cannot ultimately evaluate for a lack of an inescapable mind, a completely objective perspective or *total* understanding.

Accordingly, the geometrical metaphor for BirD that I present in the following chapter represents the lines and cycles, beginnings, ends and contiguity of human knowing and being. I cannot step outside this metaphor to assess whether or not there is an ultimate purpose to our onto-epistemological trajectories and developments. To be honest and vulnerable for a moment, my reflections on bi-relational development have at some times made the universe seem charged with a theistic sense of meaning and purpose. Perhaps a Prime Mover divided us and even 'himself' in two, so that we/He could experience what it means to be One – though at other times, the universe seems to resemble the Nietzschean and Schopenhauerian darkness, devoid of any ultimate meaning and purpose. Perhaps life and development are *just* Sisyphean journeys without God or gods, either malevolent or benevolent, to spite or please. My claim for now is that life seems to hang in the balance between these two entangled perspective-realities; indeed, life seems to proceed from this balance, though it is rarely lived in the middle. While I intend to return briefly to these speculations in Part II, my intention in this chapter was to establish a theoretical context and some defining points of departure to make sense of BirD as it is explicated in the following chapter.

In summary, BirD is an attempt to map onto-epistemological trajectories in relation to dyads and dyadic relationships. It is informed by, but seeks to further develop existing theories of human development in relation to wicked problems. Specifically, the nature of BirD is defined by its relational and contextual reconciliation of ontology and epistemology, individual and social, concrete and abstract, domain-general and domain-specific, order and chaos, and unity and multiplicity. I hope to have shown how these reconciliations that reflect the intended nature of BirD have grown out of my encounters with different and occasionally conflicting theories of development.

References

Abraham, K. (1993). *Balancing the pairs of opposites: The seven rays and education and other essays in esoteric psychology.* White City, OR: Lampus Press.

Bakhtin, M. M. (Ed.). (1981). *The dialogic imagination: Four essays.* Austin, TX and London: University of Texas Press.

Barrett, J. L. (2004). *Why would anyone believe in God? (Cognitive Science of Religion Series).* Walnut Creek, CA: Altamira Press.

Basseches, M. (1984). *Dialectical thinking and adult development.* Norwood, NJ: Ablex Publishing.

Baxter Magolda, M. B. (1992). *Knowing and reasoning in college: Gender-related patterns in students' intellectual development.* San Francisco, CA: Jossey-Bass.

Baxter Magolda, M. B. (2004). Self-authorship as the common goal of 21st century education. In M. B. B. Magolda and P. M. King (Eds.), *Learning partnerships: Theory and models of practice to educate for self-authorship* (pp. 1–35). Sterling, VA: Stylus.

Brainerd, C. J. (1978). *Piaget's theory of intelligence.* Englewood Cliff, NJ: Prentice Hall, Inc.

Broughton, J. (1987a). An introduction to critical developmental psychology. In J. M. Broughton (Ed.), *Critical theories of psychological development* (pp. 1–30). New York: Springer.

Broughton, J. (1987b). The masculine authority of the cognitive. In B. Inhelder, D. de Caprona and A. Wells (Eds.), *Piaget Today* (pp. 111–25). Hillsdale, NJ: Lawrence Erlbaum.

Broughton, J. (1986). The political psychology of faith development theory. In C. Dykstra and S. Parkes (Eds.), *Faith development and Fowler* (pp. 90–114). Birmingham, AL: Religious Education Press.

Buehl, M. M., Alexander, P. A., and Murphy, P. K. (2002). Beliefs about schooled knowledge: Domain general or domain specific? *Contemporary Educational Psychology*, 27, 415–49.

Campbell, R. L. (2006). Jean Piaget's genetic epistemology: Appreciation and critique. http://myweb.clemson.edu/~campber/piaget.html

Camus, A. (2005). *The myth of Sisyphus* (J. O'Brien, Trans.). London: Penguin Books. (Original work published 1942.)

Carey, S. (1985). *Conceptual change in childhood.* Cambridge, MA: MIT Press.

Case, R. (1992). *The mind's staircase: Exploring the conceptual underpinnings of children's thought and knowledge.* Hillsdale, NJ: Lawrence Erlbaum Associates.

Craig, W. L. (2008). *Reasonable faith.* Wheaton: Crossway.

Dawkins, R. (2006). *The God delusion.* London: Bantam Books.

De Lemos, M. M. (1969). The development of aboriginal children. *International Journal of Psychology*, 4, 255–69.

Dennett, D. C. (2006). *Breaking the spell: Religion as a natural phenomenon.* New York: Viking Penguin.

Diamond, A. (1991). Frontal lobe involvement in cognitive changes during the first year of life. In K. R. Gibson and A. C. Petersen (Eds.), *Brain maturation and cognitive development: Comparative and cross-cultural perspectives* (pp. 127–80). New York: Aldine De Gruyter.

Escher, M. C., and Brigham, J. E. (1971). *The graphic work of M.C. Escher.* New York: Ballantine Books.

Festinger, L. (1957). *A theory of cognitive dissonance.* Stanford, CA: Stanford University Press.

Flavell, J. H. (1985). *Cognitive development.* Englewood Cliffs, NJ: Prentice Hall.

Flavell, J. H., and Ross, L. (1981). *Social cognitive development: Frontiers and possible futures.* Cambridge, New York: Cambridge University Press.

Fowler, J. W. (1981). *Stages of faith: The psychology of human development and the quest for meaning*. San Francisco: Harper and Row.

Frazer, J. G. (1993). *The golden bough*. London: Wordsworth.

Freud, S. (1989). *The future of an illusion*. London: W. W. Norton & Company. (Original work published 1927.)

Harris, S. (2005). *The end of faith: Religion, terror, and the future of reason*. London: Simon and Schuster.

Hebdige, D. (1996). Postmodernism and the 'other side'. In S. Hall, D. Morley and C. Kuan-Hsing (Eds.), *Critical dialogues in cultural studies* (pp. 174–200). London: Routledge.

Hegel, G. W. F. (1991). *The encyclopaedia logic: Part one of the encyclopaedia of the philosophical sciences* (T. F. Geraets, W. A. Suchting and H. S. Harris, Trans.). Indianapolis, IN: Hackett Publishing.

Hitchens, C. (2007). *God is not great: How religion poisons everything*. New York: Twelve Books.

Hocks, R. A. (1976). 'Novelty' in polarity to 'the most admitted truths': Tradition and the individual talent in S. T. Coleridge and T. S. Eliot. In S. Sugerman (Ed.), *Evolution of consciousness: Studies in polarity* (pp. 83–97). Middletown, CT: Wesleyan University Press.

Hofer, B. K. (2002). Personal epistemology as a psychological and educational construct: An introduction. In B. K. Hofer and P. R. Pintrich (Eds.), *Personal epistemology: The psychology of beliefs about knowledge and knowing* (pp. 3–14). Mahwah, NJ: Lawrence Erlbaum Associates, Inc.

Hofstadter, D. R. (1999). *Godel, Escher, Bach: An eternal golden braid*. London: Penguin Books.

Johnson, M. (2005). *Developmental cognitive neuroscience* (2nd ed.). Cambridge, MA: Blackwell Publishers Inc.

Jung, C. G. (1970). *Myseterium coniunctionis: An inquiry into the separation and synthesis of psychic opposites in alchemy (The collected works of C. G. Jung)* (G. Adler and R. F. C. Hull, Trans., Vol. 14). Princeton, NJ: Princeton University Press. (Original work published 1955.)

Kegan, R. (1982). *The evolving self: Problem and process in human development*. Cambridge, MA: Harvard University Press.

King, P. M., and Kitchener, K. S. (2002). The reflective judgment model: Twenty years of research on epistemic cognition. In B. K. Hofer and P. R. Pintrich (Eds.), *Personal epistemology: The psychology of beliefs about knowledge and knowing* (pp. 37–61). Mahway, NJ: Lawrence Erlbaum, Publisher.

King, P. M., and Kitchener, K. S. (1994). *Developing reflective judgment*. San Francisco: Jossey-Bass.

Kitchener, K. S. (1983). Cognition, metacognition, and epistemic cognition. *Human Development*, 26, 222–32.

Kuhn, D., and Weinstock, M. (2002). What is epistemological thinking and why does it matter?. In B. K. Hofer and P. R. Pintrich (Eds.), *Personal epistemology: The psychology of beliefs about knowledge and knowing* (pp. 121–44). Mahwah, NJ: Erlbaum.

Kuhn, D. (1988). Cognitive development. In M. H. Bornstein and M. E. Lamb (Eds.), *Developmental psychology: An advanced textbook* (pp. 205–60). Hillsdale, NJ: Lawrence Erlbaum Associates.

Latour, B. (2002). *The war of the worlds: What about peace?* (C. Bigg, Trans., J. Tresch, Ed.). Chicago, IL: Prickly Paradigm Press.

Lerman, L. (2011). *Hiking the horizontal: Field notes from a choreographer*. Middletown, CT: Wesleyan University Press.

McGrath, A. (2007a). *The Dawkins delusion*. London: Society for Promoting Christian Knowledge.

114 Theory

McGrath, A. (2007b). The questions science cannot answer: The ideological fanaticism of Richard Dawkins's attack on belief is unreasonable to religion and science. Retrieved 28 May, 2008, from Times Online: www.timesonline.co.uk/tol/comment/faith/article1361840.ece

Merleau-Ponty, M. (2010). *Child psychology and pedagogy: The Sorbonne lectures 1949–1952* (T. Welsh, Trans.). Evanston, IL: Northwestern University Press.

Miller, P. H. (1993). *Theories of developmental psychology* (3rd ed.). New York: W.H. Freeman and Company.

Nietzsche, F. (1961). *Thus spoke Zarathustra* (R. J. Hollingdale and E. V. Rieu, Trans.). New York: Penguin Publishing. (Original work published 1883–91.)

Nietzsche, F. (1967). *The birth of tragedy* (R. J. Hollingdale, Trans.). Cambridge: Cambridge University Press. (Original work published 1872.)

Nietzsche, F. (1996). *Human, all too human: A book for free spirits* (R. J. Hollingdale, Trans.). Cambridge: Cambridge University Press. (Original work published 1886.)

Ormrod, J. E. (2003). *Educational psychology: Developing learners* (4th ed.). Upper Saddle River, NJ: Merrill Prentice-Hall.

Oser, F. K., and Gmünder, P. (1991). *Religious judgment: A developmental approach.* Birmingham, AL: Religious Education Press.

Pascual-Leone, J. (1987). Organismic processes for neo-piagetian theories: A dialectical causal account of cognitive development. *International Journal of Psychology*, 22(5–6), 531–70. doi: 10.1080/00207598708246795.

Perry, W. G. (1970). *Forms of ethical and intellectual development in the college years: A scheme.* New York: Holt, Rinehart and Winston.

Phillips, J. L. J. (1975). *The origins of intellect: Piaget's theory* (2nd ed.). San Francisco: W.H. Freeman and Co.

Piaget, J. (1970a). *Genetic epistemology.* New York: W. W. Norton & Company.

Piaget, J. (1970b). *Structuralism* (C. Maschler, Trans.). New York: Basic Books.

Piaget, J. (1971a). *Biology and knowledge: An essay on the relations between organic regulations and cognitive processes* (B. Walsh, Trans.). Oxford: University of Chicago Press.

Piaget, J. (1971b). The theory of stages in cognitive development. In D. R. Green, M. P. Ford and G. B. Flamer (Eds.), *Measurement and Piaget* (pp. 1–11). New York: McGraw-Hill.

Piaget, J. (1981). *Intelligence and affectivity: Their relation during child development.* Alto, CA: Annual Reviews Inc.

Piaget, J. (1995a). Explanation in sociology. In L. Smith (Ed.), *Sociological studies* (pp. 30–96). New York: Routledge.

Piaget, J. (1995b). Individuality in history: The individual and the education of reason. In J. Piaget (Ed.), *Sociological studies* (pp. 215–47). New York: Routledge.

Piaget, J. (1995c). Logical operations and social life. In J. Piaget (Ed.), *Sociological studies.* New York: Routledge.

Piaget, J., and Inhelder, B. (1958). *The growth of logical thinking from childhood to adolescence: An essay on the construction of formal operational structures* (A. Parson and S. Milgram, Trans.). New York: Basic Books.

Reich, K. H. (1989). Between religion and science: Complementarity in the religious thinking of young people. *British Journal of Religious Education*, 11(2), 62–9. doi: 10.1080/0141620890110202.

Reich, K. H. (1990). The relation between science and theology: The case for complementarity revisited. *Zygon®*, 25(4), 369–90. doi: 10.1111/j.1467-9744.1990.tb01116.x.

Reich, K. H. (1995). The doctrine of the trinity as a model for structuring the relations between science and theology. *Zygon®*, 30(3), 383–405. doi: 10.1111/j.1467-9744. 1995.tb00080.x.

Reich, K. H. (2000a). The dialogue between religion and science: Which God? *Zygon®*, 35(1), 99–113. doi: 10.1111/0591-2385.00262.

Reich, K. H. (2000b). Scientist vs. believer?: On navigating between the scilla of scientific norms and the charybdis of personal experience. *Journal of Psychology and Theology*, 28(3), 190–200.

Reich, K. H. (2002). *Developing the horizons of the mind: Relational and contextual reasoning and the resolution of cognitive conflict*. Cambridge: Cambridge University Press.

Reich, K. H. (2003). Developing the horizons of the mind: Reich's response to the commentators. *Zygon®*, 38(2), 459–66.

Reich, K. H. (2005). *Relating science to religion / theology: Which approach?* Paper presented at the Science and Religion: Global Perspectives, Philadelphia.

Riegel, K. F. (1979). *Foundations of dialectical psychology*. New York: Academic Press Inc.

Schopenhauer, A. (1969). *The world as will and representation* (E. Payne, Trans., Vol. 1). New York: Dover Publishing Inc.

Schraw, G. J., and Olafson, L. J. (2008). Assessing teachers' epistemological and ontological worldviews. In M. S. Khine (Ed.), *Knowing, knowledge and beliefs* (pp. 25–44). Netherlands: Springer.

Shulman, V. L., Restaino-Baumann, L. C. R., and Butler, L (Eds.). (1985). *The future of Piagetian theory: The neo-Piagetians*. New York: Plenum Press.

Siegler, R. S. (1996). *Emerging minds: The process of change in children's thinking*. New York: Oxford University Press.

Sinnott, J. D. (1981). The theory of relativity: A metatheory for development? *Human Development*, 24(5), 292–311. doi: 0.1159/000272708.

Sinnott, J. D. (1984). Postformal reasoning: The relativistic stage. In M. L. Commons, F. A. Richards and C. Armon (Eds.), *Beyond formal operations: Late adolescent and adult cognitive development* (Vol. 1, pp. 298–325). New York: Praeger Publishers.

Sinnott, J. D. (1996). The developmental approach: Postformal thought as adaptive intelligence. In F. Blanchard-Fields and T. M. Hess (Eds.), *Perspectives on cognitive change in adulthood and aging* (pp. 358–383). New York: McGraw-Hill.

Sternberg, R. J. (1990). *Wisdom: Its nature, origins, and development*. New York: Cambridge University Press.

Streib, H. (2001). Faith development theory revisited: The religious styles perspective. *The International Journal for the Psychology of Religion*, 11(3), 143–58. doi: 10.1207/S15327582IJPR1103_02.

Streib, H. (2003). Religion as a question of style: Revising the structural differentiation of religion from the perspective of the analysis of the contemporary pluralistic-religious situation. *International Journal for Practical Theology*, 7, 1–22.

Tabak, I., and Weinstock, M. (2008). A sociocultural exploration of epistemological beliefs. In M. Khine (Ed.), *Knowing, Knowledge and Beliefs* (pp. 177–95): Springer Netherlands.

Taylor, C. A. (1996). *Defining science: A rhetoric of demarcation*. Madison, WI: University of Wisconsin Press.

Teske, J. A. (2003). Varieties of reasoning: Assessing adequacy. *Zygon®*, 38(2), 441–9. doi: 10.1111/1467-9744.00509.

Tillich, P. (1957). *Dynamics of faith*. New York: Harper and Brothers Publishers.

Vygotsky, L. S. (1978). *Mind in society: The development of higher psychological processes*. Cambridge, MA: Harvard University Press.

Vygotsky, L. S. (1986). *Thought and language*. Cambridge, MA: MIT Press.

Wilber, K. (2000). *The eye of spirit: An integral vision for a world gone slightly mad*. Boston: Shambhala Publications.

Chapter 5

A theory of Bi-relational Development (BirD)

The purpose of this chapter is to introduce the archetypal regions, positions, trajectories and dynamics of Bi-relational Development (BirD). BirD is a theory of onto-epistemological development that is relevant to the recognition and (re) solution of wicked problems. More specifically, BirD maps diverse human trajectories of development in relation to the *creation*, pre-dyadic *emergence*, pro-dyadic *opposition*, post-dyadic *convergence*, *collapse* and *trans-position* of dyadic constituents on the premise that particular dyads (e.g. subjective/objective, nature/culture) and dyadic relationships (e.g. negation, unity, opposition, synthesis) are relevant to the recognition and (re)solution of wicked problems. For example, BirD can be used to represent how a politician or constituency approaches a socio-political issue (e.g. immigration) in relation to the conservative/liberal dyad; how a teacher or educational system approaches a pedagogical issue (e.g. lesson structure) in relation to the transmission/discovery dyad; how a physician or system of medicine approaches a patient's illness (e.g. anorexia nervosa) in relation to the mind/body dyad; how a CEO or corporation approaches a socio-ecological issue (e.g. pollution) in relation to the nature/culture dyad; and how a cleric or congregation approaches a socio-religious issue (e.g. creationism) in relation to the spiritual/material dyad. The bi-relational dynamics of human conflicts are ubiquitous and significant and my hope is that BirD will contribute to the recognition and (re) solution of some of our wickedest problems.

To this end, the chapter is divided into seven sections that include: (a) visual and symbolic representations of BirD's archetypal regions, positions, trajectories and dynamics; (b) definitions and explications of archetypal regions; (c) a brief description of the drivers of development; (d) definitions of key bi-relational dynamics; (e) a conceptual tool for mapping bi-relational trajectories; (f) a hypothetical illustration of bi-relational development; and (g) some common metaphors for understanding bi-relational development. Collectively, these sections establish a basis for the illustrations and educational applications of BirD found in Parts II and III respectively.

A visual and symbolic representation of BirD

BirD's primary visual representation (Figure 5.1) and symbolic representation (Table 5.1) identify archetypal regions, positions and trajectories of development

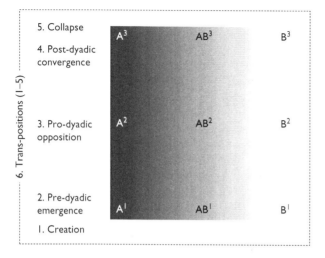

Archetypal positions (A/B) and regions (1–6) of development

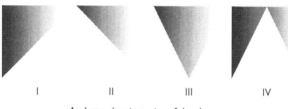

Archetypal trajectories of development

Figure 5.1 A visual representation of Bi-relational Development (BirD). The figure represents archetypal regions, positions and trajectories of a bottom-up onto-epistemological development in relation to dyadic constituents (i.e. A[black]/B[white]). Each trajectory represents an expansion that develops from a unique point of origin (i.e. creation) to the encompassment of a common spectrum (i.e. collapse) at a point that is most differentiable from the point of origin. The encompassment of the spectrum allows for a trans-positional perspective on onto-epistemological development that informs the recognition and (re)solution of wicked problems.

in relation to dyads. As 'archetypes', they are organised and presented symmetrically according to the principle 'all things being equal'. However, given that *each* thing is rarely exactly average or symmetrical in real life, the archetypes are best understood as general orientations for comprehending diverse trajectories on a continuum and *in-context*. Accordingly, BirD's primary visual representation adopts a greyscale metaphor, uses abstract generalisations to reveal concrete particularities, offers unified elements to reveal multiple realities and discrete positions to illuminate continuous developments. Collectively, these aspects of the visual metaphor offer an insight into the nature of wicked problems and their (re)solutions through the reconciliation of 'opposites'.

118 Theory

The key aspects of BirD's primary visual representation are as follows:

- The figure represents the constituent parts of a dyad (i.e. A and B) as black or white respectively. These constituent parts (i.e. black and white) may be seen in degrees of combination as shades of grey (i.e. AB). This visual metaphor helps to reconcile binary differentiations that conceptualise all knowing into two categories (i.e. A/B, black/white) with spectral differentiations that (de)categorise knowing into infinitely divisible shades of grey. Accordingly, grey areas can be seen as degrees of combination between white and black (i.e. grey = white + black).

- The figure represents a bottom-up sequence of development through archetypal positions marked by increasing differentiation and expanding awareness of shades on a spectrum between black and white. Accordingly, positions A_1, AB_1 and B_1 are less developed (i.e. less differentiated and expansive) than positions A_3, AB_3 and B_3, which subsume them.

- The figure represents four archetypal trajectories of development through each of the five positions (i.e. creation to collapse). The trajectories each form an isoscelean triangle that develops from a single point on the spectrum towards a full accommodation of the spectrum. The archetypal trajectories are differentiated by their points of origin or creation. They are also archetypes or aggregates of multiple trajectories that collectively identify an individual or group.

- Table 5.1 provides a symbolic description of the four archetypal trajectories. Trajectory I begins with a disposition for the left dyadic constituent (i.e. black); Trajectory II begins with a disposition for the right dyadic constituent (i.e. white); Trajectory III begins with a disposition for an undifferentiated middle position (i.e. grey); and Trajectory IV highlights the 'opposing self', where the most contrastable constituents simultaneously originate and develop in the 'same' individual or group. The trajectories end in complete conflation with each other at the point of collapse (i.e. region 5).

- The absolute collapse or conflation of the final stage of each trajectory represents a perceptual and semantic paradox that enables Reality to be complementarily described and interpreted as a negation, union, tension, synthesis or infinite differentiation and multiplication of 'opposites'. This paradox enables the trans-positional choice of a particular position-in-context informed by a relational understanding of the spectrum between positions.

Description of archetypal regions

The purpose of this section is to further define and explicate BirD's archetypal positions so that they can be used to analyse and synthesise almost any onto-epistemological trajectory or wicked problem that relates to a common dyad or set of dyads.

Table 5.1 Symbolic representation of Bi-relational Development (BirD)

Regions	Archetypal trajectories			
	I	II	III	IV
6 (1–5) 5	$A \Leftrightarrow AB \Leftrightarrow B$			
4	$A_3 \geq (AB_3/B_3)$ $A_3 > A_2$ $A_3 \neg (B_2/AB_2)$	$B_3 \geq (AB_3/A_3)$ $B_3 > B_2$ $B_3 \neg (AB_2/B_2)$	$AB_3 \geq (A_3/B_3)$ $AB_3 > AB_2$ $AB_3 \neg (A_2/B_2)$	$A_3 \geq AB_3$ $B_3 \geq AB_3$ $A_3 > A_2$ $B_3 > B_2$ $A_3 \neg AB_2$ $B_3 \neg AB_2$
3	$A_2 \neg (AB_2/R_2)$	$B_2 \neg (AB_2/A_2)$	$AB_2 \neg (A_2/B_2)$	$A_2 \neg AB_2$ $B_2 \neg AB_2$
2	A_1	B_1	AB_1	A_1 B_1
1				

In summary, BirD's six broadest archetypal regions include:

1 a point of *creation* or inception that while being without form and void signals the meaningful potential for bi-relational divisions of knowledge (e.g. potential for A in relation to B);

2 a *pre-dyadic region* that locates the emergence of specific dyadic constituents that are not yet consciously located in relation to each other (e.g. emergence of A_1 without relation to B_1; emergence of middle AB_1 without relation to poles; emergence of B_1 without relation to A_1);

3 a *pro-dyadic region* that locates the intersection and opposition of dyadic constituents with each other and an exclusive middle position (e.g. opposition of A_2 in relation to B_2; opposition of exclusive middle position $[AB_2]$ in relation to A_2 and B_2; and opposition of B_2 in relation to A_2);

4 a *post-dyadic region* that locates the interpenetration and convergence of dyadic constituents and the complication of binary oppositions (e.g. interpenetration of A_3 in relation to B_3; interpenetration of middle position $[AB_3]$ in relation to A_3 and B_3; interpenetration of B_3 in relation to A_3);

5 a point of absolute *collapse, conflation* or *equivalence* of dyadic constituents (e.g. A_3 is equivalent to B_3 and AB_3). This point of collapse may be understood and experienced as a negation, union, duality, synthesis and/or infinite differentiation of knowing and being.

6 a *trans-positional* perspective or potentiation of any position or combination of positions understood in relation and applied in context (e.g. $A_1, AB_1, B_1, AB_1, AB_2, AB_3, B_1, B_2, B_3$).

Collectively, these archetypal orientations provide an analytical framework for understanding onto-epistemological developments and wicked problems in everyday contexts. The following sub-sections offer further explications of each region.

Creation (inception, origin, potentiation)

Creation is most synonymous with *zero* as a number that precedes anything that can be known, experienced and counted. It is the position before the manifestation and division of content and form that enables an onto-epistemological identity. This is not to say that the individual is *tabula rasa* as there may be genetic and cultural dispositions to particular ways of being and knowing that will relationally position an individual from a very early age. Creation represents the potential for knowledge and knowing but precedes conscious differentiation and action through the formation of dyads (e.g. left/right, up/down). Creation is a point (rather than a phase or stage) characterised by potential for, but lack of, a cognitive capacity with which to actively construct a way of knowing about the world and being in the world. It precedes the accumulation and organisation of individual empirical experience that accompanies the emergence of a human life. *Creation* is the first *in-utero* and the antipode of the *point of collapse;* they are paradoxically opposite and apposite.

Most traditional theories of development maintain their linear nature by avoiding or bracketing out the more esoteric beginnings and endings of life. In fairness, it is sometimes best to say nothing about that which cannot be known or precedes knowing. However, my claim is that we *do* know of and experience the ambiguity, mystery, relativity and absurdity beyond the ambiguous beginning and ends of life in ways that powerfully shape our journeys in-between. We may live in a sort of 'middle earth' most of the time, where binary oppositions help us to make sense of the world and feel at home within it. However, an occasional tumble down the rabbit holes beyond the boundaries of the middle provides a brief glimpse of the ways and reasons we draw these boundaries at all. BirD acknowledges these more esoteric positions or rabbit holes (i.e. *creation* and *collapse*), fully aware of the awkwardness and clumsiness of language necessary to describe them, but also aware of the impossibility of understanding the everyday middle without them. They provide a brief glimpse of the deeper ways human societies have responded to the apparent absurdity beyond beginnings and endings.

The creation point is part of a singularity with the point of collapse. Singularity is paradoxically nothing and something, beginning and end. This position is concerned with the potential for beginning and expansion. The singularity is the point of potential for the separation of light and darkness. In Camus's (2005) terms, 'There is no sun without shadow and it is essential to know the night' (p. 119). The metaphor of singularity is appropriated from modern cosmology where it is a point of infinite density with zero volume:

> The speck from which space emerges is not located in anything. It is not an object surrounded by emptiness. It is the origin of space itself, infinitely compressed. Note that the speck does not sit there for an infinite duration. It appears instantaneously from nothing and instantly expands.
>
> (Davies, 2013, p. 47)

I am cautious in appropriating the terminology of modern physics (i.e. singularity), but such metaphors already have affinities with the metaphors of more ancient mythologies – for example, the dot, jot, tittle, monad or *bindu*:

> As the centre and source of everything, the dot is imagined as giving rise to all opposing tendencies: above and below, male and female, hot and cold. And it is also the place where they can be reconciled, the still place at the centre of life's multiplicity.
>
> (Martin, 2010, p. 706)

In onto-epistemological terms, this point of creation could be represented with the prefix *ante-* (before) or *non-* (without) as it refers to a point characterised by a relative lack of faculty or cognitive capacity with which to engage with the world, or actively construct a way of knowing about the world and being in the world. It is before knowledge and without knowledge, before dyads and without dyads. The point of creation precedes the accumulation and organisation of experience that accompanies the emergence of life and the development of identity. In ontological terms, creation is the point of conception and the origin of potential. It provides a silence and space, without which it is difficult to comprehend the emergence of epistemology and ontology. Representing onto-epistemological development without points of creation and collapse is like representing the physical development of an individual without a point of conception and death.

In common discourse, the difficulty of ascribing existence, sentience, meaning and potential to *an individual* at a point of creation gives rise to debates over the beginning of life, contraception and abortion. Later in the lifespan, these debates are reflected in debates over ages of accountability and levels of intellectual disability. They are then mirrored at the end of life with debates about mortality, euthanasia and cremation. Such debates represent wicked problems because they are based on central paradoxes and entangled 'opposites' that do not lend themselves to one-sided victories. Debates over euthanasia invoke hope and despair; debates over abortion and contraception invoke freedom and control; and debates over mortality invoke quality and quantity. Thus, even the origins and ends of life, like the creation and collapse of dyads, are subject to different ways of knowing and being.

Pre-dyadic region (emergence, differentiation, formation, accumulation)

The *pre-dyadic region* is most synonymous with the number *one*, which knows itself as whole because it has not yet encountered other parts. It is a relatively pre-conscious period of knowledge accumulation. Structures of knowledge are not well differentiated, and ways of knowing tend to be preoperational, egocentric, literal, concrete and in-the-moment. The *pre-dyadic position* is a period of onto-epistemological innocence, or naiveté, as ways of being are not yet perceived as choices or relative positions. The region represents a period of experience accumulation that initiates the early development of knowledge structures and schemes. The accumulation of knowledge through experience both precedes and prompts equilibration between the complementary processes of assimilation and accommodation. Thus, the emergence of dyadic constituents serves an adaptive function in that it begins to create a consciousness and language for choice and evaluation. The conscious use of dyads that both enables and proceeds from the active construction of knowing emerges for the first time and may be characterised by basic constituents (e.g. hot, fast, big) that are later brought into relationship with their 'opposites' (e.g. hot/cold, fast/slow, big/little). Needless to say, some dyads (e.g. hot/cold) are brought into conscious relationship before others (e.g. subjective/objective).

The pre-dyadic region represents the emergence or outgrowth of one or two of the constituent parts of a dyad *before* the parts are consciously conceptualised in a dyadic relationship. During this period of emergence, life experience is creating and consolidating the 'stuff and substance' that will soon be categorised in dyadic relationships. Traditional developmental theories related to knowing describe the early part of this phase variously as *undifferentiated* (Fowler, 1981), *sensory-motor* (Piaget, 1971), *pre-religious* (Oser and Gmünder, 1991), *naïve realist* or *pre-absolutist*. Alternatively, some theories neglect the early emergence of knowledge altogether because the development of knowledge implies that something known is something structured. During the pre-dyadic phase, knowledge is collected but the categories and structures it is packaged in are not well developed or differentiated from the knowledge itself. The level of differentiation and decentration is low, but nonetheless emergent with the increasing accumulation of knowledge itself. Thus, the region is characterised by the relative strength of the passive reception of knowledge over the active and conscious construction of meaning.

Pre-dyadic emergence is implicitly recognised in debates over nature and nurture, the age of accountability and the emergence of self-awareness. Does a child have a *pre*-conception or a *mis*-conception and are they *pre*-sponsible or *re*-sponsible? Abstract adult categories like good/evil, right/wrong and meaningful/meaningless carry little relational meaning for a child during the pre-dyadic phase. They are retrospective impositions and behaviouristic transmissions that serve to position and guide a child before s/he enters the pro-dyadic phase. I use *child* here to normalise the logic of development that would move from pre-consciousness to consciousness; however, I do this with the assumption that we are all 'children' (i.e. pre-conscious) in relation to many more abstract and complex dyads. That is, we may not be consciously aware that we have a position or disposition in relation to others in a particular domain, and may be mystified by their interactions with us, or our feelings towards them.

A theory of Bi-relational Development   123

Arguably, we each have a *natural* disposition that differentiates us in relation to others. This disposition emerges in the pre-dyadic phase in relation to our social, cultural and physical environments or *nurturing* influences. The nurture of these environments, whether they accommodate, assimilate or reject us, can powerfully affect our onto-epistemological trajectories. For example, just as we will experience being heritably shorter or taller, heavier or lighter than others, we may be more conservative than liberal, introverted than extroverted, passive than active and cognitive than affective in relation to others. The expansiveness of our environments will affect our sense of fit and value and our perceptions of others' fit and value. Dyads and dyadic relationships offer a way of recognising ourselves in relation to others. The pre-dyadic phase represents our early pre-conscious but still deeply felt initiations into and/or alienations from the dominant dyadic values of our family, community and culture. As such, it is an important place to look for the early formative influences that give shape to the later oppositions that exacerbate wicked problems. For example, the dominant masculinity that destructively asserts its power in all contexts and seeks to subordinate the feminine emerged in a particular context, where it may once have made sense. Similarly, the dominant anthropocentricity that destructively asserts its power over nature emerged in a particular context, where it may once have made sense. The (re)solution of wicked problems requires an appreciation for the past contexts from which present oppositions emerged.

Pro-dyadic region (intersection, opposition, dichotomy)

The *pro-dyadic region* is most synonymous with the number *two* in that the self, which perceives itself as whole, must maintain its integrity in confrontation with that which it knows it is not. It represents the epistemic potential for division and binary opposition between the constituents of a dyad (e.g. conservative *or* liberal, freedom *or* control, absolute *or* relative). The parts of a dyad are dispositionally seen as opposite, but not yet relative, interdependent or complementary. Pro-dyadic opposition sees a potential onto-epistemological tendency to assimilate knowledge into either one dyadic constituent (e.g. conservative) or another (e.g. liberal). The region is still characterised by the ego-centricity and immediacy of the earlier region but is now served by a newly found binary oppositional logic (i.e. either/or thinking). Thus, knowing and being are predisposed to separating or feeling alienated, dichotomising, opposing or feeling opposed, defeating or suffering defeat. In BirD's visual-spatial representation, a knower in the pro-dyadic position perceives absolute opposition between the dyadic constituents (e.g. liberal and conservative), but is relatively oblivious to their interdependence, continuity, relativity and contextuality. Its late stages may see the revolutionary substitution of one constituent for another (i.e. a binary inversion) after previously violent suppression and opposition. However, the pro-dyadic region can also be a period of naïve and simplistic balanced opposition.

124 Theory

This naïve middle position reflects a relative onto-epistemological disposition to approach problems using an exclusively middle position between but against left and right.

The pro-dyadic phase concerns the separation and application of binary oppositions as a form of dyadic relationship that imbues life with meaning. In fact, life can appear particularly certain in this position as wicked problems do not appear so wicked. The position is characterised by the dichotomised knowledge of right versus wrong, true versus false, good versus evil and black versus white, which admits few shades of gray or degrees of difference. Slow or fast, big or small, short or tall, forward or back, east or west, left or right, mind or body and liberal or conservative are absolute choices to be made, rather than tensions to be held. There is little perceived difference between 'slow or fast' and 'slower or faster than X'. The pro-dyadic phase is absolutistic, dichotomising and dualising, even in its middle position, which is characterised by an aversion or blindness towards the 'shades of black and white' at the extremities. It represents an either/or approach to knowledge and knowing that is driven by newly acquired structures and operations.

The pro-dyadic region admits few questions concerning purposeful or meaningful applications of knowledge that extend beyond localised dichotomies (e.g. black vs. white) and personal or provincial preferences (e.g. Manchester United vs. Liverpool). Rather, the region sees the unquestioning extension or projection of binary oppositional certainties established through provincial experiences far beyond their original reach and relevance. It is the stage of ideology where ideology is the perseverance of a one-sided idea beyond its counterbalancing origins in time and context.

The absolutism of this pro-dyadic region is usually found in the most provincial domain of knowledge that has been experienced during the pre-dyadic phase. Tabak and Weinstock (2008) refer to this dynamic as 'epistemological socialisation' and argue that 'immersion-in and privileging of a domain can cultivate absolutist positions' (p. 188). Interestingly and importantly, Tabak and Weinstock's study identified absolutist thinking in scientific *and* religious domains as the result of epistemological socialisation. Even cultures with multiplistic or relativistic content can be held in absolutistic ways. For example, socialisation through cultures of diversity, relativity and uncertainty can lead to these concepts being held in characteristically absolute or oppositional ways. For example, Tabak and Weinstock (2008) identify school socialisation 'in broader societal narratives of the postmodern era, which evoke a sense of uncertainty and pluralism' (p. 186), and argue that an overemphasis on uncertainty can restrict students from appreciating relative certainty and evaluation of better or worse answers:

> Recognizing that there is 'no one right answer' does not necessarily imply that one answer cannot be better than the other, and learning the criteria

A theory of Bi-relational Development 125

within each domain for evaluating competing claims is an important part of subject–matter learning, and of epistemological development.

(2008, p. 186)

This is an important and poorly recognised dynamic. The content of a discourse can disguise its structure. Absolutistic content can hide relativistic ways of knowing and relativistic content can disguise absolutistic ways of knowing. Tabak and Weinstock (2008) suggest that some multiplistic ways of knowing are a 'backlash to ... authoritarian transmission models' (p. 186). BirD represents this 'backlash' as a lateral movement or pendulum swing that can precede or arrest development beyond exclusively binary oppositional ways of knowing and being.

The pro-dyadic region is a place of absolute separation between knowledge and knowing in the knower's mind. It is the region where binaries are held widest apart and knowing is characterised by conflict between clearly defined oppositions. It is a region defined by a general disposition to know and engage the world through binary oppositions, regardless of context. Here, the knower pits subject against object, reality against perception, cognition against emotion, conservative against liberal and left against right in absolute terms. This leads to a disposition to exacerbate wicked problems because they are approached with a disposition to a one-sided or narrow middle solution.

The pro-dyadic phase has many manifestations in common discourse. It is characterised by grand contests between right and wrong, good and evil. It is evidenced in debates over the success or failure of a person or program and in calls for a return to or departure from old ways – as if each can be measured against an unspoken imperative or an objective rule and decided for all time. It is the region for the authority of folk wisdom like 'strike while the iron is hot' and 'many hands make light work' as opposed to 'slow and steady wins the race' and 'too many cooks spoil the broth'. It is the region for the demonisation or dismissal of the other. It is the region of powerful and polarising ideologies that push combatants beyond themselves to fight for a group not yet big enough to contain their enemies.

Post-dyadic region (interpenetration, convergence, integration, dialectic)

The *post-dyadic region* is most synonymous with the number *three* as it is the first realisation that there is a commonality between the two that were formerly held to be unequal. It refers to an awareness of interpenetration and integration between 'opposites', where the distances that create and separate binary oppositions (e.g. reality vs. perception) begin to shrink as degrees of difference and shades of grey appear in context. Post-dyadic convergence precipitates significant realisations of the equality, relationality, contextuality, symmetry and codependency of dyadic constituents (e.g. reality *and* perception). It is a position where the image of one constituent may be dimly perceived in the other. However, these developments may still 'appear' to be binary in some positions as one dyadic constituent expands to accommodate and absorb the degrees of difference that are claimed by the other, without acknowledging the reciprocal possibility. For example, more and more 'truth' may be understood and differentiated in terms of *perception* without acknowledgement that the same ground can be understood and differentiated in terms of *reality*. Thus, a relativist may argue that all reality is perception without allowing that all perception can be seen as a reality. And, a realist may argue that all perception is a reality without allowing that all reality can be seen as a perception. Similarly, while the middle position of the early post-dyadic region begins to encompass the degrees of difference between polarities, it can still fail to appreciate the extent of these polarities and the possibility that its own degrees of difference can be mostly accommodated from well developed left or right positions.

The post-dyadic phase refers to the period where dualisms begin to dissolve, contrasts begin to contract and the separation between knowledge and knowing begins to implode. It can still be a period of strong opposition and distinction, but even then opponents are fighting to explain common ground rather than claim it from a distance, as in pro-dyadic positions. The knower begins to see their image mirrored in the opposing pole. Paradoxically, the more they seek to distance themselves from their opposing pole the closer they may come to know it. Gradual for some, revolutionary for others, the inter-penetration brings the former enemies of the pro-dyadic region into closer encounters with each other and onto common ground.

Collapse (conflation, equivalence, entanglement)

The point of *collapse* is the revolutionary realisation of the equivalence, conflation and entanglement of opposites. It can be perceived and encountered in different ways that are synonymous with the numbers *Zero*, *One*, *Two*, *Three* or *Infinity* as complementary representations of the absolute breakdown of binary oppositional knowledge and understandings. However, these numerical metaphors are qualitatively different to those of the preceding positions. For example, collapse can be understood and experienced as the negation (i.e. *Zero*) of opposites. It is a point without form and content that reveals the absurdity of everything that comes before it. It is not the *Zero* of creation, which has no form to begin with. It is the zero of a development through everything that has found it to be 'much ado about nothing'. The collapse can also be experienced as a unity (i.e. *One*) of opposites. It is a point where everything can be seen as one thing; a single indivisible source. It is not the *One* of the pre-dyadic or pro-dyadic phase, which belies its partiality by defining its oneness only by denying the oneness of another. It is the one that is the sum of all parts. Furthermore, the collapse can reveal a duality (i.e. *Two*) of opposites. It is an illusory middle point that reveals only the irreducible struggle of two equal and co-defining sides that bring everything else into existence. It is not the *Two* of a binary opposition where one can be seen to defeat the other once and for all. The collapse can also be seen as a triad (i.e. *Three*) formed by the synthesis of opposites. This is not the *Three* of the previous phase, where the middle is given primacy over the two extremities, as if it could be relatively independent from them; it is a third space – a momentary point of creative synthesis between two that gives birth to a third thing in the presence of two. Finally, the collapse can be experienced as an implosion of constraining opposites and categories that precedes an explosion of multiple possibilities (*Infinity*). The extinction of two constraining boundaries frees up explorations into the messy multiplicity of reality. Collectively, these perspectives on the point of collapse reveal something of the shape and nature of onto-epistemological development The following paragraphs further unpack these numerical metaphors.

Negation (*Zero*). The collapse of opposites can represent the negation or complete reversal of opposites that renders them absurd (e.g. subject *is* object, self *is* other, relative *is* absolute, perception *is* reality). At this point the collapse of dyads may make all knowledge seem absurd, meaningless, illusory or nihilistic. It is the blinding realisation that the paradigm one has been committed to for a lifetime has no more exclusive claim to truth than the paradigm it has been defined in contradistinction to. Thus, the point of collapse can be onto-epistemologically disorientating and undermining. It is a well recognised and well documented point in many sources of literature. For Camus (2005), 'This vicious circle is but the first of a series in which the mind that studies itself gets lost in a giddy whirling' (p. 15). The epistemological journey between creation and transposition is captured by Huneker's (n.d.) metaphor: 'Life is like an onion; you peel off layer after layer and then you find there is nothing in it'. While it is a difficult place to stay, the point of *collapse* is perhaps an even more difficult place to move from, as any movement beyond can seem onto-epistemologically meaningless.

At the point of collapse, as in a vacuum, there seems nothing to push against and no way or reason to gain momentum. In Nietzsche's words:

> What were we doing when we unchained the earth from its sun? Whither is it moving now? Whither are we moving? Away from all suns? Are we not plunging continually? Backward, sideward, forward, in all directions? Is there still an up or down? Are we not straying as through an infinite nothing?
> (quoted in Reginster, 2006, p. 27)

Nietzsche's lament belies a solution to the disorientation – a will to move by recognising that disorientation exists as present knowledge in relation to past orientations.

The preoccupation with nothingness finds as much expression in modern physics as in Schopenhauer's pessimistic philosophy. For Schopenhauer (1969), 'this very real world of ours with all its suns and galaxies, is – nothing' (p. 412). And yet, *nothing*, as Schopenhauer knew quite well, is not quite *no-thing*:

> Schopenhauer will drop the bottom out of the ontology of generosity. What remains is, quite simply, nothing. No overflowing life force, no pantheistic becoming, no immanent principle of life running throughout all of Creation. Just nothing. But nothing is, of course, never simple; it is also nothingness, or emptiness, or the void, and it quickly becomes a paradoxical and enigmatic something.
>
> (Thacker, 2011, p. 24)

The dependence of nothingness on somethingness as an inversion of traditional orders of dyadic development is taken up by Schwartz:

> Whereas ancient philosophers and modern scientists share the assumption that "Nothing" is prior to "Being" — chaos precedes cosmos, void is anterior to the emergence of things — Bergson demonstrates that each of these negative terms issues from, and depends upon, the positive term it supposedly precedes. The same relation holds for other oppositions such as absence/presence, emptiness/fullness, disorder/order.
>
> (2009, pp. 64–5)

Similarly, modern theoretical physicist Brian Greene (2004) writes in anticipation of the Higgs ocean, 'The emptiest empty space need not involve a state of absolute nothingness' (p. 269). Thus, there seems to be a sense in which nothing and something, like all other dyads, are at least entangled if not mutually definitive.

The collapse of knowledge and being into nothingness is a significant perspective in the recognition and resolution of wicked problems. There is a sense in which all wicked problems with a dyadic dimension can be seen to be 'much ado about nothing' in that they arise as problems where each side has vainly sought to account for everything. Thus, the single-minded pursuit of riches in a finite world necessarily creates poverty; the single-minded pursuit of immortality devalues the very life it seeks to preserve; the single-minded pursuit of happiness intensifies the experience of sadness; the single-minded quest to subdue the environment for human habitation makes it uninhabitable; and the single-minded search for profound meaning can pluck all significance from mundane things. Paradoxically, it is the negation of opposites that charges them each with meaning, such that there is something in nothing after all.

Unity (*One*). Accordingly, there is a sense in which the collapse of opposites can be seen as a combination or unification where *One* is the whole of two, the sum of parts and the unity of everything. There is a significant onto-epistemological development between the *one* as part and the *One* as whole that is well recognised in mythological as well as psychological thinking:

> Psychologically, the experience of oneness is a natural state before the child becomes aware that he or she is an individual ... Such experiences of fusion are lost with increasing age and awareness, with the necessity to develop a clear sense of self and individuality ... Yet the sense of the deeper connectedness of all things, that 'the multiplicity of the empirical world rests on an underlying unity' (CW 14:767), can return in maturity when it may be sensed that male and female, spirit and body, inner and outer consciousness and the unconscious, the I and the Thou, are One.
>
> (Martin, 2010, p. 710)

BirD is another explicit framework that attempts to represent the onto-epistemic developments and trajectories between these two understandings of *one*.

The perception of the collapse of opposites into a single unity provides a complementary alternative to their total negation. For Nietzsche (quoted in Reginster, 2006), the collapse of opposites that sustain value and knowing and meaning need not collapse the universe in which they were produced: 'Once we have devaluated [these highest values], the demonstration that they cannot be applied to the universe is no longer any reason for devaluating the universe' (p. 55). Similarly, Eliade (1961) observed, 'In the homogeneous and infinite expanse, in which no point of reference is possible and hence no orientation is established, the hierophany reveals an absolute fixed point, a center' (p. 21).

The unity of opposites is a significant perspective in the (re)solution of wicked problems. It introduces the idea of entanglement and interdependence to the conceptualisation of problems. The realisation of unity provides a caution against solutions that are based on the extinctions or ostracisms of a part, as if the part could somehow be completely separated from the whole. Thus, the single-minded pursuit of masculinity or femininity, self or other, global or local, nature or culture, liberal or conservative, is intrinsically self-harming.

Duality (*Two*). Another perspective that the point of collapse brings is duality. This is not the duality of a binary opposition where one dominates the other, this is the duality of two equally powerful opposites that hold each other in necessary tension. For Hesse (2012), the conceptualisation of a human as two-fold is an improvement on the illusion of personal unity but a barrier to the reality of multiplicity: 'Now, even if some human beings advance only to the point where they replace the imagined unity of the self with a broader two-fold entity they are already close to being geniuses, or at any rate interesting exceptions' (pp. 61–2). However, for Hesse, the inability to count beyond two is the root of human suffering because it binds one to live in contradiction: 'He is acting like some savage, say, who is incapable of counting beyond two' (p. 64). Thus, opposites that are not reconciled or equated will simply be at war with

130 Theory

each other. And yet opposites enable movement and choice, to move left or right. Without them, there are no choices or options – just lifelessness.

Heraclitus and Nietzsche can be seen as the defenders of one and two. For the pre-Socratic philosopher Heraclitus, Reality was the *One* that became the two that seek to become *One*: 'Couples are wholes and not wholes, what agrees disagrees, the concordant is discordant. From all things one and from one all things' (Fragment 51). Likewise, Nietzsche (1962), influenced by and in agreement with Heraclitus, writes, 'the diverging of a force into two qualitatively different opposed activities . . . seeks to re-unite' (p. 5). Thus, one (i.e. unity) and two (i.e. division or separation) are powerful metaphors for onto-epistemological positions. That is, some people have a disposition to emphasise one (i.e. unity), others have a disposition to emphasise division (i.e. two). Still others, like Heraclitus and Nietzsche, have a disposition to emphasise the interdependence of one and two (i.e. unity and division).

Synthesis (*Three*). While Heraclitus and Nietzsche seemed to deny the necessity of a 'third' position between or beyond the two, Aristotle (1970) and Jung (1970) invoke the number *Three* – a trinity or *triarchy*. For Jung, this third thing lies beyond or perhaps *between* the two as a synthesis, necessary middle, or mediator, without which there can be no sense of purpose or direction for action for the union of two. Speaking of opposites (i.e. two), Aristotle (n.d./1970) writes, 'both of them must operate on a third something' (p. 189). That is, there is a transcending medium for the struggle between opposing forces. So, the dueling past and future becomes the triadic past–present–future; mind and body becomes mind–soul–body; birth and death becomes birth–life–death; heaven and hell becomes heaven–earth–hell, and so on. For some, the third thing makes ultimate sense of the struggle and union between two – a sense that charges the relationship with meaning and purpose. The presence of this third space brings the possibility of a complementary or entangled relationship into consideration where previously there has been only opposition. It also allows for interplay, creative interaction and synthesis.

This *third* perspective is important in the recognition and (re)solution of wicked problems because it encourages integrative syntheses and solutions that are made possible by the meeting of two that are otherwise seen exclusively in opposition. In this third space, conflict produces creative solutions and developments. Thus, life is created and lived out between birth and death, male and female, spirit and flesh, and heaven and hell.

Multiplicity (*Infinity*). For some, the false stability of oppositions may eventually collapse into the disorientating but liberating realisation that reality is a multitude of infinitely divisible and discoverable things. As Hesse (2012) writes of his protagonist's tendency to divide the world into two: 'A human being is an onion consisting of a hundred skins, a fabric composed of many threads' (p. 64). Hesse's images powerfully illustrate the dynamics of development – at and beyond the collapse of dyads. Not only are the polarities reconciled beyond mere binary opposition, but the middle ground is included. Thus, there is no longer a gap between polarities. All degrees of difference, all shades of grey, all colours are realised. There are numerous polarities, shades of black, grey or white and a potentially infinite number of trajectories between them.

In BirD, the realisation of multiplicity is not a priori a final maturity that proceeds beyond the realisation of a unity that has in turn proceeded from the realisation of duality. Rather, it is one side of a mature figure. Nothing (*Zero*) can be maddening, unity (*One*) can be constraining, duality (*Two*) can be violent, triarchy (*Three*) can be confusing and multiplicity (*Infinity*) can be paralysing. And yet nothing can be peaceful, unity can be purposeful, duality can be sustaining, triarchy can be creative and multiplicity can be liberating. So, even the final conceptualisations of bi-relational development must be relationally and contextually understood. BirD represents the dexterity to move relationally and contextually between these perspectives as a *trans-position*.

Trans-positions (re-entry, re-commitment, re-iteration)

Trans-positions emerge from the realisation that opposites can be conflated and collapsed in different ways (i.e. negated, unified, equated, synthesised and multiplied) that collectively and complementarily express reality. Trans-positions enable the recreation of dyads – the beginning of a new epistemology and ontology. Trans-positions realise the potential for the re-diffusion and re-emergence of the dyads that produce and sustain knowledge and understanding. Thus, when one finds oneself in the middle of nowhere, one may begin to find oneself; the end is just the beginning; complete darkness heightens the perception of light; and knowledge emerges from absurdity. The point of collapse can reveal that the boundaries of context in space and time can be shown to be (n)either absolute (n)or relative. It is a point of ground shift between dyadic constituents. Thus, collapse allows for a trans-positional recreation of dyads to meaningfully participate in the world that has either collapsed into meaninglessness, seems wholly indivisible or infinitely divisible. The *trans-position* simultaneously embraces the paradoxical and relational status of dyadic constructs and commits to a particular dyadic position in context. The trans-position approaches wicked problems using relational perspectives of the left (e.g. knowledge as concrete, subjective, local, synthetic, holistic, dynamic) *and* the right (e.g. knowledge as abstract, objective, universal, analytic, reductive, fixed) in order to select and act on a particular position in context. Trans-positions can be characterised by a seemingly effortless and unified *flow* between dyadic locations and relations *in context*. Thus, trans-positional movement is dexterous but not erratic. It is evaluativistic, able to draw on all positions, including oppositional positions, with an awareness of the fluidity of context and an adaptive ability to change, oppose or affirm different positions at different times.

Trans-position entails relational and contextual selections of particular positions informed by choices between all positions. The final stages of traditionally linear theories of development rarely accommodate the intense conflicts that can exist between mature versions of different onto-epistemologies. Here,

132 Theory

I have in mind the commonalities and differences between Zen Buddhist negations, pantheistic unities, Daoist dualities, the Christian Trinity and the empirical multiplicities and infinities of some secular cosmologies. Either these onto-epistemologies have to be assigned different levels of development or the later stages of development need to be able to accommodate such differences. BirD represents these positions as potentially mature and complementary understandings that arise from the reconciliation of opposites. Accordingly, BirD represents positions that can help us to understand the structure of wicked problems and the complementary differences between well developed (re)solutions.

The movement from the collapse of knowledge to the trans-positional return to knowing and being can be an intensely difficult step. To sustain life at the point of collapse is impossible, but there is sense in which the experience of dyadic collapse or extinction is the beginning of life; nothing is entangled with the creation of something. The cycle must be escaped altogether or re-entered in a line that admits the separation of dyads that allow meaningful choice and agency. Not to move is to risk freezing to death or dying of onto-epistemological starvation. This realisation, that the lack of movement or knowledge is itself a position in relation to other positions may well provide the motivation to re-enter the journey, to re-walk the line. The full realisation that the loss of meaning and knowing is itself relative to all that was known or meant provides the potential and possibility that what is unknown may be purpose enough for knowing again. Silence, stillness, absence, and nothingness can only exist in relationship with sound, movement, presence and *thingness*. Paradoxically, *nothing* may be something after all. This realisation may be the beginning of a post-formal or trans-positional re-entry into the cycle of knowing and knowledge.

This re-entry through trans-positions is found in many forms. It is the beginning of Ricoeur's (1981) *second naiveté*, Kierkegaard's (1992) leap *to* faith, Sinnott's (1984) *postformal* development, Hegel's *aufhebung*, Plato's *metaxy*, Latour's *amodernism*, Epstein's (1997) *trans-*, Turner's (1996) *post-post-modernism*, Jung's (1971) *enantiodromia*, the Hindu *moksha*, the Buddhist *nirguna* and Nietzsche's (1961) 'will to power'. In a modern context, Epstein writes:

> In considering the names that might possibly be used to designate the new era following "postmodernism," one finds that the prefix "trans" stands out in a special way. The last third of the 20th century developed under the sign of "post," which signalled the demise of such concepts of modernity as "truth" and "objectivity," "soul" and "subjectivity," "utopia" and "ideality," "primary origin" and "originality," "sincerity" and "sentimentality." All of these concepts are now being reborn in the form of "trans-subjectivity," "trans-idealism," "trans-utopianism," "trans-originality," "trans-lyricism," "trans-sentimentality" etc.
>
> (1997, p. 2)

So, the trans-positions represent a return to life and its inherently wicked problems, though with a broader repertoire of possibilities and a purposeful sense of timing.

A theory of Bi-relational Development   133

This trans-positional development is expressed in almost all religious and secular traditions, including that most 'disorientatingly orientating' passage of religious literature, Ecclesiastes 3:1–8 (New International Version):

> There is a time for everything, and a season for every activity under the heavens;
> a time to be born and a time to die,
> a time to plant and a time to uproot,
> a time to kill and time to heal,
> a time to tear down and a time to build,
> a time to weep and a time to laugh,
> a time to mourn and a time to dance,
> a time to scatter stones and a time to gather them,
> a time to embrace and a time to refrain from embracing,
> a time to search and a time to give up,
> a time to keep and a time to throw away,
> a time to tear and a time to mend,
> a time to be silent and a time to speak,
> a time to love and a time to hate,
> a time for war and a time for peace.

Thus the trans-positional return to onto-epistemological life is characterised by a relational and contextual disposition. The trans-positional individual or culture is dexterous and can live and speak in the blacks or whites or greys of wicked problems, not schizophrenically or haphazardly, but with meaning and purpose.

Drivers of development

A premise of BirD is that, over time and in context, interactions between key locations produce identifiable and powerful onto-epistemological developments, dispositions and dynamics in everyday lives. A bi-relational approach to development makes several important, if seemingly obvious, assumptions of the aging individual and culture:

a   The aging individual and culture will have to reject or coordinate an increasing number of contents accumulated and encountered through life experience.

b   Dyadic structures represent a simple and ubiquitous way of conceptualising and coordinating these contents.

c   The aging individual and culture will be able to form more complex relationships between contents by applying more advanced and accurate processes to dyadic structures.

d   Cognitive-epistemic structures (e.g. dyads) and processes (e.g. binary oppositional relating) that interact with contents will be progressively more recognisable through the act of *meta-cognition* (i.e. thinking about thinking). Through meta-cognition, the structures and processes of thought are brought into consciousness and become part of *what* and *how* we know. This consciousness creates the classic subject–observer dilemma. Knowing about our thoughts and defining epistemological locations changes the way we see and know objects. Arguably, the perception and (re)solution of this dilemma prompts onto-epistemological developments beyond the naïve realism that separates subject from object, reality from perception.

In metaphorical terms, the continuance of life compels us to walk over more terrain. To stay upright generally requires the progressively dexterous differentiation, integration and coordination of feet (i.e. left foot/right foot) or *dyads*. It may be useful to replace *feet* with *wings* in keeping with the book's avian acronym (i.e. BirD) – the meaning is the same. The development of dexterity, our self-awareness of its development and the coevolution of knowing and being provide a basis for the study of onto-epistemological development. There is a logical and, arguably, empirical reason for suggesting that a naïve disposition for binary oppositions (i.e. *pro-dyadic region*) comes before an awareness of the interpenetration of oppositions (i.e. *post-dyadic region*), equivalence of oppositions (i.e. *collapse*) and the relationality and contextuality (i.e. *trans-positions*) of oppositions.

We all have powerfully formative life experiences that may predispose us to identify more generally with one polarity than the other. However, when we engage with others who have different experiences that cause them to relate to a different polarity, we see the production of conflict and/or an onto-epistemological development characterised by an appreciation for the interdependence and contextuality of value. BirD offers a way to represent such dynamics and trace the developments and trajectories in context and over time. For example, what onto-epistemological dynamics help to describe changes from conservative to liberal political affiliations, or from liberal political affiliations to a post-conservative way of knowing and being political? Or what onto-epistemological dynamics are involved in religious conversions or deconversions that may help us to better understand wicked problems such as the separation of religion and state or religious violence?

Dynamics of development

This section offers basic definitions of the key dynamics that characterise movement and relations between BirD's archetypal positions. In folk epistemology, bi-relational dynamics are evidenced in common sayings such as 'swinging the pendulum', 'finding common ground', 'sitting on the fence', 'being one-eyed, or short-sighted', 'taking things too far', 'taking two to tango', 'opposites attracting',

A theory of Bi-relational Development   135

'being poles apart', 'removing the training wheels' and 'cutting off one's nose to spite one's face'. Such sayings signify important structural developments and dynamics that reflect and create how we know and act in relation to dyads. At the very least, such sayings imply common onto-epistemological changes and dynamics that warrant closer attention.

Different positions meet and engage each other in different ways such that there are dynamics between positions. In abstract terms, bi-relational development can be stable or volatile, gradual or revolutionary and can involve polarisation, opposition, reclusion, conversion, repulsion, consolidation and inversion between positions. In concrete terms, these dynamics can be used to describe the interactions between dyads such as male/female, nature/nurture, matter/spirit and subjective/objective. They can provide relational understandings of dynamics such as *radicalisation* in the context of religious violence, *polarisation* in debates over gay marriage and *sustainability* in approaches to environmental conservation and development. These dynamics provide ways of speaking about and understanding onto-epistemological developments in relation to wicked socio-cultural problems. In keeping with BirD's organising principle, the following dynamics can be conceptualised as bi-relational dynamics because they relate to movements between polarities or dyadic constituents (i.e. A/B).

BirD's archetypal positions imply dynamics. There is a spatial dimension to the relationship between dyadic constituents. That is, A and B can be conceptualised in directional terms as moving and doing in relation to each other. For example, the pro-dyadic phase implies acts of 'intersecting', 'opposing' or 'contradicting', while the point of collapse implies acts of 'negating', 'unifying', 'dualising', 'synthesising' and/or 'multiplying'. Accordingly, the following glossary identifies and defines BirD's primary dynamics in order to facilitate the bi-relational analysis of wicked problems.

The first six sets of terms relate to the dynamics most directly implicated in each of BirD's six archetypal regions:

1   **Creating:** the act of conceiving or originating a thing that precedes the division of its parts.

2   **Emerging:** forming and growing a part before its conscious differentiation from other parts.
    Polarisation: movement towards a particular dyadic pole.
    Consolidating: reinforcing an emerging or existing position.

3   **Opposing:** expressing a contradiction between undifferentiated and independent parts.
    Binary opposition: the representation of conflict through two mutually exclusive positions with relatively little continuity, degrees of difference or interdependence between them and the assumption that one is a priori more correct or valuable than another.

136 Theory

Retreat: return to a position after a negative experience with a different position.

Reclusion: negative fear of a different position without experience of that position.

Repulsion: leaving of a position from within with little attraction from without.

Polar inversion: a rapid shift of exclusive identification from one polarity to another.

Exclusive middle: a middle position that is exclusively held in binary opposition to polarities.

Enantiodromia: the unconscious emergence of a polarity through the privileging of the opposite polarity.

4   **Converging:** expressing the inter-penetration and co-accommodation of interdependent parts.

Depolarisation: movement from a particular dyadic pole.

Naïve balance: balancing two positions for the sake of balance.

Immirroring: recognising aspects of a position in an opposing position.

Entanglement (interdependence): the realisation that one dyadic constituent cannot be changed without a related change in the other dyadic constituent.

Relativistic disorientation: the experience of an absurd and debilitating relativism and subsequent immobilisation.

Dyadic reflexivity: an awareness of dyadic relationships that influences those relationships.

Ubiquitisation: the sense that a dyad has a profound interconnectedness with other dyads or relevance across domains of knowledge.

5   **Collapsing:** expressing the equivalence of opposing parts.

Negating: expressing the mutual extinction of equally opposing parts.

Unifying: expressing the subsuming whole of equal and complementary but opposing parts.

Dualising: expressing the perennial tension between equal and opposing parts.

Synthesising: creating a third thing from the combination of opposing parts.

Multiplying: expressing the infinite division and differentiation of parts.

6   **Trans-positioning:** the act of taking a side or committing to a particular action in context with a simultaneous appreciation for the ultimate value and interdependence of an opposing part.

Relational: pertaining to the interdependence of parts.

Contextual: pertaining to the most immediate and salient aspects of a situation.

Counterbalancing: deliberate identification with a position in context in order to rectify a perceived imbalance with its counter-position.

Bi-relational development also has a temporal dimension in that movement and development of dyadic constituents takes place over time.

Stable: a period of consistent identification with a position.

Transitioning: movement from one position to another.
Gradual: a period of gradual transition between positions.
Volatile: in a period of extreme tension that precedes a violent change of position.
Revolutionary: in a state of rapid and violent change of position.

The time period for bi-relational development depends significantly on the degree of formative influence that different experiences have on individuals and cultures over time. Some events and experiences can be catalytic to bi-relational development.

Formative experiences: real or perceived experiences that influence an individual or group's onto-epistemological identity or development.

Positively reinforcing: an experience that makes a position intrinsically more attractive.
Negatively reinforcing: an experience that makes a position more attractive by making an opposing position less attractive.

Impact: the level of influence of an experience on bi-relational development.
Intense: a powerfully formative experience in relation to a position.
Moderate: a mildly formative experience in relation to a position.

Frequency: the amount of times an experience is reinforced.
High: many experiences that accumulate to affect a position.
Low: one or a few experiences that affect a position.

Collectively, these terms and their organisation in relation to BirD's archetypal positions provide an analytical framework for understanding and (re)solving wicked problems.

A conceptual tool for identifying bi-relational dynamics

The identification of bi-relational positions and dynamics requires an understanding of onto-epistemological trajectories over time. BirD's visual metaphor identifies archetypal positions, but it can be adapted to identify actual positions, explore developmental dynamics and form and test hypotheses about bi-relational development. Accordingly, Figure 5.2 provides a conceptual grid for mapping actual onto-epistemological trajectories and positions in light of BirD's archetypal positions. This particular grid represents 10 time periods that can be designated at any meaningful interval over days, weeks, years or even centuries for trajectories of cultural development. Each time period contains nine possible identifications in

138 Theory

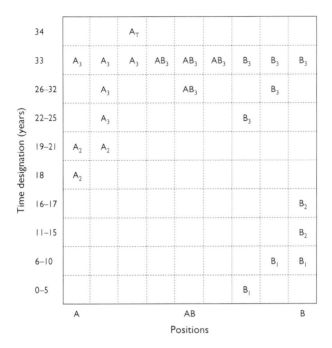

Figure 5.2 A representation of bi-relational positions over time.

relation to the dyadic poles. Unlike a standard Likert scale, one or more identifications can be made per time period to recognise the potential homogeneity or diversity of individual and group ways of knowing and being.

This particular grid could represent the development of a specific individual and be juxtaposed over the positions and regions of BirD in Figure 5.1. Thus, ages 6–10 could represent the pre-dyadic emergence of a disposition; ages 11–21 could represent a period of pro-dyadic *opposition* with a polar inversion occurring around the age of 18; ages 22–25 could represent a period of internal division and tension between equal but separated opposites; ages 26–32 could represent the post-dyadic *convergence of opposites*; age 33 could represent a *collapse of dyads*; and age 34 could represent the beginning of a trans-positional return to a particular issue-in-context. These positions represent one possible onto-epistemological trajectory through the wicked problems of a particular individual. However, the grid could also be used to represent different trajectories between individuals, within groups or between groups that provide an insight into the dynamics of wicked problems.

BirD and the representation of wicked problems

BirD offers an insight into the structure and development of wicked problems. The wickedness of many problems lies in the difficulty and complexity of first recognising and then reconciling the 'opposites' that define the problem. Socio-cultural problems are particularly wicked because reconciling destructive imbalances that have been established and culturally embedded, possibly over centuries, comes at great human cost as livelihoods, identities and even lives are threatened. While re-equilibration in the face of injustice is usually warranted for a greater good, too often the way this is done either swings the proverbial pendulum to create a new set of injustices for future generations or corrals everyone into an anaesthetised middle. We burn bridges today that we may well need to use tomorrow. True equilibration or 'sustainability' is an ongoing act that requires vigilant dexterity in dynamic contexts. In general terms, recent Western generations have struggled to re-equilibrate the masculine dominance of the feminine, the cultural dominance of the natural, the global dominance of the local, the material dominance of the spiritual, the conservative dominance of the liberal, the competitive dominance of the collaborative and the rational dominance of the intuitive. Of course, there are pockets of society and historical antecedents where these dyadic struggles are reversed. However, perhaps the greatest challenge for any individual or group is the ability to know and live the difference between the reconciliation of opposites in the face of great injustice and the mere reversal of opposites that merely creates a new injustice.

Another feature of wicked problems is that, as individuals, we are born and raised into cumulative dispositions towards one or the other pole. It can be a natural onto-epistemological challenge for an 'alpha male' to co-value the broader social role of his male and female antitheses and vice-versa. It can be a natural onto-epistemological challenge for a 'left-wing liberal' to co-value the broader social role of his or her 'right-wing conservative' antitheses and vice-versa. Our developmental task as individuals and groups is to reconcile our own roles and dispositions with the different roles and dispositions of others, without completely losing ourselves or absolutely destroying others.

A further feature of wicked problems relates to the semantic difficulty of differentiating positions. Part of the (re)solution of wicked problems relates to the disentanglement of positions to identify who or what is actually being opposed. This is why the developmental differentiation of the 'same' position is so important. We can identify ourselves as liberal and/or conservative, male and/or female, traditional and/or alternative and rational and/or intuitive in epistemologically different ways. BirD differentiates these ways as A_1, A_2, A_3; AB_1, AB_2, AB_3; and B_1, B_2, B_3, where the third positions are more onto-epistemically expansive than the first positions. Wicked problems are often exacerbated by a failure to differentiate exactly who or what is in opposition because it is easier to recognise the same overarching identifiers (e.g. male/female, liberal/conservative, subjective/objective) than it is to recognise the epistemically different ways of knowing them (e.g. binary oppositions, complements or constraining categories). Thus, A_3 may be opposing B_2 while they appear to be opposing B_3, and B_3 may better oppose A_2 by opposing B_2. BirD's archetypal positions help to conceptualise such dynamics. While these

140 Theory

positions and dynamics are more generally illustrated and applied to real wicked problems in later chapters, I include a brief hypothetical scenario in the following section.

An illustration of bi-relational development

This scenario focuses on a fictional individual (i.e. Andrew) in relation to a liberal/conservative (i.e. A/B) dyad. The onto-epistemological trajectory of development is based on the particular trajectory identified in Figure 5.2.

> **Scenario part 1.** Andrew is raised in a relatively self-identifying 'conservative' family and community. Throughout his childhood and adolescence, he develops a strong sense of national identity that, through familiarity, he associates with white protestant ways of working, dressing, eating, worshipping, marrying, speaking and playing. His ways of knowing and being are strengthened by his negative but provincial experiences of *the other* (e.g. other religions and races). Accordingly, he has a distrust of 'blacks', who he sees as disproportionately responsible for petty crime, violence and welfare dependency in the community. He learns to encapsulate his provincial values and attitudes with the term 'conservative' and to identify sympathisers with the other as 'liberal'. These labels are entangled with other identifiers that are used in Andrew's discourse, such as democrat/republican, traditional/progressive and left/right.

> **Analysis.** Andrew's early life represents a period of *dyadic stability* as a relatively significant period of time in a general position. The stability is consolidated through *negative reinforcement* (i.e. negative experiences of the opposite pole) and/or *positive reinforcement* (i.e. positive experiences with the pole). The position represents a half-truth – a binary oppositional approach to knowing and being that is characteristic of the pro-dyadic phase. It is true based on the realities it sees but false based on the realities it ignores. For example, Andrew sustains his racial attitudes based on the present provincial realities he sees (e.g. crime and welfare dependency) but what he does not see is the entangled relationship between the past actions of his community and the present situation, the other realities beyond his immediate social context and the possibilities and potential for a different future. For Andrew, A and B are not yet entangled or interdependent. Black is black and white is white; black is bad and white is good.

> **Scenario part 2.** Andrew's identification with conservative values is violently disrupted in a single year when the pastor of his local church is disgraced for infidelities and his racial stereotypes of the other are challenged by new experiences and a friendship formed after an overseas mission trip. He feels personally betrayed by his pastor and reacts by rejecting his community as hypocritical and narrow-minded in light of the realisation that many of his

A theory of Bi-relational Development 141

personal stereotypes do not accurately describe or allow him to deeply engage with the other. He begins to reconstruct a fragmented identity by identifying against the mores of his childhood and adolescence and assuming what he sees as more 'liberal' values and attitudes. Ironically, his new identifications are still largely informed by the opposite stereotypes he had constructed. So, as he moves town and enters university at the end of the year, he adopts a permissive approach to most socio-political issues, which he identifies as 'liberal'. His tastes in dress, music, peers and lifestyle also change in accordance with a general rejection of his 'conservative' past. He estranges himself from and is estranged by his parents, who attribute his changes to the corrupting influence of a secular university.

Analysis. Andrew's eighteenth year sees a *revolutionary polar inversion* that represents a rapid and intense change of position from one dyadic pole to another. This is similar to a *pendulum swing* in common terms. The polarity swing could represent *dyadic repulsion* from a period of *dyadic stability*. Here, *stability* at a particular pole creates a proportionately strong but brittle identity subject to *dyadic volatility* that often precedes a *polar inversion* or *enantiodromia*. Thus, a strong binary oppositional disposition (i.e. B) creates the very opposition that it will inevitably become (i.e. A) if it is rapidly and violently pushed over its clear boundaries from within, as happens to Andrew. Changing sides while keeping the same structure is the only way that the identity stops itself from structurally shattering into a million pieces in this position. However, the new position can be consolidated or *negatively reinforced* by *expulsion* from the previous group.

Scenario part 3. Andrew's immersion in and enthusiasm for 'liberal' discourses lasts for a while but is slowly problematised in relation to several new experiences. He has a confrontation with an old friend from his community over 'the legalisation of marijuana', who suggests that his judgemental attitudes and stereotypes have merely been reversed, rather than challenged. He also experiences some conflict with current friends who tease him as still being too politically conservative, and he begins to be troubled by the relativity of such labels. He embraces the social conscience of his new group through anti-racism, marriage equality and environmental-activism campaigns. However, given his conservative past, he experiences some discomfort at the group's caricatures of realities he knows better. He sometimes feels as if the harsh realities he saw on the mission field are glossed over in the idealism that his relatively affluent friends espouse. Andrew is occasionally struck by the similarities between the hypocrisies and hatred of his new group and the approaches of his old group. He has fleeting but disconcerting insights that common problems are exacerbated by the mutually exclusive ways his current liberal friends and former conservative friends try to resolve them. The more he engages in socio-political debate and activism on campus, the more he struggles to identify individuals, groups and positions as unambiguously liberal or conservative, right or wrong. While attending a particularly divisive student debate on 'intelligent design', Andrew has the absurd feeling that the sides were somehow creating each other. Later that semester he engages a tutorial debate on retribution and rehabilitation in a criminal law subject; here, he is chided by some friends as being 'too conservative' and others as being 'too liberal' for the same stance on the same issues.

Analysis. Andrew experiences a *gradual depolarisation* from the left dyad. This depolarisation could be the result of *inmirroring*, which is the experience and perception of symmetry between different poles. Andrew has come from relatively polarised positions in a short period of time. The experience of de-identifying from a second polarity is potentially disorientating as he experiences a stalemate between opposites with little experience of middle ground. He has begun to realise the abstract value of both poles (i.e. liberal and conservative) but struggles to reconcile or bring them together on common ground.

Scenario part 4. Andrew completes his studies, but increasingly his new socio-political disorientation spills over into his professional life as a lawyer. The more he struggles to orientate himself politically, the more this disorientation spills over into other domains of life. He struggles to practise confidently because he finds he has lost much of the moral conviction that guided his early studies and inspired his advocacy for the disadvantaged. His partner and family relationships struggle as he begins to question his identity as a man and his effectiveness as a parent. Friends describe him as a 'fence sitter' – able to see others' perspectives but not really having one of his own. Andrew realises this but cannot seem to escape from his general feeling that all roads lead to nowhere. He experiments with various forms of escape including intoxication. Professionally, Andrew finds himself participating in his legal cases more as a dispassionate observer, caring little for the outcome. He becomes increasingly politically, socially and professionally disengaged.

Analysis. After his studies Andrew experiences a period of *relativistic disorientation* akin to having to move both feet or both hands against each other to move at all. There is a sense in which Andrew becomes a divided self and is unable to reconcile this division. This divided self is not easily accommodated by past structures, and new accommodations can be socially and emotionally costly. It can seem impossible to move, commit or choose to act.

Scenario part 5. After several light but pointed comments from friends and colleagues, Andrew becomes more aware that he is 'detached', 'depressed' and 'simply not caring about anything'. Such comments lead him to realise that his disillusioned detachment *from* the world is still a way of being *in* the world. His sense of stalemate between conservative and liberal values has led him to be more pessimistic than optimistic, more detached than attached and more passive than active. But he begins to see this. He sees, too, that his relatively new vices *are* his response to his self-perceived inability to respond to the vacuum of life he experiences. He begins to appreciate that others have different responses to the same vacuum. Seeing his response as one *among* the many rather than one *above* the many paradoxically opens new choices, positions and possibilities. In metaphorical terms, Andrew starts to appreciate that blacks and whites are needed to make shades of grey.

Analysis. There is some evidence of *dyadic ubiquitisation* and *dyadic affinity* as Andrew realises that his struggle to orientate himself politically is a more basic and pervasive human struggle that affects and is affected by, to a greater or lesser extent, his whole orientation to life and his relationships with others. He often feels lost and disorientated. However, at other times Andrew experiences the entanglement and inter-penetration of opposites that characterise post-dyadic developments. Once clear separations and binary divisions are complicated by glimpses of relationality and common ground that have meaning in context. Andrew begins to appreciate that a return to context can help him to move again. He sees that he will be able to move more deliberately and dexterously than before with the spectrum between 'opposites' that his life journey has created.

Scenario part 6. Andrew begins to experiment and choose between different positions more deliberately than before. As a voter, lawyer, parent and partner he becomes more rationally and intuitively discriminating in the actions he takes. He no longer lets his tendency to observe experiences detract from his ability to participate in them. This new openness allows him to participate more fully but more discerningly. He re-engages with life politically, socially and professionally, though with a broader range of positions and possibilities than were available to him before. He re-invokes distinctions to make life choices but they are more differentiated than before. He feels the need to make relational and contextual choices without having to decide ultimately between being liberal or conservative, traditional or progressive, right or left, a realist or idealist. Over time, some friends and colleagues notice a change in Andrew. His characterisations as 'detached', 'depressed' or 'aloof' are replaced with characterisations as 'balanced' and 'even-handed'.

Analysis. The last position could represent the beginning of a more *trans-positional* disposition that abstractly embraces multiple positions while concretely and contextually evaluating and choosing between positions. This disposition is marked by the ability to observe the world more objectively in order to participate more subjectively. Discriminating choices are

144 Theory

made with an appreciation for the relationality of opposites and the contextuality of actions. Here, life hangs in the balance but rarely in the middle.

This brief hypothetical illustration of one onto-epistemological trajectory preempts the more authentic illustrations of bi-relational development in subsequent chapters. To conclude this chapter as an explication of BirD, the following section offers some general metaphors that highlight some important aspects of a bi-relational approach to onto-epistemological development.

Metaphors for understanding BirD

Obviously, all presentations of an idea like BirD are metaphorical to a degree, including academic prose. However, while this book appropriates the relatively more literal and, for many, more inaccessible language of academia as its dominant metaphor, I hope that the following common metaphors will shed further light on a bi-relational approach to wicked problems.

Feet, hands and eyes

One of the most obvious metaphors for understanding BirD is feet. In allegorical terms, the left foot and the right foot represent the two constituents, or parts, of any pair or dyad. Of course, the allegorical coordination of left and right hands and eyes would serve just as well. The metaphor encourages the dexterous use of both feet for ease of movement and warns against the mixing up of feet in the pursuit of balancing. Creation is potential for the development of feet with which to traverse the diverse terrains of life.

The pre-dyadic region is the emergence of left footedness or right footedness before coordination or differentiation of both feet. It is a time for crawling and scooting, with particular reliance on the lead of others. Imagine trying to navigate a difficult terrain with only one foot, while dragging the other behind.

The pro-dyadic region involves the opposition of the left foot and right foot. This opposition serves to strengthen both legs as an individual stands upright, but if this tension is not broken and one foot is allowed to lead the other depending on the terrain, then this opposition ultimately restricts movement in complex terrains. In opposition, the left foot walks away from the right foot or stands against it – seeking a different path but not realising it shares a common body such that it ends up doing the splits or standing still.

The post-dyadic region sees an extension and differentiation of the range of motion. The left foot can extend its range well beyond the centre of balance, as can the right foot, though one may still tend to dominate the other in every terrain, restricting full motion. Or one foot can mirror the other with great range, which is good for jumping and hopping but still not particularly efficient for traversing uneven ground for long periods. The end of this stage involves near full use of left and right foot, but still lacks coordination with the changing terrain. It is dexterous but not deft, enjoying running, jumping, leaping, ducking, weaving and hopping but without full range or regard for the obstacles in its path and the nature of the terrain.

The point of collapse involves a spinning and mixing of feet. It is the realisation that left foot can become right foot can become left foot in a tighter and tighter pirouette on a point closest to collapse. It is the ultimate detachment of movement from space and time – a dervishian whirling where differentiations between left and right make little sense. However, paradoxically, this union of left and right feet at the point of collapse is the creation of a newly found dexterity that allows for a trans-positional 'dance of opposites'.

Here, left foot and right foot are differentiated and integrated, dexterous and deft, paradoxically balanced through multiple imbalances, able to step left, right or pirouette. The trans-positional traveller remembers that life is a balancing act. There is necessity in space and time to run, jump, hop, skip, twist, turn and even whirl a little along the way.

The brightness-illusion metaphor

The brightness illusion (Figure 5.3) reveals how context influences perception and provides a powerful metaphor for understanding BirD as a theory of development towards the reconciliation of opposites. Out of context, A and B are identical shades of grey; however, in contrast with their respective backgrounds, A appears lighter than B.

BirD represents the developmental nature of this realisation and the archetypal positions that constitute it. It does this on the assumption that the same archetypal positions and developments apply to more concrete dyads (i.e. male/female, pleasure/pain, liberal/conservative) in real-life contexts. Furthermore, it proposes that these different positions and developments can help us to understand the inherent wickedness of wicked problems while finding better ways of (re)solving them.

Developmentally, the subjective perception that the shades are different seems to come before the objective awareness that the shades are the same. In BirD, these perspectives are represented as pro-dyadic oppositions that grow out of pre-dyadic experience in context such that A is seen as better than B or B is seen as better than A. Eventually, however, experience of different contexts may

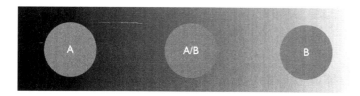

Figure 5.3 The brightness illusion.

146 Theory

start to bring the role of context into focus and begin to relativise or at least problematise the absolute contrast between A and B. BirD represents this development as a post-dyadic phase as the two begin to converge. The absolute convergence occurs when A and B are removed from context altogether and their equality is revealed. BirD represents this as a point of collapse. Developmentally, it may seem at this point as if the objective view is superior to the subjective view and represents a final development. That is, A and B should be treated as if they are the same. However, a further development sees collapse as giving primary value to the abstraction from context and not the context itself. Trans-positions seek to rectify this by rebalancing and reintegrating abstract and concrete, objective and subjective.

In summary, the relationship between A and B and their context can be understood in terms of BirD's archetypal positions and developments, as follows:

1   Creation: potential for perception of A and B.
2   Pre-dyadic emergence: perception of A or B before relationship.
3   Pro-dyadic opposition: perception of A and B in opposing relationship.
4   Post-dyadic convergence: perception of A and B in dependent relationship in context.
5   Collapse: equation of A and B across contexts.
6   Transpositions: relation of A and B in and across contexts.

BirD's application to wicked problems is based on the premise that similar developments and dynamics relate to a range of common dyads that present as opposites. So, consider the previous structural description repeated with the masculine/feminine dyad. Developmentally, the perception in context that masculinity and femininity are of different value seems to come before the awareness across contexts that they are the same value. In BirD, pro-dyadic oppositions grow out of pre-dyadic experience in context such that masculinity may be seen as better than femininity or femininity may be seen as better than masculinity. Eventually, however, experience of different contexts may start to bring the role of context into focus and begin to relativise or at least problematise the absolute contrast between the value of masculinity and femininity. BirD represents this development as a post-dyadic phase as the two begin to converge in value. The absolute convergence occurs when A and B are removed from context altogether and their equality is revealed. BirD represents this as a point of collapse. Developmentally, it may seem at this point as if the objective view of gender equality is superior to the subjective view and represents a final development. That is, masculine and feminine should be treated as if they are the same. However, a further development sees collapse as giving primary value to the abstraction from context and not the context itself. Trans-positions seek to rectify this by rebalancing and reintegrating abstract and concrete, objective and subjective. This means that masculine and feminine are treated as equal and complementary across contexts but may be differentially valued in a particular context.

The rabbit and the duck

Ambiguous images and figure–ground-shift images offer useful visual metaphors for understanding BirD. Though there are numerous examples, a vintage favourite is the ambiguous rabbit-or-duck image (Figure 5.4). Here, the 'same' picture can be seen as a rabbit or a duck. I have used the figure and others like it with many different students over the years to introduce concepts like *constructivism*, *paradigm* and *epistemology*. The diversity of actual and possible perceptions is useful in illustrating some of BirD's archetypal locations.

Obviously, from creation to early pre-dyadic stages and ages it probably makes little sense to consider the figure at all, though there may exist influences that will affect later responses, such as exposure to ducks or rabbits. However, late pre-dyadic responses to the picture presented with no context, title or question (e.g. 'Is this a rabbit or a duck?') could take the following forms:

- What a nice duck!
- That's an interesting scribble!
- What a nice rabbit!

In each case, the perception is simply reported in the absence of closely competing perceptions.

However, responses that are representative of the pro-dyadic region are formed in the company of competing perceptions.

- I clearly see a duck so you can't possibly see a rabbit!
- I clearly see a scribble so you can't possibly see a rabbit or a duck!
- I clearly see a rabbit so you can't possibly see a duck!

Such competitions and exclusions can be fought most fiercely when more than rabbits and ducks are at stake. But when they do not lead to death, such contestations lead often to deep dialogue and close scrutiny that begins to narrow the distance between perspectives.

Figure 5.4 Rabbit or duck? (Original source: Jastrow, 1899.)

148 Theory

Often inspired by dissonance and opposition, responses that are representative of the post-dyadic region typically take the following forms:

- Though I can hear parts of what you are saying and see much of what you are seeing (e.g. ears that look like a duck's beak), I can explain everything you say and see as belonging to a rabbit.
- Though I can hear parts of what you are saying and see much of what you are seeing, I can explain everything you say and see as belonging to a scribble.
- Though I can hear parts of what you are saying and see much of what you are seeing (e.g. a beak that looks like a rabbit's ears), I can explain everything you say and see as belonging to a duck.

The more detail one sees of the other's perspective, the closer one gets to the point of ground shift. For example, training to see a duck's bill protruding forwards as a rabbit's ears protruding backwards can bring the perceiver of a duck one step closer to being a perceiver of a rabbit.

The act of image reversal is usually fun in the context of visual illusions that flip rabbits and ducks. However, the experience of reversal between subject and object, reality and perception, relative and absolute, right and wrong, faith and reason can be deeply disorientating if not disturbing if one has deep social and emotional ties to a particular perspective.

The equivalence of the two opposites can be experienced in different ways, as represented at BirD's point of collapse.

- I can see a rabbit and a duck so maybe I really see *no-thing* at all (Zero).
- I can see a rabbit and a duck that must be part of *one* thing (One).
- I can see a rabbit and a duck so there must be *two* things (Two).
- I can see a rabbit and a duck produce a *third* thing (Three).
- I see a rabbit or a duck, depending on my perspective, so there may actually be an *infinite* number of things to see (Infinity).

Thus, the monist sees a union or *Oneness* in the meeting of dyadic constituents: the perception of a rabbit by some and a duck by others suggests that they are both reflections of the same 'One' thing. The dualist sees a division or twoness: the rabbit and the duck both exist. The nihilist sees a negation or collapse of meaning in the meeting of dyadic constituents: the perception of a rabbit by one and a duck by another can be used as grounds to suggest that neither a rabbit nor duck 'really' exist, for where is the 'all seeing eye' to know that there are two? For others, the experience of being blind but now seeing opens up an infinite number of possibilities. I once posed the figure with the title 'Rabbit, duck or elephant?' to a lecture theatre of over 100 students. Two claimed to see the elephant, one claimed to 'sort of see it' and ten agreed that it was there even if they could not see it, because others could. The rabbit-or-duck is a simple visual metaphor and, although I may have extended it a little too far, the onto-epistemological locations it represents are identified in BirD as a way to approach and appreciate some of life's more significant wicked problems.

Conclusion

In summary, this chapter has presented a theory of bi-relational development (BirD) as a culmination of Part I. The aim of the following part is to illustrate and apply BirD's archetypal regions, positions and dynamics to a range of wicked problems. The following chapter offers bi-relational analyses of wicked problems as they are experienced in individual lives, before the subsequent three chapters explore wicked problems as they are expressed on a global stage. My subsuming claim for these illustrations is that many wicked problems can be understood in terms of onto-epistemological differences and that these differences are powerfully revealed in bi-relational developments towards a reconciliation of opposites.

References

Aristotle. (1970). *Physics, Bks I–II* (W. Charlton, Trans.). Oxford: Clarendon Press.

Camus, A. (2005). *The myth of Sisyphus* (J. O'Brien, Trans.). London: Penguin Books. (Original work published 1942.)

Davies, P. (2013). The day time began. In J. Webb (Ed.), *Nothing: From absolute zero to cosmic oblivion – amazing insights into nothingness* (pp. 44–54). London: New Scientist.

Eliade, M. (1961). *The sacred and the profane: The nature of religion* (W. R. Trask, Trans.). New York: Harper Torchbooks.

Epstein, M. (1997). *The place of postmodernism in postmodernity*. Paper presented at the After Post-Modernism Conference. www.focusing.org/apm_papers/epstein.html

Fowler, J. W. (1981). *Stages of faith: The psychology of human development and the quest for meaning*. San Francisco: Harper and Row.

Greene, B. (2004). *The fabric of the cosmos*. London: Penguin.

Hesse, H. (2012). *Steppenwolf*. (D. Horrocks, Trans.). Kindle edition. Retrieved from Amazon.com. (Original work published 1927.)

Huneker, J. G. (n.d.). Thinkexist.com. [wuotation]. Retrieved from http://thinkexist. com/quotation/life_is_like_an_onion-you_peel_off_layer_after/166083.html

Jastrow, J. (1899). The mind's eye. *Popular Science Monthly*, 54, 299–312.

Jung, C. G. (1970). *Myseterium coniunctionis: An inquiry into the separation and synthesis of psychic opposites in alchemy (The collected works of C. G. Jung)* (G. Adler and R. F. C. Hull, Trans., Vol. 14). Princeton, NJ: Princeton University Press. (Original work published 1955.)

Jung, C. G. (1971). *Psychological types, collected works of C.G. Jung* (Vol. 6). Princeton, NJ: Princeton University Press.

Kierkegaard, S. (1992). *Concluding unscientific postscript to the philosophical fragments* (H. V. Hong and E. H. Hong, Trans.). Copenhagen: University Bookshop Reitzel. (Original work published 1846.)

Martin, M. (Ed.). (2010). *The book of symbols: Reflections on archetypal images*. Cologne: Taschen.

Nietzsche, F. (1962). *Philosophy in the tragic age of the Greeks* (M. Cowen, Trans.). Washington, DC: Henry Regnery Company. (Original work written in 1873.)

Nietzsche, F. (1961). *Thus spoke Zarathustra* (R. J. Hollingdale and E. V. Rieu, Trans.). New York: Penguin Publishing. (Original work published 1883–91.)

Oser, F. K., and Gmünder, P. (1991). *Religious judgment: A developmental approach.* Birmingham, AL: Religious Education Press.

Piaget, J. (1971). The theory of stages in cognitive development. In D. R. Green, M. P. Ford and G. B. Flamer (Eds.), *Measurement and Piaget* (pp. 1–11). New York: McGraw-Hill.

Reginster, B. (2006). *The affirmation of life: Nietzsche on overcoming nihilism.* London: Harvard University Press.

Ricoeur, P. (1981). *Hermeneutics and the human sciences: Essays on language, action and interpretation* (J. B. Thompson, Trans.). Cambridge: Cambridge University Press.

Schopenhauer, A. (1969). *The world as will and representation* (E. Payne, Trans. Vol. 1). New York: Dover Publishing Inc.

Schwartz, S. (2009). *C. S. Lewis on the final frontier: Science and the supernatural in the space trilogy.* New York: Oxford University Press.

Sinnott, J. D. (1984). Postformal reasoning: The relativistic stage. In M. L. Commons, F. A. Richards and C. Armon (Eds.), *Beyond formal operations: Late adolescent and adult cognitive development* (Vol. 1, pp. 298–325). New York: Praeger Publishers.

Tabak, I., and Weinstock, M. (2008). A sociocultural exploration of epistemological beliefs. In M. Khine (Ed.), *Knowing, Knowledge and Beliefs* (pp. 177–95). Amsterdam: Springer.

Thacker, E. (2011). Darklife: Negation, nothingness, and the will-to-life in Schopenhauer. *Parrhesia*, 12, 12–27.

Turner, T. (1996). *City as landscape: A post post-modern view of design and planning.* London: Taylor & Francis.

Part 2

Illustrations

Chapter 6

Illustrations of bi-relational development in life narratives

Wicked problems are usually defined and explored as global issues (e.g. poverty, sustainability and racism) and I intend to discuss some of these in later chapters. However, in this chapter I want to show that wicked problems are also experienced as individual issues that have deeply affective and existential dimensions. Accordingly, this chapter illustrates BirD with extracts from life narratives collected using a semi-structured survey. The purpose of such illustrations is to illuminate the theoretical regions, positions and dynamics introduced in Chapter 5 as they relate to individual human experiences and ways of being in the world. I hope that they will provide snapshots of the diverse ways that dyads and dyadic relationships manifest in everyday wicked problems.

For many of us, our appreciation of particular dyads and dyadic relationships will grow out of formative and often difficult life experiences that wed epistemology and ontology. Most of us who live long enough are likely to have to wrestle with the wicked relationship between hope and despair, happiness and sadness, good and evil, change and stability, and pleasure and pain. The experience of entanglement can come as an existential shock when we are cocooned by popular cultures that pursue happiness, pleasure, hope, good and stability as if they are somehow separable from their co-defining opposites. Education that privileges global and social over local and individual expressions of wicked problems risks missing out on some of the most powerful opportunities for learning in and about the world.

The narratives I have used are generally between 150 and 400 words in length. They were collected using a paper-based and online open-ended questionnaire as part of an Epistemic Mapping Project in the School of Education at James Cook University. The basic questions and instructions from the online questionnaire are summarised below:

> Choose one pair from the list provided that has been most significant in your own life. Please share your view and story about one of the pairs you have chosen. There is no wrong or right answer and no maximum word limit (200 words minimum recommended) as all views and details you provide are valuable. The questions below may guide your response.

a   What is your basic understanding or definition of each part of the pair?
b   What is your view of the relationship between the parts of the pair?
c   Do you see one part of the pair as more valuable or true than the other?
d   Have you always held this view or has your view changed throughout your life?
e   What specific life experiences or events do you think have influenced your view?
f   How do you think your views have affected your actions or relationships with others?

Approximately 120 of the 200 participants were enrolled in the same Bachelor of Education degree. The list of dyads provided is similar to the list provided in Chapter 1. Out of 67 dyads the most popular choices were: future/past (7%), physical/mental (7%), mind/body (7%), nature/nurture (6%), teach/learn (6%), feeling/thinking (5%), sadness/happiness (5%), change/stability (5%), subjective/objective (3%), freedom/control (3%) and wrong/right (3%). Needless to say, I cannot hope to cover all of the dyads the participants chose, but I have included a selection for the purposes of illustrating bi-relational development in relation to everyday wicked problems. I have chosen to structure this illustration using different dyads rather than different locations or dynamics. Given the previous chapter's relatively theoretical and domain-general focus, this allows me to focus on actual domains of knowledge in individuals' real-life contexts. Hopefully, this way of structuring the chapter will bring participant voices and experiences to the foreground. To recall, BirD posits six archetypal positions that describe the creation, pre-dyadic emergence, pro-dyadic opposition, post-dyadic convergence, collapse and trans-positioning of dyads.

Light/dark

One of the most common metaphors of bi-relational development – indeed, the basis of BirD's primary visual metaphor – concerns the separation of dark and light and black and white into seemingly infinite shades of grey. For this reason, the illustration begins with an analysis of some responses to the dyad dark/light. There is an affinity between light/darkness and many other dyads that relate to one of life's most wicked existential problems: suffering.

Participant 115 notes an affinity between dark/light and different dyads by capitalising one constituent of multiple dyads:

A few more concepts originating from light and dark have been explored in my art are listed – Good/bad White/black Day/night Sun/shade Water/fire Something/nothing Yes/no Positive/negative Happy/sad Giving/taking On/off Life/death Love/hate Shallow/deep Light/heavy Seen/unseen.

This participant's response is a particularly clear example of *ubiquitisation*: the sense that a dyad or dynamic has a profound interconnectedness with other dyads or dynamics across domains of knowledge:

> My understanding of light and dark is very broad and begins at the simplest basic level and grows from there. I extend the words to hold multiple meanings as metaphors and concepts which feature across many areas of my life . . . Light and dark is the concept itself in some artworks and enables my expression from within to help understand larger concepts ... All aspects of my life connect to each other and with light and dark, all that is needed is time to reflect to observe this.
>
> (115)

Perhaps unsurprisingly, this ubiquitisation is correlated with a relatively sophisticated trans-positional disposition that allows for relational and contextual choices.

This trans-positional disposition is recognisable in the same participant's descriptions of the relationship between light and dark:

> Knowing light and dark as opposite concepts allows for a consideration of the grey areas in between and beyond (and grey matter for that matter). As uncomfortable as grey areas can be, I believe they are a fundamental positioning to maintain balance and harmony throughout one's life. Recognising the full spectrum helps to hold the balance between light and dark evenly weighted.
>
> (115)

These descriptions suggest a paradoxical appreciation for opposition, degrees of difference on a spectrum, ambiguity of grey areas and an abstract sense of balance. Participant 165 expresses a similarly paradoxical perspective:

> You cannot have light without some darkness around the edges, and even in the darkest of dark there is still a hint of light somewhere to be found. One thing existing with the other, because they need each other while being polar opposites.

Given the relative rarity of late post-dyadic and trans-positional ways of knowing, it is worth looking more deeply at the life worlds in which they have developed.

The life worlds that reflect these sorts of onto-epistemological dispositions tend to show two things: deeply difficult and intense formative experiences and access to rich symbols for the expression and exploration of these experiences. Participant 115's responses to the question 'What specific life experiences or events do you think have influenced your view?' offer some examples. In the

156 Illustrations

first instance, she describes the loss of a close family member to suicide. This type of experience (i.e. tragedy and trauma) highlights the educative power of suffering that raises profoundly difficult but potentially transformative questions about the nature and purpose of life:

> Such emotional depths of darkness and negativity were reached in the grief that followed but were subsequently transformed to light, positivity and healing ... Knowing basic concepts such as light and dark have helped to understand more difficult concepts such as life and death.
>
> (115)

This perspective is shared by other participants' reflections on the light/darkness dyad. For example, Participant 165 recalls her slow descent into darkness after a formative bullying incident:

> I used to be a carefree kid, not overly boisterous, but fairly independent and confident . . . Life was great; nothing bad existed . . . It was in grade 3 when I was bullied for the first time at a school social night. An older student, from grade 5 or 6, came up to me and started calling me names and making fun of my dancing, which started a chain reaction of others coming up to me and teasing me that night. I'd never experienced anything like it before and it crushed me. I quit dancing, afraid that I would do something that would make people laugh at me or call me names. I'd spend afternoons at my Nonna's house, where she would spoil me with chocolate biscuits and sweets. I put on weight and got glasses, which created more ammunition for the bullies. By grade 5, I was lost. I immersed myself in books to escape reality and had no friends . . . I was wary of anyone who showed me any kindness. Did they really want to be my friend, or did they just want something from me? My knowledge of darkness stems from this. Depression, social anxiety, low self-esteem and low self-worth.

A gradual depolarisation from this state throughout young adulthood and university informed her later reflections:

> I have experienced both darkness and light and I understand that you require both to truly understand the world and the people who inhabit it ... It is essential to understand that life has only begun to be lived when you have experienced both total darkness and total light.

This ability to appreciate and engage the difficult questions posed by tragedy and trauma requires rich and expressive symbols.

These symbols can take many different forms and I appreciate that this book itself relies on a particular symbolic set that will resonate with some and seem alien to others. BirD represents a few ways of expressing bi-relational

Bi-relational development in life narratives   157

developments amid the plethora of symbols that grow from the furthest flung seeds of life. In terms of rich symbols, Participant 115 reflects on her experience as an artist working with colour and shade: 'I am an artistic person and my life has centred on creative endeavours. Light and dark concepts are explored in my art where tone and shade of colour is concerned'. Similarly, Participant 165 writes:

> My first and most important ray of light came to me in high school. My best friend who saved me with her genuine care and compassion. We understood each other so perfectly because we both went through the same thing. We encouraged each other's creativity and passion for art. She saved me from the horrible darkness in my mind that was consuming me. My second light was going to university for the first time. Studying graphic design and photography, I was able to put some of the images moving through my head into physical view.

Participant 190 draws on natural imagery to help her express her changing relationships between light and darkness:

> My understanding of darkness and light has changed throughout my life. As a child I believed that light was far better than darkness, and if darkness could be avoided this was the best way. As I have grown and matured though, I have realised that they need to work together to bring out the best of its contrasting partner . . . a life experience that shaped my view of this was living in the country away from the depths of the city lights. Learning about things such as nocturnal animals and star constellations brought a new meaning of darkness as I grew up.

It is also important to note the formative influence of this natural environment in the realisation of new relationships between light and dark that permeate broader ways of knowing and being. Such images and symbolic sets provide a language for the conscious construction of meanings that accompany onto-epistemological developments.

A premise of BirD is that dyads provide a relatively ubiquitous structure for understanding onto-epistemological development and its expressions in diverse symbolic systems. The symbolic dyad (e.g. natural light/darkness) helps to mediate real-world experiences and more abstract reflections on meaning. The rest of Participant 190's response reveals this relationship clearly:

> I realised that everything that is there in the dark is there in the light and it makes no difference. I find that this can relate to people as they mature and go through difficult times. When a person is going through a 'dark' or down stage in life everything is bad in their eyes, what they don't realise is that everything they see when the light finally flicks on was always there

158 Illustrations

with them through the darkness of their lives. Though, many times this is not realised until they have experienced the concept of darkness and light in their lives.

Collectively, these extracts highlight the educative importance of rich symbols and metaphors for the expression and development of complex ways of knowing and being in relation to wicked problems. They also demonstrate the diversity of domains where deep onto-epistemological dispositions can develop. Onto-epistemological development is by no means the exclusive domain of the formally educated, and I suspect that formal education in some forms can be as blinding as enlightening and as hampering as sponsoring of development.

Sadness/happiness

The attainment of happiness is a wicked problem that has a profound effect on individual and societal trajectories of development. Arguably, the material pursuit of happiness, decoupled from its necessary entanglement with sadness, is counterproductive. The more we pursue exclusive happiness in a binary oppositional way, let alone happiness through exclusively material gains, the more elusive it can seem. In bi-relational terms, it is a case of *enantiodromia*, where the exclusive pursuit of happiness paradoxically intensifies the experience of sadness when it is never found, found and lost again or found only by those who fail to see how their happiness is built on the sadness of others.

Many participants identified a form of *entanglement* between sadness and happiness that reflects *post-dyadic* ways of knowing and being. For example, 'Without happiness what would be the point to life? But in saying that you cannot feel true happiness without some sort of sadness' (214); 'I can't see happiness without sadness or vice-versa because as a pair they [have the] same value, and balance each other out' (208); 'Sadness and happiness are directly related and can feed into each other, as well as being emotional opposites' (186).

For some participants, this realisation is deeply linked to formative experiences and affects new experiences and the way that they are perceived:

> I realised how important my pain was to my life experiences and how it has made me the person who I am today. When I was 10 months old, my dad decided [to] leave my mum and me, and I have not seen him since. As a child I always thought it was my fault and that he left because of me. Understandably I had very low self esteem, and I was always filled with sadness. I think overcoming this and becoming a stronger person has influenced this. I would not be able to be so confident and enjoy life as much if I hadn't experienced this.
>
> (203)

Bi-relational development in life narratives   159

As an onto-epistemological trajectory, it seems logical and chronological that this realisation would come later in life and after some deep struggles with sadness. Participant 186 recalls, 'As a child and as a young teenager, I think I believed that the only way a person could want to stay alive is if they were actually 100 percent happy'. Such thinking reflects a *pre-dyadic* or very early *pro-dyadic* way of knowing, where happiness is not yet held in relationship with sadness, even if in opposition or deliberate separation.

For Participant 186, the deeper post-dyadic co-ordination of the dyad came after several difficult years. However, the realisation of dyadic *entanglement* came out of the experience of *being* in both states of happiness and sadness:

> This overlapping of past and plausible future happiness sustained me emotionally while my current experiences were tedious and depressing. At the same time, I believe that the sadness I experienced as a young and as an older teenager enabled me to develop a deeper understanding of life, the world and some of the aspects within it.

Other participants emphasised the opposition and separation between happiness and sadness that is indicative of the *pro-dyadic* position:

> I believe happiness is more valuable than sadness. Why live a life being gloomy and miserable when you can be happy and enjoy life? Being happy reduces stress, makes you feel better, form a stronger relationship with your partner and family, become more successful in life and work and last of all you generate positivity towards others; a simple smile can brighten a stranger's day!
>
> (164)

Arguably, this separation tends to precede an appreciation of the entanglement that characterises the post-dyadic positions.

Participant 131 reflects a trajectory that moves from happiness to sadness to a post-dyadic understanding of their interdependence. 'As I have gotten older and grown as a person, I have gained an understanding and appreciation for sadness and its place in our lives'. Participant 186 reflects a similar position: 'I am also more equipped to deal with the everyday ups and downs of life from now on, as I have been through many of them before and have managed to come through the other side'. Here, we see the development of a new disposition towards the wicked problem of the attainment of happiness that has moved beyond an exclusively binary oppositional approach. The new onto-epistemological disposition adaptively equips one to *experience* the ups and downs of life and its wicked problems, rather than merely neutralise them.

The early neutralisation of opposites is different to a reconciliation of opposites in that it entails a sort of opposition to extremes – a truncation of the full spectrum that leaves an inert middle. Participant 131 reflects on the ontological effects of taking medication for depression in relation to this dyad:

> The medication certainly made me less sad, but it didn't make me happy either. I was stuck in the middle, feeling numb all the time. After nearly a year of feeling this way, I came to the realisation that I would rather deal with the bad days and also get to enjoy the good days, than feel nothing constantly.

Here, the life-giving and defining necessity of opposition or balanc*ing* as a verb is replaced with a neutral point of balance. This neutrality is like a nihilistic anaesthetic that can accompany the middle point of any region or the collapse of dyads. The dyadic relationship between happiness and sadness is collapsed into a meaningless single (middle) point, a no-thing that represents the middle point of the pro-dyadic region.

One of the great challenges of any transition or development is to adaptively accommodate, rather than maladaptively reject, previous positions. In plain terms, the transitional danger is well recognised as 'throwing the baby out with the bathwater'. Participant 211 provides a good example of the adaptive capacity to retain the pro-dyadic ability to separate and oppose dyadic constituents while still enabling development to more paradoxical and complementary dyadic relationships:

> It is my belief that the two parts of sadness and happiness as a pair can be seen in two contrasting ways. Firstly, they can be described as a dichotomy as they are two contradictory parts of a pair. This is illustrated by the fact that sadness can be defined as unhappiness. The emotions can be viewed as mutually exclusive because it is possible to argue that they cannot be felt at the same time. Secondly, in contrast it could be argued that certain situations, happiness and sadness can in fact be felt concurrently. It could also be claimed that an individual cannot give meaning to the emotions in this pair until both emotions have been experienced.

This two-way approach to relating dyads indicates a *post-dyadic development* that moves beyond mere separation and opposition without collapsing them. It is interesting that these two views are described as 'contrasting' without also being described as complementary or paradoxical in light of the view that they are both valued by the participant. Nonetheless, the opposition and reconciliation of dichotomous and codependent approaches to happiness and sadness is evident in this extract. In ontological terms, the participant later reflects on how this way of knowing about happiness and sadness helps her to appreciate the highs and lows of moving countries and living away from her extended family.

Interestingly, Participant 211 does not recall any preceding or different ways of knowing about sadness or happiness: 'I cannot remember a time in my life when I did not hold the above views of sadness and happiness'. Arguably, this ability to accommodate dichotomous and dialectical approaches comes from either overcoming great challenges in developing beyond a particular onto-epistemological position or is a quiet progression that seems quite natural in the absence of intense onto-epistemological challenges. Without significant onto-epistemological challenges (i.e. circumstances of great sadness or happiness) in the past, it may well seem as if one has always thought in a particular way. As the participant later reflects, this may simply be 'due to a lack of memory of the way in which the concepts became apparent to me as a child' (211).

Participant 114 offers more recall of childhood understandings that seem to reflect an onto-epistemological trajectory from the emergence of dyadic constituents in the pre-dyadic position to the experience of opposites in the pro-dyadic position, and then to the post-dyadic understanding of interconnectedness:

> My view of this has constantly changed. From when I was a child, the concept of sadness and happiness was unknown to me, all I knew was that I was feeling these things. One was good, and one was bad. Then I began to learn about how we become who we are today, and what defines us. That's how it's changed. Going through these constant ups and downs in life has helped to make me understand and build my own belief of sadness and happiness . . . Sadness and happiness belong hand in hand. Even though sadness is unpleasant for most people, and most people wish we could not feel sadness, how would the world be if we couldn't react to troublesome moments? And without them, who would we be?

This particular extract highlights the deep connection between epistemology (how we know in relation to dyads) and ontology (i.e. who we are and how we experience reality) that characterises BirD's approach to wicked problems.

Hope/despair

I have briefly included two responses to the dyad despair/hope, given its dyadic affinity with happiness/sadness. The despair/hope dyad helps to define a set of wicked problems that relate to our individual places in social contexts and our society's place in the cosmos writ large. Like sadness/happiness, the binary oppositional divorce between hope and despair seems to have unanticipated consequences. Participant 71 writes, 'I see despair and hope as the extremes on an emotional scale', and reflects on the dangers of separation at both polarities:

> I tend to think of despair as a self-pitying response to reality; a bad state in which to live your life. But I think too hope can be dangerous because of the great disappointment it can lead to. Hope is very positive in the moment but it can prevent you from being able to find happiness if things don't go according to plan.

162 Illustrations

Here, the participant sees 'reality' as a mediating influence on hope and despair and the danger of separating one or the other in a way that does not allow for a co-relationship between reality and the state of hope or despair.

It is worth noting that Participant 71 related their position to a formative experience with chronic fatigue:

> I think I have always held this view, but I possibly have more conviction in it than I used to. I have had Chronic Fatigue Syndrome for almost seven years and have desperately wished to get better all that time. But that hasn't happened. It can be more frightening to always be waiting and nothing ever coming, than to just face my illness head on. I don't think this is something that most of the people around me understand.

The last comment powerfully illustrates the onto-epistemological isolation that a person can feel when surrounded by well intentioned hope. As an example of enantiodromia, the pursuit of hope that has been separated from despair can paradoxically exacerbate feelings of despair. This recognition that there are dangers at both extremes provides some evidence of immirroration: the recognition of the entanglement between polarities (e.g. excessive hope can lead to despair).

Immirroration and enantiodromia can precede later post-dyadic developments towards the extinction of binary oppositions altogether. For example, Participant 110 reflects that 'the greatest hope will often cause the greatest despair'. This is a late post-dyadic reflection that can lead to an unsettling relativisation and then extinction of meaning. If 'despair can cause hope can cause despair', how does one orientate oneself to being and knowing anything at all? Participant 110 uses images of light, darkness, tunnels, circles and spirals in her response and writes:

> Despair and hope are antonyms of each other and seem to have a Yin/Yang manner to them. As in, there cannot be one without the other – there has to be a balance of some sorts. But these two aspects of life and the human psyche can just lead a person round, and round in never ending circles ... place/s where one would go to seek help and find hope, but are instead blamed, ridiculed, and demonised and are consequently sent in to a steep spiral of despair. What is a person to do, when the very systems that are in place to prevent and cure despair and in turn provide hope, instead exacerbate the problem? What happens to that individual, or that group? Should they still have hope?

The participant's response reflects one of BirD's most significant and elusive regions: collapse. More specifically, it represents a form of collapse found in the negation of opposites. This way of being and knowing can repulse people at pro-dyadic positions and confuse or irritate people at early post-dyadic positions.

A person in this position can appear subversive and cynical with a logic that seems like madness (i.e. A is B), attacking the 'very systems that are in place to prevent and cure despair'.

Needless to say, some individuals live out or cut short a lifetime in this position. However, BirD recognises the possibility of an onto-epistemological development beyond this position. The final extinction of the despair/hope dyad comes with the realisation that *nothing* cannot be defined despairingly (i.e. with something) and still be counted as nothing. When the last piece of despair is removed to the point where nothing remains, *everything* seems possible and even meaningful if one can find a possible reason for the existence of such a simultaneous separation and union of opposites. As I shall explore in more detail in later chapters, I think this is one of the most complex, powerful and pervasive dyadic dynamics affecting wicked socio-cultural, socio-ecological and socio-religious problems.

Change/stability

The Greek philosopher Heraclitus is famously quoted as saying 'No-one steps into the same river twice' as a way of emphasising change as the one constant in life. The relationship between change and stability applies in many contexts and to many wicked problems, but is often most deeply felt in relation to our own sense of self in relation to the world around us. Some seek stability to escape from the uncertainties and fragmentations of change. Some seek change to escape from the monotony of stability. For some participants, the relationship between stability and change was a significant abstraction that reflected their life experience. Most participants valued change over stability; some valued stability over change, though almost all acknowledged development towards an understanding of the codependency of the two.

Participant 132's reflection is representative of those who experienced change rather than sought it, and then, much later, learned to appreciate it:

> Change is a persistent teacher. Many changes are not welcome but they won't let us be. We rail against them, try to ignore them and hope the situation will just go away. However when we emerge from the other side, battered and bruised but alive and kicking we can find ourselves more resourceful and adaptable than we had ever felt the need to be before someone moved the goal posts.

Similarly, Participant 143's reflection is representative of those who see the interdependence of the two: 'change has created a new form of stability in my life. There is always change, whether it is small or big and you will always end up with stability'.

Participant 218 claims that 'everyone aims for stability in their lives' but acknowledges that changes are occasionally necessary to bring stability: 'I am changing something by choosing to study which will then produce stability for me in my later years of life'. For this participant, the necessity of change was heightened by her experience of family illness, which led her to see that 'life is too short, and to live for each moment and not to be scared of making choices that are life changing'. In onto-epistemological terms, fear can breed a certain type of 'reclusive stability' that far from being in balance with change exists in binary opposition to it as a principle of life. However, it can be the more ultimate threat of dying or decaying in stability that effects a polar inversion between stability and change for some.

For Participant 209, stability is of primary value, 'as it creates emotions of confidence, predictability and, self-reliance'. This participant grew up in a military family and experienced the instability of multiple postings. As a parent, she places a 'high value' on stability but is concerned that 'at times, this has affected the way my children respond to change'. We see in such descriptions that childhood experiences can be powerfully formative and defined by the emergence of one dyadic constituent over another. These early formative experiences form the basis for decisions in later years. A bad experience of change can negatively reinforce an approach to stability, and a negative experience of stability can negatively reinforce an approach to change. As Participant 209 appreciates in relation to the 'challenge she faces as a parent', the onto-epistemological challenge of development is to appreciate the range of possibilities in-between the dyadic poles and to choose between them carefully in context, rather than impose the pro-dyadic oppositions from our childhoods onto our own children.

For Participant 215, change is more valuable than stability, though the two are interrelated. This view reflects a gradual change of her previous position, which saw the benefits of stability:

> I didn't like change when I was growing up ... I was brought up by conservative parents who worked hard for what we had and looked after their children the best they could. It was a very stable environment for us to grow up in.

However, she later describes her parents as 'very set in their ways' and sees this as contributing to their later divorce. A tentative analysis would suggest that stability for stability's sake might eventually effect a form of enantiodromia where repression of change leads paradoxically to the revolutionary expression of change. For Participant 215, the perception of this dynamic in her parents' divorce seems to have contributed to the valuing of change.

Another participant reflected on the counterproductive efforts and mechanisms needed to protect stability from change. He suggests that some individuals over-stabilise by externalising problems or waiting for external solutions, rather than internalising the need for change. The same participant also recognised the difficulty of experiencing change and stability simultaneously: 'It seems that we want both, the benefits of the new plus the best of the status quo – these are often mutually exclusive'. In dyadic terms, there is a sort of necessary opposition between equally powerful constituents. This perspective reflects the dualism of BirD's point of collapse, where two equally skilful and powerful opponents wrestle for an eternity. It is post-dyadic in the sense that one reflects the image of the other and each can inter-penetrate the other's space for a time. In this interpretation, there is opposition, but it is not binary in the pro-dyadic sense, where one is ultimately valued over the other.

Feeling/thinking

Feeling/thinking is a common dyad invoked in many discourses, some of which pose them as opposites competing for primacy in human development. It is a dyad implicated in many wicked problems, which are exacerbated by attempts to singularly think or feel our way to solutions. For the thinkers, feelings are emphasised distractions that produce irrational decision-making and gross distortions of reality. Feelings are at best relegated to artistic and aesthetic domains. At worst, they are the remnant neurotransmitters of primitive limbic structures that an evolved species could do without. For the feelers, thinking is emphasised as the impotent dissection of a reality that one fails to live. The premise of BirD is that our onto-epistemological dispositions are powerfully revealed in our ways of relating the polarities of feeling and thinking.

Participant 191 describes thinking and feeling as being in a 'symbiotic relationship', whereas Participant 169 claims to 'value feeling over thinking' after formative experiences with 'thinking types' who used logic to use her. This onto-epistemological disposition towards feelings reveals a common dynamic in which negative formative experiences associated with one polarity make it difficult to appreciate the broader or even symbiotic value of that polarity.

Participant 158 reflects on the order of development, where feelings were seen to dominate actions during adolescence, while thinking began to influence feelings more in adulthood: 'In my teenage years most of my actions were governed by my feelings. And as I've grown into a mature adult, my thoughts have gradually had more influence over my feelings'. Her response suggests a post-dyadic appreciation of their interdependence and inter-penetration, 'Our thoughts influence our feelings and our feelings influence our thoughts'. Arguably, this trajectory has a neurobiological dimension in the mylinisation of axonal projections from the prefrontal cortex to the amygdala that allow conscious regulation and processing of instinctively generated emotions. The timing of the process is often cited in correlation with adolescent risk-taking and catastrophising.

Arguably, as Participant 169 suggests, 'both thinking and feeling are techniques of judgement'. In this sense, impulsive feelings are highly evolved but generalised judgements – the most adaptive responses based on past judgements. Fight or flight can be immediately adaptive responses to environmental hazards. However, experience (nurture) and mylinisation (nature) of adulthood enable a more contextualised application and regulation of these generalised and impulsive judgements such that thinking and feeling enter a more symbiotic cycle of co-development. This is an important onto-epistemological dynamic that may be applicable to many dyads. There is a sense in which feeling emerges before thinking in a pre-dyadic phase of development. However, this is only from an individual perspective. Across generations of individuals, feeling is thinking is feeling.

The understanding of causal interchange between dyadic constituents is a mark of late post-dyadic thought that often precedes the collapse of dyads altogether. Participant 108 observes feeling and thinking in a 'dynamic relationship' where the causal order can be flipped:

> It doesn't necessarily begin with thinking which creates feeling, sometimes the feeling is at the start . . . I haven't always held this view. I always thought feelings came from thought processes, which were unchangeable.

The understanding of dyadic interchangeability and bi-directional causality arguably suggests a deeper onto-epistemological development than exclusively oppositional or uni-directional approaches to causality. As Participant 108's later recollections reveal, these 'deeper' ways of knowing cannot be separated from depth of being through life experience. For this participant, deep anxieties (feelings) were locked in a cycle of thoughts about the inadequacy of her thinking:

> My thinking was happening in a vicious cycle bringing about feelings of inadequacies. After seeking professional help I have been able to start to change the way I think, which is changing the way I feel.

The reason I have combined ontology and epistemology in BirD is to recognise this bi-directional causality in our ways of knowing and being in relation to wicked problems.

Future/past

One of the most popular dyads chosen by participants was future/past. I suspect it is one of the most familiar and encompassing dyads. Again, it is a dyad that is implicated in many wicked problems. In relation to dyadic relationships most participants had a similar perspective to that of Participant 139: 'The terms future and past are mutually dependent terms that cannot exist without each other'. However, due to different life experiences, some participants valued both constituents equally, some past more than future and some future more than past. Most participants described a trajectory where the future dominated perception in the early years to be replaced by an appreciation for its dependence on the past in later years. Arguably, this is an obvious effect of the

Bi-relational development in life narratives   167

accumulation of life experience. For example, Participant 135 reflects, 'as I've grown older the more I've understood that it does play a role in my identity, and it is not something that can be repressed'. Participant 156 describes a similar perspective that reflects an early post-dyadic integration of past and future:

> Due to certain experiences that have happened recently I have now realised that the past is just as important as the future. I used to believe that once something had happened, it should be left in the past and forgotten about. I now realise that it is better to reflect on what has happened and learn from it in order to have a successful future.

Participant 62 suggests that the depolarisation from the future orientations of childhood is to do with the intrusion of reality making them seem unrealistic: 'During childhood you dream about [the] future and [are] very ambitious and have unreal expectations. Once you are an adult you see them [as] unreal'.

One participant, who claimed to have always held a view as to the interdependence of past and future, twice attributed this to her parents' explicit teaching: 'My view on past and present has held for as long as I can remember as it is an aspect that has been taught to me from a young age' (129). Arguably, early education on the interdependence of dyadic constituents can provide a scaffold for accommodating the inevitable short-term polarisations of experience that life presents. BirD provides a basis to inform deeper explorations as to what this sort of education could look like, if it is possible at all.

Mind/body

Mind/body is one of the most common dyads in popular culture. It is implicated in a range of wicked problems, including everyday concerns such as eating disorders and the effects of stress, technological concerns such as artificial intelligence, medical concerns about pharmacological and holistic treatments, and more philosophical speculations about neurobiological correlations with concepts like consciousness, freewill, spirit and soul. Most participants adopted a dualistic approach to the mind/body dyad and made the assumption that they there were separate but interacting parts, but not parts of the same thing. Participant 127 responded that the 'the mind is the brain' (127) but the brain (mind) and the body are separate but interacting. He described the equal value of parts in terms of brain death and disability, arguing that a brain-dead person could be physically functional but was like 'a hollow shell' – and that a physically disabled person could still have a fully functioning mind. It is worth noting that this participant reported that his experience with Klein Levine syndrome and narcolepsy had 'greatly influenced' these views.

Participant 67's response contained aspects of dyadic opposition, separation, interaction and unity in a single paragraph. She described mind as 'significantly more powerful than body' but also related mind and body as 'two parts in a person's life', 'all ONE', 'not separate', 'all one person's being' and able to be 'synced' and 'reunited'. The participant's response also highlights the ubiquitisation of dyads (the perception of affinity between different dyads) by suggesting that the synchronisation of mind and body would cause 'any other listed pairs that were options [to] come into conflict'. Finally, the same participant reflects on the contextual nature of the synchronisation of dyads as dependent on the distance of separation and the actual life-embedded imbalances that are to be addressed: 'a person would only see whichever [is] working stronger as being valuable'. Though somewhat fragmented, this response is arguably one of the more conceptually dense and sophisticated, revealing a level of dyadic reflexivity that many other responses lack. While the participant does not go into detail, it is worth noting her description of past 'trauma' as the catalyst for her conceptual understanding. The depth and intensity of formative life experiences seems to be linked to the conceptual sophistication of dyadic relationships. Again, this is why BirD attempts to recognise the entanglement of ontology and epistemology in the recognition of wicked problems.

Participant responses revealed multiple trajectories towards the post-dyadic convergence of mind and body. Some participants noted the emergence and continuance of early dispositions related to family interests. Participant 175 valued 'mind over body' and acknowledged that 'a sporting discourse has always been an important part in my life' such that 'mind over body is always something I tell myself when I feel it is too tough'. For others, a pre-dyadic and pro-dyadic identification with the value of the body gradually came into relationship with an appreciation of mind. For example, Participant 80 reflects:

> For many years I believed that physical health was achieved almost exclusively from sound nutrition and physical exercise . . . Over the years I have become increasingly aware of the extent to which our mental health affects our physical health.

I have previously rationalised the inclusion of individual narratives in a discussion of wicked problems that are usually understood in global terms on the basis that they are different levels of the same thing. Indicatively, Participant 80's individual response reflects the basis of wicked problems that I introduced more globally in Chapter 2's review of dyads in health and medicine.

While some participants emphasised the power of the mind in controlling the body, others maintained a degree of realistic separation. Participant 126 emphasised both the usefulness and limitations of coordinations between mind and body: 'If you have a broken leg, only time will heal it, no matter how many positive thoughts you have about it healing quicker' and linked this to her ongoing experience with chronic fatigue. The potential for onto–epistemological conflict between different dispositions is noteworthy here. Some therapies and healing systems can force a 'mind over body' approach onto patients whose needs are deeply physical. Other therapies and healing systems can force a 'body before mind' approach onto patients whose needs are better recognised as psychological. As with many onto-epistemological conflicts, they play out in individual, institutional and cultural interactions.

Pleasure/pain

Perhaps one of the dyads most central to onto-epistemological development and wicked problems is pleasure/pain. Its primacy is evident in the doctrines of suffering that define most major religions. For example, in Buddhism this focus is apparent in the four noble truths, and in Christianity suffering presents in Christ's crucifixion and in theological formulations concerning the 'the problem of evil'. In many individual participants' lives, the pre-dyadic emergence of a pleasure focus seems to be sustained through a period of pro-dyadic opposition (i.e. all suffering is to be opposed) and then later reconciled with pain and suffering in post-dyadic ways of knowing and being. Ways of knowing that move beyond exclusively oppositional or pro-dyadic relationships are characterised by metaphors of complementarity and interdependence. For example, participants describe the relationship between pleasure and pain in many ways such as 'like twins in our life' (51), 'not mutually exclusive' (99) and 'two sides of the same coin' (144).

The basic development towards such ways of knowing finds expression in participant narratives, too. For example, Participant 144 reflects on the development from pro-dyadic separations of pleasure and pain to post-dyadic entanglements:

> As children we usually associate pain as a form of wrong-doing and pleasure with a form of 'good' behaviour. As we grow older though, we start to understand the deeper relationship the two sensations have. As our life experiences develop from just getting in trouble as a child to falling in love or losing a loved one, so too does our view on the connection between pleasure and pain. As children we fear pain, and react positively to pleasure such as rewards. Into our adolescence we connect pain with our first break up or a sports injury and pleasure as getting that good grade in school you know will make your dad happy. Into our later years there is no greater pain than loss and no greater pleasure than new life. The relationship between pain and pleasure really depends on what stage of life you are in ...You cannot have one without the other; they coexist, and sometimes coincide.

Similarly, Participant 21 reflects the development from a pre-dyadic focus on pleasure to its more 'mature' or post-dyadic reconciliation with pain that reflects what she describes as 'the nature of the world':

> Probably as a little girl I would not call pain valuable but as you mature you do see things in a different way regarding certain things ...I think they are both valuable and true in their own way.

170   Illustrations

She reflects on the passing of a loved one as a formative experience that helped her to appreciate the relationship between how much pleasure and love a relationship brings and how much pain results when that relationship is lost.

Self/other

The reconciliation of self with other is one of human development's defining tasks and the basis of many wicked problems. Participant 48 demonstrates an ability to separate self from other while recognising the need for negotiation between the two. The move beyond opposition between self and other as a general disposition requires reciprocation or immirroration: seeing an image of self in the other by seeing other as self. For example, she reflects 'while I am "the self" to me, I am the "other" to someone else', and perceives her reception by the other as relational rather than absolute:

> They will find ways to connect with me and seek me out to agree with them, and if I do they will open the fold, and 'my self' will be a kindred spirit, permitted a sense of belonging to a subculture or group. If I differ from them, I may be pushed to the fringe or margin, only sought when there is no other option, or ignored. The list of things that may make me the 'other' to people may relate to my appearance (skinny cow! or fatty!), my way of thinking (she is so down to earth – or – I just can't understand a word she says).

The sense of opposition and separation between self and other is accommodated into a broader way of knowing and being that recognises the role of difference in the sustenance of self: 'I am often reliant on a number of people very different from myself to ensure that society is positively productive'.

This way of knowing about the other extends to this participant's ways of being a self in relation to social systems and structures created by the other. Specifically, she reflects on this dynamic in relation to her experience with apartheid while living in South Africa:

> [G]rowing up in apartheid South Africa, transitioning to post apartheid and diversity, and then emigrating to another nation have been very insightful and at the core of my journey and progress . . . I think I have lived in those 'interesting times' but am less defined by the hegemony in which I now find myself, and more acceptant of it as a form of social structure that allows for peaceful and productive co-existence. The other may have chosen this social shape, my 'self' chooses to navigate their life through it.
>
> (48)

While these reflections are post-dyadic in the sense that they move beyond pro-dyadic oppositions and separations towards negotiation and navigations,

Bi-relational development in life narratives   171

the response does not really collapse the self and the other (i.e. the other is part of my self is part of the other) or relate to this collapse as is characteristic of late post-dyadic ways of knowing and being.

Conservative/liberal

Participant 57 reconciles subjective and objective dimensions of onto-epistemological identity by recognising their subjective disposition (i.e. 'I've always been fairly conservative') *and* a more objective status (i.e. 'they enhance one another'):

> Neither is more valuable than the other, but they enhance one another. I've always been fairly conservative. I think my upbringing, environment and personality have all influenced my leaning in that direction.

This reflects a post-dyadic way of knowing and being that accommodates the pre-dyadic emergence of one polarity (i.e. conservative upbringing, environment and personality) but moves beyond the pro-dyadic opposition of this polarity with liberal ways of being that could otherwise occur by a simple generalisation of individual identity.

Reality/representation

Another post-dyadic representation is found in Participant 24's reflection on the relationship between reality and representation: 'It is this cycle of reality and representation that runs the world; to step outside the cycle and observe it is to know the world'. The response is post-dyadic in that it has moved beyond exclusively linear and oppositional metaphors. It reflects an attempt to 'step outside', which is a post-dyadic characteristic. However, the broader response does not recognise the difficulty or circularity of 'stepping outside', which characterises late post-dyadic ways of knowing before the total collapse or extinction of dyads.

Faith/doubt

Participant 55's response reflects a pro-dyadic separation of faith and doubt. It is framed within a particularly evangelical Christian discourse that, at least in some forms, is characterised by a similar tendency to treat doubt in opposition to, rather than in composition with, faith:

> Faith and doubt are inversely related as the opposite of faith is doubt and vice versa. Being that we were created by the all knowing God, it is imperative for Christians to exhibit the attitude of faith in any circumstance they find themselves as he always responds to those who trust him.

172   Illustrations

As I have written elsewhere, I suspect that the onto-epistemological positions of different individuals and subgroups within the 'same' belief systems can cause much dissonance, communicative confusion and even conflict. And, as I have also suggested previously, these epistemic differences may underlie many seemingly superficial differences between the contents (e.g. rituals, symbols, ethics, doctrines) of different cultures or traditions.

Freewill/determinism

Participant 128's response demonstrates a depolarising trajectory from an initial pre-dyadic disposition to assume freedom of choice. This is followed by a pro-dyadic polarisation to believe in the primacy of determinism in contrast to freewill: 'I have always thought that my decisions were free and my choices were up to me. Throughout my life experiences, I realised that my perspective was naïve ... Therefore, I value more determinism than free-will'. The disposition seems pro-dyadic as it is relatively uncomplicated by the interdependence of the concepts or degrees of difference. While determinism is given primacy, it is not yet inflated so as to be able to subsume a particular understanding of freewill; rather, it is inflated only in opposition to freewill. 'I believe that these two concepts contrast with each other ... I am convinced that my personal choices were determined by a chain of events'. The pendulum swing or binary inversion constitutes a development, but a relatively lateral one that substitutes one polarity for another without appreciation for the depth of their interpenetration.

Freedom/control

Many participants reflect on the development of their insights into the abstract balance and contextual choice between dyadic constituents. For example, Participant 174 reflects on the need to find 'perfect balance' between freedom and control. But this is a form of balance that appreciates the contextual value of the relative control of boarding school during her adolescence and the relative freedom and autonomy of her young adulthood. This seems to reflect a post-dyadic position. However, Participant 72 defines control in dominantly negative terms that seem linked to his experience of 'very controlling parents'. This participant has experienced *repulsion* from one dyadic position (i.e. control), which has led to affinity with freedom as a form of rebellion against this control. The participant's suspicion of parental control extends to the dominant religion of the country he left. These are relatively intense formative experiences that can lead to revolutionary changes (i.e. rebellion). Arguably, the participant's current onto-epistemological position reflects a pro-dyadic opposition between freedom and control.

Dyads reflecting wicked problems in formal education

I have selected the last set of dyadic responses to reflect on the formative role of purposeful education in onto-epistemological development. While an educator by profession, I am critical of the common divorce of educational theories, systems and techniques from the contexts in which they are applied and from which they are derived. I do not think that education has any intrinsic or a priori value and believe it is often 'over-rated' in formal settings. However, this is a counterbalancing statement based on my personal and professional experiences as a schoolteacher and academic. This said, I think that formal education can have a powerfully facilitating role in onto-epistemological development. It does not do this by providing exclusively didactic and transmissive approaches to onto-epistemological theory, but by using such theory to construct experiences that facilitate the internalisation and critique of theory in light of learners' real-world concerns and interests. This co-developmental approach is implicit in many of the narratives previously analysed in relation to the teaching/learning dyad. While I elaborate and illustrate this co-developmental approach in Part III, the following dyads serve to illustrate the formative influence of formal education on onto-epistemological trajectories.

Teaching/learning

Onto-epistemological relationships between teaching and learning manifest in the ways individuals and societies educate their children. How best to educate our children and ourselves is a wicked problem that demands close attention to the relationship between teaching and learning. Different dyadic relationships manifest themselves in diverse pedagogical approaches and radically different models of schooling. There are deep dyadic affinities between teaching/learning and other dyads like behaviourism/constructivism, transmission/discovery, traditional/progressive, competitive/collaborative and teacher-centred/student-centred approaches to schooling.

Participant 221 notes a complex interaction between teaching and learning that reflects a post-dyadic way of knowing in relation to the dyad (i.e. teaching/learning). She also differentiates this way of knowing from a more *pre-dyadic* approach that somewhat naïvely assumes that teaching 'automatically' includes learning, without looking for evidence of learning:

> My perception of how people discuss the pair is that often people talk about teaching and seem to assume that teaching automatically includes learning. It is as if the very act of teaching means that learning must also occur. My view is that teaching occurs when learning occurs. If a teacher presents material to a student but no learning has occurred then I believe that no teaching has occurred either. This does not mean that the teacher is a poor practitioner but rather represents my view of the complex nature of both learning and teaching.

(221)

While the participant notes the interaction between teaching and learning, his definition of teaching and a teacher reflects a traditional conceptualisation, such

174   Illustrations

that 'learning can occur without teaching'. Thus, *learning* is expanded beyond formal education but *teaching* is limited to formal education. This expansion of learning reflects an epistemological development beyond the separate and limiting definitions that tend to dominate the *pro-dyadic* position.

The participant goes on to recall experiences teaching maths and science that *negatively reinforced* the interaction between teaching and learning:

> Over time, I could see a pattern that for many students the issue was not the science or mathematics but rather their own confidence in their ability to learn science or mathematics. I would often hear comments like 'the teacher rushed through the material', 'I don't know why we did this', 'we moved onto a new topic and I still do not understand X'. It seems to me that the students often did not understand why they had to do particular steps and the students seemed either embarrassed to ask their teacher or saw asking the teacher as a waste of time.
>
> (221)

These formative experiences seem to have affected the participant's *ontological disposition* as it relates to their ways of teaching and being with learners in a school context:

> To me, teaching requires the practitioner to consider the material from the viewpoint of the learner. What does the learner know and understand? What are their prior experiences? What prior experiences will they need in order to achieve learning? How can I make the material interesting and relevant? What will the learner consider success to be? How high can I make the expectations of this success?
>
> (221)

The comment shows a complex *post-dyadic* interaction between teaching and learning. It reflects a different way of being a teacher that moves beyond *naïve pro-dyadic separations* of teaching and learning where a teacher assumes that a student has been taught without looking at what they have learned.

Participant 220 reflects similarly complex post-dyadic interaction between teaching and learning in her observation that 'a valuable teacher will also see themselves as a perpetual learner'. This participant's formative experiences reveal how personal struggles as a learner can eventually produce deep understanding of the nature of teaching. These struggles were reflected in her own learning, and her daughter's learning experiences at school:

> Throughout school I experienced learning difficulties. Before long I had developed strategies to ensure my learning difficulties were not discovered by my peers or teachers ... my daughter has twice made it to the end of

Bi-relational development in life narratives   175

the school year without the teacher realising she had not learnt a thing. During parent teacher interviews I would often wonder if they would be able to pick her out of a line up.

(220)

Rather than retreating from teaching altogether after a negative experience as a learner, some learners use their negative experiences to become better teachers who recognise the deep interdependence of teaching and learning:

I can't help but wonder how many students don't get the learning environment that they need, to learn. As a teacher I will endeavour to recognise these students as a true measure of my teaching ability.

(220)

In dyadic terms, this represents a transition from pro-dyadic separations of teaching and learning to post-dyadic reconciliations through a process of negatively induced development. In plain language, this dynamic is similar to 'turning a negative into a positive'. Someone who remained in a pro-dyadic disposition would tend to live with a sustained and undifferentiated opposition to teaching, conceptually defining the whole only in light of negative experiences with some of its parts.

Literal/symbolic

Perhaps one of the most onto-epistemologically ubiquitous dyads concerns literal and symbolic meanings. The developmental awareness of the degrees of difference and relationality of literal and symbolic meanings can be revolutionary. The awareness can be the difference between enslavement to language and mastery of language. Arguably, there is a developmental trajectory from literal understanding to symbolic understanding and then to a relational balancing of both. As Participant 125 reflects, 'At a young age we understand literal statements as they are delivered as rules, facts and information. Our understanding of symbolism develops with age and experience'. The challenge is to be dexterous in our perceptions and descriptions of the literal and symbolic function of language in context.

Participant 125's response is illustrative of the role of education in the development of dexterity on the spectrum between literal and symbol functions. She first defines the pair:

The pair (symbolic/literal) relates to the relationship between semantics and the symbols, shapes, colours, images, language, etc., used to convey or represent concepts/ideas. Meaning can be symbolic (with layers of meaning) or the literal representation of a concept (fixed interpretation).

176 Illustrations

The broader response then illustrates a post-dyadic appreciation for the codependency and value of the concepts. For example, she reflects:

> These terms are connected as they encourage individuals to think in both concrete and abstract terms. As a society we require meaning that is both symbolic and literal, in order to make sense of the world. Literal thinking is very focused and constrained, whereas symbolic thinking encourages depth and the formation of new connections.
>
> (125)

What role can formal education play in the facilitation of such ways of knowing?

Participant 125 credits her own experiences with formal education as facilitating this understanding:

> Education is the main setting in which individuals are taught and encouraged to think in layers of meaning and how they are shaped by context. English is the main subject that I personally believe helped shape my understanding of what is literal and symbolic, through critically analysing film adaptations of novels and reading literature written by Shakespeare. In my opinion, semantics and context are the two concepts introduced in high school that really influence our perception of things literal and symbolic.

The challenge for educators is to facilitate these ways of knowing in concert with the contexts and interests that shape the life worlds of individual students. As every teacher and generations of students know well, Shakespeare can be nauseatingly boring or intensely stimulating depending on the relational fit between teacher and student. Reflecting on my own experience as a highschool English teacher, I can appreciate the importance that dexterity between literal and symbolic functions has in the success or failure of formal education.

Art/science

Two of the more poignant examples of the formative role of formal education in onto-epistemological development were provided by Participants 122 and 187 in response to the art/science dyad. Art/science is a secondary dyad, but I included it on the list of dyads because of its ubiquity and relation to important primary dyads that may not otherwise be recognised. For example, Participant 122 identifies art/science as having affinities with creativity/ criticality, imagination/logic and innovation/replication:

> For me the terms art and science have always been about an individual's way of thinking. I define art as having the creative ability to imagine, express and innovate something original, without limitations and various constraints of particular protocols. Whereas science is the opposite to art, in

having to think critically and decisively to hypothesise, experiment and solve ideas to either prove or disprove a thesis, with the awareness of limitations to scientific theories and concepts. In other words, from my understanding science requires a logical mindset and art requires an imaginative mindset.

This definition characterises a pro-dyadic position that focuses on the separation of dyadic constituents (i.e. art and science). Participant 187's response provides interesting points of similarity and difference:

[Science] embodies a linear thinking process in which set algorithms are followed to meet a pre-determined answer. However it is also exploration, new ways of working, new ways of thinking, inventing and creating. Is it that far removed from the world of art? I do not believe that one of these pairs is of more value than the other. I also do not believe that they are polar opposites but rather two ways of thinking or being that continuously overlap.

The first response is relatively dichotomising and the second is relatively dialectical.

These dyadic relationships play out in broad socio-political discussions concerning the respective value of the arts and the sciences. In school contexts, as in broader social contexts, these tensions are often reflected in debates over funding allocations, space and scheduling allocation, curriculum focus and teacher status. The ways in which art and science are conceptualised in school contexts can have a powerful affect on students' onto-epistemological dispositions. As many educators appreciate, though others exacerbate the 'problem', the legacy of this effect in post-school society is grossly underestimated. The danger is that art and science are used to exclusively 'silo' different ways of knowing and thinking about the world. Here, artists are 'imaginative, creative and innovative' and scientists are 'logical, critical and replicative'. Such siloing serves a purpose and can facilitate the development of such ways of knowing. However, if there are no spaces for the exchange and even inversion of these characterisations (i.e. science as inextricably linked to imaginative, creative and innovative ways of knowing and art as inextricably linked to critical, logical and replicative ways of knowing) then we arrest the development of both and the whole of which they are parts.

Participant 122 illustrates the arresting influence of a type of formal schooling that silos art and science into the mutually exclusive ways of knowing that typify pro-dyadic positions:

If there is one significant lesson I take from my schooling (which has been a part of my life thus far, as I only finished high school last year) it is the different cognitive abilities needed to excel in the study areas, art and science ... It was due to the schooling system I went through that shaped my view of art and science, as having opposing ways of thinking.

The participant recalls an early love for art in primary school, which was later challenged in secondary school when 'plummeting grades' led him to believe that he 'did not have the cognitive ability to do well in art'. The participant recalls:

> I was in the school art room with my best friend who was talented in the subject. I was observing one of the many art pieces that decorated the room and could not figure out what the painting portrayed (to me it looked like a bunch of colours and shapes). 'It's called abstract,' my best friend told me. It really struck me how different minds could perceive paintings. Where on one hand, my straightforward, logical thinking could not make any meaning from looking at the painting, and on the other hand my best friend's imaginative mind could think of many intricate messages from looking at it.
>
> (122)

In this instance, the educative message received from the participant's formal schooling was that science and art require opposing ways of thinking and are separate subjects. There is truth in this message, but it is insufficient truth because it does not reveal exposure to the dialectical space between art and science that sees them grow as much together as apart. The participant's experience suggests the possibility of a formal education that has neglected the creative, divergent, imaginative and innovative ways of knowing that generate hypotheses for testing, problems for solving and applications for using – or it neglects the logical, critical, replicative and analytical ways of knowing that inform the selection of artistic media, mastery of technique, crystallisation of ideas and development of process that contribute to even the most abstract forms of art. Both represent pro-dyadic separations of knowledge.

Participant 187's experience reveals a similar experience of separation and opposition:

> In my own schooling I tended to see the world through artistic glasses. I identified with creative subjects such as Art, Drama, English and Music but struggled in subjects requiring rote learning of facts, figures and scientific process. During school however, it was drilled into us that we were not academically intelligent if we did not excel in these areas. In light of this I held a belief that I was not as intelligent as other students.

For Participant 206, the experience of separation during schooling was challenged by the experience of travel abroad:

> The life experience that changed my view was when I travelled through Italy and I saw that art and science could share some aspects. Some of the most famous art work such as sculptures, would have needed the artist to have some scientific knowledge of the material the sculpture was made of,

Bi-relational development in life narratives   179

also some of the inventions certain artists made started as sketches and were inspired by artistic ideas, but could only be realised with the correlation of science.

There is probably an age-related tendency to separate subjects or to accept separations literally before integrating them that exacerbates the divisions of formal education. However, the challenge for teachers, school administrators, teacher educators and the public they represent is to know when to draw lines that separate art and science, when to draw circles that encompass them and when to erase the lines and circles altogether. Each form has its function, and an education – if not a society – is impoverished by a disposition towards drawing lines between art and science, or circles around art and science, and the ways of knowing they relate to.

Theory/practice

Perhaps one of the most cited dyads in commentaries on formal education is theory/practice. Unfortunately, a common perception of formal education is that it is 'just theory' and that true learning occurs from practice in 'real life'. Arguably, there is a reciprocal error of judgement in reversing the primacy of one constituent over another (e.g. practice over theory). In dyadic terms, this polar inversion drives a way of knowing and being from one pole to another as an act of repulsion that results in little net growth. The binary opposition between theory and practice remains, even if the tables have been turned. One polarisation perpetuates another, such that the 'theorisation' of formal education as separate from practice will eventually inspire a counter-revolution that threatens its value.

Participant 63 reflects on development in relation to this dyad: 'Both have their vital place. This is a view I have come to over my lifetime. I once would have harboured suspicion about the real usefulness of "theory"'. However, a gradual appreciation for the role of theory now sees them 'urging closed-minded "practice" persons to step back for a moment and bone up on the relevant theory about the issue they are trying to resolve'. The response demonstrates the onto-epistemological ability to counterbalance in context (e.g. emphasising theory vs. practice) while acknowledging the ultimately 'vital place' of both constituents (e.g. theory and practice).

The role of individual educators in facilitating such developments is evident in Participant 141's response to the theory/practice dyad in the context of physical education. He reflects: 'my view on the relationship between theory and practice is that one cannot be achieved without the other ... it is clear that neither one is more valuable than the other, and in fact one cannot work without the other'. On the development of this position, he writes:

I have not always had this view on theory and practice. As a young boy in primary school, I loved to play sport so at that age, I believed that practice was more important than theory because I was able to go outside and have fun with practice rather than sitting in a classroom doing "boring" theory. As I got older and started high school, I started to learn that theory had some vital information that I could use to improve my practice and since then, I have always believed that they are both equally important.

Regarding the formative experiences that contributed to this development, he reflects:

In grade 11 however, I was blessed to be a part of one of the best classes in my schooling life. This was my senior PE class who had a teacher with a strong emphasis on theory and practice being linked. I believe that it was this teacher who has influenced me to believe that both theory and practice are equal in regards to importance.

(141)

Again, the formative influence of formal education and individual teachers cannot be underestimated in the facilitation of onto-epistemological development.

Separate/connected

This educative influence is reflected in many responses that reveal the capacity for any subject to contribute to the development of ways of knowing and being that exist 'outside' the subject. For example, Participant 107 reflects on the separate/connected dyad:

I learnt the relationship between the pairs, separate and connected at an early age when I learnt the basics of foundation mathematics. For instance, a whole can also be made up of separate parts called fractions. The same principle applies for people living in communities. We are all dependent on nature to survive. Water, food and oxygen are essential to our survival on earth. People are all separate individuals living as part of a global community that connects us together as one race of people on the planet.

The perennial challenge for formal education is to find ways of separating that paradoxically facilitate deeper connections and ways of connecting that inform our separations.

Mercy/justice

Formal education has a powerful influence on the ethical dimension of our onto-epistemological dispositions – and this dimension has one of the most ubiquitous and long-lasting influences on the ways societies direct and reflect educational systems. Perhaps one of the most powerful, perennial and socially definitive dyads is mercy/justice. How we relate the parts of this pair can profoundly affect the lives we live and the societies we live in.

Participant 119's reflections on this relationship are illustrative of a broader social struggle to reconcile mercy and justice. While positioning mercy and justice as 'equally' valuable, she perceives her schooling as having a disposition to mercy, which is perplexing in relation to situations she has faced that seem to warrant justice:

> The reason this pair spoke to me, as a relevant one in my life is my upbringing in a school founded by The Sisters of Mercy. A very significant part of both my primary and secondary schooling has been to determine the differences between mercy and justice. Although in my Catholic faith I understand the importance of showing mercy no matter the circumstance, I am also somewhat perplexed in how I respond to providing justice for people affected by the actions of another who maybe does not 'deserve' any mercy. In my education and family upbringing I have always understood the importance of acceptance, forgiveness and unconditional love. I believe these are the branches of mercy. I have been confronted in situations in my life where although I love a person and want to show mercy, I have strongly believed they need to pay for their actions so others feel justice has been served. This is a complex situation for me as I am faced with the beliefs of my religion and my own individual thoughts on a situation.

The potential for disparity between individual and institutional ontologies and epistemologies in a shared space is a significant dynamic. In Participant 119's case, as in most cases, this disparity is resolvable through some minor compartmentalisation (e.g. my religion and myself), or is minor enough not to need a definitive resolution. However, while onto-epistemological conflict is inevitable, in many cases the conflict can result in a mutually destructive divorce of identities that sustains binary oppositional ways of knowing and being. In the context of religion, this is the antagonistic relationship between the apostate and the former fold – or in an educational context, this can be the antagonism between an individual who 'hated school' and the broader institutions of formal education.

I have little hope for the formative value of exclusively formal, theoretical and compartmentalising types of education and teaching. However, in concert and communication with informal, practical and holistic types of education and learning I believe that formal education can help to facilitate onto-epistemological development beyond merely oppositional ways of knowing and being. These ways of knowing and being are essential to the (re)solution of wicked problems.

Conclusion

My intention in this chapter has been to illustrate some of the archetypal regions, positions and dynamics that define BirD while again highlighting the ubiquity of dyadic structures. Perhaps my most common focus has been on the differences between pro-dyadic dispositions that lend themselves to binary oppositions, and post-dyadic dispositions that balance, correlate or even begin to collapse dyadic oppositions. However, I have tried to illustrate the polarisations, depolarisations, inversions, repulsions, attractions, reinforcements and revolutions that accompany these broader developments. I have tried, too, to wed the ontological and the epistemological in the contexts of wicked problems to highlight the importance of the life worlds from which they emerge.

There are similarities and differences in the myriad experiences of participants' lives. I have drawn attention to the unlikely places and spaces in which onto-epistemological developments occur. The participants have generously and honestly shared their experiences with death, abuse, guilt, love, hope and joy in reflecting on their ways of knowing and being in the world. They have reflected on their family, friends, jobs, hobbies and education in connecting their ways of being to their ways of knowing. Collectively, these brief narratives reveal the necessity of structure and content for the description of human ways of knowing and being. Ultimately, it does not make sense to ascribe primacy to one or the other in descriptions of human identity because, to borrow my participants' analogies, 'they are twins', 'both sides of the same coin' and 'ends of the same spectrum'.

It may appear that I have selectively emphasised post-dyadic positions, and this is true to the extent that the usable narratives are somewhat self-selecting. Some participants see no connection to write about or, more commonly, see a very literal separation and describe the terms accordingly. Obviously, their accompanying experiences and understandings of relationality are particularly sparse. For some, this may represent a late pre-dyadic inability to see a connection or an early pro-dyadic tendency to recognise a dyad but not appreciate why it is a dyad, even as opposition. For others, the available dyads may simply lack significance in the moment or altogether.

The final groups of dyadic narratives were selected to foreground the role of formal education in arresting or sponsoring onto-epistemological development. I hope to explore this role more deeply in Part III and introduce some practical ways for facilitating deep onto-epistemological exchanges in formal educational contexts towards the (re)solution of wicked problems.

Finally, while many of the extracts are sufficient to reveal developmental trajectories, I have deliberately framed them as mere illustrations and snapshots of BirD's core positions and dynamics. Bi-relational dynamics offer an important insight into our ways of knowing and being in relation to the wicked problems that define our everyday lives. The two detailed interview transcripts analysed in Part III may serve to demonstrate more deeply how these positions and dynamics can come together to constitute onto-epistemological developments in individual lives. However, the next three chapters shift the focus from individual lives to some of the wicked socio-cultural, socio-ecological and socio-religious problems that define the twenty-first century. Needless to say, in light of BirD's developmental premise, this is a shift of focus within the same picture.

Chapter 7

Bi-relational development and wicked socio-cultural problems

Some of the most defining dyads of the modern milieu have arisen to describe the cultural challenges, opportunities and wicked problems of globalisation. Thus, we find 'oppositions' such as local/global, unity/diversity, relative/absolute, inclusion/exclusion and public/private working their way into debates around immigration, multiculturalism and trans-national corporatisation. Of course, these dyads are as old as cultural conquests to expand and occupy the known world; however, modern technologies have exponentially increased the speed and scope of cultural exchange. Rapid advances in geographical mobility (e.g. physical transportation and migration) and technological mobility (e.g. web communications) are enabling unprecedented levels of cultural exchange. As Ross-Holst (2004) suggests:

> Virtually all aspects of modern life – our jobs, our culture, our relationships with one another – are being transformed by the profound forces of globalization. Goods and people flow across national borders, and data and information flash around the world, at an ever-accelerating rate.
>
> (2004, p. ix)

While some voices champion the cause of globalisation with its promises of highly coordinated and efficient organisation, equitable wealth distribution and a common humanity, others caution against the potential loss of rich cultural diversity and the evolutionary dangers of homogenising the future. Either way, the new cultural interfaces produce apparent oppositions that must be fought and won or reconceptualised and reconciled. Accordingly, there is a sense of educative urgency by commentators who recognise the epistemic dimension of such exchanges. Hofer (2008) urges accordingly: 'Increased migration, globalisation, and multiple examples of intercultural conflict on this planet call for attention ... to awareness of differing epistemic assumptions, views of authority, and understandings of what it means to know' (p. 18). This chapter offers a broad bi-relational sketch of the opposites that characterise our wicked socio-cultural problems and the ways they may be reconciled.

Understandably, dyads such as global/local, traditional/progressive, monocultural/multicultural, egalitarian/hierarchical and individual/collective have arisen in socio-cultural discourses to capture the range of positions, tensions and trade-offs that can describe and inform our directions in the seemingly unstoppable 'progress' to a more global culture. Bi-relational development recognises that the ways we conceptualise these dyads (e.g. as oppositions, complements or negations) can exacerbate or facilitate the (re)solution of the wicked problems they relate to and describe. For example, our dyadic conceptualisations of unity and diversity can manifest in our approaches to a range of socio-culturally complex issues, including immigration, multiculturalism and bi-cultural schooling.

Globalisation and cultural interfaces

As defined in the précis to the 'Understanding Globalization' issue of the *International Journal of Social Inquiry* (2008): 'Globalization is a highly challenged and debated concept. The term is often loosely used to refer to the increasing depth and speed of interconnectivity of people, finances, ideas, culture, power and technology across the world' (n.p.). 'Interconnectivity' is perhaps the most benign description of cultural exchanges that can also be neglectfully indifferent and sometimes brutally oppositional. Exchange is not always of pleasantries. As Geert Hofstede, one of the foremost researchers on cultural difference, is often quoted, 'Culture is more often a source of conflict than of synergy. Cultural differences are a nuisance at best and often a disaster'. Globalisation presents a range of wicked socio-cultural problems mostly concerned with the distribution of power at cultural interfaces. Cultural power distributions obviously affect basic needs such as food and water supply, shelter and physical security, but they also powerfully affect psychosocial needs such as identity, social belonging, existential purpose and efficacy. Thus, there is much at stake concerning how the 'opposites' revealed at cultural interfaces are recognised and reconciled.

Conceptualisations of cultural exchanges are present in everything from immigration policies to school curricula. Hierarchical, 'might is right' approaches to the meeting of cultures ignore the relative interdependence of cultures, but exclusively horizontal, 'we are one' approaches can ignore the relative independence of cultures. Arguably, a bi-relational approach can help to make sense of and coordinate the 'number of contesting perspectives' in a way that retains the integrity of different perspectives while perhaps reducing the level of contestation due to epistemologically limited conceptualisations of difference. Accordingly, the purpose of this chapter is to apply a bi-relational approach to help identify and engage some of the defining socio-cultural challenges of the twenty-first century.

My premise is that the decisive choices our generations must make, given our capacity for rapid globalisation, are best informed with (a) an appreciation for the spectrum of possibilities available to us and (b) an understanding of the bi-relational dynamics that our choices will bring into play. For example, it may be that the more we pursue a global identity, the less the sacrifice of our local identities will seem worth it (global > local). Inversely, perhaps the more we retreat from cultural interfaces and exchanges, the more stagnant, maladaptive and impotent our local cultures will be (global < local). BirD represents the ways in which these bi-relational problems are likely to be engaged by different individuals and groups. Exclusively pro-dyadic separations and polarisations (i.e. local vs. global, monocultural vs. multicultural) are likely to exacerbate socio-cultural conflicts and limit our choices. Similarly, early and undifferentiated post-dyadic appeals to balance and unity may be destructive (i.e. local and global, monocultural and multicultural). Whereas trans-positional ways of approaching problems at the cultural interface may help us to make more specific contextual choices from a broader range of possibilities. Arguably, such ways of knowing and being can help us to live within tensions rather than exacerbating conflicts by trying to choose ultimately between opposites or negate them altogether. Accordingly, trans-positional ways of knowing can never choose the ultimate primacy of egalitarian, global, collective, united and progressive approaches to culture over hierarchical, local, individual, diverse and traditional approaches to culture or vice-versa.

Socio-cultural dyads and wicked problems

Many scholars invoke dyads and dyadic relationships to frame what could be conceptualised as wicked socio-cultural problems. Perhaps the most ubiquitous dyad used to explore wicked problems in socio-cultural contexts is individual/collective (e.g. Green *et al.*, 2005; Schwartz, 1990; Montuori and Purser, 2000; Munro, 1985), though there are many more. Hofstede (1980, 1991; Hofstede *et al.*, 2010) identifies dyads including individual/collective, masculine/feminine, hierarchical/egalitarian, certainty/uncertainty, long term/ short term and indulgence/restraint. Nakata (2007) and Battiste (2002) explore the Western/Indigenous dyad. Latour (2002) frames the clash of civilisations using dyads such as unity/diversity, subjective/objective, village/cosmos, myth/reality, peace/conflict and appearance/reality. Stiglitz (2002) discusses globalisation in light of dyads such as markets/government and capitalist/ socialist. Bidois (2013) illustrates the structural relationships of Pakeha/Maori and self/other. Gans (2012) invokes the culture/structure dyad. Nisbett *et al.* (2001) use the holistic/analytic dyad to point out cultural differences, while Chick (2012) refers to tight/loose cultures. Some of these dyads are secondary dyads (e.g. Western/Indigenous) but they are useful starting points for the identification of the primary dyads (e.g. analytic/synthetic) that inform them. My purpose is to illustrate the usefulness of dyadic structures for identifying wicked socio-cultural problems and the relevance of dyadic relationships and dynamics in (re)solving these wicked problems.

Dyadic structures and relationships are particularly useful in the conceptualisation of cultural differences. Hofstede's seminal work *Culture's Consequences*

(1980) elaborated his *cultural dimensions theory* on the basis of a survey of over 100,000 participants from nearly 50 different countries. He found that cultures differ in relation to power distance expectations (e.g. hierarchical/egalitarian), social value (e.g. individual/collective), uncertainty avoidance (e.g. risk/security) and gender value (e.g. masculine/feminine). In later studies (1991; Hofstede *et al.*, 2010), Hofstede added cultural differences related to time horizon (e.g. long-term/short-term) and impulse control (e.g. indulgence/restraint). Examples of his findings include a relatively high power distance for Latin, Asian and Arab countries, and a relatively low power distance for northern European countries such as the UK and Sweden. Nordic countries have a relatively low masculinity index compared to Japan, which has a relatively high masculinity index.

Hofstede's dyadic structures are useful for the identification of relative cultural differences, but they are implicitly instructive concerning dyadic relationships as they prompt us to consider the compatibilities, tensions and trade-offs between different cultures. Pro-dyadic dispositions tend to assume the a priori primacy of one or the other dyadic constituent such that, for example, a global culture should be more masculine, egalitarian, long-term-focused and restrained. Early post-dyadic dispositions tend to assume the a posteriori value of all positions such that there is no danger in bringing highly masculine, hierarchical, restrained and risk-averse cultures into direct contact with highly feminine, egalitarian, indulgent and uncertain cultures. Trans-positional dispositions appreciate the possible range and value of positions while considering the dynamics of cultural exchanges between different positions (e.g. the possibility for Hofstede's 'disastrous consequences'). In summary, Hofstede's implicit and explicit dyadic structures provide a useful example of dyadic representations relevant to wicked socio-cultural problems.

One of the interesting developments of Hofstede's cultural dimensions theory concerns attempts to move 'beyond' the individual/collective dyad. While Hofstede's use is already post-dyadic in that it assumes the relative value of constituents and the degrees of separation between them, others (e.g., Lim *et al.*, 2011; Montuori and Purser, 2000; Munro, 1985) have also recognised the entanglement and interdependence of the constituents (i.e. individual and collective). For example, Lim *et al.* invoke *holism* as a way of engaging the dialectical relationship between individualist and collectivist cultures:

> As a subsystem of a larger system is a system in itself, a sub-whole of a bigger whole is a whole in itself. As the digestive system of the human body system is a system, a member of a family him/herself is a whole, too. Different from collectivism, which discourages members from pursuing their personal interests, holism encourages and even pushes members to seek their individual goals as complete wholes. Collectivism presumes contradiction between 'We' (group) and 'I' (individual) and thus, for the

best interest of the group, members need to put their personal issues aside. Holism, however, operates on the assumption that 'We' and 'I' are, or rather must be, compatible.

(2011, p. 25)

In BirD, this represents a trans-positional way of understanding cultural differences. The integrity of 'I' (individualism) and 'we' (collectivism) is maintained only in relation to each other. Thus, contextual choices (i.e. whether to act collectively or individualistically) are made with the understanding of their interdependence.

Government/market (social/economic) in globalisation

One of the most significant dyads that appears in the literature on globalisation conceptualises a relationship between market and government influences. These terms (i.e. market/government) are affiliated with capitalist, economic, and conservative influences on the one hand and socialist, environmental and liberal influences on the other. BirD's main thesis is that coordination of these opposing influences represents a wicked problem that needs re(solving), and that an exclusively binary oppositional approach to this resolution will simply exacerbate conflict.

Stiglitz's (2002) *Globalization and its Discontents* offers one illustration of this dyad that reflects BirD's trans-positional appreciation of the entanglement of apparent opposites. As the US President's economic adviser and chief economist of the World Bank, Stiglitz first recognises the wicked nature of the problem of globalisation: 'The world is a complicated place. Each group in society focuses on a part of the reality that affects it the most' (p. 217). He then recognises the danger of attempts to solve the wicked problem by defeating one or the other dyadic constituent such that a country allows government or market to dominate at all costs. Stiglitz's logic reflects a deep reconciliation of opposites. He begins with an acknowledgement of the good intentions of each side but shows how a binary oppositional approach turns these good intentions into devastating consequences:

> They genuinely believe the agenda that they are pursuing is in the *general interest*. In spite of evidence to the contrary, many trade and finance ministers, and even some political leaders, believe that everyone will eventually benefit from trade and capital market liberalization. Many believe this so strongly that they support forcing countries to accept these 'reforms'.
>
> (2002, p. 216)

When these intentions are pursued at the expense of government they represent a form of 'market fundamentalism' (p. 219), which, Stiglitz claims, 'flies in the face both of economics, which emphasizes the importance of trade-offs, and of ordinary common sense' (p. 221). Here, the use of 'trade-offs' shows an appreciation of the entanglement of opposites that characterises wicked problems. The recognition of opposites is the first step in identifying trade-offs; however, it is a step too often prematurely truncated by the application of a binary oppositional approach. As Stiglitz writes, 'those responsible for managing globalization, while praising these positive benefits, all too often have shown an insufficient appreciation of this adverse side, the threat to cultural identity and values' (p. 247). Arguably, the movement from binary oppositions (i.e. government < market) to relational and contextual coordinations (i.e. government <=> market) represents a bi-relational development worth educating for. Stiglitz's (2002) expression of a dyadic relationship reflects the language of coordination and reconciliation:

> I have advocated a balanced view of the role of government, one which recognizes both the limitations and failures of markets *and* government, but which sees the two as working together, in partnership, with the precise nature of that partnership differing among countries, depending on their stages of both political and economic development.
>
> (2002, p. 220)

Here, we see the equality of 'partnership' that dominates early post-dyadic developments identified in BirD but also the further development of contextually 'dependent' and 'precise' choices that characterises trans-positional approaches to wicked problems. The global market's 'threat to cultural identity and values, which Stiglitz claims needs be taken more seriously by the market mindset, is often most recognised in socio-cultural literature exploring the legacies of colonialism.

Colonialism's wicked legacy

Many post-colonial commentators suggest that the plight of Indigenous peoples in the modern world is the legacy of Western binary oppositional ways of knowing and being that enabled the subjugation of cultures that were *different*, on the grounds that they were somehow *deficient*. Conceptualised in terms of BirD, this is a pro-dyadic form of cultural dominance, where the relative and relational values of one culture (e.g. individualism) are totalised and imposed on another (e.g. collectivist) as if they are somehow separate and superior in opposition. The danger for post-colonial movements is that in attempting to correct the errors of the past, they merely invert the error in the future. Thus, the values of the dominant culture become subordinated and the values of the subordinate culture become dominant. I suspect that this dynamic forestalls much development in intercultural relations and reconciliations as pro-dyadic proponents on both 'sides' fear subordination, while failing to comprehend the possibility of *sublation* (i.e. Hegel's mutually beneficial transformation) in a bi-relational sense.

The problems of globalisation are most pronounced when it brings cultures with different values and opposing dispositions into the same space. Pro-dyadic or binary oppositional dispositions can be found in different cultures representing relatively different polarities (e.g. individual > collective, collective > individual), such that it can be very difficult for any individual or group to navigate between cultures. For example, Australian academic Martin Nakata writes of his personal and professional attempts to coordinate 'Western and Indigenous interpretations of experience':

> It is often the case that Indigenous learners are unsettled and confined by both the accepted or orthodox Western and Indigenous interpretations of their experience ... But they cannot easily forge a deeper understanding without being called into alignment with one position or the other ... Thus it is difficult to work through the inherent tensions of the everyday world.
>
> (2007, p. 222)

There are many lists of these 'inherent tensions' in both scholarly cross-cultural studies and educational materials. Consider some general examples from the Aboriginal Human Resource Council (2007), where the first constituent is said to represent traditional cultural values and the second is said to represent Western cultural values:

- Community foremost value/Individual foremost value
- Future is dominant/Present is dominant
- Mythical understanding/Scientific understanding of world
- Patient attainment of goals/Aggressive attainment of goals
- Communal ownership/Individual ownership for hard work
- Aging as wisdom/Aging as decay and loss
- Faith in harmony with nature/Faith in scientific control of nature
- Extended family/Nuclear family

Such tensions form the basis of many wicked problems, not the least of which affect Indigenous educational outcomes in credential-inflating Western societies. Such problems include Indigenous student participation in science curricula (mythical/scientific), study and family-life commitments (extended/nuclear family) and performance in individual merit-based school systems (individual/collective).

Consider, the study of chronemics, which highlights the meeting of cultural subjectivities concerning time that can challenge the pro-dyadic separation of past and future. Chronemics is the study of cultural and personal differences in the experience and perception of time. For example, some modern Western cultures tend to be monochromic, with highly regulated and compartmentalised perceptions of time and divisions of past and future, whereas many traditional cultures tend to be polychromic, with more fluid perceptions of time and overlapping states of past and future. As Cohen writes:

> Traditional societies have all the time in the world. The arbitrary divisions of the clock face have little saliency in cultures grounded in the cycle of the seasons, the invariant pattern of rural life, community life, and the calendar of religious festivities.
>
> (1997, p. 34)

Understandably, the coordination of culturally and personally different onto-epistemological dispositions towards the past/future dyad can be a difficult task. Time is one of numerous dyads that can help us to recognise wicked cultural problems and reconcile cultural differences. Arguably, there are affinities between these dyads. For example, are dominant Western ontologies that segment and objectively measure time it in order to control it related to dominant Western epistemologies of thinking as reductive and analytical? Here, it is noteworthy that Junker (2003, p. 18) records a dyadic collapse of feeling and thinking (i.e. feeling *is* thinking) as a linguistic feature of the East Cree culture of North America. It is not unreasonable to suggest that there are culturally diverse ways of relating feeling and thinking and onto-epistemologies of time. BirD offers a way of locating and coordinating such diversity in ways that can move beyond mere binary oppositions.

As many scholars of Indigenous studies note, these differences have been dominantly related in binary oppositional forms by Western colonial powers, with Western ways of knowing and being privileged over Indigenous ways of knowing and being. Battiste laments:

> For as long as Europeans have sought to colonize Indigenous peoples, Indigenous knowledge has been understood as being in binary opposition to 'scientific,' 'western,' 'Eurocentric,' or 'modern' knowledge. Eurocentric thinkers dismissed indigenous knowledge in the same way they dismissed any socio-political cultural life they did not understand.
>
> (2002, p. 5)

My claim is that approaches like BirD can assist in the working through of globalisation's 'inherent tensions' and facilitate development beyond binary oppositions. It does this by recognising the dispositions that exacerbate opposites and bring them into conflict *and* the dispositions that bring 'opposites' into more dialectical or interdependent relationships.

Trans-positional ways of knowing and being begin to move beyond pro-dyadic separations and simplistic binary oppositions to recognise not just the shades of grey or colours on the spectra between polarities, but also the (re) constitutions of cultural identities in dynamic interplay. For example, Milian (2013) claims to explore 'how multidirectional processes of Latinness travel, break, and alter at the level of meaning, geographies, and peoples' (p. 1). She rejects the simplistic separations of the black/white binary and observes that 'Blacks, browns, and dark browns enter, move into, and interfere with one another's color lines, and not unidirectionally either, horizontally, vertically as well' (p. 5). Elsewhere, she utilises strong post-dyadic metaphors like 'multiple interwoven discourses' and 'panethnic space' to describe the dynamic interaction between ethnicities that would otherwise be grouped into two mutually exclusive categories:

> Latinities offer a conceptual shift in multiple interwoven discourses and how these shape the subject. They are a 're-articulatable' panethnic space where the subject is constituted in relation to blackness, brownness, and dark brownness but also in terms of language, ethnicity, nation, class, gender, sexuality, and race, depending on the context.
>
> (2013, p. 15)

Such conceptualisations of culture and ethnicity highlight the complexity and polysemy of cultural interfaces and the opportunities that a reconciliation of opposites can bring. While culturally dichotomising typologies (e.g. Western vs. traditional perspectives) are useful in understanding the 'inherent tensions' and inevitable conflicts at globalisation's cultural interface, Milian's approach reminds us of the creativity of cultural exchanges that generate the infinite richness of a spectrum between them and possibilities beyond them.

Of course, bringing cultures and their differences into relationship does not mean ignoring their abstract tensions; rather, it means making decisions in context without an a priori commitment to one or other set of values (e.g. individual or collective). For example, Gladwell (2008) provides a lucid example of cultural tensions and contextual choices in his discussion of the cultural origins of plane crashes from Korean airlines. Air-crash investigator David Greenberg found that culturally and linguistically embedded nuances were leading to increased incidences of Korean airlines plane crashes. The Korean cultural characteristic of silent deference to authority (i.e. a relatively high power-distance index on Hofstede's scale) was overriding on occasions where it would have been appropriate for a co-pilot or traffic controller to challenge or question a pilot's decision. Thus, air crashes were more frequent for Korean airlines. Gladwell comments:

> Greenberg wanted to give his pilots an alternate identity. Their problem was that they were trapped in roles dictated by the heavy weight of their country's cultural legacy. They needed an opportunity to step outside those roles when they sat in the cockpit ... he knew that cultural legacies matter – that they are powerful and pervasive and that they persist, long after their original usefulness has passed. But he didn't assume that legacies are indelible part of who we are.
>
> (2008, p. 219)

A trans-positional approach is that the cultural characteristics must be valued or devalued in context. Greenberg did not devalue the socially deferential and hierarchical character of Korean culture a priori. He devalued it in a particular context. As Gladwell notes, this is a difficult project that can offend cultural sensitivities:

> But first we have to be frank about a subject that we would all too often ignore ... Why are we so squeamish? Why is the fact that each of us comes from a culture with its own distinctive mix of strengths and weaknesses, tendencies and predispositions, so difficult to acknowledge? Who we are cannot be separated from where we're from – and when we ignore that fact, planes crash.
>
> (2008, p. 221)

Cultural sensitivities are arbitrarily ignored and opposed in binary oppositional approaches to wicked problems, but they are too often left unchallenged in early post-dyadic or multiplistic approaches that attempt to value all positions all the time. Cultural exchange in everyday life is often messy and often involves conflict. However, my claim is that trans-positional dispositions to the wicked problems of globalisation can help us transform conflicts that have the capacity to destroy everything into more purposeful, relational and contextual choices between values and ideas.

Beyond the socio-cultural

While 'socio-cultural' is a classification of convenience, the cultural differences I have briefly touched on have a deep connection to the wicked socio-ecological and socio-religious problems discussed in the following chapters. In many and profound ways, our cultural identities are an expression of our onto-epistemological approaches to nature and the cosmos writ large. The dyads that are commonly used to define cultures (e.g. collective/individual) and discuss cultural expansions (e.g. local/global) are deeply connected to the dyads we use to define our relationship with nature (e.g. nature/culture) and existence (e.g. subjective/objective, universal/relative). For example, linear cosmologies may be manifest in a more immediate sense and control of time than cyclical or infinite cosmologies, which may cede control of time to seasons to be lived within, rather than resisted or circumvented. Bi-relational development represents the interconnectivity of different dyads and thus warrants some reflection on the relationship between globalisation (e.g. local/global) and cosmic purpose (i.e. despair/hope) at the cultural interface.

French philosopher Bruno Latour offers one of the most provocative and lucid commentaries on culture and cosmology in the twenty-first century. Latour (2002) invokes a series of dyads (e.g. subjective/objective, hope/despair, unity/diversity) to describe the wicked problems of globalisation in his reflection on the post-September 11 'clash of civilisations' and 'war of worlds'. His analysis reveals a deep appreciation for the entanglement of dyadic constituents that is needed to grapple with and (re)solve the wicked problems of globalisation. He begins by addressing modernity's hope in privileging the *objective* to emphasise unity:

> There always remained the hope that differences of opinion, even violent conflicts, could be eased or alleviated if one only focused a little more on this unifying and pacifying nature and a little less on the divergent, contradictory and subjective representations humans had of it.
>
> (2002, p. 8)

However, the convergence and collapse of dyads always reveals a darker side or a trade-off to the previously championed position. Latour identifies such a trade-off, for modernity ends violent conflicts by making them 'devoid of meaning': 'Objective facts in their harsh reality could neither be smelled, nor tasted, nor could they provide any truly human signification. The modernists themselves were fully aware of this, and even acknowledged it with a sort of sado-masochistic joy' (p. 11). Thus, the apparent failure of modernity, with its emphasis on unity, gave rise to a new emphasis on diversity, as if somehow the failure of one (i.e. unity) can be remedied by its substitution with an opposite (i.e. diversity).

The entanglement of opposites and the strange inversions that occur when one is pursued at the expense of the other characterise Latour's analysis of cultural relativism as a rejection of modernism. Here, the void of meaning is only exacerbated by appeals to cultural relativism that emphasise diversity:

> 'You possess meaning, perhaps,' they were told, 'but you no longer have reality, or else you have it merely in the symbolic, subjective, collective, ideological form of mere representations of a world that escapes you, although *we are able to grasp it objectively*. And don't be mistaken, you have the right to cherish your culture, but all others likewise have this same right, and all cultures are valued by us equally.' In this combination of respect and complete indifference, we may recognize the hypocritical condescension of cultural relativism.
>
> (2002, p. 10)

Latour's reflections highlight the indissoluble tensions and irreducible paradoxes between the constituents of dyads such as unity/diversity, subjective/objective, village/cosmos, myth/reality and peace/conflict. His questions and descriptions cast doubt on the optimism of modernist objectivism and postmodernist relativism as separate ends in and of themselves. Bi-relational development offers a generic representation of this movement from either/or to both/and/either/or ways of being and knowing in relation to cultural diversity. It suggests that approaches to the wicked problems of globalisation must begin with an appreciation for the entanglement and interdependence of opposites like unity/diversity and subjective/objective.

On education

It is worth emphasising the role for education in relation to the socio-cultural problems of globalisation. Arguably, there is a facilitative role for educators in the development of the trans-positional logics needed to appreciate these entanglements in real-world contexts. While I explore more general approaches to bi-relational development in education in Part III, I note here some of the existing calls for formal education to engage more deeply and directly with the onto-epistemological challenges that globalisation presents. For example, Ross-Holst argues in *Globalization: Culture and Education in the New Millennium:*

> What educators and policy makers need are models that can more readily take advantage of the challenges and opportunities offered by globalization ... These new opportunities suggest to me that educators are more relevant to the project of education that ever before: to scaffold new ways of knowing; to help children and youth reach higher levels of understanding, and to guide students to achieving greater appreciation for cultural complexity and diversity.
>
> (2004, p. x)

BirD offers one such model, one such approach to scaffold new 'ways of knowing' that can facilitate encounters with wicked problems.

Gardner (2004) suggests of the problems posed by globalisation: 'Perhaps it will be necessary to institute psychological studies of the synthesizing or inter-disciplinary mind' (p. 250). BirD offers a relatively accessible and contextualisable structure (i.e. dyads) for such studies. More specifically, in light of Gardner's principles for such studies, bi-relational development offers a potential scaffold to facilitate:

1 Understanding of the global system
2 Capacity to think analytically and creatively within disciplines
3 Ability to tackle problems and issues that do not respect disciplinary boundaries
4 Knowledge of and ability to interact civilly and productively with individuals from quite different cultural backgrounds – both within one's own society and across the planet
5 Knowledge of and respect for one's own cultural tradition(s)
6 Fostering of hybrid or blended identities
7 Fostering of tolerance.

(2004, pp. 253–5)

Dyadic structures can help us to appreciate the breadth of an evolving spectrum of possibilities. A repertoire of dyadic relationships can help us to move beyond exclusively binary oppositional approaches to the wicked socio-cultural problems posed by globalisation by filling in the gaps and noting the degrees of difference and entanglement between them.

In summary, I have attempted to provide a bi-relational analysis of some of the oppositions that most characterise wicked socio-cultural problems. The same bi-relational principles that apply to the wicked socio-cultural problems of globalisation apply to the wicked socio-ecological problems that confront a species with the increasing capacity to influence its *natural* environment. Globalisation forces us to reconcile our individual and collective cultural goals; however, it also forces us to reconcile our species' goals with the collective goals of all life as we discover more and more deeply how entangled these can be.

References

Aboriginal Human Resource Council. (2007). Differences between traditional Aboriginal cultures and mainstream Western culture. Retrieved from http://www.aboriginalhr.ca/en/resources/getstarted/cultures

Battiste, M. (2002). *Indigenous knowledge and pedagogy in first nations education: A literature review with recommendations.* National Working Group in Education, Canada.

Bidois, V. (2013). A genealogy of cultural politics, identity and resistance: Reframing the Maori-Pakeha binary. *AlterNative: An International Journal of Indigenous Peoples,* 9(2), 142–54.

Chick, G. (2012). Culture, leisure, and creativity: Anthropological and comparative perspectives. *Creativity and Leisure: An Intercultural and Cross-disciplinary Journal (CLICJ),* 1(2). doi: 10.3850/S2010469320120000184.

Cohen, R. (1997). *Negotiating across cultures.* Washington, DC: US Institute of Peace Press.

Gans, H. J. (2012). Against culture versus structure. *Identities,* 19(2), 125–34. doi: 10.1080/1070289X.2012.672850.

Gardner, H. (2004). How education changes: Considerations of history, science, and values. In M. M. Suarez-Orozco and D. B. Qin-Hillard (Eds.), *Globalization: Culture and education in the new millennium* (pp. 235–58). Berkeley: University of California Press.

Gladwell, M. (2008). *Outliers: The story of success.* New York: Little, Brown.

Green, E. G. T., Deschamps, J. C., and Páez, D. (2005). Variation of individualism and collectivism within and between 20 countries: A typological analysis. *Journal of Cross-Cultural Psychology,* 36(3), 321–39. doi: 10.1177/0022022104273654.

Hofer, B. K. (2008). Personal epistemology and culture. In M. S. Khine (Ed.), *Knowing, knowledge and beliefs* (pp. 3–22). Amsterdam: Springer.

Hofstede, G. (1980). *Culture's consequences.* Beverly Hills, CA: Sage.

Hofstede, G. (1991). Management in a multicultural society. *Malaysian Management Review,* 25(1), 3–12.

Hofstede, G., Hofstede, G. J., and Minkov, M. (2010). *Cultures and organizations: Software of the mind* (3rd ed.). New York: McGraw-Hill.

International Journal of Social Inquiry. (2008). Retrieved from http://globalartmuseum.de/site/newsitem/82

Junker, M. O. (2003). A native American view of the mind as seen in the lexicon of cognition in East Cree. *Cognitive Linguistics,* 14(2–3), 167–94. doi: 10.1515/cogl.2003.007.

Latour, B. (2002). *The war of the worlds: What about peace?* (C. Bigg, Trans., J. Tresch, Ed.). Chicago, IL: Prickly Paradigm Press.

Lim, T.-S., Kim, S.-Y., and Kim, J. (2011). Holism: A missing link in individualism-collectivism research. *Journal of Intercultural Communication Research*, 40(1), 21–38. doi: 10.1080/17475759.2011.558317.

Milian, C. (2013). *Latining America: Black-brown passages and the coloring of Latino/a studies*. Athens, GA: University of Georgia Press.

Montuori, A., and Purser, R. (2000). *In search of creativity: Beyond individualism and collectivism*. Paper presented at the Western Academy of Management Conference, Hawaii. http://ciis.bigmindcatalyst.com/cgi/bmcDL.pl/montuori/insearchofcreativity.pdf.

Munro, D. J. (1985). *Individualism and holism: Studies in Confucian and Taoist values*. Ann Arbor, MI: The University of Michigan Center for Chinese Studies.

Nakata, M. (2007). *Disciplining the savages; Savaging the disciplines*. Canberra: Aboriginal Studies Press.

Nisbett, R. E., Peng, K., Choi, I., and Norenzayan, A. (2001). Culture and systems of thought: Holistic versus analytic cognition. *Psychological Review*, 108(2), 291–310. doi: 10.1037/0033-295X.108.2.291.

Ross-Holst, C. (2004). Preface. In M. M. Suarez-Orozco and D. B. Qin-Hillard (Eds.), *Globalization: Culture and education in the new millennium* (pp. ix–xi). Berkeley: University of California Press.

Schwartz, S. H. (1990). Individualism-collectivism: Critique and proposed refinements. *Journal of Cross-Cultural Psychology*, 21(2), 139–57. doi: 10.1177/0022022190212001.

Stiglitz, J. (2002). *Globalization and its discontents*. New York: W. W. Norton & Company.

Chapter 8

Bi-relational development and wicked socio-ecological problems

Some of the most salient wicked problems of the modern era concern the relationship between human activity (i.e. culture) and the natural environment (i.e. nature). The purpose of this chapter is to engage the bi-relational dimension of socio-ecological challenges in relation to dyads such as nature/culture and technological/ecological. Furthermore, it explores how onto-epistemological developments can reconcile opposites that otherwise exacerbate problems in exclusively binary oppositional forms. These dyadic relationships are all the more salient for the modern spectre of anthropogenic climate change, which demands a deep and decisive dialogue about the relationship between humans and the environment. However, I also hope to show that to understand the level of polarisation this dialogue is prone to, we must appreciate and explore the dyadic affinities between cultural (e.g. local/global), ecological (e.g. nature/culture) and cosmological (e.g. matter/spirit) concerns.

Arguably, the modern socio-ecological dialogue began with post-WWII realisations of the global scale of human activity in relation to pollution and nuclear capabilities. Glass's early lament reflects one of the more apocalyptic expressions of this realisation:

> There is indeed grave peril that ere long – maybe in the 21st century – the human species will have destroyed its entire delicate biosphere, if not by nuclear war, then by callous treatment of the environment, treatment destroying the balance of nature. We must learn very soon to endure the thought that human survival itself, not merely our pleasure or comfort, depends on the preservation of our relations with the rest of life on earth and on the maintenance of the great cycles of nature that restore the life-giving properties of our environment.
>
> (1977, p. 278)

There are implicit traces of dyadic relationships (e.g. 'balance of nature', 'great cycles of nature') in this conceptualisation of environmental problems. My claim is that these relationships need to be made much more explicit to illuminate deep structures that create and reflect the ways we interact within our environments.

Unsurprisingly, the nature/culture dyad is one of the most prevalent and salient in environmental discourses. The related problems (e.g. anthropogenic climate change, environmental pollution, species extinction, population pressure) all have a wicked dimension. They are multidisciplinary: that is, they involve the social sciences (e.g. psychology and sociology), natural sciences (e.g. earth sciences and biological sciences) and formal sciences (e.g. logic and mathematics). They involve complex subject-to-subject (i.e. social) relationships. And they invoke deeply divisive answers to existential questions (e.g. what is the purpose of life?) that are embedded in individual and collective identities. My claim is that solutions and (re)solutions to wicked socio-ecological problems require attention to dyadic relationships as represented in BirD. For example, too often the socio-ecological dialogue is derailed when formal problems that may be best handled by the harder sciences are conflated with dialectical ones that may be best handled by the social sciences and humanities. Understandably, natural scientists working with relatively well defined object-to-object problems can be frustrated when their findings are relativised or trivialised in subject-to-subject exchanges such as socio-political commentaries on climate change. However, social scientists working with relatively relational and contextual subject-to-subject systems can be equally frustrated when these systems are objectified or trivialised, as if what 'ought' be done with 'the facts' from natural sciences is simple and self-evident. For example, while Green commends natural scientists for 'commonsensically' raising the moral issue of environmental responsibility, he observes:

> although scientists have tended to assume the existence of a responsibility to the future, they have not commonly discussed the more abstract question of the nature of that responsibility, its basis, extent, or limits ... [such as] why should there be obligations to nonexistent persons?

> (1977, p. 260)

BirD provides a framework for appreciating the logics (i.e. ways of knowing) required to identify and engage wicked socio-ecological problems. It offers a way to relationally locate the different ways of knowing and being that inevitably contribute to socio-ecological (re)solutions.

Common dyads

While there are few explicit analyses of the role of dyadic structures in socio-ecological dialogues, there are many attempts to frame socio-ecological problems in terms of specific dyads. I have already introduced nature/culture as one of the most encompassing and ubiquitous dyads. It is worth identifying this and other dyads in relevant literature to see how the study of dyadic relationships represented in BirD is useful for representing wicked socio-ecological problems.

There are many dichotomous classification systems for understanding different approaches to socio-ecological problems that relate to the nature/culture dyad. Table 8.1 offers some examples of dyads found in socio-ecological literature. For example, Naess (1973) and Eckersley (1992) classify deep and shallow ecologies that reflect individualistically driven concerns and interdependently driven concerns respectively. Gagnon Thompson and Barton (1994) identify an anthropocentric/ecocentric dyad that reflects an extrinsic value of nature for human benefit and an intrinsic value for nature regardless of human benefit respectively. O'Riordan (1989) and Eckersley (1992) identify technocentric and ecocentric ways of knowing and being that emphasise open and closed approaches to resources and systems respectively. Gough *et al.* (2000) argue for a balance of anthropocentrism and ecocentrism that is more able to account for cultural pluralism than O'Riordan's approach. Collectively, these dyads support BirD's premise that dyadic structures pervade most domains of knowledge and that dyads are deeply interconnected and useful in delineating and (re)solving wicked socio-ecological problems.

BirD provides a framework for exploring the developments and dynamics between dyadic constituents. It offers a language that helps to name and recognise divisions and oppositions that can otherwise tacitly stall the description and (re)solution of wicked socio-ecological problems. It provides a diverse set of dyadic relationships with which to move beyond exclusively binary oppositional approaches to dyads such as nature/culture.

Illustrations of dyadic relationships

Where there are dyads there are dyadic relationships. Most commentators explore these dyads as historically situated binary oppositions where the constituents have been held as mutually exclusive and one valued more than the other. In much environmental discourse, the root problem is often seen as human culture dominating and subduing nature (i.e. culture > nature), ultimately and ironically at its own expense. A common call is for a reintegration and reunification of the dyadic constituents. The negation, union, equation, synthesis and expansion of dyads described in BirD's trans-positions represents a repertoire of relationships that can help to coordinate opposites that otherwise find expression only in conflict. Consider Moscovici's reconciliation of the nature/culture dyad:

> Man's single-handed conflict with nature should be seen as a confrontation *within* nature ... The notion that nature is inhuman and man unnatural is totally invalid. No part of man is or ever was closer than any other to an ever-changing nature.
>
> (1976, Introduction)

Table 8.1 Examples of dyads in socio-ecological literature

Wilshire (1989)	**Tàbara and Pahl-Wostl (2007)**	**Walker (2000)**
Nature/Culture	Nature/Culture	Subjective/Objective
Emotion/Reason	Ecological/Social	Intuitive/Rational
Ignorance/ Knowledge		Aesthetic/Scientific
Occult/ Accepted Wisdom	**Keulartz (2005)**	Opaque/Transparent
Lower/Higher	Nature/Culture	Specific/Totalised
Negative/Positive	Practice/Theory	Homogenous/ Heterogeneous
Body/Mind	Value/Fact	
Earth/Spirit	Body/Mind	**Hamilton (2002)**
Chaos/Order		Intuitive/Rational
Spontaneity/ Control	**Yanarella and Levine (1992)**	
Subjective/Objective	Country/City	**O'Riordan (1989)**
Metaphorical/Literal	Nature/Humankind	**Eckersley (1992)**
Process/Goals	Environment/ Economy	Ecocentrism/ Technocentrism
Darkness/Light		
Myth/Logic		**Birkeland (2002)**
Public/Private	**Luke (2001)**	Nature/Culture
Attached/Detached	Nature/Society	Organic/Technical
Holy/Secular	Environment/ Organism	Abstract/Concrete
Cyclic/Linear		Public/Private
Fluctuations/ Permanence		Body/Mind
Dependent/ Independent	**Lehman (2002)**	Cyclic/Linear
Social/Individual	Nature/Humanity	Lateral/Hierarchical
Integrated/Isolated	Society/ Corporations	Organic/Mechanistic
Soft/Hard		Qualitative/Quantitative
Whole/Dualistic		Subjective/Objective
		Holistic/Reductionist

Moscovici absorbs the opposition within a union that problematises the idea of a war against nature. To reiterate here, the general premise of BirD is that onto-epistemological development reveals the relational and interdependent nature of knowledge, while paradoxically locating the need to reflect on and choose the best (re)solution possible in a given context. BirD represents such developments as transitions from pro-dyadic binary oppositional ways of knowing and being to post-dyadic integrations and convergences. The following paragraphs offer contextualised illustrations of pro-dyadic and post-dyadic relationships in socio-ecological discourse.

Sheets-Johnstone identifies human/non-human as an 'ordering principle of western human thought' and claims:

> Subsumed in its compass are the oppositions nature/culture, mind/body, thinking/doing, reason/emotion. Subsumed are also subsidiary oppositions,

ones having to do generally with behaviour or behavioural capability ascriptions such as learned/instinctual, future planning/ immediate action, articulate/mute, and the like.

(1996, p. 57)

She attacks an exclusively pro-dyadic way of knowing and being that 'is evidentially unsound, myopically self-serving, and for philosophers especially, a particularly thin justification for cherishing their [i.e. human] species' (p. 57). This post-dyadic dissolution of binary oppositions such as nature vs. nurture is seen by many natural scientists as imperative inasmuch as binary separations create distances and vacuums where empathy and interconnectivity perish.

Wicked socio-ecological problems need (re)solving because they are constantly (re)created through different forms of imbalance between natural and cultural forces. Human cultures grow from natural conditions but over time they become so divorced from these conditions, unresponsive to changes in these conditions and dominating of these conditions that they may inadvertently threaten their own survival. Arguably, anthropogenic climate change is a global manifestation of this problem where cultural technologies, beliefs and attitudes that perhaps originated as useful protections from naturally 'threatening' weather or conditions become so divorced from these origins that they are blind to the negative effects of a binary inversion of power. As Simmel argues:

We speak of culture whenever life produces certain forms in which it expresses and realizes itself ... But although these forms arise out of the life process, because of their unique constellation they do not share the restless rhythm of life, its ascent and descent, its constant renewal, its incessant divisions and reunifications ... They acquire fixed identities, a logic and lawfulness of their own; this new rigidity inevitably places them at a distance from the spiritual dynamic which created them and which makes them independent.

(quoted in Gare 1996, pp. 375–93)

This explanation fits neatly into BirD's framework, whereby pre-dyadic constituents emerge or 'arise out of the life process' only to reify and 'acquire fixed identities' that evolve into separations and oppositions in the forgetting of origins. The recognition of the dynamism and iterativity of many socio-ecological problems is a significant development in being able to effectively and adaptively (re)solve such problems.

Dyads can help to clarify some of the most manifestly complex tensions. For example, O'Riordan (1989) uses the terms *technocentrism* and *ecocentrism* to talk about the two major orientations of current environmental politics. Eckersley uses similar dyads and argues:

The essential difference between these two approaches is that the former values the non–human world for its instrumental or use value to humankind (whether material or otherwise) whereas the latter also values the non-human world for its own sake, irrespective of its value to humans.

(1990, p. 70)

Eckersley's definition suggests some incommensurability between the views that underlies the difficulty of reconciling them in practice. In some anthropocentric cosmologies, humans are the teleological pinnacle of evolution or creation. In some of these narratives, the very existence of the human species is the story of survival *against* a nature that is 'red in tooth and claw'. The fear for proponents of this cosmology is that environmentalism is essentially anti-human, willing to sacrifice humanity for the sake of 'lesser' species and inanimate objects. For example, Guha (1997), while offering a dialectical approach to the nature/culture dyad, argues in *The Authoritarian Biologist and the Arrogance of Anti-humanism* that modern conservationism is 'an ecologically updated version of the White Man's Burden' (p. 15). Writing of the conflict between tribal survival and tiger preservation in the North Indian context, Guha's thesis is that modern Western conservationism has occasionally inverted rather than reconciled the nature/culture opposition:

The present philosophy and practice of conservation is flawed in a scientific as much as a social sense. National park management in much of the Third World takes over two axioms of US wilderness thinking: the monumentalist belief that wilderness has to be 'being continuous wilderness', and the claim that all human intervention is bad for the retention of diversity.

(1997, p. 19)

BirD recognises this dynamic as a polar inversion that can characterise the pro-dyadic position. Instead of conceptualising solutions to problems in terms of post-dyadic dialectics (which may still involve counterbalance), problems are exacerbated by a simplistic inversion of oppositions (i.e. human > non-human *to* non-human > human). I suspect that this onto-epistemological dynamic frustrates authentic sustainability more than any other. More sustainable is action and choice taken and made within a broader framework that recognises the interdependence of dyadic constituents (e.g. human <=> non-human). Guha's argument reflects this post-dyadic voice:

These conflicts must not be reduced, however, to a contest over which discipline privileges which species. More sociologically-sensitive biologists, for instance, have warned of the dangers involved when wilderness and wildlife conservation programmes neglect the concerns of those communities who live in and around protected areas.

(1997, p. 18)

The reciprocal fear for proponents of ecocentric cosmologies is that humans have indeed sacrificed many other species and many natural environments for their

204 Illustrations

own survival. Both ecocentric and technocentric positions can be held in relatively binary oppositional ways that reflect pro-dyadic positions in BirD. However, there is also a post-dyadic way of bringing these positions closer together. For example, some cosmologies recognise the interdependence of human and non-human species' survival. Human survival and well-being depends on the survival of coexistent species and care for the environment. Both of these positions move towards post-dyadic ways of relating nature and culture, ecology and technology.

One of the more explicit and creative attempts to bridge the nature/culture divide is seen in Sowards' discussion of orangutans and human identity. Sowards explores the symbolic place of the orangutan as enabling reconnection and reconciliation between 'opposites':

> The nature/culture dualism has long been criticized for constructing social beliefs, attitudes, and behaviors that fail to respect and value the natural world. . . . Ultimately, orangutans are an effective rhetorical metaphor for bridging nature/culture dualisms by representing the natural world from which we have become rhetorically separated
>
> (2006, pp. 45–6)

This approach is one example of an educative attempt to facilitate post-dyadic development beyond pro-dyadic separations that are otherwise seen to alienate humans from the nature that contains and sustains humanity.

The ways that socio-ecological dyads are related have implications in almost all fields of human endeavor. For example, Birkeland's call for 'ecological design' reflects a post-dyadic attempt to bridge the nature/culture divide in architecture:

> The nature-culture division in Western thought is a fundamental dualism reflected in our anthropocentric (human-centred values). The growing realisation that culture and nature exists in an inseparable and reciprocal relationship has not found real expression in building design . . . Ecological design would represent a rebalancing of these two systems.
>
> (2002, pp. 116–17)

Birkeland's ecological design demonstrates an awareness of dyadic ubiquitisation in recognising the interdependence of dyads such as nature/culture, public/private, cyclic/linear and organic/mechanistic.

Wilshire's use of dyads is also ubiquitising and reflexive as it explores the ways of knowing privileged in Western epistemology. For Wilshire, the nature/culture divide is the legacy of Aristotelian hierarchical dualisms that have privileged reason, masculinity and humanity over intuition, femininity and ecology:

> Western epistemology is both hierarchical and pyramidal. This system gives some kinds of knowing more value than others, demeans some, and elevates

one kind to a position of highest value and independence from the others. Science and philosophy strive to achieve and defend this ultimate, most desirable kind of cognition: objective, factual, Pure Knowledge.

(1989, p. 92)

Her (re)solution reflects a distinctively post-dyadic way of knowing and being that encompasses rather than simply inverts the opposition:

> This system needs to be rethought and re-visioned, for in my experience knowledge, or a healthy awareness of the world, comes from many kinds of knowing working together or taking turns, with no one kind ultimately more valuable than any other. Knowledge is, in a sense, like diet, for many food ingredients – vitamins, amino acids, minerals, proteins – must also all work together to provide us with proper nourishment. With knowledge, as with diet, each component or ingredient is essential to goodness; no one manner of knowing – not disinterested cognition, intuition, inspiration, sensuous awareness, nor any other – is sufficient unto itself to satisfy our need to know ourselves and the world.

(1989, p. 92)

It is rare to find analyses of binary oppositions that explicitly encompass rather than simply invert the opposition. The vacuum of a more explicit bi-relational logic and language for the recognition and reconciliation of opposites means that the potential for constructive dialogue is arrested at the lowest common denominator of binary oppositions, which is characterised by destructive diatribes. Again, BirD recognises the all important distinction between these positions and developments as central to the types of dialogue needed to recognise and (re)solve socio-ecological problems.

Hamilton makes a similar case for moving beyond binary oppositional separations that characterise the pro-dyadic position in BirD. He identifies an intuitive/rational dyad as fundamental to human ways of knowing and being in the environment:

> This paper argues that there are two forms of knowledge, intuitive and rational. Duality refers to the separation of the two and the trivialisation of intuitive knowledge, the form that has historically governed the inner relationship of humans to the natural world ... While recognising the value of reason, the well-spring of environmentalism is intuitive knowledge. Environmentalism seeks to transcend duality, reassert the cosmic unity and breathe life back into Nature ... Environmentalism arises from the reintegration of the two forms of knowledge so that reason is informed by intuitive knowledge, and the duality that divides our inner and outer worlds is transcended.

(2002, pp. 89–90)

206   Illustrations

Hamilton uses late pro-dyadic concepts of 'transcendence' and 'reintegration' and generally avoids the onto-epistemological danger of 'swinging the pendulum' (i.e. to intuition) that can frustrate rather than facilitate the reintegration of the formerly dominant part (i.e. reason). Such post-dyadic positions acknowledge the co-evolution and codependency of reason and intuition, the failures of their totalisation (e.g. the detachment of reason and the imprecision of intuition), and the success of their contextual separation (e.g. the precision of reason and the attachment of intuition).

Another interesting example of post-dyadic thinking in environmental discourse relates to 'industrial ecology' – an examination of the symbiotic relationships between industries and between industries and the environment. Ehrenfeld and Gertler (1997) note the emergent focus on ways of thinking and knowing in relation to environmental problems and industrial ontologies: 'Environmental thinking has recently focused on a consciousness of the intimate and critical relationships between human actions and the natural world, and reflects limits in the current reliance on command-and-control regulation in much of the industrialized world' (p. 68). Their argument is that industries have tended to operate as open systems somehow separate from nature, while, in reality, they are part of a closed system such that any outward action (e.g. pollution) will eventually affect the source (i.e. the industrial polluter). They identify the problem in dyadic terms as concerning the relationship between product and process: 'As long as attention is limited to products and processes viewed in isolation, larger systemic problems, such as the accumulation of persistent toxic materials, will not be addressed' (p. 68). In structurally similar terms, Walker argues for the reintegration of material and spirit in industrial design:

> The suppression of this "other half" has led to a materially abundant but spiritually impoverished world.It is argued here that greater acknowledgement of this "other half" in industrial design can lead to products that are expressive of a more balanced understanding of human needs. Such a shift would not only contribute to a culturally richer material environment, it would also allow us to more effectively address the principle of sustainability.
> (2000, p. 52)

In terms of BirD, this is a post-dyadic expression of the need to reintegrate dyadic constituents that have been separated in pro-dyadic cultures of knowing. Environmental volatility is related to dyadic volatility, wherein a prolonged period of polarisation (e.g. dominance of culture) serves merely to intensify the eventual reaction and rebellion of the repressed polarity (e.g. nature). The development from linear ways of knowing that characterise pro-dyadic positions to more cyclical ways of knowing that characterise post-dyadic positions is implicit in their observation that 'Moving from linear throughput to closed-loop material and energy use are key themes in industrial ecology' (Ehrenfeld and Gertler, 1997, p. 68). Again, the point of this analysis is to suggest the role for more explicit accounts of bi-relational dynamics (i.e. BirD) in understanding wicked socio-ecological problems.

The environmental focus on industrialised ways of knowing and being is related to commentaries on 'political ecology' in design and technology education. Scholars are beginning to question the current value of traditional methods of design that emerged in industrial economies. For example, Petrina invokes dyads such as technocentric/ecocentric, skills/process, universal/local and private/public, arguing that a polarised Western bias towards the first constituent of each dyad has come at great environmental cost:

> As researchers in education, design, cultural psychology, and sociology have shown, design and technological methods are neither conducive to student work nor ontologically sound. These methods are rooted in a psychology of the private, Euro-centric intellect rather than in the everyday, sociopolitical mediation of culture and nature. I argue here that these methods are also inadequate for modelling good practice in the face of cultural change and environmental degradation at dawn of the twenty-first century.
>
> (2000, p. 207)

The implicit use of dyads illustrates their usefulness in identifying dominant ways of knowing and being in a particular field (e.g. industrial design and technology). However, where there are dyads there are usually implicit beliefs about dyadic relationships. For example, Petrina's (2000) call is for development from simple to complex, linear to cyclic, separate to interconnected ways of knowing design and being designers. These implied developments reflect the explicit development from pro-dyadic separations and simplifications to the early post-dyadic integrations represented in BirD.

Education for socio-ecological sustainability

One of the most widespread discourses in modern socio-ecological literature concerns *sustainability*. And one of the more popular definitions of the term is from a World Commission on Environment and Development (1987) report: 'Sustainable development is development that meets the needs of the present without compromising the ability of future generations to meet their own needs' (p. 8). In more generic definitions, the term implies balance or dynamic equilibrium in the presence of tensions and fluctuations between intricately connected systems (e.g. past/future, economy/environment). As with any grand term (e.g. God, Science, Religion, Truth, Nature), the range of onto-epistemological dispositions that seek to infuse it with meaning can lead to a 'Babel effect', where the same term is appropriated by different groups speaking into the same space in contradictory ways. Thus, for some, the term *sustainability* is synonymous with a form of environmentalism that defines itself against, or in binary opposition to, economic development and the political right. This presents a wicked problem for educators who may find themselves stuck in messy semantic spaces dominated by standard dualisms (e.g. economy vs. environment, conservation vs. development, nature vs. culture). The educative task and the basic rationale for BirD's abstract representation of onto-epistemological development is to help to (re)solve such confusions by representing them relationally and contextually. For example, if economic concerns have been separated from environmental concerns and allowed to subordinate them, then there may indeed be a period of counterbalance where environmental concerns are re-emphasised and models of dominance are attacked. However, there is a profound onto-epistemological difference between inverting an opposition (e.g. environment < economy *to* economy < environment) and re-engaging interdependent polarities. The first invokes violent and hostile conflicts, while the second invites equilibration. Arguably, there is a development between the two that represents an important educative task. As Tàbara and Pahl-Wostl write in the context of sustainability education:

> Sustainability learning entails overcoming many of the prevalent dualisms that now inform assessment and decision making with regard to the perception and use of social-ecological systems. These include dualisms between the individual and the collective, between human and natural systems, between structure and change, between internal and external system properties, and between human agency and natural conditions. A more hybrid, relational, and co-evolutionary holistic understanding of human–natural interactions is needed.
>
> (2007, p. 11)

One rationale for BirD is that conceptual models can help to facilitate such 'hybrid understandings' when used in context.

Learners can benefit from representations and metaphors that 'break up dualisms' and introduce 'degrees of difference' as conceptual schemas that are intricately related to their experiences in the life world. As Keulartz suggests:

> The first pragmatic strategy to make persistent conflicts manageable is breaking up dualisms. Pragmatism is an anti-dualistic movement of thought. Both Western philosophy and Western common sense are dominated by dualisms like theory and practice, fact and value, body and mind, nature and culture. These dualisms encourage 'black-and-white' thinking, which brings conflicts to a head and leads debate to reach a total deadlock and to get stuck in childish 'does not'– 'does too' exchanges. One method to break up dualisms is gradualization: thinking in terms of degrees instead of boundaries.
>
> (2005, p. 49)

A premise of BirD is that evaluative thinking in terms of degrees of difference and the break-up of dualities requires more complex ways of relating and conceptualisaing polarities, rather than the total destruction of dyads altogether. The developmental task is to paradoxically pull polarities further and further apart to see the 360 degrees of difference between them that will bring them circuitously closer together. Lehman (2002) ponders the role for such 'dialectical analysis' in late modern capitalist societies: 'the question seems to concern the extent to which a critical and dialectical analysis can provide an escape pathway in a world where relationships are often defined as dualisms—humanity/nature, corporations/society and civil society/state' (p. 227). Similarly, Luke highlights the necessity of the educative task in the school context:

> Whether one looks at K-12 classrooms or colleges of natural resources, the dualistic misconstruction of nature and society as green and brown zones, separate and apart, is a major intellectual distortion in most environmental education ... Environment is put to one side in its own closed black box, and organism/society/community/economy is placed on another.
>
> (2001, p. 193)

I have taken up this general educative challenge in later chapters to illustrate some of the ways BirD can be actualised in formal education.

Never far from the discourse of sustainability is the discourse of science. Accordingly, a related educative task for development beyond socio-ecological dualisms involves the conceptualisation of *Science* and the *sciences*. While I have addressed this issue elsewhere, and it is beyond the scope of this chapter to explore in detail, the domain-specific or field-related ways of defining, claiming or rejecting science have significant implications for how these fields are perceived in public discourse and coordinated for the (re)solution of wicked socio-ecological problems. *Science* defined exclusively in terms of particular fields of knowledge that then devalue and alienate other fields of knowledge will simply exacerbate binary oppositions. Science needs to be narrowed to certain fields as one way of knowing alongside others or expanded across all fields as a ubiquitous way of knowing – or both of these, where the uses are carefully differentiated. Such differentiation can build bridges between ways of knowing, even within common sciences, which are traditionally suspicious of each other.

Mauz and Granjou (2013) provide an interesting educative example of a post-dyadic approach to ways of knowing represented by field naturalists and modelling ecologists. They invoke dyads such as qualitative/quantitative, descriptive/predictive, past/future and technological/natural to describe epistemic differences between the two sciences and acknowledge the space for interfacing and dialectic: 'This culture is characterised by the merging of the chief epistemic values of both ways of knowing: collecting, comparing and computing for natural history, and objectivity, quantification and precision for experimentalism' (p. 5). Mauz and Granjou's approach is implicitly post-dyadic in that it recognises a need for the contextually based separation and integration of these sciences:

> Overall, we found that, in the case we studied, the arrival of modelling ecologists had opened up new perspectives for field naturalists and their way of knowing. Our study therefore confirms that ways of knowing can

support each other, at least at some point in their respective development. This invites us to analyse how, like public problems (Hilgartner and Bosk, 1988), ways of knowing interact and form a system or an ecology. It also invites us to be wary of grand historical narratives staging the domination of a specific way of knowing at a given time.

(2013, p. 26)

My point, as illustrated by Mauz and Granjou's example, is that an understanding of bi-relational dynamics can help to facilitate the development of science as it pertains to the (re)solution of socio-ecological problems. Once we expand our appreciation of the ways of knowing that contribute to *science* we can more usefully, and less contentiously, expand *science* into the collective consciousness. As Glass observes in the context of ecological catastrophe:

What is needed by mankind in the present juncture is not a retreat from scientific ways of thinking, but an expansion into the consciousness of every man of the ways in which science and technology may be directed toward the prevention of Pandora's evils.

(1977, p. 278)

However, *science* that is reduced to a grand historical narrative dominated by a specific way of knowing (e.g. exclusively reductive, analytical, empirical, positivistic, objectivistic) – and therefore not so 'grand' – will only serve to polarise the ways of knowing it seeks to define itself against.

Mathews (2006) articulates a similar approach to science and ecology in her attempt to establish a third way or post-materialist metaphysic: 'Post-materialism doesn't reject science, or the innumerable benefits for humanity that science has delivered. Rather, it looks beyond science, not by embracing the supernatural, but by seeking the subjectival interior of the natural' (p. 96). Such onto-epistemological repositionings of science and ecology are important for a conceptualisation of wicked socio-ecological problems that is broad enough to engage the full spectrum of human ways of knowing and being. Any lesser conceptualisation (e.g. socio-ecological problems are all to be dealt with by objective sciences) will simply alienate and disorientate different parts of the same body.

At some point, the ways of relating dyadic constituents like nature and culture, traditional and modern, ecological and economic, and spirit and matter invokes answers to metaphysical and existential questions that, while to be approached with caution in formal education, are ignored at a substantial cost. As Le Grange (2002) observes in the context of environmental education: 'Educational ideologies have shaped different approaches to environmental education, and have influenced its implementation in formal education' (p. 83). Neglect of the metaphysical dimension of such ideologies limits a language for recognising and communicating what is often the elephant in the classroom.

As the physicist Bohm (1969) shrewdly observes, 'the practical "hard-headed" individual has a very dangerous kind of metaphysics, i.e. the kind of which he is unaware' (p. 41). Bourdieu too recognises the powerful voice of the silent metaphysic in the context of education:

> Nothing seems more ineffable, more incommunicable, more inimitable, and, therefore, more precious, than the values given body, *made* body by the transubstantiation achieved by the hidden persuasion of an implicit pedagogy, capable of instilling a whole cosmology, an ethic, a metaphysic, a political philosophy, through injunctions as insignificant as "stand up straight" or "don't hold your knife in your left hand".
>
> (1977, p. 94)

My argument is that concepts like *sustainability* imply significant dyadic relationships (e.g. balance, dynamic equilibrium) that are rarely made explicit or discussed in relation to the deep metaphysical ways of knowing that play a major role in shaping behaviour.

EfS (Education for Sustainability) is an approach to socio-ecological problems that prompts deep reflection on the relationships between society (i.e. culture) and environment (i.e. nature) that can positively influence more sustainable ways of being (Kemmis *et al.*, 1983). As Gare notes in *Nihilism Inc: Environmental Destruction and the Metaphysics of Sustainability*:

> Environmental philosophers have had to go beyond ethics and social philosophy and engage in the fundamental issues of cosmology, metaphysics, epistemology and logic. The atomistic or mechanistic view of nature has been rejected in favour of a conception of the world which emphasizes inter-dependence. Ecological theory in particular has been pressed into service for this task, supplemented by the metaphysical ideas of such philosophers as Spinoza, Schopenhauer, Nietzsche, Whitehead and Heidegger and by Eastern religions and Amerindian cultures.
>
> (1996, p. 59)

BirD provides one framework for explicit examination of relations between *two* (i.e. bi-relations or dyadic relations) that are relevant to identifying and understanding the metaphysical stances that affect engagement with EfS. Accordingly, the following chapter shows the interdependency between socio-ecological problems and socio-religious responses to ultimate questions.

Conclusion

In summary, I have attempted to do three things in this chapter. First, I have attempted to illustrate the ubiquity of dyads in socio-ecological literature (e.g. nature/culture, technology/ecology). These dyads help us to define some

212 Illustrations

of the most pressing problems and challenges that define the discourse – namely, pollution, climate change, population growth, resource depletion and species extinction. Second, I have tried to illustrate the relationship between the conceptualisation of socio-ecological problems and the (re)solution of socio-ecological problems. Using the dynamics and positions identified in BirD, I have argued that exclusively pro-dyadic separations and oppositions of dyadic constituents exacerbate environmental problems. However, while acknowledging the usual suspects (i.e. culture > nature in Western instrumental materialism), I have also suggested that inverted separations (i.e. nature > culture) can be equally destructive if wedded to a metaphysic that alienates rather than accommodates its 'opponents'. Third, I have attempted to highlight the significance of the metaphysical dimension of socio-ecological problems, especially in relation to environmental education. Socio-cultural, socio-ecological and socio-religious problems are interdependent. BirD highlights the cross-disciplinarity (i.e. *ubiquitisation*) of dyads that appear in socio-ecological literature and offers a way to conceptualise dyadic relationships that moves beyond mere oppositions and the environmental destruction they cause and reflect. Accordingly, while the next chapter focuses on the recognition and reconciliation of dyads related to wicked socio-religious problems (e.g. spirit/matter, faith/reason), I hope to reveal its contiguity with the socio-cultural and socio-ecological problems already discussed.

References

Birkeland, J. (2002). *Design for sustainability: A sourcebook of integrated ecological solutions.* New York: Earthscan Publications Ltd.

Bohm, D. (1969). Some remarks on the notion of order. In C. H. Waddington (Ed.), *Towards a theoretical biology.* Edinburgh: Edinburgh University Press.

Bourdieu, P. (1977). *Outline of a theory of practice.* Cambridge: Cambridge University Press.

Eckersley, R. (1992). *Environmentalism and political theory: Toward an ecocentric approach.* New York: State University of New York Press.

Eckersley, R. (1990). The ecocentric perspective. In C. Pybus and R. Flanagan (Eds.), *The rest of the world is watching* (pp. 68–78). Sydney: Pan Macmillan.

Ehrenfeld, J., and Gertler, N. (1997). Industrial ecology in practice: The evolution of interdependence at Kalundborg. *Journal of Industrial Ecology*, 1(1), 67–79. doi: 10.1162/jiec.1997.1.1.67.

Gagnon Thompson, S. C., and Barton, M. A. (1994). Ecocentric and anthropocentric attitudes toward the environment. *Journal of Environmental Psychology*, 14(2), 149–57. doi: 10.1016/S0272-4944(05)80168-9.

Gare, A. (1996). *Nihilism Inc. Environmental destruction and the metaphysics of sustainability.* Sydney: Eco-logical Press.

Glass, B. (1977). The scientist: Trustee for humanity. *BioScience*, 17(4), 277–8. doi: 10.2307/1297704.

Gough, S., Scott, W. and Stables, A. (2000). Beyond O'Riordan: Balancing anthropocentrism and ecocentrism. *International Research in Geographical and Environmental Education*, 9(1), 36–47. doi: 10.1080/10382040008667628.

Green, R. M. (1977). Intergenerational distributive justice and environmental responsibility. *BioScience*, 27(4), 260–5. doi: 10.2307/1297701.

Guha, R. (1997). The authoritarian biologist and the arrogance of anti-humanism: Wildlife conservation in the Third World. 14–20. www.uvm.edu/rsenr/wfb175/guha_wildlife.pdf.

Hamilton, C. (2002). Dualism and sustainability. *Ecological Economics*, 42(1–2), 89–99. doi: 10.1016/S0921-8009(02)00051-4.

Kemmis, S., Cole, P., and Suggett, D. (1983). *Orientations to curriculum and transition: Towards the socially-critical school.* Melbourne: Victorian Institute for Secondary Education.

Keulartz, J. (2005). *Boundary-work: The tension between diversity and sustainability.* Paper presented at the Prague Conference of the Forum of University Teachers, Prague.

Le Grange, L. (2002). Towards a 'language of probability' for environmental education in South Africa. *South African Journal of Education*, 22(2), 83–7.

Lehman, G. (2002). Global accountability and sustainability: Research prospects. *Accounting Forum, 26*(3–4), 219–32. doi: 10.1111/1467-6303.00087

Luke, T. W. (2001). Education, environment and sustainability: What are the issues, where to intervene, what must be done? *Educational Philosophy and Theory*, 33(2), 187–202. doi: 10.1111/j.1469-5812.2001.tb00262.x

Mathews, F. (2006). Beyond modernity and tradition: A third way for development. *Ethics and the Environment*, 11(2), 85–114.

Mauz, I., and Granjou, C. (2013). A new border zone in science. Collaboration and tensions between modelling ecologists and field naturalists. *Science as Culture*, 22(3), 314–43. doi: 10.1080/09505431.2012.753047.

Moscovici, S. (1976). *Society against nature: The emergence of human societies* (S. Rabinovitch, Trans.). Brighton: Harvester Press.

Naess, A. (1973). The shallow and the deep, long-range ecology movement. A summary. *Inquiry*, 16(1–4), 95–100. doi: 10.1080/00201747308601682.

O'Riordan, T. (1989). The challenge for environmentalism. In R. Peet and N. Thrift (Eds.), *New Models in Geography* (Vol. II). London: Unwin Hyman.

Petrina, S. (2000). The political ecology of design and technology education: An inquiry into methods. *International Journal of Technology and Design Education*, 10, 20737.

Sheets-Johnstone, M. (1996). *Human versus non-human: Binary opposition as an ordering principle of western human thought.* Paper presented at the Pacific Division meetings of the Society for the Study of Ethics and Animals, Seattle.

Sowards, S. K. (2006). Identification through Orangutans: Destabilizing the nature/culture dualism. *Ethics and the Environment*, 11(2), 45–61, Article 3. www.ecologyandsociety.org/vol12/iss2/art3/

Tàbara, J. D., and Pahl-Wostl., C. (2007). Sustainability learning in natural resource use and management. *Ecology and Society*, 12(2).

Walker, S. (2000). How the other half lives: Product design, sustainability and the human spirit. *Design Issues*, 16(1), 52–8.

Wilshire, D. (1989). The uses of myth, image, and the female body in revisioning knowledge. In A. M. Jaggar and S. M. Bordo (Eds.), *Gender / body / knowledge: Feminist reconstructions of being and knowing* (pp. 92–114). New Brunswick: Rutgers University Press.

World Commission on Environment and Development. (1987). *Our Common Future.* Oxford: Oxford University Press.

Yanarella, E. J., and Levine, R. S. (1992). Does sustainable development lead to sustainability? *Futures*, 24(8), 759–74. doi: 10.1016/0016-3287(92)90105-O.

Chapter 9

Bi-relational development and wicked socio-religious problems

Perhaps the most difficult question that preoccupies human consciousness and culture is the perennial 'Is there a God?'. Arguably, this ultimate question more than any other has preoccupied and shaped human minds and societies since we first evolved the ability to ask it. The question seems no less poignant in the twenty-first century than it was in the most primitive stages of human consciousness. Indeed, some of the primary and secondary dyads that most characterise the question (e.g. spirit/matter, faith/reason and science/religion) are of utmost importance in the identification and (re)solution of some of our most wicked personal and global problems. There are correlations between our answers to this ultimate question and our positions on everything from gay marriage to anthropogenic global warming. I have alluded to this importance in the previous two chapters by demonstrating the affinity of dyads that characterise wicked socio-cultural problems (e.g. local/global) and socio-ecological problems (e.g. nature/culture) with dyads that characterise socio-religious problems (e.g. spirit/matter). Our grandest narratives about *God* can reflect and construct our everyday ways of knowing and being in relation to everything from immigration to climate change. My hope is that a bi-relational approach to the wickedest question can help to chart and coordinate some archetypal positions and dynamics towards the recognition and (re)solution of such related wicked problems. Accordingly, the following chapter provides (a) a general bi-relational perspective on secular and religious answers to the question 'Is there a God?', (b) a bi-relational attempt to reconcile 'opposing' appeals to *faith* and *reason* and (c) a bi-relational discussion of *spirit* and *matter* that reveals the dyadic affinities between socio-religious and socio-ecological problems.

My bi-relational thesis is that the question 'Is there a God?' has longevity and ubiquity because its answers are relational and contextual; they are interdependent even in, perhaps especially in, the most violent of oppositions. While we may wrestle with and choose between answers to the question in everyday life (e.g. whether or not to pray before a meal or send our children to a religious school), any ultimate victory (e.g. matter > spirit, faith > reason) is a pyrrhic victory in which the victor either negates its own existence or has to become the very enemy it has defeated. This thesis offers some explanation for the historical persistence and modern poignancy of the contest between faith and reason, matter and spirit and, the secondary dyad, science and religion. In an abstract sense, the dyadic constituents are structurally interdependent such that one can never defeat or escape the other once and for all.

This is not to neglect the very real and specific oppositions that can and should be fought between God-beliefs correlated with science or religion as they exist in context. The reconciliation of opposites does not destroy oppositions; it contextualises and coordinates them in the service of something bigger. BirD's trans-positions include oppositions as significant and valid ways of knowing and being. However, the trans-positional use of opposition differs from the pro-dyadic use of binary oppositions in that its ways of opposing aim to restore equilibrium, dialectic, rightful place and balance of power between primary dyadic poles in real-world contexts. Trans-positional ways of opposing fight battles to restore a balance of power. Pro-dyadic ways of opposing fight battles as if they were wars to end all wars. Binary opposition in the pro-dyadic phase tends only to want to destroy its opposition once and for all. Perhaps nowhere are these dynamics more manifest than in wicked socio-religious problems related to encounters between *science* and *religion* and the primary dyads these encounters reflect (e.g. literal/symbolic, spirit/matter, faith/reason, hope/despair).

One manifestation of the opposition between science and religion concerns the wicked problem of origins. Here, there are two codepedent battles that should rightly be fought from a trans-positional stance. One battle is to wrest religious mythology from unwittingly materialistic interpretations that literalise essentially symbolic content. The other is the battle against the assumption that material explanations necessarily reduce all possible spiritual interpretations. The battles are co-definitive. For example, six-day young-Earth creationists may attempt to defend a *spirit* that they fear has been attacked by the secular scientism of militant atheists or that they have exclusively linked to a particular interpretation of scripture; and atheists may attack any conceptulisation of *spirit* in an attempt to defend the *matter* that they fear has been attacked by religious fundamentalists. Each is right in one sense, but wrong in the sense that they tend to take their opposition's particular appropriation of an opposing concept (i.e. faith, reason, matter, spirit) as the only possible appropriation of a concept, thus neglecting a basic discovery of onto-epistemological development – that the 'same' term may be known and experienced in different ways. As Haught reflects in the introduction to *God and the New Atheism*:

> The deeper I became involved in the writing of this book, the more evident it became to me that I was offering a critique not only of the new atheism but also to the kind of religious thought, ethics and spirituality against which it is reacting.
>
> (2000, p. xv)

The relationality and contextuality of conflict needs to be assumed at the outset of any analysis.

A bi-relational approach offers an understanding of developmentally different ways of knowing and relating dyadic constituents that can help to identify and (re)solve wicked socio-religious problems and conflicts. A bi-relational approach cannot choose a priori between science or religion, spirit or matter; rather, it views them relationally and contextually as co-definitive terms that can be dexterously coordinated. Therefore, targeted attacks on particular expressions of science or religion may be warranted as a defensive or preventative response to an aggressive imperialism that stems from a binary oppositional way of knowing one or the other. However, the more indiscriminate such attacks are, the more they will end up reflecting the very image they seek to destroy and the more resistance they will encounter. I would suggest that this is true whether the wicked socio-religious problem presents itself in the form of terrorism or creationism. As the emergence of neo-atheism suggests, expressions of faith have persisted well beyond the historical Age of Reason. A bi-relational analysis can help us to understand why this persistence reveals something more complex than the death throes of faith and the triumph of reason.

Onto-epistemological development *to* or *from* religion?

Beyond faith?

One of the most significant and contested questions is whether human development leads *to* or *from* religion or the practice of God-beliefs. In dyadic terms, does human development lead from spirit to matter, faith to reason and religion to science or vice-versa? Atheistic philosophers such as Ludwig von Feuerbach directly proposed the claim that development leads *beyond* religion. Reflecting on the development of his own thought, Feuerbach (in McEnhill and Newlands, 2004) delivered his famous aphorism: 'God was my first thought; Reason my second; Man my third and last thought' (p. 120). Feuerbach's developmental logic was further elaborated by Freud:

> If one attempts to assign to religion its place in man's evolution, it seems not so much to be a lasting acquisition, as a parallel to the neurosis which the civilised individual must pass through on his way from childhood to maturity.
>
> (2008, p. 6)

The question and debate surrounding development beyond religion, initiated by Feuerbach and elaborated by Freud, has been revitalised by relatively recent research into the cognitive evolutionary origins of religion (e.g. Atran, 2002; Barrett, 2000, 2002, 2004; Boyer, 1994, 2000, 2001) and the neuropsychology of religious experience – more popularly known as *neurotheology* (Joseph *et al.*, 2003; Newberg *et al.*, 2001; Persinger, 1987; Ramachandran and Blakeslee, 1998).

Boyer (2001) notes the rare cognitive and cultural conditions that enable a reductive explanation of religion in *Religion Explained: The Evolutionary Origins of Religious Thought*. It is implied in Boyer's approach that, though rare, these conditions represent the most developed position and warrant the relegation of religion to an earlier developmental state. Likewise, Persinger's position is that the neurological explanations for religious experience enabled by scientific and cognitive development explain religion away:

> All religions are counterfeit organisations of explanation, dictate, and ritual. Churches, synagogues, and mosques are completely irrelevant to the God Experience. The Bible, Koran, and Book of the Dead are pages of absolute nonsense ...These neutral stimuli become important because they are associated with the person's temporal lobe displays.
>
> (1987, p. 97)

The 'development beyond religion' thesis finds its most recent and robust expression in the writings of the neo-atheists, including Richard Dawkins (2006), Daniel Dennett (2006), Sam Harris (2005) and the late Christopher Hitchens (2007). Dawkins, the former Charles Simonyi Chair for the Public Understanding of Science, echoes Feuerbach and Freud's perspective:

> In childhood our credulity serves us well. It helps us to pack, with extraordinary rapidity, our skulls full of the wisdom of our parents and our ancestors. But if we don't grow out of it in the fullness of time, our ... nature makes us a sitting target for astrologers, mediums, gurus, evangelists, and quacks. We need to replace the automatic credulity of childhood with the constructive skepticism of adult science.
>
> (1998, pp. 142–3)

Collectively, these claims assume that development leads beyond religion, faith and spirit. However, there are alternative claims concerning the direction of development.

Beyond reason?

Can the claims that development leads *beyond* religion be subsumed within an even 'more developed' typology that sees a development *back* to religion? Feuerbach's claim can be considered against Francis Bacon's (2008) counterclaim, 'It is true, that a little philosophy inclineth man's mind to atheism; but depth in philosophy bringeth men's minds about to religion' (p. 1). Likewise, Boyer's claim can be considered against Barrett's (2004) counterclaim: 'Concepts of a superpowerful, superperceiving, superknowing, and immortal supreme God receive further support and encouragement by the character of natural human conceptual development ... Compared to theism, atheism is relatively

218 Illustrations

unnatural' (p. 108). Persinger's claim can be considered against Ramachandran and Blakeslee's (1998) counterclaim that the goal of science 'is to discover how and why religious sentiments originate in the brain, but this has no bearing one way or the other on whether God really exists or not' (p. 185). And, in the modern context, Dawkins' claim can be considered against Haught's counter-claim that the new atheists' claim to reason and evidence:

> is a profession of faith known as *scientism*, a modern belief system that has the additional mark of being self-contradictory.
>
> Why self-contradictory? Because scientism tells us to take nothing on faith, and yet faith is required to accept scientism. What is remarkable is that none of the new atheists seems remotely prepared to admit that his scientism is a self-sabotaging confession of faith.
>
> (2008, p. 17)

So, is it possible to reconcile such competing claims towards the (re)solution of wicked problems?

A bi-relational approach to socio-religious dyads (e.g. faith/reason)

To reiterate the question subsuming these claims and counterclaims: does development lead beyond, back or through to faith or 'religion'? BirD offers a way to approach the question beyond an exclusively binary oppositional answer by differentiating ways of knowing a common referent (e.g. God, matter, faith, spirit, science). My central claim is that lexically identical referents can be known in different ways as represented by BirD's archetypal positions. Table 9.1 provides a representation of this idea that can be understood in relation to Table 5.1 and Figure 5.1.

Table 9.1 A symbolic representation of the relationship between faith (F) and reason (R)

Regions		Archetypal trajectories				
		I	*II*	*III*	*IV*	
6 (1–5)	5	$F \Leftrightarrow FR \Leftrightarrow R$				
	4	$F_3 \geq (FR_3/R_3)$ $F_3 > F_2$ $F_3 \neg (R_2/FR_2)$	$R_3 \geq (FR_3/F_3)$ $R_3 > R_2$ $R_3 \neg (FR_2/R_2)$	$FR_3 \geq (F_3/R_3)$ $FR_3 > FR_2$ $FR_3 \neg (F_2/R_2)$	$F_3 \geq FR_3$ $F_3 > F_2$ $F_3 \neg FR_2$	$R_3 \geq FR_3$ $R_3 > R_2$ $R_3 \neg FR_2$
	3	$F_2 \neg (FR_2/R_2)$	$R_2 \neg (FR_2/F_2)$	$FR_2 \neg (F_2/R_2)$	$F_2 \neg FR_2$	$R_2 \neg FR_2$
	2	F_1	R_1	FR_1	F_1	R_1
	1					

The key concept of Table 9.1 is that *faith* and *reason* must each be internally differentiated before being related. More specifically, they are onto-epistemologically differentiated using the symbols $F_{1,2,3}$ and $R_{1,2,3}$. Of course, this can be done for any dyad relevant to the recognition and (re)solution of wicked problems. The subscript of each constituent differentiates the extent to which it is developmentally mature. Accordingly, symbols F_1, FR_1 and R_1 represent perspectives from a growing or emerging part that is indicative of the pre-dyadic region; symbols F_2, FR_2 and R_2 represent the region of intersecting parts that are most likely to meet in binary opposition and is indicative of the pro-dyadic region; and symbols F_3, FR_3 and R_3 represent the region of interpenetrating or equalising parts towards a whole that is indicative of the post-dyadic region. My claim is that the wickedness of many socio-religious problems arises when these different positions (i.e. understandings of dyadic constituents) are left undifferentiated. Even as I present these problems in relatively symbolic and abstract ways that reflect epistemological development, I appreciate the deep pleasures and pains of the life-world experiences that create and reflect them. Such epistemological dynamics can underlie very real socio-religious conflicts that play out everywhere from the family dinner table to the Gaza Strip. The tiniest epistemological perturbations in our onto-epistemological webs can reverberate through our whole beings, whether we are conscious of this or not.

Consider the use of Table 9.1 for a brief bi-relational analysis of the aforementioned conflict between neo-atheists (e.g. Richard Dawkins) and their theistic critics (e.g. John Haught). Haught (2008) suggests that neo-atheism is largely a response to a particular type of religion that he identifies as 'fundamentalist'. Fundamentalism can be seen to represent a pro-dyadic way of knowing and being in relation to faith that is synonymous with position F_2. Fundamentalism represents a way of knowing and being that opposes an expanded *reason* (i.e. R_3) it does not understand to defend an impoverished faith (i.e. F_2) that it does. This is the type of 'faith' that Dawkins (1992) describes as 'the great cop-out, the great excuse to evade the need to think and evaluate evidence. Faith is belief in spite of, even perhaps because of, the lack of evidence' (n.p.). However, fundamentalism is greatly enabled in this opposition by an impoverished form of reason (i.e. R_2) that opposes an expanded form of faith (i.e. F_3). This is the *reason* that foolishly tangos without a partner because the available partners look other than itself. This 'mono-tango' is perhaps the most common and destructive dance of life – one that is difficult to step in on as the divided half thinks itself whole. Haught identifies this type of *reason* (i.e. R_2) with 'scientism' (p. 38) and attempts to defend against Dawkins' apparent rejection of all faith: 'The new atheists are saying in effect that if God exists at all, we should allow this God's identity to be determined once and for all by the fundamentalists of the Abrahamic religious traditions' (p. xvi). Can these positions be reconciled at any level?

Arguably, Haught's position represents an expanded type of *faith* (i.e. F_3) that is compatible with an expanded type of *reason* (i.e. R_3) but which attacks the form of *reason* (i.e. R₂) that opposes *faith* (i.e. F₃). So, both Dawkins and Haught may at least agree that *faith* (i.e. F₂) is destructively and unnecessarily oppositional. However, given the wickedness of such terms, Haught would probably prefer not to call it faith at all, preferring *fundamentalism*. And Dawkins would probably agree that 'scientism' (i.e. R₂) is destructively and unnecessarily oppositional. Reciprocally, Dawkins' would probably prefer not to call 'scientism' by any name that implicates science or reason. So far, the 'opposites' are reconcilable. From here, my thesis is that Dawkins has a post-dyadic conceptualisation of science, reason and matter (i.e. R₃) that is able to inflate these terms to accommodate much of the space that Haught would argue can be occupied by religion, faith and spirit (i.e. F₃). Reciprocally, Haught has a post-dyadic conceptualisation of religion, faith and spirit (i.e. F₃) that is able to accommodate much of the space that Dawkins would argue can be occupied by science, reason and matter (i.e. R₃). Dawkins tangos with faith (i.e. F₃) and calls it reason; Haught tangos with reason (i.e. R₃) and calls it faith.

In BirD, this expansion towards the other is identified as a post-dyadic convergence or interpenetration of 'opposites'. However, the expansion is not always semantically conciliatory as increasing the explanatory power of one polarity (e.g. reason) may give the appearance that the other (e.g. faith) is diminishing in explanatory power. This is especially true if the other is being defined loudly and exclusively in terms of its pro-dyadic expressions. Thus, Dawkins' expansion of *reason* (i.e. R₃) is proportional to his diminishment of *faith* (i.e. F₂). This type of interpenetration can go a long way towards the reconciliation of opposites; however, it can *appear* binary so long as it is expressed in grand terms (e.g. faith, God, science) that are not epistemically well defined, either by the creator or the perceiver.

Dawkins (2003) seems perplexed and frustrated by calls for the convergence of science and religion: 'Are science and religion converging? No. There are modern scientists whose words sound religious but whose beliefs, on close examination, turn out to be identical to those of other scientists who straightforwardly call themselves atheists' (p. 146). Here, Dawkins seems unable or unwilling to recognise an understanding of *faith* (i.e. F₃) that can shift the perspective on his very detailed view of an arguably ambiguous figure. Dawkins' justifiable resistance to this convergence may be related to his sense that defenders of *faith* (i.e. F₃) like Haught have not done enough to renounce the destructive *faith* (i.e. F₂) of those who worship under the same church roof and in the same name of 'God'. Dawkins' attack on religion and faith can be seen as proportional to religion's provincialism. It ultimately serves faith (i.e. F₃) by destroying its idols (F₂). This is an overlooked dynamic of wicked problems and their inherent oppositions. Sometimes a critical enemy may be more helpful than an uncritical friend.

The neo-atheist claim that some theists engage in semantic sophistry to redefine science as religion is not a one-way street. Dawkins (2003) accuses such theists: 'You have *redefined* science as religion, so it's hardly surprising if they turn out to "converge"' (p. 147). However, my claim is that some neo-atheists

(R$_3$) have redefined important aspects of religion (i.e. faith [F$_3$]) such as imagination, mystery, awe, wonder and purpose to accommodate them under science. This redefinition serves one purpose in rescuing these aspects from being lost in faith (F$_2$) but defeats another in keeping them from being found in faith (F$_3$). Conversely, some theists (F$_3$) have redefined important aspects of science (i.e. reason [R$_3$]) such as quantum entanglement, uncertainty and singularity to accommodate them as religion. Similarly, this redefinition may rescue some control of these aspects from reason (R$_2$) but may fail to appreciate how these same aspects have been misappropriated by less developed forms of faith and already richly accommodated by more developed forms of reason (R$_3$). These dynamics suggest that one of the major features of wicked socio-religious problems has to do with the complexity of their definitions. Bi-relational analyses can help to differentiate some of these terms to show who is actually disagreeing with whom, for it is not always as clear as it may first seem. So, there is a paradoxical sense in which Dawkins (R$_3$) and Haught (F$_3$) strengthen each other by exposing each other's more proximate enemies. At this point we may wonder if it is possible for faith and reason, science and religion to interpenetrate or converge fully as represented by BirD's point of collapse (i.e. F $\Leftrightarrow$ FR $\Leftrightarrow$ R).

What happens if we allow science and religion, faith and reason, matter and spirit to converge into each other (i.e. Science is Religion is Science)? BirD represents the end point of this convergence as the complete *collapse* of dyads. Some see this as a great union of opposites (i.e. One); some see it as an absurd and disorientating negation (i.e. Zero). My sense is that the point of collapse gives a glimpse of the relatively ineffable referent of the language of science and religion, faith and reason, matter and spirit. The ineffability of this referent invokes ironic terms used by theologians like Paul Tillich (1951) such as 'God beyond God', 'Ultimate Reality' and 'Ground of Being'. For example, Tillich (1951) writes, 'God does not exist. He is being-itself beyond essence and existence. Therefore, to argue that God exists is to deny him' (p. 205) and 'It is as atheistic to affirm the existence of God as it is to deny it. God is being-itself, not *a* being' (p. 237). Such descriptions are characteristic of the collapse of dyads where the referent (i.e. Ground of Being) cannot be adequately described by dyadic distinctions such as immanent/transcendent, male/female and human/divine unless they are simultaneously applied.

For some, this is mere sophistry and semantics that dress nothing as something; for others, this is a glimpse at a profound *Reality* from which springs forth all understandings of *reality*. Proponents of *two* may find it instructive that even the point of collapse can be seen as *nothing* by some and *everything* by others. Understandably, and perhaps indicatively of the point of collapse, Tillich is described as a theist by some and an atheist by others. Again, this is a dynamic that BirD attempts to represent. It is difficult to know and to live at the point of collapse. Everyday life requires movement, choice and communication, albeit 'through a glass darkly', which gives rise again to degrees of difference orientated between dyadic polarities such as faith and reason. However, the crucial difference between the pro-dyadic use of dyads before their collapse and the trans-positional use of dyads after their collapse concerns the relationality, contextuality and dexterity of their use. The post-dyadic disposition may expand one polarity by absorbing another. The point of collapse is where total absorption makes one polarity indistinguishable or simultaneously distinguishable from the other such that a full spectrum exists both within and between them. The trans-positional disposition returns with a sense of purpose to the real world of wicked problems where it 'weighs in' with a new respect for the relationality, contextuality and life-giving purpose of 'oppositions'. This trans-positional approach is sensitive to the affinity between the dyads of socio-religious problems (e.g. spirit/matter) and the dyads of wicked socio-ecological problems (e.g. nature/culture) and socio-cultural problems (e.g. local/global).

The 'religious' dimension of wicked socio-eco-cultural problems

This section offers a cumulative integration of some of the dyads discussed in this and previous chapters (i.e. nature/culture, matter/spirit). I intend to integrate these dyads in the context of some of our most pressing wicked problems. The previous chapter concluded with a brief transitional discussion of the relationship between the nature/culture dyad and the matter/spirit dyad in relation to socio-ecological challenges. The discussion highlighted the interrelationship between different dyads and the domains of knowledge they represent, and I now hope to extend it here to re-emphasise the deep connection between cultural, ecological and religious and/or spiritual domains of knowledge. Ecology and religion are deeply linked. The ubiquitisation of dyads, not least in dyads related to the environment, always leads back to metaphysics – even the metaphysics that metaphysics is dead. My claim is that socio-ecological problems will not be effectively identified or engaged without reference to the metaphysical systems of the individuals and societies who co-create and (re) solve them. As Coates implicitly recognises, metaphysical questions arise in the context of the nature/culture dyad:

> Why are we here? What is the proper human-Earth relationship? These are questions concerning our ultimate meaning and purpose that, in light of environmental destruction and social injustice, call for a new consciousness and, as such, can be seen as essentially spiritual questions.
>
> (2012, p. 63)

Similarly, Mathews' (2006) paper, *Beyond Modernity and Tradition: A Third Way for Development*, highlights the socio-religious-spiritual dimension of socio-ecological problems and the importance of dyads and dyadic relationships in conceptualising such problems. She suggests 'How we understand the world (our metaphysical premise) determines, to a large degree, how we treat it' (p. 86) and invokes dyads such as spiritual/material, internal/external, connected/detached,

Wicked socio-religious problems 223

mental/physical and subjective/objective in her analysis of traditional and modern modes of knowing and being.

Arguably, environmental education must engage in more encompassing cosmological and metaphysical discussions, not least because socio-ecological discussions that attempt to situate environmental problems in a 'more ultimate reality' often highlight the fundamental differences that quickly bring such discussions back to earth. For example, Kahan *et al.*'s (2011) *Cultural Cognition Project* illustrates the deep and pervasive influence of cultural values and metaphysical beliefs, finding 'correlational and experimental evidence confirming that cultural cognition shapes individuals' beliefs about the existence of scientific consensus, and the process by which they form such beliefs, relating to climate change, [and] the disposal of nuclear wastes' (p. 1). Cultural values and metaphysical beliefs are deeply interconnected and cannot be ignored in the identification and (re)solution of socio-ecological problems.

One of the most current examples of the interdependence between socio-ecological and and socio-religious problems is climate change. For example, a relationship between religious identity and conceptualisations of climate change has been recognised by environmental researchers (e.g., Fien, 2002; Mortreux and Barnett, 2009), psychosocial commentators (e.g. Tracey, 1995), historians (e.g. Collins, 1995) and policy analysts (e.g., Hildén, 2011; Wardekker *et al.*, 2009). Fien (2002) notes tensions in different religions that 'give rise both to environmental respect and disregard on different occasions' (p. 152). In their study of responses to climate change in Tuvalu, Mortreux and Barnett (2009) observe, 'Faith in God's protection shaped responses to climate change for the young and old alike' (p. 110). Collins (1995) argues that 'religion and ethics will have to become an essential part of our ecological rethinking' and that 'modern ecology is absolutely central to the future of religion' (p. 3). Likewise, Wardekker *et al.* (2009) note that 'religious discourses add a deeper dimension to the public debate on climate change, and seem to resonate with large audiences. This is what makes religious discourse powerful and an important object for study in the context of climate-policy analysis' (p. 519). Needless to say, there is a significant relationship between socio-cultural, socio-ecological and socio-religious domains. More needful to say is that there is a lack of relational and contextual approaches (e.g. BirD) in education that can help to represent and (re)solve the wicked problems that span these domains.

One of the post-dyadic challenges of environmental movements is to articulate a metaphysical premise that moves beyond mere blanket rejections of modern or traditional ways of knowing and being. Failure to understand modern ways of knowing and being tends to produce pendulum swings rather than development towards more dexterous ways of knowing and being in context. It dissolves old dualisms (e.g. nature/culture) but replaces them with new ones (e.g. modernity/sustainability). Here, Mathews' (2006) pan-psychic approach to wicked socio-ecological problems is worth briefly analysing in terms of BirD for its post-dyadic and trans-positional ways of knowing and relating religion, culture and ecology. Mathews defines traditional modes as religious ways of knowing and being characterised by revealed authority, divine intentionality and petitioning as a way of coping with a lack of technical control over the environment. These ways of knowing tended to self-perpetuate the lack of control of nature by hindering the development of more scientific and instrumental ways of knowing that later characterised modernity. However, she argues that the modernist mode sacrificed the 'sense of being plugged into the sources of Creation [and the] effortless connectedness and belonging' of traditional modes' (p. 88). She refers to the result of this decoupling of spiritual connectedness from materialist instrumentalism and the privileging of the latter as 'the catastrophic impact of materialism on non-human species and the natural environment' (pp. 92–3). Mathews recognises the need for a metaphysic for sustainability and calls for 'a third way for development' (i.e. post-materialist) beyond modernity and tradition (p. 87). While describing the third, post-materialist way as 'beyond', her discussion is also framed in dialectical terms as 'into', 'between' and 'a combination of' the modalities of *traditional* and *modern*, while recognising that it is also a rejection of some aspects of these modalities.

Accordingly, Mathews' third way, or post-materialist society, clearly reflects some important aspects of post-dyadic ways of knowing, including contextuality, interpenetration and equality of opposites. Her approach to what I have termed 'wicked socio-ecological problems' illustrates contextuality (e.g. 'decoded afresh in every situation' (p. 95)) and tension and paradox between freedom and control (e.g. 'nonauthoritarian [with] additional restrictions' (p. 95)) that reflect post-dyadic ways of knowing. Ways of living in tension and paradox are implicit in other passages, for example, in the call for 'a spiritual attitude to "nature" … combined with the equal insistence on the irreducible plurality of approaches to questions of deeper life-meaning' (p. 93). This necessary tension or synergy is also expressed in Mathews' reflections on passive observance and active participation that together allow for 'an essentially creative mode [that] draws forth the new without contradicting the old' (p. 102).

Gandy (1997) expresses a similar post-dyadic position in his article 'Postmodernism and environmentalism: Complementary or contradictory discourses?': 'More dialectic approaches to nature which eschew the essentialist and transcendental trappings of the past may lead to new fusions of nature and culture which celebrate the possibilities for new interactions between human creativity and nature' (p. 152). As represented in BirD, late post-dyadic ways of knowing and being *regulate* rather than *relegate* oppositions and tensions within broader ways of knowing and being.

The breadth and connection of dyads in Mathews' work further indicates the sort of dyadic reflexivity and ubiquitisation that characterises BirD's late post-dyadic thought:

> It is important to note that the scope of post-materialism is not merely ecological but *cosmological*. In consequence, our thought and action in *every*

context of life, not merely in the environmental context, must be consistent with the conativity of reality, and must leave the world intact ... In other words, if we adopt the post-materialist ethos in every department of life, we will not need any special department of environmentalism.

(2006 pp. 95–6)

Thus, there is a sense in which the 'environmental metaphysic' must transcend ecology and the environment as fields or disciplines if it is to be truly metaphysical. This 'transcendence' leads to the dyadic oppositions and tensions that define religious and spiritual discourses (e.g. spiritual/material, faith/reason, nothing/something, absurdity/meaning) and find expression at the *collapse* of dyads and trans-positions represented in BirD.

Socio-cultural contexts reflect responses to such dyads and dyadic relationships in ways that affect environmental action. For example, Gare argues that modernity reflects an implicit nihilism (i.e. absurdity > meaning; nothing > something) that affects the way it relates nature and culture. He suggests a need for 'modes of thought' that can deeply engage such complex relationships in relation to ultimate questions and metaphysical stances:

The environmental crisis reveals the need for developing modes of thought capable of analysing the inter-relationships between such diverse problems and for appreciating the significance and meaning of life. And it raises fundamental ethical and social issues. Why should people concern themselves with non-human life, future generations, oppression in the economic peripheries or the plight of the poor? And why in fact do so few people do so? In raising these issues environmental problems reveal the nihilism pervading modern civilization.

(1996, p. 31)

The relationship between nihilism, modernity and environmentalism raises especially important considerations for educators in sustainability who seek (re)solutions to socio-ecological problems. The relationship is being recognised and explored in different ways, most recently by scholars (e.g. Kelsey, 2011) attempting to understand the affects of a relatively dominant 'doom and gloom' discourse in environmental education. A new vocabulary is emerging that recognises the existentially pessimistic affects of this trend. For example, concepts such as 'environmental grief' (Kevorkian, 2004), 'environmental depression' (Kelsey, 2011) and 'environmental apathy' (Twenge *et al.*, 2012) are encouraging educators to reconsider dyadic relationships between constituents such as *hope* and *despair* in the context of education for sustainability.

I once participated in a symposium on education and climate change, where a presenter gave an expansive natural history and future of the solar system ending with the death of the sun. The call was for 'pedagogies of hope', with the assumed rationale that life is precious because it is incredibly rare and finite.

226 Illustrations

I wondered aloud, and still do, at the leap of *faith* between the materialist metaphysic presented and the assumption that it necessarily inspires hope (or is indeed *true*). My expectation is that such a future predicament, presented as a metaphysic, could be interpreted as much in terms of despair and meaninglessness as it could be in terms of hope and purposefulness. Some individuals are inspired by imagining – 'no hell below us; above us only sky' – while others experience the wild-eyed Nietzschean madness that accompanies proclamations of the death of God. I suspect Nietzsche's personal descent into madness is of much interest to scholars as much for its spiritual implications as its material explanations.

BirD represents both the opposition and entangled collapse between these seemingly opposing experiences of the death of God. This collapse is represented in BirD as the extinction of dyads – a point where meaning, purpose, existence, metaphysics and knowledge seem to collapse altogether into a disorientating darkness beyond the certainties of formal logic and the separations, oppositions and balances of pro-dyadic and post-dyadic ways of knowing and being. For many people and professions, this point seems distant and incomprehensible; it is pre-consciously held or quickly dismissed as a figment of philosophers' imaginations with no practical importance. However, there is a sense in which this point of negation has a gravitational pull that draws actions and thoughts towards it, whether we are conscious of it or not. As Haught suggests to the neo-atheists:

> If you're going to be an atheist . . . go all the way and think the business of atheism through to the bitter end; before you get too comfortable with the godless world you long for, you will be required by the logic of any consistent skepticism to pass through the disorientating wilderness of nihilism . . . you would have to experience the Nietzschean Madman's sensation of straying through 'infinite nothingness' . . . Are you willing to risk madness? If not, then you are really not an atheist.
>
> (2008, p. 24)

Scholars such as Gare (1996) seem to appreciate that how we understand and interpret this 'infinite nothingness' can affect our ways of recognising and (re)solving wicked socio-ecological problems.

For example, one paradox of instrumentalist materialism in the West, enabled by a particular interpretation and application of science, is that it seems to co-develop with a pervasive nihilism or negation of Ultimate meaning. As Weinberg (1977) writes at the end of his cosmological work *The First Three Minutes*, 'The more the universe seems comprehensible, the more it also seems pointless' (p. 154). There is an obstacle to coordinated responses to socio-ecological problems, especially through formalised EfS. The obstacle is that seemingly opposing sides (i.e. liberals on the left and conservatives on the right) each claim the other to be the nihilistic cause of environmental degradation. Indeed, it can be surprising for some liberal environmentalists, who see the unsustainable materialism of the industrial West as metaphysically nihilistic, to be seen as themselves nihilistic by some conservatives on the grounds of misanthropic worship at the idol of nature. Reciprocally, it can be surprising for some conservatives, who see the deep ecology movement and radical environmentalism as inherently nihilistic, to be seen as themselves nihilistic by some liberals on the grounds of the origins of Western instrumentalist materialism in a dominant form of Judeo-Christian theism characterised by a patriarchal, hierarchical, anthropocentric ethic that encouraged subjugation more than stewardship, and separation from, rather than interdependence with, the natural environment. The left has a tendency to emphasise the benevolence of nature and the malevolence of a culture which has destroyed it, while the right has a tendency to emphasise the malevolence of nature and the benevolence of a culture which has tamed it. A bi-relational (re)solution of such conflicts recognises the reality of this opposition, while encouraging reciprocal understandings of the relationality and degrees of diversity between these positions. Arguably, environmental problems are exacerbated when the constituents of dyads such as conservative/liberal, matter/spirit, nature/culture and technology/ecology are separated, reified and pursued as independent ends. The irony and tragedy of this dyadic independence is that the pursuit of one constituent at the expense of the other actually costs both.

However, we may expand the category of nature to include our human selves, and we may expand the category of our human selves to include all of nature, such that we are its teleological aim. In both claims we see the gradual inflation of one dyadic constituent to the point where it fully encompasses the other and the two become one, such that nature *is* culture *is* nature. My point is that neither of these views lends itself to any a priori ethical stance that the other could not also attain. Viewing human culture as encompassing nature may as much warrant the conservation of nature as viewing nature as encompassing human culture. This is a difficult dynamic to comprehend but one I suspect to be most important in directing dialogues about socio-ecological sustainability. My claim is that dialogues between advocates for matter or spirit, nature or culture will quickly dissolve into polemic and monologue if each claims to have an exclusive a priori moral authority or environmental ethic. Haught's (2008) association of atheism, madness and absurdity, and Gare's (1996) association of modernity and nihilism are warranted only inasmuch as atheists reject God and not all gods. But I suspect that such rejections interdepend on the certainty with which many theists accept gods as God. Onto-epistemological development recognises the possible expansion and transformation of either position into the other. These inversions and exchanges are as relevant and related to the dyad matter/spirit as they are to nature/culture.

Mathew's pan-psychic claim that all matter is intrinsically the expression of spirit is similar to the astronomer James Jeans' (1937) observation that 'The stream of knowledge is heading towards a non-mechanical reality; the Universe begins to look more like a great thought than like a great machine' (p. 137).

Arguably, both claims represent a relational reaction to the post-Enlightenment dominance of a rational, reductive and mechanistic form of materialism. Mathew's (2006) pan-psychic restoration of mind and spirit in the modern era is largely a rebellion against the perceived relationship between instrumental materialism and the destruction of the material environment. In a modern case of enantiodromia, the successful expansion of materialism paradoxically allows some to see the whole of matter in terms of spirit without recourse to naïve notions of divine intervention, the miraculous or the supernatural. This dyadic (re)union also allows post-materialists to break the naïve and unwarranted alliance between materialism and unbounded human consumption.

This transformation (i.e. matter to spirit) is not complete unless the inverse is also true (i.e. spirit to matter). It is possible for the category of spirit to become so encompassing of the whole of reality that we are inspired to examine the parts and wondrous workings of the great mind, only to come to the ultimate conclusion that the spirit moves in decidedly *mechanical* (i.e. predictable) ways – so much so that it might as well be called *matter*. This dyadic (re)union allows materialists to see the whole of spirit in terms of matter and break the unholy alliance between religion and divine petitioning as the only shelter from natural threats. My simple, but hopefully not overly simplistic claim, is that the (re)solution of some of our greatest socio-ecological problems will come from paradigms that can coordinate spiritual and material ways of knowing about the world and our place within it. Paradigms that adopt an exclusively either/or approach will offer attractive but short-term solutions that in the long term will paradoxically exacerbate the wicked socio-ecological problems they set out to resolve.

Conclusion

The purpose of this chapter was to sketch out a bi-relational approach to some of the socio-religious challenges of the twenty-first century. My claim again is that a bi-relational approach to development provides a useful way to conceptualise and (re)solve some of the wicked problems that arise in relation to dyads such as faith/reason, matter/spirit and, though I use the secondary dyad with caution, religion/science.

Furthermore, I hope to have highlighted the dyadic affinities between cultural, ecological and religious problems. And, finally, I hope to have highlighted the need to approach these problems relationally and contextually with an acute awareness that the 'same' referents (e.g. nature, culture, spirit, matter) may be known in deceptively different ways.

References

Atran, S. (2002). *In Gods we trust: The evolutionary landscape of religion.* New York: Oxford University Press.

Bacon, F. (2008). Of atheism. Athenaeum Reading Room. http://evans-experientialism. freewebspace.com/bacon02.htm

Barrett, J. L. (2000). Exploring the natural foundations of religion. *Trends in Cognitive Sciences*, 4(1), 29–34. doi: 10.1016/S1364-6613(99)01419-9.

Barrett, J. L. (2002). Dumb Gods, petitionary prayer and the cognitive science of religion. In I. Pyysiänen and V. Anttonen (Eds.), *Current approaches in the cognitive science of religion* (pp. 93–109). New York: Continuum.

Barrett, J. L. (2004). *Why would anyone believe in God?* (Cognitive Science of Religion Series). Walnut Creek, CA: Altamira Press.

Boyer, P. (1994). *The naturalness of religious ideas: A cognitive theory of religion*. Berkeley: University of California Press.

Boyer, P. (2000). Evolution of the modern mind and the origins of culture: Religious concepts as a limiting case. In P. Carruthers and A. Chamberlain (Eds.), *Evolution and the human mind: Modularity, language and meta-cognition* (pp. 93–112). Oxford: Oxford University Press.

Boyer, P. (2001). *Religion explained: The evolutionary origins of religious thought*. New York: Basic Books.

Coates, J. (2012). Prisoners of the story: A role for spirituality in thinking and living our way to spirituality. In J. Groen, D. Coholic and J. R. Graham (Eds.), *Spirituality in social work and education: Theory, practice, and pedagogies* (pp. 57–76). Waterloo, Canada: Wilfred Laurier University Press.

Collins, P. (1995). *God's Earth: Religion as if matter really mattered*. Blackburn, Australia: HarperCollins.

Dawkins, R. (1992). [untitled lecture]. Edinburgh International Science Festival.

Dawkins, R. (1998). *Unweaving the rainbow: Science, delusion and the appetite for wonder*. London: Penguin Books.

Dawkins, R. (2003). *A Devil's Chaplain: Reflections on hope, lies, science, and love*. Boston: Houghton Mifflin.

Dawkins, R. (2006). *The God delusion*. London: Bantam Books.

Dennett, D. C. (2006). *Breaking the spell: Religion as a natural phenomenon*. New York: Viking Penguin.

Fien, J. (2002). Synthesis: A cross-cultural reflection. In J. Fien, D. Yencken and H. Sykes (Eds.), *Young people and the environment: An Asia-Pacific perspective* (pp. 151–71). Dordrecht, The Netherlands: Kluwer Academic Publishers.

Freud, S. (2008). *Moses and monotheism*. Retrieved 23 May, 2008, from http://psychology.about.com/od/sigmundfreud/p/freud_religion.htm (Original work published 1939.)

Gandy, M. (1997). Postmodernism and environmentalism: Complementary or contradictory discourses? In M. Redclift and G. Woodgate (Eds.), *The international handbook of environmental sociology* (pp. 150–7). London: Edward Elgar.

Gare, A. (1996). *Nihilism Inc. Environmental destruction and the metaphysics of sustainability*. Sydney: Eco-logical Press.

Harris, S. (2005). *The end of faith: Religion, terror, and the future of reason*. London: Simon and Schuster.

Haught, J. F. (2008). *God and the new atheism: A critical response to Dawkins, Harris, and Hitchens*. Louisville, KY: Westminster John Know Press.

Hildén, M. (2011). The evolution of climate policies – the role of learning and evaluations. *Journal of Cleaner Production*, 19(16), 1798–1811. doi: 10.1016/j.jclepro.2011.05.004.

Hitchens, C. (2007). *God is not great: How religion poisons everything*. New York: Twelve Books.

Jeans, J. (1937). *The mysterious universe*. Cambridge: Cambridge University Press.

Joseph, R., Newberg, A., Albright, C. R., Rausch, C. A., Persinger, M., James, W., and Nietzsche, F. (2003). *Neurotheology: Brain, science, spirituality, religious experience.* San Jose, CA: University Press.

Kahan, D. M., Jenkins-Smith, H., and Braman, D. (2011). Cultural cognition of scientific consensus. *Journal of Risk Research*, 14(2), 147–174. doi: 10.1080/13669877.2010.511246.

Kelsey, E. (2011). *Beyond 'Doom and Gloom': Nurturing hopeful narratives in the age of climate change and environmental despair.* Invitational Seminar on Climate Change Education Proceedings, Cairns, Australia.

Kevorkian, K. (2004). *Environmental grief: Hope and healing.* PhD dissertation. Union Institute and University, Cincinatti, Ohio.

Mathews, F. (2006). Beyond modernity and tradition: A third way for development. *Ethics and the Environment*, 11(2), 85–114.

McEnhill, P., and Newlands, G. (2004). *Fifty key Christian thinkers.* London: Routledge.

Mortreux, C., and Barnett, J. (2009). Climate change, migration and adaptation in Funafuti, Tuvalu. *Global Environmental Change*, 19(1), 105–12. doi: 10.1016/j.gloenvcha.2008.09.006.

Newberg, A., D'Aquili, E., and Rause, V. (2001). *Why God won't go away: Brain science and the biology of belief.* New York: The Ballantine Publishing Group.

Persinger, M. (1987). *Neuropsychological bases of God beliefs.* New York: Praeger.

Ramachandran, V. S., and Blakeslee, S. (1998). *Phantoms in the brain: Human nature and the architecture of the mind.* London: Fourth Estate.

Tillich, P. (1951). *Systematic theology* (Vol. 1). Chicago, IL: University of Chicago Press.

Tracey, D. J. (1995). *Edge of the sacred: Transformation in Australia.* Blackburn, Australia: HarperCollins.

Twenge, J. M., Campbell, W. K., and Freeman, E. C. (2012). Generational differences in young adults' life goals, concern for others, and civic orientation, 1966–2009. *Journal of Personality and Social Psychology*, 102(5), 1045–62.

Wardekker, J. A., Petersen, A. C., and van der Sluijs, J. P. (2009). Ethics and public perception of climate change: Exploring the Christian voices in the US public debate. *Global Environmental Change*, 19(4), 512–21. doi: 10.1016/j.gloenvcha.2009.07.008.

Weinberg, S. (1977). *The first three minutes.* New York: Basic Books.

Part 3

Applications

Chapter 10

General applications of bi-relational development in education

The final chapters of this book consider the educational applications of bi-relational development. While I am hesitant to promote a developmental imperative as a basis for education, I see no reason to ignore the significant role that formal education plays in either facilitating or hampering onto-epistemological development needed to (re)solve wicked problems. Education can never separate itself from critique and I concur with Gopnik (2013) that 'Science may or may not find the one true origin for human symbol-making, but criticism, in caves and classrooms alike, will always have to learn to count to two' (n.p.). As I have argued previously, there is a bi-relational dimension to the conceptualisation of education as traditional or progressive, subjective or objective and as art or science. My trans-positional approach is that it can be both, and that the matter or degree should take into account the relationality of the two and the context of the problem. The totalisation of either approach at the expense of the other is likely to hamper development. If our ways of knowing and being are presented in overly universal terms and taught with exclusively traditional, transmissive and authoritarian pedagogies then we and our children are likely to exacerbate the wicked problems we seek to engage. Alternatively, if our ways of knowing and being are presented in overly relativistic terms and taught with exclusively progressive, constructivist and collaborative pedagogies then we and our children are likely to experience a loss of direction that can unite us in our diversity. Formal education gets into trouble when it decouples these approaches and chooses a 'one size fits all, once and for all' approach. Accordingly, this chapter provides a range of general strategies and pedagogies for the facilitation of bi-relational development.

My rationale for using BirD as an educational tool is that it promotes onto-epistemological dexterity. BirD represents more encompassing ways of knowing and being in order to facilitate more discriminating evaluations and actions. It offers a broader range of possibilities from which to identify or shape specific realities. And BirD offers a way to identify and (re)solve wicked problems in a variety of domains and contexts. I have explored these applications elsewhere in the context of sociocognitive conflict in school-based contexts (e.g. Adam, 2008b, 2010), onto-epistemological conflict in higher education

234 Applications

(e.g. Adam, 2011a, 2012a, 2012b, 2015), and sociocognitive conflict and religious/secular developments (e.g., Adam, 2003, 2007a, 2007b, 2008a, 2009a, 2009b, 2011b, 2013).

I frame my claim that formal education has a role to play in the engagement of wicked problems in the context of similar approaches to epistemological development that acknowledge the transformative and facilitative role of developmental theories in education. For example, Abraham (1993) offers a broad approach to the development of relational modes of thinking in education. Similar to BirD's core positions, he identifies a development between (1) unconscious unity, (2) conscious separation and duality and (3) conscious unity in the lifespan. More specifically, Reich (2002) identifies an approach to 'stimulating RCR in the classroom' (p. 160). To help students engage with dialectical problems he suggests encouraging (a) *differentiation* by using figure–ground shift and ambiguous-figure resources such as the young woman–old woman picture, (b) *integration* of dual concepts of time (e.g. linear and non-linear) using mechanical clocks and stimuli such as Dali's 'melting clocks' and (c) *different logics* such as formal dyadic logic and dialectical logic.

One of the few online resources for teachers relating to bi-relational development is the Imaginative Literacy Program, which offers the following rationale that I endorse in the broader project of education for the facilitation of dyadic development:

> We would be wise to be suspicious of the simple claim that young children and people in oral cultures are 'concrete thinkers;' the prevalence of this odd belief has obscured the sense in which they are also, and perhaps primarily, abstract thinkers. We can employ this powerful tool that all children have to help them in learning. This doesn't mean that we are going to teach them that everything is made up of binary opposites or to deal only with abstract concepts, but rather it might guide us to see how we can often introduce topics in binary terms, in order to provide a clear and comprehensible access to it. We can also make sure that topics are built on powerful abstract oppositions underlying them. Once access has been gained, then we can mediate between the opposites, and elaborate the content in all kinds of ways.
>
> (2013, para 9)

I have used BirD formally and informally in a variety of contexts over the last few years and seen its usefulness in reframing problems that were previously seen as intractable and situations often seen as hopeless. However, these applications presuppose some cautions.

By its very nature as a theory, I am cautious about the educational applications and implications of BirD. Some of this caution is due to the dual ontological-epistemological nature of the theory. Should BirD be taught formally as a decontextualised framework for 'how we know', it is as likely as any other theory to be known only in pro-dyadic ways: that is, over-simplified, abstract,

General applications in education 235

literal, rigid, all encompassing and prescriptive. As a lecturer in educational psychology I am acutely aware of the tendency for lecturers to present theories, and students to receive them, in such ways. Another reason for caution is that I do not think education to be, though as a lecturer this may seem heretical for me to say, intrinsically 'good'. The danger of students deeply understanding a theory is that they may be offended by it or challenged by it in ways that, at least in the short term, can cause intense growth pains or even pain without growth. I share Basseches' (1984, p. 29) recognition that certain ways of thinking can challenge 'intellectual security' in ways that are not easily identifiable as aiding 'psychological well-being'. Similarly, Abraham (1993) cautions against educational and pedagogical methods that are insensitive to the integrity of each developmental position or dominated by one position and argues: 'The over-emphasis of the present educational systems, generally speaking, is on the stage of intellection [i.e. separation], characteristic of a civilization that has lost for the most part its spiritual connection' (p. 121). I am mindful of the danger of 'intellectualising' bi-relational development and extracting it from the affectively, socially and 'spiritually' complex worlds of individual students and teachers. Kegan (1982) rightly warns educators who see themselves as facilitators of development through deliberate disequilibrium: 'The greatest limit to the present model of developmental intervention is that it ends up being an address to a *stage* rather than a person' (p. 277). More often than not, our intellectual securities are firmly attached to our ontological securities, and our psychological well-being is firmly attached to our social relationships and identity. Nonetheless, I see these cautions as refining rather than confining pedagogies that bring bi-relational approaches to wicked problems into the classroom.

Schools and universities, classrooms and lecture theatres are contested spaces for the clash and exchange of ideas. However, the ways educators create these spaces, facilitate these exchanges and engage in exchange themselves can powerfully influence learners' experience and development. In the context of dialectical thinking, Basseches provides a general but powerful description of a developmental approach in education:

> For an educational experience to promote development, it must challenge those structures of reasoning which the individual uses to make sense of the world. It must first engage the individual's existing structures and, with them, the individual's emotional and cognitive investment in the experience. Then it must stretch those structures to their limits, and beyond, to the point where they are found wanting. At the same time, the experience must provide the elementary material out of which the individual can construct new, more sophisticated cognitive structures.
>
> (1984, pp. 302–3)

How, then, is it possible to 'challenge those structures of reasoning' and facilitate the development of trans-positional ways of knowing and being?

236 Applications

Given the endless possibilities, I hope to provide some general examples of bi-relational pedagogy in the following sections and chapters.

I have organised these examples into two sections, each with three sub-sections (rationale, resources, activities). The first section is designed to facilitate the development of learners' dyadic vocabulary: that is, the range of dyads (i.e. oppositions, antonyms) that they can identify in context. The second section is designed to facilitate the development of dyadic relationships that move into and beyond binary opposition. Finally, as a general principle, bi-relational pedagogies should be used 'bi-relationally', such that: (1) *abstract* concepts help us to understand *concrete* contexts which generate *abstract* concepts, (2) *simple* representations help us to understand *complex* realities which generate *simple* representations, (3) *transmission* aides the *discovery* of knowledge which prompts its *transmission* and (4) *teaching* is a measure of *learning* which informs *teaching*.

Improving dyadic vocabulary

Rationale

This section focuses on reasons, resources and activities for improving learners' dyadic vocabularies. In more common terms, this vocabulary is known as a list of opposites or antonyms. One of the earliest developmental tasks is binary categorisation. So, as children we learn to distinguish between hot and cold, left and right, up and down, and heavy and light. This stage is marked by the transition from pre-dyadic to pro-dyadic ways of knowing. This identification of opposites does not end in childhood and should not be relegated to childhood. The identification of opposites (i.e. a dyadic vocabulary) is a lifelong task. We move from simple opposites such as big/small to more complex ones like objective/subjective as our conceptual awareness and self-awareness develops. The accumulation of polarities is educationally useful as it allows us to understand, to make decisions within and to integrate new domains of knowledge. However, while the need to identify dyads continues, the premise of BirD is that the way we relate dyadic constituents develops or expands beyond simple binary oppositions as we develop. Arguably, this development does not extinguish the need for dyads; rather, it is understood in relation to dyads. Accordingly, this first section explores resources and activities to assist in the lifelong identification of dyads. There is perhaps a need for more advanced resources in secondary and tertiary education as failure to recognise the inherent 'opposites' at work in life's later problems can merely frustrate attempts to find solutions.

Resources

There are many age-appropriate lists and presentations of opposites available online or in book form. For example, some children's books such as Meredith's

General applications in education 237

(2011) *Left or Right* focus on a particular dyad. Some children's books such as Cook's (1989) *Word Study Fun: Like and Opposite Meanings* contain worksheets of synonyms and antonyms. Other books such as MacRae and Odriozola's (2006) *The Opposite* and Dr Seuss' (1990) *Oh the Places That You'll Go* integrate the idea of opposites into a story. There are also websites with lists of opposites that provide a range of interactive exercises. For example, the *Manythings* (Kelly and Kelly, 2010) site contains interactive quizzes on lists of opposites, and I have listed some others below.

- http://www.manythings.org/vocabulary/lists/2/words.php?f=opposites

Similarly, the Picture Dictionary for Kids (2011) site contains interactive videos and flash cards of opposites.

- http://englishwilleasy.com/english-through-pictures/dictionary-children/opposites-words/

For older children and adolescents there are online antonym generators such as:

- http://www.synonym.com/antonyms/

There are also many online videos that introduce children to the concept of opposites using songs and visual representations. For example:

- http://www.youtube.com/watch?v=TW4OQxUVjiE
- http://www.youtube.com/watch?v=BjQT1kpBwcg
- http://www.youtube.com/watch?v=LMEIyTwuj4w

Such textual and online resources can assist teachers in the identification of dyads. Nonetheless, the human resources that exist in any educational setting may be invaluable in generating dyads. Of course, the provision of lists is of little pedagogical value without the 'real world' contextualisation of dyads through activities.

Activities

Pairing: in these activities, learners find the pair (i.e. opposite, complement) for a dyadic constituent (e.g. hot, small, heavy). This can be done in many ways, including:

- pair flash cards where the paired constituent is spoken aloud
- pair flash cards where multiple learners match pairs by turning over matching pairs in successive turns
- antonym word associations where the pair is spoken aloud, written or typed in a blank space
- dyadic crosswords where the clue is the antonym of the answer

238 Applications

Induction and illustration: in these activities, learners explore texts, places and spaces to find implicit or explicit dyads and/or look for instances of prefigured dyads. For example:

- early childhood teachers can use storybooks (e.g. *Beauty and the Beast*) and fables (e.g. *The Tortoise and the Hare*) to help children identify simple dyads (e.g. beautiful/ugly, fast/slow)
- adolescents and young adults can identify dominant dyads in movies, novels, plays, computer games, songs or poems, popular television or magazine advertisements (e.g. rich/poor, fail/succeed, male/female)

At any age, excursions can be used to immerse learners in environments and experiences for the induction of dyads. For example:

- children can identify dyads that are relevant at a zoo or farm (e.g. big/small, tall/short, common/rare, wild/domestic).
- adolescents and young adults can identify dyads that are relevant at a sporting event (e.g. winner/loser, skill/strength, defend/attack, theory/practice) or meeting (e.g. formal/informal, soft/loud, structured/chaotic, authoritarian/egalitarian).

The dyads and examples identified in these activities can be presented using lists, dialogues, essays, mash-ups, posters, interactive presentations or even online movies. Collectively, these resources and activities can aid the identification of dyads. This is perhaps the first step in development of dyadic relationships.

Developing dyadic relationships

Rationale

A key premise of this book and the application of BirD is that the facilitation of development beyond binary oppositional ways of knowing is essential for the adaptive (re)solution of many wicked problems. Many teachers are uncomfortable with using binary oppositions, as illustrated by an extract from the Imaginative Literacy Program:

> Some of the teachers we've worked with have been initially reluctant to try out this particular tool. Some said that they didn't want to encourage the children to see the world in terms of opposites, and they were especially wary of using such opposites as good/bad. They felt that it led to stereotyping and simplifying when the aim of education was to give children a more complex view of things. Also, they said, nothing was simply good or bad and no one was simply courageous or cowardly; that such opposites were always mixed.
>
> (2013, para 7)

General applications in education   239

The teachers' concerns are warranted if the educative experience begins and ends with the identification of binary oppositions. However, my claim is that pro-dyadic binary oppositions are a natural and necessary point of departure for more nuanced and complex post-dyadic relationships. Young or old, implicitly or explicitly, learners use dyads. The pedagogical challenge is to dissolve binary oppositions by filling in the blank spaces that sustain them with degrees of difference, shades of grey, continua and spectra. However, I maintain that removing the ends, or polarities, of the spectrum altogether is as maladaptive as removing the connection between them.

As a former English teacher at a time of transition between modern and postmodern curricula, I can recall the discontent experienced by students and teachers when the novelty of deconstruction that was ideologically endorsed in the then new English syllabus evolved into a sort of relativistic cynicism. Students and teachers longed to construct again, rather than endlessly deconstruct children's fairytales with a sort of malicious objectivity. In hindsight, I think that the deconstruction movement in education, which reveled in exposure of binary oppositions, got tangled in its own polarisation towards deconstruction and pessimism in relation to construction and optimism. Perhaps the time was right and the abuses and counter-polarisations of the past had warranted the intensity of such deconstructions, but, in hindsight, it affirmed for me the need to move between the binary into order to move beyond it. Accordingly, the following resources and examples offer ways of representing and bridging binaries to move beyond mere opposition.

Resources

Visual metaphors. One of the most effective ways to help learners conceptualise dyadic relationships is to represent them with age-appropriate visual metaphors. As evidenced in previous chapters, many of these metaphors are also common in everyday communication, helping learners to implicitly and tacitly think about dyadic relationships. Some of these metaphors can be manipulated to represent a range of dyadic relationships. For example, a see-saw, scales, wings, feet, hands and piano keys all represent polarities with an almost infinite number of possibilities for coordination and movement between them. Feet can step left or right and up or down to navigate complex terrains; wings can flap in unison to move forward, or turn into the wind to move left or right; left and right hands can play black and white notes to create music; and so on. Each metaphor emphasises the abstract balance but contextual selection between dyadic constituents. Other metaphors such as perspective shapes, ambiguous figures and figure–ground-shift pictures can be used to emphasise the difficulty but importance of seeing multiple perspectives in the description of reality. Some metaphors such as the ladder and stairs may help to represent linear, hierarchical or sequential relationships between polarities in different contexts. Some metaphors such as the bridge help to represent the gap between polarities, while others like the pendulum help to represent the continuation between

240 Applications

polarities. Collectively, the metaphors can be used to expand on otherwise simplistic and exclusive binary oppositions.

Symbols. The dyadic symbols mentioned in Chapter 2 (e.g. cross, labyrinth, yin–yang) can also be used to reveal the ubiquity of dyads in human belief systems or worldviews. These metaphors and symbols can be engaged as visual representations or physical artifacts to mediate the use of general bi-relational approaches to specific wicked problems.

Allegories. There are also many extended metaphors and allegories that are useful to explore dyadic relationships. For example, poems such as Saxe's *The Blind Men and the Elephant* can be used to explore the complexity of subjective/objective relations. Film representations can also be powerful. For example, a scene in the film *Dangerous Minds* (Simpson and Bruckheimer, 1995) depicts two groups of rival students lined up to face each other across a line in the classroom. Their teacher reads questions (e.g. 'Who has had someone they know injured or killed in an act of violence?') to which students indicate an affirmative response by taking a step towards their enemy. By the end of the questioning, the clear lines between the rival groups are blurred and the space is disrupted as many come face-to-face with the deep similarities and affinities they share with their 'enemies'. Short videos like *Prickles and Goo* (Watts, n.d.), an animation of a monologue on the relationship between intellect and intuition, can be used to explore dyadic relationships between different types of personalities or professions with older learners.

Vote Compass. An excellent resource relevant to dyadic relationships and wicked problems for Australian learners in particular is the national broadcaster's *Vote Compass* project (ABC, 2013). This project collected over 1.4 million voter responses to statements related to key issues in the national 2013 election. Responses to 30 issue-based questions were collected using a five-point Likert scale with a 'don't know' option. The questions included:

- The Australian constitution should recognise indigenous people as Australia's first inhabitants. (Indigenous People)
- The government's parental leave pay should be the same for all working mothers. (Gender Equality)
- There should be fewer restrictions on coal seam gas exploration. (Natural Resources)
- Students in government and non-government schools should receive the same amount of federal funding. (Education)
- How much should the federal government do to tackle climate change? (Climate Change)
- Asylum seekers who arrive by boat should not be allowed to settle in Australia. (Asylum Seekers)
- How accessible should abortion services be in Australia? (Conscience)

The questionnaire also collected demographic data and general political-orientation data, for example: 'In politics people sometimes talk of left and

General applications in education   241

right. Where would you place yourself? (0 = left, 10 = right)'. The project offers a range of analyses, including a personal orientation in relation to major political parties visually mapped between a horizontal axis (economic left/economic right) and a vertical axis (social liberalism/social conservativism) and a video and map of Australia's most left-leaning and right-leaning seats. Such resources offer powerful demographic and geographic insights into dyadic relationships related to socio-political dyads (e.g. conservative/liberal) that are relevant to a wide range of wicked problems. Most importantly, such resources offer a powerful link between abstract dyadic analyses and concrete real-world problems.

Online educational videos. There are few resources for more direct engagement with dyadic relationships, though I have cited some relevant books that explore explicitly dyadic approaches in earlier chapters (e.g. Reich, 2002; Basseches, 1984; Riegel, 1979). There are also several short online video discussions of binary oppositions that may be useful for older learners. For example, the Investigative Education Research Group's (IERG, 2015) *Binary opposites* video offers a short discussion of practical ideas for teachers. The Institute of Art and Ideas' (IAI, 2015) video *Everywhere and nowhere: Are binary oppositions real?* is a panel discussion that offers multiple perspectives on the existence and usefulness of binary oppositions.

Cartesian See-saw. There are also more abstract models that represent dyadic relationships. Obviously, BirD is one of these models. Choices, judgements or decisions require valuing and evaluation – a weighing up of the positive and negative values of available information. BirD explores the onto-epistemological dimension of such evaluations and offers a bi-relational way of representing them that I have called the Cartesian See-saw (CSS) (Figure 10.1). The CSS is a particularly useful model for representing different dyadic relationships in a variety of contexts with older learners. It can be used to identify onto-epistemic positions in relation to particular dyads and to explore interactions (e.g. conflicts) between different positions.

The CSS is a basic representation of evaluations or weightings between dyadic constituents (e.g. conservative, liberal; traditional, progressive). The representation can help us to consider and identify some of the dynamics most relevant to development. Valuation or weighing between dyadic constituents guides everyday action and being and is the equation of quadrants, each representing the positive and negative dimensions of a dyadic constituent. In this visuo-spatial metaphor, the lower the constituent (e.g. like a person on a see-saw), the more weighting or privilege it has. In more symbolic terms, onto-epistemological disposition (d) is the sum of the positive disposition towards the left (A^+) and the negative disposition towards the left (A^-) compared to the positive disposition towards the right (B+) and the negative disposition towards the right (B-), such that:

$$d = (A^+ + A^-) >=< (B^+ + B^-).$$

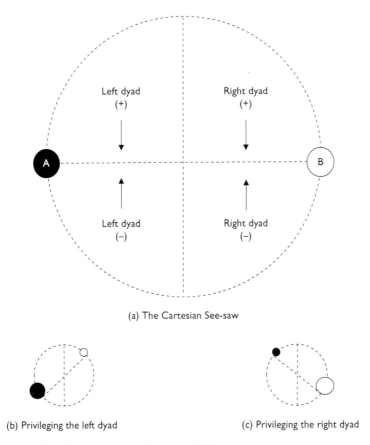

(a) The Cartesian See-saw

(b) Privileging the left dyad

(c) Privileging the right dyad

Figure 10.1 The Cartesian See-saw (CSS).

The interdependent sides swing, or see-saw, in relation to the relative weightings. So, Figure 10b shows a weighting towards the left dyadic constituent. Here, the positive valuation of the left constituent is increased relative to the negative valuation of the right constituent. Alternatively, Figure 10c shows a weighting towards the right dyadic constituent. Here, the positive valuation of the right constituent is increased relative to the negative valuation of the left constituent.

In keeping with the see-saw metaphor, a positive association with the left dyad (10b), like the weight of a person sitting on the left, will weight the see-saw to the left. However, a positive association with the right dyad (10c), like the weight of a person sitting on the right, will weight the see-saw to the right. A negative association with the right dyad, like a person pushing up with their

General applications in education   243

legs, exerts an upward force on the right, resulting in a weighting of the left dyad. Conversely, a negative association with the left dyad exerts an upward force on the left, resulting in a weighting of the right dyad. Thus, a bad experience with the right negatively reinforces the left and a bad experience with the left negatively reinforces the right.

For example, in a liberal/conservative dyad, a person who identifies strongly with a liberal (i.e. left) position may have a relatively strong identification *with* liberal values and *against* conservative vices, and a weak identification with conservative values and against liberal vices. When applied across contexts, the more polarised the product of these four dimensions, the more binary oppositional and absolutist (i.e. pro-dyadic) the onto-epistemological disposition of the individual or group tends to be.

I have previously used a variation of the CSS as a pedagogical tool to facilitate onto-epistemological exchanges between pre-service teachers (Adam 2012b). Participants identify and record formative life experiences, evidence and attitudes in relation to a domain-specific dyad (e.g. nature/nurture, intrinsic/ extrinsic [motivation]) in order to explore: (1) the complexity of relationships between dyads and their constituents, (2) the relativity and contextuality of dyads, (3) the diverse experiences that produce identity in relation to particular dyads and (4) the role of structure in the organisation of experience and the expression of onto-epistemological identity. Individual and group engagement with the CSS, or with the dyadic structure it represents, reveals intra-individual and inter-individual dynamics. A simpler abstract representation of different positions is the bi-relational scale introduced as the basic building block of Figure 5.2, where learners can identify single or multiple positions at or between polarities in a given context.

Venn diagrams. For all learners, Venn diagrams can provide a useful introduction to the idea of dyadic relationships and a point of departure for considering basic post-dyadic integrations and exchanges. Venn diagrams can graphically demonstrate different relationships between two sets contained in different circles that are positioned within a universal set, usually a rectangle. These relationships can include:

- A
- B
- Not B
- Not A
- A and not B
- B and not A
- A and B
- If A then B

- A if and only if B
- Not A and not B
- If B then A
- Not (A and B)
- A if and only if not B
- A or not A
- A or B
- A and not A

244 Applications

Collectively, these resources provide abstract representations with which to engage the concrete contexts where dyadic relationships are expressed.

Activities

The main elements of bi-relational pedagogy include (1) a dyad (e.g. conservative/liberal), (2) an abstract representation of dyadic relations (e.g. a CSS) and (3) a concrete context for application (e.g. Australian immigration policy in the context of boat arrivals and offshore processing). The following activities offer examples of these aspects in context.

Wall walk. This is a common activity used by teachers with adolescent learners. A physical representation of a polarity scale is set up in a room. The teacher reads out statements relating to a particular dyad and the learners physically position themselves on the scale. The learners may then volunteer to speak to their position. For example, a teacher in a senior Modern History class may use a wall walk to engage learners in discussion on the conservative/liberal dyad in the context of current issues such as gun control, immigration, mandatory sentencing or social welfare. For example, learners could position themselves in relation to immigration-related statements such as 'Asylum seekers who arrive by boat should not be allowed to settle in Australia'. Learners can also be allocated different roles to help them identify, empathise with and debate multiple positions. It is also useful in older groups to facilitate a meta-discussion as to what general factors are likely to cause differences of opinion on the issues. For example, it can be powerful for learners to see how demographic factors (e.g. age and gender), formative life experiences (e.g. knowing a refugee) and personality traits can be predictors of particular positions. Perhaps one of the most onto-epistemically transformative factors is the realisation of the general integrity and sincerity of mutually opposed parties. Demonisation of the *other* is one of the characteristics of binary oppositional ways of knowing and being. Activities such as the wall walk bring different learners into common spaces to understand and reflect on the origins of difference.

Scales. A similar activity can be done using scales and counters. In this activity, a set of scales representing polarities is positioned at the front of class or centre of a group. Participants are allocated a number of counters (i.e. plastic discs) with which to represent the strength of their position on an issue. They then speak or write to the issue or statement and allocate their counters to either side of the scales (or both), depending on the strength of their position. This particular activity is useful for younger secondary learners to see how different political systems allocate power in different ways as represented by the initial distribution of counters.

Venn diagrams. As already discussed, Venn diagrams can help learners to represent and complicate bi-relational categories. They are particularly useful for facilitating early steps beyond binary oppositional ways of grouping. Teachers can use pen and paper diagrams or physical representations (e.g. plastic

General applications in education   245

hoops, chalk on concrete, rope) to explore concrete problems. For example, Venn diagrams can be useful for complicating gender (i.e. male/female) oppositions and racial oppositions (e.g. black/white) by foregrounding intersecting spaces and commonalities. Learners can generate, locate and debate each group's personal experiences and general characteristics to begin to appreciate the 'fine lines' and fluidity between 'different' groups.

Dyadic analyses. An extension of the previous activities for identifying dyads is to identify dyadic relationships. For example:

- Early secondary teachers can use storybooks (e.g. *Beauty and the Beast*) and fables (e.g. *The Tortoise and the Hare*) to help children identify dyadic relationships between identified dyads (e.g. beautiful/ugly; fast/slow). For example, are these dyads presented in pro-dyadic terms as binary oppositions (e.g. physical beauty and fastness = goodness; ugliness and slowness = badness) or do they challenge and complicate these oppositions?
- Adolescents and young adults can identify dyadic relationships in movies, websites, novels, plays, computer games, songs or poems, popular television or magazine advertisements (e.g. rich/poor, fail/succeed, male/female, conformity/creativity). For example, are the dyads that dominate a particular advertisement in a magazine presented in pro-dyadic terms as binary oppositions (e.g. rich and male = goodness; poor and female = badness) or do they challenge and complicate these oppositions? What do pro-dyadic ways of knowing 'sound' like and look like? What do post-dyadic ways of knowing sound like and look like? The basic act of deconstruction can help to inform playful and serious reconstructions of text (e.g. alternative endings, narratives in the gaps).

Such activities can provide a platform for more explicit analyses and discussions of bi-relational dynamics. These meta-analyses and discussions are important because they can facilitate abstract understandings of dyadic relationships that learners can begin to apply and reflect on in new contexts.

CSS mapping. One of the most significant barriers to (re)solving wicked problems concerns the scale and proportion of the parts that build a representation of the problem. In other words, big pictures are difficult to draw on small canvases. I have seen many dialogues between well intentioned participants break down because while both participants can appreciate the integrity of their own position, neither has a conceptual scaffold (i.e. canvas) or structural metaphor that can accommodate both positions. Activities such as perspective mapping based on the CSS introduced earlier can help interacting learners to maintain the integrity of multiple positions by positioning them in relation to each other and a larger whole. For example, a learner can visually locate their negative experience with the left polarity in the lower left quadrant while understanding how a different learner can see a positive experience with a different dimension of the left polarity, depending on context. Consider a dyad such as conformity/creativity. Learner 1 may recall a difficult experience in a particularly rigid schooling system that did not accommodate her particular artistic talents and need for creative space. However, learner 2 may recall how the rigidity of a schooling system equipped her with the skills and perseverance to identify and develop her own artistic style in later years.

The educational usefulness of such visual representations, as simple as they are, is that they can be used to facilitate development beyond binary oppositional and mutually exclusive ways of relating dyadic constituents such as creativity and conformity. Learners can begin to appreciate post-dyadic ways of knowing, where 'conformity can obfuscate or facilitate creativity', depending on the interactions between learners and systems and the artistry and science of the teachers in-between.

Dialogical speaking. Formal debates have a long and dominant tradition in Western education, one that I have been heavily involved in both as a student and a teacher. In one sense, the debate, which is structured as a binary oppositional conflict between two sides, can be said to promote dialectical thinking as the audience appreciates the strengths and weaknesses of both sides. However, I sometimes wonder if the structure of formal debating can have the opposite effect, given its emphasis on the conflict of individual versus individual, school versus school and parent versus parent. Are the wicked problems of debating topics best approached with an adversarial structure? Teachers could be open to alternative speaking structures that promote dialogical approaches to wicked problems. For example, instead of two teams of three representing A versus B, two teams of two could explore a dyad in relation to a wicked problem in a way that disrupts the usual opposition. Here speaker 1 and speaker 2 from the 'same' team could present the case for the strengths and weaknesses of one dyadic constituent (e.g. liberal) respectively, while speaker 1 and 2 from the opposing team could present the case for the strengths and weaknesses of the complementary constituent (e.g. conservative). This structure disrupts or complicates the oppositional approach of traditional debating. It incorporates binary oppositions and dialectical approaches.

Illustrative applications. There are numerous bi-relational resources and activities. So far, I have attempted to provide a very small and general selection of examples to highlight many possibilities for the broader bi-relational project in the domain of formal education to facilitate more effective engagement with wicked problems. Though loosely formulated in the early stages of this project, I have adopted and applied an implicitly bi-relational approach in past educational projects, which may be summarised as follows:

- a bi-relational approach to the design of an interactive online rubric to support first-year students' academic literacy (Adam, 2015)
- a bi-relational approach to pedagogy in a primary mathematics classroom conceptualised in the cultural context of the 'Math Wars' (Adam and Chigeza, 2014)

- a bi-relational approach to pre-service teachers' pedagogical identity in a philosophy-of-education subject (Adam, 2012b)
- a bi-relational approach to the design and delivery of a behavior-management subject for pre-service teachers (Adam, 2010)
- a bi-relational approach to teachers' management of students' sociocognitive conflict in the face of cultural difference (Adam, 2008b)

Each of these projects relates to the wicked problems that teachers encounter in schools and universities as particularly diverse sites of socio-cultural engagement. While not explicitly in the context of formal education, I have also implicitly explored bi-relational dynamics and developments in relation to academic identity (Adam, 2012a) and socio-religious diversity, particularly in relation to religious fundamentalisms (e.g. Adam, 2007b, 2008a, 2009a, 2009b, 2011b, 2013). While it has taken a long time to crystallise my current approach to bi-relational development through these few projects – an approach that will no doubt change and 'develop' in the future – I hope to have seen the potential for a more explicitly bi-relational approach to wicked problems in formal educational settings.

Conclusion

It is important to note that the general and specific examples of bi-relational pedagogies and strategies I have provided here are by no means quick fixes or crash courses for ontologically entangled epistemological developments. Rather, they are facilitative and catalytic tools for teachers who mostly recognise that learning is never contained by school gates or within university corridors. Likewise, the wicked problems of education have little respect for classroom walls. Wise teachers cannot transcend the wicked problems of their own and students' lives by living safely on mountain tops or sheltering in caves; rather, they 'playfully' but purposefully move between transcendent perspectives and immanent concerns: 'One need not think of this process as involving a transcendence to a metaphysical realm, but a more limited self-transcendence that arrives at a new *betweenness* with the world' (Csikszentmihalyi and Rathunde, 1990, p. 39). To further highlight this 'betweenness' and the entanglement between the ontological and the epistemological dimensions of *teacher* development, the following chapter provides two case studies of professional educators reflecting on their bi-relational development and its influence on their ways of teaching.

References

ABC. (2013). Vote Compass project. Retrieved from http://www.abc.net.au/votecompass/

Abraham, K. (1993). *Balancing the pairs of opposites: The seven rays and education and other essays in esoteric psychology.* White City, Oregon: Lampus Press.

248 Applications

Adam, R. J. (2003). *Fundamentalism and structural development: A conceptual synthesis and discussion of implications for religious education* [Masters (Research) thesis]. James Cook University, Queensland, Australia. Retrieved from http://researchonline.jcu.edu.au/13/

Adam, R. J. (2007a). *A cognitive developmental analysis of apostasy from religious fundamentalism* [PhD thesis]. School of History, Philosophy, Religion and Classics, University of Queensland, Australia. Retrieved from http://espace.library.uq.edu.au/view/UQ:131309.

Adam, R. J. (2007b). Towards a synthesis of cultural and cognitive perspectives on fundamentalism. *Crossroads: An Interdisciplinary Journal for the Study of History, Philosophy, Religion, and Classics*, 1(2), 4–14.

Adam, R. J. (2008a). Relating faith development and religious styles: Reflections in light of apostasy from religious fundamentalism. *Archive for the Psychology of Religion/Archiv für Religionpsychologie*, 30(1), 201–31. doi: 10.1163/157361208X317204.

Adam, R. J. (2008b). *Sociocognitive conflict and cultural diversification: Problems and strategies for teachers*. Paper presented at the Australian Association for Research in Education (AARE), Brisbane, Australia.

Adam, R. J. (2009a). 'Leaving the fold': Apostasy from fundamentalism and the direction of religious development. *Australian Religion Studies Review*, 22(1), 42–63. doi: 10.1558/arsr.v22i1.42.

Adam, R. J. (2009b). 'Losing my religion': Religious development and the dynamics of apostasy. In M. Miner, M.T. Proctor and M. Dowson (Eds.), *Spirituality in Australia: Directions and applications* (Vol. 2, pp. 36–57). Sydney: Australasian Centre for Studies in Spirituality.

Adam, R. J. (2010). Schooling for hard knocks: Using scenario-based learning (SBL) for behaviour management skills in pre-service teacher education. In E. P. Errington (Ed.), *Preparing graduates for the professions using Scenario-based Learning* (pp. 97–110). Brisbane, Qld: Post Pressed Publishers.

Adam, R. J. (2011b). An epistemic analysis of religious fundamentalism. *The International Journal for the Study of Spirituality and Society*, 1(1), 81–95.

Adam, R. J. (2011a). *Engaging the epistemic dimension of preservice teachers' identity: A pedagogical tool*. Paper presented at the Australian Teacher Educators Association (ATEA) annual conference, Melbourne, Australia.

Adam, R. J. (2012a). Conceptualising the epistemic dimension of academic identity in an age of Neo-liberalism. *Education Research and Perspectives*, 39, 70–89.

Adam, R. J. (2012b). An exploration of the epistemic dimension of preservice teachers' identity. *Online Journal Of New Horizons In Education*, 2(2), 1–27.

Adam, R. J. (2013). 'The Devil wears nada': The Simpsons and the demythologisation of the apocalypse archetype. In J. Aston and J. Walliss (Eds.), *Small screen revelations: Apocalypse and prophecy in contemporary television* (pp. 179–202). Sheffield: Sheffield Phoenix Press.

Adam, R. J. (2015). Bi-relational design: A brief introduction and illustration. *Journal of Learning Design*, 8(1), 1–20. doi: 10.5204/jld.v8i1.129

Adam, R. J., and Chigeza, P. (2014). Beyond the binary: Dexterous teaching and knowing in mathematics education. *Mathematics Teacher Education & Development*, 16(2), 108–25.

Basseches, M. (1984). *Dialectical thinking and adult development*. Norwood, NJ: Ablex Publishing.

Cook, J. (1989). *Word study fun: Like and opposite meanings/grades 2–3*. Elizabethtown, PA: Continental Press.

General applications in education   249

Csikszentmihalyi, M., and Rathunde, K. (1990). The psychology of wisdom: An evolutionary interpretation. In R. Sternberg (Ed.), *Wisdom, its nature, origins and development* (pp. 25–51). Cambridge: Cambridge University Press.

Gopnik, A. (2013). Mindless: The new neuro-skeptics. *The New Yorker*, 9 September. Retrieved from: www.newyorker.com/magazine/2013/09/09/mindless

IAI [Institute of Art and Ideas]. (2015, April 10). *Everywhere and Nowhere: Are binary oppositions real?* [video file]. Retrieved from http://www.youtube.com/watch?v=GqCUiPbzxi4.

IERG [Investigative Education Research Group]. (2015, September 9). *Binary Opposites* [video file]. Retrieved from http://www.youtube.com/watch?v=FylRwSJy7WU

Imaginative Literacy Program. (2013). More about binary opposites. Retrieved from http://www.ierg.net/ilp/teacher-resources/cognitive-toolkits/more-about-binary-opposites/

Kegan, R. (1982). *The evolving self: Problem and process in human development*. Cambridge, MA: Harvard University Press.

Kelly, C., and Kelly, L. (2010). Manythings. Retrieved from http://www.manythings.org/vocabulary/lists/2/words.php?f=opposites

MacRae, T., and Odriozola, E. (2006). *The Opposite*. Atlanta, GA: Peachtree Publishers.

Meredith, S. M. (2011). *Left or right?* Vero Beach, FL: Rourke Pub.

Picture Dictionary for Kids. (2011). Opposites. Retrieved from http://englishwilleasy.com/english-through-pictures/dictionary-children/opposites-words/

Reich, K. H. (2002). *Developing the horizons of the mind: Relational and contextual reasoning and the resolution of cognitive conflict*. Cambridge: Cambridge University Press.

Riegel, K. F. (1979). *Foundations of dialectical psychology*. New York: Academic Press Inc.

Seuss, D. (1990). *Oh, the places you'll go!* New York: Random House.

Simpson, D., and Bruckheimer, J. (1995). *Dangerous minds*. US: Hollywood Pictures.

Watts, A. (producer). (n.d.). *Prickles and Goo*. Retrieved from http://www.youtube.com/watch?v=D4vHnM8WPvU

Chapter 11

Narrative explorations of bi-relational development in education

The following examples of bi-relational development and education are based on two semi-structured interviews with practising teacher educators. Together, I hope they highlight the relationship between bi-relational development, life experience and education. After all, the ways we encounter and engage wicked problems in our own lives will ultimately be reflected in the ways we teach and learn from others.

Case one: Carolyn – teacher of dance and the arts (mind/body)

At the time of the interview, the female participant (pseudonym Carolyn) was a schoolteacher in her mid fifties, a PhD student and a sessional university lecturer who specialised in the field of dance and arts education. Carolyn selected *mind/body* from the list of available dyads as the dyad that most resonated with her ways of knowing, being and teaching.

Summary analysis

The most general level of analysis suggests a deeply introspective teacher whose life experiences and reflections have led her to a very conscious post-dyadic attempt to reconcile mind and body in her ways of teaching. Like many participants, this reconciliation is made all the more necessary but difficult by her negative experiences with one of the polarities. For Carolyn, her pre-dyadic emergence of an early identification with bodily expression through movement came into pro-dyadic conflict with a system of schooling that seemed, for her, to separate and place the two in hierarchical opposition. She valued the affective, existential and intuitive expressiveness of the physical self, but found herself and later her children to be immersed in school environments that valued the logico-mathematical intellect alone, or the aggressive physicalities of a competitive sporting culture. Her subsequent trajectory reflects a re-identification from alienated to accepted and then, more recently, a deliberate attempt to relativise and subsume both ways of identifying within a broader framework, while retaining her own identity.

Carolyn's experiences with formal schooling have profoundly shaped the ways she relates mind and body. The premise of BirD is that these ways of relating dyadic constituents can help us to understand our ways of knowing and being ourselves in relation to others. Educators have a professional as well as personal interest in the ways in which different types of schooling are experienced by different types of student. As an educator and teacher-trainer, Carolyn's ways of knowing and being are deeply linked to her ways of teaching, but these ways of teaching can only be understood in relation to her ways of being taught and taught to know. Therefore, the final section explores this aspect of her mind/body relationship to show how onto-epistemological dispositions relate to pedagogical dispositions in the context of wicked problems.

Pre-dyadic disposition and schooling

From an early age, Carolyn's onto-epistemological disposition was characterised by her need to physically move in order to express herself. She recalls herself 'as a child growing up needing to move all the time' and reflects, 'I also need to move a lot, so it's part of me'. She then provided the following example:

> I was a strange child who used to write in the air ... I didn't know until about seven years ago ... and I suddenly realised what I'd been doing as a child was various forms of figure of eight ... I realised that when I get stressed or worried about something or needed to think about something I'd start doing that in my head. I'd start doing these figure of eights in my head and that's what I was doing when I was a child. I would use that because I was extremely shy and nervous and I would do that as a way of coping. And it became a thing and it suddenly came back to me this movement I did, following this movement helps me to calm down, focus, think about things ... I've always had that.

Pre-dyadic dispositions emerge very early in life. However, they are pre-dyadic in the sense that the dispositions are not well developed enough to be compared and contrasted with others' dispositions and held in a conscious relationship. Nonetheless, these relationships may be felt and intuited.

For many children, schooling provides some of the first and most powerful experiences of difference and diversity that are needed to 'know' or 'be' oneself in relation to others. For Carolyn, the school environment was a powerful context for implicit learnings about body and mind:

> When you are a child in kindergarten or the first years of school what you're learning is how the body should be and how the body should relate

to each other and itself in a learning environment ...What do you learn about your body when you're at school. You learn a lot of things and it's the hidden curriculum.

However, these learnings are not always implicit or 'hidden' in the curriculum:

I know principals who make it clear to their staff that good learning takes place when children are sitting still and a child in a chair facing the teacher is the epitome of a good learning moment.

The types of message a child receives about their disposition in this learning environment can be powerfully formative. For a child, the school and the authorities in it are the world, and not merely one way of doing things among many. The emergence of a particular disposition is likely to be inflated positively or negatively, depending on the nature of the school environment and a particular child's disposition.

For Carolyn, the emergence of her own disposition to express herself through physical movement (i.e. what she associates with the body) was in conflict with the school environment. Her relative identification with the body emerged during childhood and was negatively reinforced by her sense of alienation and strangeness with her immediate educational contexts. She recalls feeling like 'a strange child, and always in my education, feeling out of place'. She characterises her own school environment and her son's school environment as subordinating the body to the mind. Her disposition towards the body was negatively reinforced in later life by seeing her own child experience a similar alienation from his immediate contexts that also seemed to simultaneously subordinate the body and privilege the mind: 'Seeing my own children, one of my own children in particular, struggling with school and struggling with needing to keep still as part of his learning'. On her son's experience she reflects, 'it was the school trying to train his body to do the right thing which was to keep still and to focus on the teacher and to keep the body parts ... it was a struggle for him'.

Pro-dyadic dispositions: sport vs. dance

In her own schooling, Carolyn felt that the sense of belonging was generally reserved for a kind of individualistic, brute physicality (i.e. body) that was divorced from the mind: 'I just didn't really fit in with the maybe sporty, tough kind of chicks that were around'. Here the pro-dyadic separation of mind and body is seen to impoverish both. The range of physical actions and expressions (i.e. body) and the range or applications of intelligences (i.e. mind) are narrowed through the privileging of a particular subset. It could be argued that Carolyn's pejorative characterisation of 'sporty, tough chicks' is similarly pro-dyadic in the sense that it narrows intelligence in failing to perceive it in this

Narrative explorations in education 253

form of physicality. The interviewer then pursued this theme in the context of sport, noticing that Carolyn had occasionally seemed to position sport as body without mind, and dance as mind and body. She confirmed this distinction:

> Some sports can be expressive as in ice-skating or gymnastics, but that's not its purpose. The beauty of the movements are there because they fit certain requirements and a certain look, something that is beautiful, but dance can break all of those rules down because the thing that you need to express might be expressed best with something that actually looks quite, seems quite ugly, strange and distorted ... [Sport is] for a goal, to win and to increase fitness and maybe learn some other useful skills like persistence, and so forth. But ideally the arts can do that but it can do other things as well and on top of that.

Carolyn sees a dichotomy between sport and the arts as competitive/ collaborative, goal-orientated/process-orientation and skilful/creative:

> It's creative work, it's not about competition. It's about how can we best communicate that idea and it's around expressing something, and that reason that you do that movement is not to kick that goal but to express that idea, or [you know] it's got all that other emotional stuff.

Indeed, some of her early postgraduate work examined children's perceptions of sport and dance:

> They were young people studying dance as a subject at school and I was interested in how they saw the difference between sport and dance. And a lot of them did play sport as well, but the kind of thing that they said is 'sport's just running around but dance is about expression. It's about your feelings'.

It is possible that Carolyn's earlier experience of the 'sporty, tough chicks' has sustained her relative focus on the negative manifestations of sport. When the interviewer recontextualised her characterisations of sport in light of these previous experiences, Carolyn responded that the sport of these experiences was 'total physicality for a goal'. She also reflected, 'I see dance and some people have said it involves the mind and the body and the heart at the same time. And when I tried to play netball there was something missing'. So, in context, her characterisation of sport as body separated from mind is a form of counterbalancing in a context where there is already an imbalance, and dispositions like Carolyn's are alien and alienated.

Carolyn perceives these school contexts as privileging a particularly intellectualised and compartmentalised view of the mind as a reflection of a broader institutionalised privileging of the mind in Western societies. Specifically, she

254 Applications

sees this as a legacy of a Cartesian separation of mind and body that gives rise
to a binary oppositional relationship:

> The body is basically a vehicle to carry the mind around which is a supe-
> rior part and that it's come to dominate education. It's my view that
> thinking [that] though the mind is privileged over the body ... in educa-
> tion the body is disruptive; the body gets in the way so we always try to
> control the body to allow the mind to do its work.

While it may not be philosophically accurate to describe this form of separation
as 'Cartesian', it is still an accurate description of the felt separation of mind and
body that defined her school experience. This separation characterises pro-dyadic ways of knowing and being. The great divorce of mind and body, intellect
and physicality leads inevitably to hegemonic and hierarchical structures that
are 'felt' by all of us, children included, in different ways.

Pro-dyadic reinforcements

Intense pre-dyadic experiences of acceptance or alienation can develop into
pro-dyadic oppositions and separations that either reinforce the accepting discourse or challenge the alienating discourse. However, the strength to consciously challenge an alienating discourse often requires social acceptance with
a counter-culture and the language of resistance that develops within it.

For Carolyn, the formative experiences that began to reveal an alternative
culture of acceptance involved a particular teacher and, later, travel. She recalls
the formative influence of one of her own teachers as an exception to the educational norm, a teacher who reconciled mind and body in the context of dance:

> My first teacher of dancing was a very unusual woman from Eastern
> Europe who'd been a classical ballet dancer, contemporary dancer and
> came to Australia and did a lot of expressive dance called in those days, so
> at the end of a class she would sit us down and talk about culture and art
> and connecting always the creative and philosophy and ideas, and I came to
> see that they were connected.

Carolyn's disposition towards the body was positively reinforced in other contexts involving dance and travel, which celebrated the physical movement of
the body and reduced the sense of childhood alienation. She recalled discover-
ing 'people like her' and encountering specific cultures that positively reinforced her sense of connection between mind and body. Carolyn described
Italians as being like her: '[they] wave their arms around a lot when they are
talking because they need their hands to help explain things ... we've got these
metaphors and images of the body to explain our feelings and our thoughts,
and so on. I think they [Italians] are very connected'.

Similarly, her lifelong experiences with diverse groups of people added to her sense of belonging and an appreciation for human difference and diversity: 'A lifetime of dancing and being involved with movement and involvement in working with all kinds of people with different abilities was always something kind of important to me'. Collectively, such formative experiences accumulate contents that co-evolve with the ways we structure and organise it. Perhaps one of the most difficult onto-epistemological challenges for those who have been personally and structurally alienated earlier in life is the re-accommodation of the 'other' that is held responsible for this alienation. For Carolyn, the post-dyadic challenge was to accommodate this 'other' into the diversity that she now embraces. In other words, how do the 'sporty, tough chicks' fit into her current ways of knowing and being?

Post-dyadic developments

Carolyn reflected directly on the development of her approach to the mind/body dyad and identified a period of reactionary polarization, when she privileged the body over the mind, while rejecting understandings of the body as 'brute physicality':

> I think for a while I was rejecting the mind; it's all about the body. Children have to learn through the body. That's so important whether they're in a garden or whatever, we've got to get back to our bodies because we need them. That's what we've got to live.

Understandably, this pro-dyadic separation was perhaps a reaction to past experiences with the 'sit still or play sport' school culture she perceived in childhood.

Self-awareness of this subjectivity is a powerful indicator of post-dyadic development and the collapse of dyadic separation. For Carolyn, the last few years have been an especially significant time in the (re)conciliation of mind and body. She demonstrates dyadic reflexivity, given her familiarity with the pairing of mind and body, reflecting, 'it was after taking up a research subject in order to enter postgraduate study that I became aware of this body/mind split'. This awareness seems coupled with a realisation of experiences that bring them back together after a period of separation:

> Some things that I've read and experienced have maybe brought them back together a lot more, because I've worked with some incredible people in the last couple of years ... and they really, they really did bring them back together.

This reconciliation is not the naïve balancing of early post-dyadic epistemologies; rather, Carolyn manages to maintain a late post-dyadic tension between

256 Applications

her subjective ontology and a broader interpersonal ontology that embraces even the 'other' that a part of her resists.

Dyadic collapse and trans-positions

Late post-dyadic development is characterised by the ability to appreciate the abstract unity and balance of opposites, while understanding that this unity and balancing requires counterbalancing in dynamic real-world contexts. Carolyn's reflections show clear evidence of both. She perceives the opposition between mind and body and sees the division and separation as artificial: 'In recent times by doing copious amounts of reading and practical research I've come to see that this division ... it's an artificial construct that we're separate'. This reflection demonstrates post-dyadic convergence as the separation decreases, perhaps close to collapse in the perception that the construct is artificial. Carolyn later expresses this as drawing together the ends of a line to create a circle:

> [S]o I guess I'm thinking now that it's not a line and I found something in this which I found really interesting – that when you join the ends of a line together they make a circle ... you know there's a hierarchy that when you shift that, when you flip that over on its side and then it's not a hierarchy anymore it's a line that you can travel on. And then if you go and join those then it becomes something else again.

The circular metaphor reflects an implicit awareness of enantiodromia – the realisation that some attempts to separate and oppose can lead to a transformative encounter with oneself in one's opposition.

While appreciating the cyclic, balanced, unitary relationship between dyadic polarities, Carolyn also sees herself as counterbalancing the contextual privileging of mind over body in education. Her reflexivity on this counterbalancing is a mark of late post-dyadic ways of knowing:

> [I'm] privileging the body, again it's really to redress the balance because I don't think that they are separate things ... I'm running around trying to promote and advocate for more, valuing the body more in learning than it has been up until now ... Maybe I'm trying to hold the fort for the body in a way.

There is clear evidence of reflexivity: that is, she is self-conscious of the way she positions others and is positioned herself. Pro-dyadic dispositions tend not to 'step outside' the opposition to reflect on its subjective dimension. Carolyn's counterbalancing disposition towards the body is also revealed in her claim that the body comes before the mind.

It's the thing that comes before. You know we're made to think before I am, but we are before we think and we move, the first thing we do is move so it goes right back to that for children and that's my probably my big thing, and old people.

She is clear and conscious of this counterbalancing: 'So, they're so connected, but the whole trying to put emphasis back on the body I think is to try and tip that from, maybe from being vertical back to being horizontal.' Tellingly, Carolyn identifies with a counterbalancing movement in dance that uses the term 'embodiment' to mean 'understanding through the body' and is used for 'breaking down the distinction between the body and the mind'. Arguably, this reflexivity demonstrates a post-dyadic or even trans-positional development that moves beyond mere opposition and separation.

The movement beyond pro-dyadic opposition is also reflected in Carolyn's awareness of self-contradiction between her diversity-encompassing onto-epistemic disposition and her sense of otherness from the dispositions represented by 'sporty, tough chicks'. She is still a little apologetic, as if there is a contradiction rather than a fully conscious acceptance of a subjective stance or commitment in relativity: 'You know, it's hard to explore something without feeling that you're . . . [you know that I'm] making a lot of value judgements'. The complete extinction of dyads can be brought about by the pursuit of this line of reasoning. The post-dyadic disposition is characterised by its embrace of diversity and its expansiveness beyond the binary oppositions of pro-dyadic positions. However, diversity and expansiveness are only 'known' in relation to another who is homogenous and narrow. The downward spiral towards the total extinction of dyads sees deep reflection on the possibility of encompassing that which seeks to be apart, including that which seeks exclusion, and connecting that which seeks separation.

Mind, body and pedagogy

A central assumption of BirD is that our epistemological dispositions are deeply connected to our ontological dispositions: that is, there is a relationship between our ways of knowing and being in the contexts and domains of everyday life. For Carolyn, the dyadic relationships between mind and body are manifested in the context of dance education. Her post-dyadic approach to mind and body is evident in her explanations of dance:

> I'm not talking here about just learning a dance – that's something and it's important and it's physical and it's fun and people have to work together in unison and that's all good for society, but I'm talking about something a bit different. So, I'm talking about in learning it's a kind of physical problem solving and it's expressive at the same time about something. So I'm talking

258 Applications

about dance that's about something where children or people or whoever find ways to express an idea through movement.

Here, she rejects the notion of dance as a purely physical activity (i.e. body) as opposed to a mental activity (i.e. mind). Rather, it is the bodily expression of an idea and the physical solving of a mental problem. She contrasts her approach with others she has seen that seem to privilege the body over the mind in the context of dance:

> You sometimes hear judges on reality dancing TV shows say, 'just move don't think', which I think is a wrong way to go about it because [you know thinking] they're combined, they're together, our body and our mind are in the same, you know we don't have a mind over here and a body over here.

Such extracts reflect the language of a post-dyadic disposition that brings dyadic constituents together.

However, the later post-dyadic and trans-positional developments can reconcile this bringing together with the contextual and functional use of deliberate separations. In a pedagogical sense, teachers often separate a thing in order to bring it together more fully. Carolyn reflects:

> Oh they're [i.e. mind/body] still useful and sometimes when you're teaching . . . it's good to separate and sit down and let's verbalise and let's write what we're thinking, describe what we're seeing in words and make that connection between here and here and keep making it rather than just, dancing is just exercise. It's actually a thoughtful expression, so in my teaching I'm always trying to hopefully get children to see that connection – that we're not just here doing something that's just fun or exercise.

Tellingly, she conceptualises the relationship between mind and body in metaphorical terms as relating to a Presi platform. Presi is a post-linear presentation tool that is commonly contrasted with the relatively more linear PowerPoint:

> So this body/mind thing maybe it's like a kind of giant Presi . . . you know it's all these things are floating around and you go 'vvvup'. It kind of zooms in and then [you know], it's a bit like that. Sometimes you want to focus on the mind because you want them to perceive and see. You want them to articulate what they're feeling, and so on.

This implicit reconciliation of separation and connection demonstrates a post-dyadic way of teaching. Such teaching uses analysis to inform synthesis, separation to inform connection, and reduction to inform wholeness.

Carolyn suggests that a teacher with a different onto-epistemological disposition in relation to the mind/body dyad may have been a more effective teacher

Narrative explorations in education 259

for her son: 'I think if it had been a more creative and perhaps open-minded teacher he may have been able to come to that stillness in his own way, but he was kind of forced into it'. Her own pedagogical disposition seems to reflect a collaborative rather than individual approach. It is experimental, conversational and physical, breaking down pro-dyadic oppositions between mind and body. She reflects:

> It's a kind of creativity that's not individual. People are calling it 'small C creativity' – this idea of creativity coming out of a group rather than individual genius ... they're trying out ideas and bouncing off each other and they're [kind of] in a kind of conversation, which is physical. It's quite amazing.

The interviewer asked Carolyn how she approaches students who do not identify with these ways of doing the arts. Arguably, such students can experience a form of alienation that mirrors her educational alienation as a child. A typical pro-dyadic answer would reflect an oppositional disposition such as 'I had to learn to deal with it so they should too' or 'they just need to get out of their comfort zone like I had to'. However, Carolyn's response is more post-dyadic than reverse discriminatory:

> You know some dance is not for everybody. Nothing can be. So students come into the arts subject at university with bad experiences, with negative experiences, with a view that really they're just a waste of time, the arts are just a waste of time or a terrible fear in themselves about their own body. So all sorts of reasons why they come into it wishing they didn't have to do that.

She blames a counter-collaborative culture for exacerbating the anxieties that many older students have:

> The whole idea of putting each other down is something that's embedded in youth and children's popular culture now. It's the whole Simpsons idea [like] so they find it really hard not to put themselves or each other down. They're creating some great stuff; they're coming up with great ideas, but they find it really hard to relax into that – they find it harder than kids do ... adults are terrified to admit they enjoyed something or they actually did something good, or their friends did, so that's a bit of a struggle.

Carolyn claims to respond to this alienation by using non-threatening, collaborative and play-based pedagogies:

> So how I try to help them through that experience is by making, always working as a whole group. I never single anybody out because that's probably something they remember from their schooling – I've got to stand up in

260 Applications

front of everybody else and sing a song or whatever. So all of the work is collaborative. It's all group, and when they're sharing their ideas that they've created there are little structures to help that to make it less frightening. So small groups, share with groups, we share our ideas. We structure the sharing so there's always lots of things happening and lots to look at. So, it's always playful. We play lots of games. Lots of creative stuff and the thing, it takes a while to get over.

When asked for a specific example of this pedagogical approach in the context of mind/body, Carolyn gives the following example:

It could be quite a mathematical idea that I'm always working with – what we call an improvisational tool, like a score or an idea or framework, so students have a really strong structure; they're making up a dance that's going to be based on words or images or it could even be a mathematical formula, so they're having to solve problems together that are physical and then explaining their movements in terms of the language of dance, the words, . . . what does the movement represent and why did you choose that particular form, that dynamic, that level, that shape and how does that represent this idea and constantly in the beginning it's me. I'm verbalising it all the time. When I'm talking to them maybe making that visible because the way we are used to making that visible is within words.

Her example reveals a dexterous pedagogical approach that creatively reconciles mind and body and its associated dyads, including structure/form, words/actions and representation/reality.

Carolyn further emphasised the importance of dance as process rather than product in childhood:

And they have to get over that really because what children produce as creative product – you give them the right to do that – it's not always sophisticated, it's not always going to win the Eisteddfod, but the child has gone through this amazing process of solving the problem collaboratively with their friends and then working on it and thinking about it and sharing it with somebody else. It's like they're putting themselves out there so they have to appreciate that it's not the product which they're frightened of (not being good enough), but it's the process that's more important.

At first glance, this seems to set up an opposition between process and product; however, Carolyn places the emphasis in the context of childhood.

She expresses concern that dance is linked to body and subordinated to disciplines of the mind in education:

I think in maybe the mind/body thing; that divorcing of the mind from the body might mean that we see the arts, whether it's music, dance, drama or

Narrative explorations in education 261

visual art as being solely about skill. It's not about thinking, it's not about expressing an idea, [it's] solely about being skilful.

For Carolyn, this characterisation of dance is impoverished. She recalls Howard Gardner's multiple intelligences as a way of repositioning dance as a form of kinaesthetic intelligence that reconnects body and mind. However, she again rejects the privileging of innate skill and its 'product over process' in education:

If it's just about skill then it becomes that because this kid's obviously the most talented in the class because they're the most physically adept but in education, in an education context it's not about that. It's not about who's the most skilful but it's about what we can all learn about what bodies can express and how they can say something and how they always said something throughout history; people have used that.

The interviewer probed the skill/creativity dyad here a little to see if Carolyn privileged creativity over skill in an educational context. She raised the relativity of judgements of skill and the distribution of naturally skilful and creative children in a class:

Thirty-five children, all given the same task will solve it in different ways, and some children will obviously be more skilful physically, but others will be more creative as well. And I guess there's another side to that [which] is who or what body determines is highly skilful, because that can be culturally determined ...You know there may be some beautiful graceful and trained dancers, even in a class of eight and nine year olds who've been dancing since they were three and a half, and there are other children who are clever with their bodies and interesting, and they don't fit into that model of what is seen to be a good dancer.

Elsewhere, she reflects on the workshop as an example of education that reconciled the body and mind in the context of dance:

It was all about creating and exploring different ways to express ideas, and it was named research. It wasn't assumed just by some people to be, but it was very much, this is what it's about. And that doesn't mean that you don't talk and write as well. We did writing, we did talking, we did moving, we did going from one to the other in the same class, [Yeah it really, yeah I just realised it's not you know] it's about standing up for the body because nobody else is but when you're trying to argue for the value of it you have to show that it's a package, you know, it's not this binary that it can become.

Carolyn's response again reveals a counterbalancing disposition that seeks to address the imbalanced emphasis on detached intellect, skill and product in formal education, rather than opposing it altogether.

262 Applications

Dyadic affinities and ubiquitisation

One of the characteristic tendencies of post-dyadic positions is an awareness that there is an affinity between one dyad and many others that in turn relates to the general interconnectedness of all knowledge and being. Carolyn's link to other dyads demonstrates this ubiquitisation – the growing sense of the depth of connection of her dyadic interest with other dyads and onto-epistemological domains beyond dance and education:

> This body/mind split so called, is something that appears to me to be at the basis of the grand division of research and thinking, what is knowledge and what is worth knowing, how do we come to know.

Her pedagogical approach also reflects this ubiquitisation as she uses dance to encourage deep learnings that connect beyond dance:

> And so, when they dance they have talk about what they did and talk about each others' dance, so usually there's some sort of questions. A lot of teachers are using simple questions like what did I see, what did I think, what did I wonder, not just about the dance but about what it did mean or how do I feel. So, yeah, constantly connecting the meaning of what we're doing and how we are creating that meaning, so it's not just random stuff.

Such pedagogies reveal deep connectivity between mind and body through dance. For Carolyn, dance is not simply or merely a series of technical bodily movements: it is a medium for the cognitive and affective exploration of life.

When asked about the relationship of mind and body to other dyads, especially those related to education, Carolyn characterised herself as relatively more liberal than conservative, student-centred than teacher-centred, more about freedom than control:

> You know there's all these student-centred/teacher-centred, freedom and control and so forth and conservative and liberal. I don't think it's this side and this side necessarily, but it seems to me that thinking, for example, of student-centred and teacher-centred learning that the teacher-centred side would tend to favour more the mind and learning; freedom and control, if you take a Foucauldian viewpoint that's all about control of the body; liberal/conservative ... the whole 60s thing – the liberation of the body against the control of how we should dress, how we should sit, how we should move and so forth ... those more open and inclusive and diverse ends of spectrums would tend to be ones that recognise the importance of the body that [you know] we've all got one.

Narrative explorations in education   263

Illustratively, Carolyn reflected on her subjective identification with the liberal side of the liberal/conservative dyad in light of her students' characterisations of her as 'a hippy':

> I was always told by kids at school, because they were always saying that I was hippy ... I said to a friend once, I try really hard. I just about wear a twin set and pearls to school. 'Ah miss you're a hippy miss. How's ya dope plantation going' and all this kind of thing to me ... Here's me in a little navy blue suit. I said what is it you know? I try really hard. He said 'you can't control your body, 'cause your body you know ...' Of course that's what it is – it's your body language gives you away.

Carolyn's reflections on conservative schooling and the control of the body serve to negatively reinforce or consolidate her identification with liberal, creative and emancipatory pedagogies:

> often with teachers there's a certain, maybe it's an age thing, maybe it's experience, or maybe they've been in the job too long and the children they were lining up outside and they cannot abide a child not looking directly in front, both arms down. It's like they spend an inordinate amount of time on making children understand what it is to be in school, which is, you know to control that body ... I've been teaching a dance class. I thought it was going swimmingly and they [conservative teachers] can't help it, they're always trying to discipline the kids ... and the teachers are freaking out because they can't cope. They can't cope with the kids not being like that ... I think it's a lot about control – control of the body and separating, separating the body out ... Bodies are scary things. They do scary things. You know, they do things that they're not supposed to so a lot of people freak out about it.

Carolyn reflected on one of her own lessons for a supervising teacher. Her reflection demonstrates the difference between teachers who emphasise factual recall as indicators of success and teachers like Carolyn who tend to emphasise or co-value affective response and deep connected understandings:

> I asked them to find movements, to vary. We're talking about greetings, handshakes, high-fives, played around doing different things then took that movement from that person that person that person. We put them together and we created a sequence; then they had to go with their partner and make changes and add things and take way things and create a beginning and an ending. That was our class. Pretty simple. At the end the teacher wanted to know what did you learn. Well what she wanted was more like facts like 'I learned high level and low level' or whatever it was. That's fine

but then the first child put her hand up and said 'I learnt that you don't have to be perfect'. I thought, 'kid, you're on my team'.

Collectively, Carolyn's examples serve to qualify her earlier concession in relation to opposing pedagogical approaches: 'I don't think it's this side and this side necessarily but . . .'. While these examples cannot be separated from other more general counterbalancing statements, Carolyn's experiences seem, understandably, to have left a residual opposition to relatively physical pursuits like sport and relatively control-based pedagogies. While the structure of balance is there in many of Carolyn's statements, it is possible that it is yet to be fully inhabited and applied in domains where she has experienced the deepest oppositions to her dispositions. In other words, her reconciliation of opposing pedagogies is an ongoing journey simultaneously into and beyond her natural and nurtured dispositions with liberal, artistic, collective and collaborative ways of knowing, being and teaching. Needless to say, this is the general trajectory of every journey towards the dynamic reconciliation of subjective and objective ways of knowing and being. Inasmuch as this journey can be understood in developmental terms, Carolyn consistently reflects from a post-dyadic position.

Carolyn's ubiquitisation or extension of mind/body relations also reflects a post-dyadic development. She reflected for some time on the place of the body in socio-technical futures that seemed to her to threaten its significance and existence. She noted first of all a social movement that is revaluing the body: 'in a weird way we're all very aware of our bodies and everybody's into health'. However, she sees this in contradistinction to a polarisingly technicist movement in education that is re-distancing mind from body and bodies from each other:

> Weirdly in education we're going away from the body and more to mediated forms of learning, distancing ourselves from each other . . . weirdly because of technology it's [i.e. education] doing that job again of privileging the mind because it's taking the body out of it again.

Here, Carolyn refers to the current radical shift in education towards online modes of learning and away from traditional face-to-face modes of learning. She refers to this shift as a form of 'disembodiment' where mind is again divorced from the bodily physicalities it is wedded to.

When asked what could go wrong with a technicist movement towards disembodiment in education, Carolyn responds that schooling and life after school produces understandings that are derived from body language and relationships. She argues that disembodiment will cause the loss of a powerful dimension of human relationships:

> We become so divorced from understanding body language in other people and relating to other people in the real sense, not the virtual sense, that we'll be finding those relationships more difficult.

Narrative explorations in education 265

Here, the interviewer picks up on Carolyn's dyadic opposition between real and virtual and asks whether the problem of disembodiment is transitional or perennial:

> So what about someone who says that we're just in a transitional period and the virtual world will become more and more 'real' as we learn to replace body language cues with more subtle and nuanced understanding of virtual cues and the use of emoticons and all those sorts of things. Do you think, I guess even in theory that it's possible to disembody through technology and that that could get to the point where it's a good thing, whatever that means?
> (Interviewer)

Carolyn's response seems to suggest a post-dyadic or trans-positional commitment within relativism or a (re)creation of dyadic equilibrium that acknowledges but resists the future for the sake of the past:

> My resistance is probably some kind of deep gut feeling that we still are bodies at this point in history until we get the – what's that word when we will fuse with technology – you know that machine and man will come together?

She indicates another dyadic opposition (logic/intuition) when reflecting on her resistance to disembodiment:

> That's probably got nothing to do with logic or what's going to be better for the planet in the long run, but maybe it is just a gut reaction that somehow once you lose that then you can't go back to it. And will the future always provide us with a technologically marvellous world that we can inhabit in that way? What if it doesn't? . . . I don't know largely, it's probably, I don't know, a kind of quasi-religious thing I've got about the body that doesn't rely on logic at all.

Carolyn's dyadic structures suggest she has a dyadic affinity between 'body, real, social, tacit and feeling' and 'mind, technology, artificial, individual, articulated and logical'. That she seems more focused on the loss of body than the loss of mind in AI futures illustrates her disposition towards the body. Furthermore, she sees an affinity between body and expressiveness, the social, collaborative, creative, interpersonal and innate: 'I think I'm relating body more to expressiveness. Well it's very social. It's very interpersonal. It seems to be something so innate'. Throughout this section of the interview, Carolyn invoked the oppositions and separations (e.g. logic/intuition, real/virtual) that dominate the pro-dyadic position. However, her self-awareness of this way of thinking as revealed in her reflexive analysis of her subjectivity (e.g. 'My resistance is probably . . . maybe it is just a gut reaction') suggests a post-dyadic use

266   Applications

of opposition to question the pro-dyadic certainties of the disembodied other. Thus, her oppositions are more counterbalancing and cautionary than absolute and dichotomising.

Conclusion

Perhaps the clearest statements reflecting Carolyn's post-dyadic way of knowing and being in the world were recorded towards the beginning and end of the interview. Both statements reveal dyadic reflexivity – the conscious awareness of dyadic structures that create and reflect the ways we know about the world and act within it. Characterising the ways of knowing that she seeks to avoid, at the beginning of the interview, Carolyn lamented:

> we tend to think of something as being better as in good or evil, freedom/ control, or you know in binaries, love and hate or whatever, we tend to see it as a hierarchy, something is better. You know the mind it's the higher part physically and the body here [points lower].

Her story reflects a common trajectory in relation to a less common dyad: first, the pre-dyadic emergence of a contextually unique identity related to bodily expressiveness; then, the experience of alienation within a system that subordinates this identity through its hierarchical separation of mind and body; then, the validation of identity that gave her the confidence to express a pro-dyadic counter-opposition; finally, the gradual and ongoing post-dyadic reunification of mind and body in the context of dance.

Indicatively, Carolyn's final unsolicited comment after the close of the interview was, 'I've, like, come round in a circle'. As I've explored in earlier chapters, the circle is a powerful post-dyadic metaphor that moves beyond exclusively linear separations and oppositions. In BirD, the circle is a metaphor that is developmentally more complex than linear metaphors, but contains and integrates them rather than replacing them. The primacy of body may precede the primacy of mind, but the onto-epistemological impetus is to re-coordinate and reconcile the two in ways that enhance the development of each and the appreciation of an infinitely divisible *One*. Carolyn's personal encounters with the wicked problems of schooling are a microcosm of the wicked problems of education on a global scale. Her ways of reconciling the opposites most salient to her life offers a powerful example of bi-relational development and the sorts of pedagogy it can inspire.

Case two: Simon – teacher of science and mathematics (concrete/abstract)

At the time of the interview, the male participant (pseudonym Simon) was a lecturer at an Australian university in his mid forties, who specialised in the fields of mathematics and physics education. Originally from Zimbabwe and of Shona heritage, Simon has often found himself reflecting on complex cultural interfaces. Now a teacher educator, Simon has taught and been taught using a range of pedagogical approaches. He formerly worked as a teacher; and while he was schooled within a traditional Western form of education, he retains strong ties with his traditional village culture. Simon selected *concrete/abstract* from the list of available dyads as the dyad that most resonated with his ways of knowing, being and teaching.

Summary analysis

The most general level of analysis suggests that Simon has consciously attempted to reconcile oppositions between concrete and abstract ways of knowing and teaching throughout his teaching career. His onto-epistemological trajectory is characterised by a post-dyadic realisation of the interdependence and con-textuality of concrete and abstract representations of mathematical knowledge and his ongoing attempts to overcome their separation and hierarchical organ-isation in traditional education. He has clearly moved beyond simplistic pro-dyadic separations and oppositions of concrete and abstract approaches. While the emergence of his appreciation for abstract approaches to education is related to his particularly traditional form of Western education at a mission school, his ability to see and his desire to understand experience-based learn-ing seem to be related to his teaching experiences with Indigenous students. Simon's current academic research explores the spectrum of representations available to teachers and students beyond exclusively abstract forms of mathe-matics. He uses a range of post-dyadic metaphors to express the continuous and contextual relationship between concrete and abstract. However, his way of knowing is often characterised by the admitted confusion that can accom-pany the extinction or collapse of dyads (i.e. concrete *is* abstract *is* concrete). While such confusion can be epistemically immobilising, Simon seems to use it as a source of humility concerning his own development and empathy for the development of students who experience confusion and often anxiety when engaging with mathematics.

Pre-dyadic and pro-dyadic dispositions and formative experiences

Simon selected concrete/abstract because of its relevance to his teaching – in particular, his field of mathematics education. He initially defined *concrete* as 'hands on' and involving 'concrete materials like counters' and later expanded this definition to include 'physical experience' in real-life contexts. He contrasts this with *abstract*, which he defines as concerning the use of 'written symbols, symbolism and equations'. Simon understandably defines the terms in relation to their polarities. He does this in order to describe some of the polarisations

268 Applications

he has observed in mathematics education and to orientate his own more nuanced understandings of the relationship between the two.

BirD emphasises the centrality of formative life experience on our trajectories of dyadic relationships. Simon's early life trajectory was defined by the pre-dyadic exposure to abstract ways of knowing mathematics:

> Reflecting back, I was sort of introduced to mathematics when I moved to a mission school ... I was one of the students who was really struggling in that classroom, why, because I had limited language as everyone was taught in English and it was my third language ... And people tried to explain things and symbolise things and it would not mean anything to me ... somehow I passed then went to university and still the same experience ... I don't know why I majored in maths and physics. I always thought that there was more to this than the symbolism we were just doing.

Pro-dyadic separation can grow naturally out of a dominant way of knowing, being and doing things. For Simon, the abstract way of knowing mathematics dominated his own teaching because he knew simply no other way. Accordingly, he recalls: 'My first four years I actually taught the way I had been taught'. However, the separation between concrete and abstract ways of knowing and learning mathematics never amounted to full opposition for Simon, perhaps because he was appreciative of the opportunities that his traditional abstract-orientated opportunities had afforded him.

While Simon's education and early teaching was dominated by abstract representations of mathematics, he recalls some formative experiences that began to challenge this pro-dyadic separation and hierarchical arrangement of concrete and abstract ways of knowing. One of these experiences related to a young student whose tacit understanding of the Bernoulli principle made Simon rethink the hierarchical relationship between concrete and abstract representations of mathematical knowledge. He recalls:

> We were always going out fishing when I was working at this Indigenous college and you know I did have a lot of experience on the dinghy ... it was on a very big river, flowing into the sea. We were on a dinghy and the engine packed [it in] ... and one of the Aboriginal boys who was in year 10 ... the boy struggled to write his name, white people would say he's illiterate if you actually want to use that word ... As we were sort of going down the river and the engine had packed up I started panicking, alright, then he really took control of everything.

Simon recounts his panic as 'the dinghy began to sink' and two of the girls considered jumping into the river. However, the boy quickly explained that the sinking effect was simply due to the narrowing of the river and that the dinghy would be more buoyant soon after the river expanded again. Simon was struck by the boy's tacit knowledge of the Bernoulli principle, which relates to the pressure decrease and velocity increase of a fluid, and the failure of his own explicit knowledge in application to the situation:

> I had read about the Bernoulli effect ... but it was this boy who actually applied it. He'd actually lived it. I'd only imagined it ... the moment I lived that experience I actually understood the Bernoulli effect ... And I actually sat down with him and I said 'do you know that a lot of people who are studying to be pilots are struggling with this concept?'.

For Simon, the experience was intense and revolutionary to his understanding of the relationship between theory and practice and concrete and abstract representations of knowledge. The old pro-dyadic separations and hierarchies of knowledge were complicated, and his more explicit development to post-dyadic ways of knowing began. The connection between ways of knowing and ways of being is revealed in Simon's pedagogical transformations. He began to see his own alienation from formal education in his students' alienation, especially in the context of mathematics: 'I actually find that when students are out there in the ... abstract world. I think they actually struggle to understand what mathematics is all about'. Subsequently, he recalls becoming more interested in and engaged with his students' life worlds and cultural identities (e.g. 'I think the students tell you what they need, if you interact with the students'), an interest that eventually led him into doctoral studies.

Simon recalls a particular six-month period that began to explicitly challenge the dominance of abstract ways of knowing mathematics implicit in curricula materials. He recalls his sense of frustration when teaching Indigenous students at an Australian school and again characterises his inherited pedagogies as reflecting an abstract way of knowing:

> I think, if I can use this pendulum kind of thing ... I was sitting on this side you know, and when I came to Australia and started working with Indigenous students ... I got so frustrated ... When I was working with some of these students one afternoon teaching me how to play some of these Indigenous games ... why is this not being translated in the classroom context? ... I think it was those six months. When I went to this school I was mainly dealing with years 10, 11 and 12, but the students really were around grade five levels. And I went to the principal and said look you know this is pointless.

This was a particularly formative period in Simon's career as it began to crystallise a problem that he later explored through a PhD thesis examining Indigenous students' representations of scientific knowledge.

Post-dyadic and trans-positional metaphors

Onto-epistemological dispositions are powerfully represented in our use of relational metaphors. Simon's ways of explaining his understanding of the relationship between *concrete* and *abstract* contain metaphors that reveal his transition from pro-dyadic to post-dyadic ways of knowing and being. He variously refers to 'putting things in boxes', 'divorcing', 'balancing', 'see-saws', 'pendulums' and 'fulcrums':

> I used the see-saw, fulcrum, balance, pendulum a lot ... I'm kind of like a pendulum depending on the context ... if I am with preservice teachers hopefully I am at the centre making them realise that you can use mathematics this way by representing mathematics that way.

Though these metaphors are not always consistently expressed, the intention is clear enough to see Simon's relational and contextual ways of knowing concrete and abstract approaches to mathematics.

At some points of the interview Simon expresses frustration with the over-simplification of curricula and pedagogy that move from concrete to abstract representations of mathematical knowledge according to year level:

> And I actually struggle even with the syllabus when they highlight that from year eight to nine was mostly working in the abstract domain with symbolism and equations, not realising that the equation and my physical world are just two sides of the same coin.

And elsewhere:

> I've gone to conferences where ... there's a distinction between primary and secondary sectors ... and when you attend the conferences with more eminent educators they are talking much more about a lot of concrete materials being used in the lower primary ... the same academics are attending sessions for the senior secondary they actually talking about it from an abstract ... like students have already moved from this concrete kind of experience and they're now in the abstract experience ... people looking at it in the hierarchical you actually have to start at the concrete, you move to the abstract ... yet for me it's still much more horizontal. That abstract conceptualisation has to mean something in the concrete context you know, and that concrete has to mean something in the abstract.

Simon challenges the hierarchical arrangement, arguing instead for their horizontal relation: 'it should be more or less horizontal'. However, he has moved beyond naïve appeals to a static balance or a self-negating middle position: 'I don't want to use the word horizontal, as nothing in life is horizontal'. Instead he observes, 'students are in different positions at different times ... I always come to the see-saw, you know the pivot-fulcrum kind of thing'.

For Simon, both concrete and abstract expressions of mathematics are representations. One is not necessarily superior to, or separate from, the other. As he emphasises at one point in the interview, 'an equation is just a story'. Such statements illustrate a post-dyadic tendency to converge previously separated dyadic constituents:

> When people talk about representing mathematics in an abstract concept I think that people's understanding is very different from my understanding ... they look at your every day physical world – fine, I understand that as concrete ... and then when you want to represent it as a story you use a word equation and them using symbols. I actually see it as a continuum. I struggle to see it as boxing it – we are not in the concrete domain, we are now in the abstract domain.

The post-dyadic ability to see the continuous connection between dyadic constituents (i.e. concrete/abstract) enables a sort of polar inversion and immirroring where one constituent is seen in terms of another. For example, referring to the interviewer's folder on the table, Simon makes the point that mathematical abstractions like quantity, density and weight can affect the way the concrete object is actually concretised:

> Even if it's a concrete thing just sitting there, it depends on how I want to look at it ... concrete doesn't necessarily mean simple ... it's the lens you use to look at that concrete thing ... Instead of trying to look at volume, density or weight of that folder you draw it like an art form or abstract of that. I don't see it very differently from trying to represent it in a kind of symbolic way.

Here, he implicitly refers to the entanglement between subject and object. This entanglement is indicative of post-dyadic ways of relating dyadic constituents.

Dyadic collapse

However, this polar inversion and immirroring – the realisation that one person's concrete can be another person's abstract – is a point that can signal the collapse or extinction of dyads. BirD represents this point as being potentially disorientating and even nihilistic, especially when it is approached from the relative securities and certainties of pro-dyadic and even post-dyadic ways of knowing. Simon's narrative signals this disorientation at several points:

> But what confuses me is ... the moment we try to put something in boxes concrete/abstract I struggle with that ... I actually get confused with looking at it from a totally abstract perspective or from a concrete perspective.

272 Applications

This comment suggests that Simon has experienced the *interpenetration* of opposites: that is, that one can come close to defining a whole spectrum in terms of one polarity. However, while interpenetration 'comes close' it can never 'totally' subsume a whole spectrum without the confusing acknowledgement that the 'opposing term' could be similarly used to do the same. This interpenetration and subsequent confusion can precede the collapse of dyads.

Later in the interview, Simon relates concrete and abstract representations to social constructivist and objectivist ways of knowing respectively. He reflects, 'I'm getting more confused because I'm comfortable with both'. The juxtaposition of 'confusion and comfort' is indicative of the disorientating collapse of dyads represented in BirD. The comfort comes from a more expansive spectrum of possibilities that dissolves the former oppositions that cause tension and conflict. However, the confusion can come from the seemingly impossible task of having to act and to choose from an extended range of possibilities in ever changing and boundless contexts. The confusing dilemma that presents itself with the collapse of dyads is why and how to re-enter the onto–epistemological cycle of life, without seeming to make absurd, arbitrary and ungrounded choices. The (re)solution, for many, is to recognise the dilemma itself in dialectical terms. The extinction and negation of dyads is itself a polarisation towards the first constituent of dyads like extinction/creation, nothing/something, relative/absolute, fluid/fixed. Arguably, this is largely because the movement towards the extinction of dyads is a development away from the pro-dyadic certainties, absolutes and sense of cosmic purpose that sustain oppositions and choice. The trans-positional re-entry into this cycle requires the understanding (tacit or explicit) that the cycle was never really escaped or transcended at all. These seemingly esoteric dynamics are probably most explicitly explored in small pockets of philosophy, religion, science and art. However, it is possible that they can be tacitly felt by almost anyone, even if for a fleeting moment. For a teacher, the extinction of dyads can be experienced as a loss of belief in the ultimate purpose and power of education, or fatigue at the seemingly impossible logistical and practical constraints one has to make meaningful choices within.

Simon expresses confusion or disorientation as to how to discern which representation is most relevant when a spectrum of choices is available and context is difficult to define:

> I'm honestly confused with mathematics as a way of representing the world ... When I look at this I really get confused as to where I am or where I want to go really ... if I look at mathematics I look at it as something which really has to mean something to me ... When you talk about real mathematics or pure mathematics which is out there, outside experience, to me, how do I know it exists if I can't experience it – you know what I mean.

Narrative explorations in education 273

Arguably, this confusion is a characteristic of late post-dyadic development – a form of uncertainty that is felt all the more strongly for the pro-dyadic certainties that have been left. When asked about the usefulness of binary terms like pure/applied, concrete/abstract, Simon replies: 'For me they are not necessary. That is an aspect that confuses not only me but many maths teachers. I'm not saying I've got a solution'. Here, Simon expresses the difficulty of having to navigate realities and communicate in contexts that otherwise have no clear conceptual boundaries. The wicked problem of Simon's mathematics teaching has this same structural element as all wicked problems. It can be difficult to live with binary oppositions and it can be difficult to live without them. A trans-positional stance requires renewed commitment to make choices, draw boundaries, move left or right. However, these new trans-positional movements are characterised by a sense of irony, paradox, play, flow relationality and contextuality.

Conclusion

Simon's final comments illustrate a commitment to (re)enter the world of mathematics teaching having transcended and reconciled one of its most definitive oppositions (i.e. concrete/abstract):

> I take different identities in different contexts. I actually realise that in some contexts mathematics needs to be much more hands on ... others are more abstract ... they have travelled this journey to actually get to this point ... for me I'm always thinking mathematics should be on the whole spectrum.

Elsewhere, Simon discusses the need to find a space where one is comfortable, while recognising the many possible spaces that others may occupy and that are still available at other times and in other places:

> We have to represent mathematics differently to different groups of students depending on context ... I'm actually very comfortable with that ... But when we look at mathematics at one end of the spectrum we deny others the pleasure of experiencing all of these different representations of mathematics ... I think that's where the beauty of mathematics is. And of course you finally get your spot and say I'm now comfortable to operate in this space.

Such comments reflect a dialectical 'betweenness' that can reconcile subjective and objective ways of knowing, being and teaching. This is not a final state or stage as much as it is an ongoing process. It is a commitment to 'balancing' as an act rather than simply balance as a position, because, to reiterate Simon's own words, 'nothing in life is horizontal'.

These teachers' journeys illustrate the relationship between ways of knowing, being and teaching. In this chapter, I have attempted to loosely plot these journeys in relation to BirD's archetypal positions. No doubt, BirD will continue to co-evolve with such journeys and others that may challenge its current formulation. However, I hope to have at least affirmed the significance of the general project in the context of education. Teachers are in a unique position to facilitate or inhibit their students' ability to recognise and (re)solve wicked problems. Needless to say, the position comes with great responsibility.

Chapter 12

Conclusion and final reflections on bi-relational development

My hope is that this book brings the heuristic of bi-relational development into the broader discussion of wicked problems. Our human tendency to bifurcate the universe is nothing new, but there is always a need for new metaphors and models that help us to recognise and 'reconcile the opposites' inherent in wicked problems. As I have argued previously, the stakes for (re)solving wicked problems have been raised by the sheer scale of human interactions enabled by modern technologies in the context of globalisation. As I have illustrated with extracts from individual life narratives, in-depth interviews, scholarship and literature, these ubiquitous bifurcations and their various transformations can help us to understand the nature and construction of some of life's most wicked problems. How we construct and describe the universe affects the problems we see and create, and the ways we (re)solve them. I hope to have sketched out some of the dyads that help to define grand socio-cultural problems in the context of globalisation, socio-ecological problems in the context of sustainability and socio-religious problems in the context of fundamentalisms. However, I have also tried to explore the dyads and dyadic relationships that give meaning to individual lives. My central claim is that wicked problems are best fought, and complex terrains best navigated, with dexterous coordinations of left and right. Accordingly, I have proposed a bi-relational approach (i.e. BirD) to help us understand the ubiquity of dyads and the development of dyadic relationships in the midst of our most personal and public problems

Summary

I have structured my introduction to bi-relational development into three parts. Part I introduced the concept of dyads and dyadic relationships in relation to the recognition and (re)solution of wicked problems. Chapter 1 conceptualised wicked problems as onto-epistemological concerns. Chapter 2 illustrated the ubiquity of dyads across many different domains of knowledge, including education, law, medicine and politics. Chapter 3 explored the origins of dyads and classifications of dyads. Chapter 4 sketched a brief theoretical background to the original approach to onto-epistemological development introduced in

276 Applications

Chapter 5: Bi-relational development (i.e. BirD). BirD was introduced as model for identifying archetypal regions, positions, dynamics and trajectories of development between the creation and collapse of oppositions.

Part II was used to illustrate BirD's archetypal positions and dynamics in authentic contexts. The illustrations in Chapter 6 involved a range of dyads (e.g. hope/despair, teaching/learning, art/science) and dyadic relationships (e.g. binary oppositions and complements) explored in the context of different individuals' life experiences of wicked problems. The remaining chapters offered a broader bi-relational perspective on some of the wicked problems that occupy modern societies. Chapter 7 explored the socio-cultural tensions and trade-offs between local and global in the context of globalisation. Chapter 8 explored the socio-ecological coordination of nature and culture in the context of sustainability. And Chapter 9 offered a bi-relational approach to socio-religious problems that concern the ways we conceptualise and engage ultimate questions. These chapters culminated in a discussion that highlighted the bi-relational connections between wicked socio-cultural, socio-ecological and socio-religious problems.

Finally, Part III discussed some of the applications of a bi-relational approach in the context of formal education. It explored educational opportunities and limits in the facilitation of bi-relational development. Chapter 10 provided a range of general educational strategies, while Chapter 11 offered two illustrations of experienced teachers' bi-relational development in the domains of the arts and the sciences respectively. Together, these illustrations served to highlight the importance of teachers' onto-epistemological development for the ways they interact with different learners and facilitate the deep engagement of wicked problems.

Collectively, the parts of this book have introduced and illustrated BirD as a useful approach for recognising and (re)solving wicked problems in the real world. I hope to have demonstrated that the recognition and reconciliation of opposites is an individual and a social task that needs more serious attention, especially in the context of formal education.

Future directions

Every book is a work in progress, even when it is 'finished' and bound between covers. The purpose of this penultimate section is to suggest some future directions for this progress. Even the most lucid authors probably have a sense that they have expressed themselves 'through a glass darkly' and I do not claim to be the most lucid writer. However, I would hope to see my pixellated intuitions and blurry visions of bi-relational development and wicked problems more clearly expressed by scholars more scientific and artistic. There is room for more quantitative explorations, complements and refinements to the largely qualitative expressions of BirD I have used for introductory purposes. I would dare to add that even the more esoteric positions identified in BirD could be explored

Conclusion and final reflections   277

and 'enlightened' with quantitative methodologies. The sort of 'big data' capacities of Hofstede's (1980) cultural identity surveys (Chapter 7) and the ABC's (2013) Vote Compass project (Chapter 2) highlight the possibilities for quantitatively exploring different individuals' and cultures' bi-relational ways of knowing and being. Such explorations are increasingly important in the age of globalisation as cultures, like individuals, meet each others' ways of knowing and being and ask anew the question – where to from here?

Furthermore, while I encourage future quantitative developments of bi-relational development, I hope that explorations of the way we know are not left to, or merely taken over by, the harder sciences with their particular metaphors. Well funded scientific explorations sometimes plant flags in places that artists have long visited. So, I hope also to see artistic expressions of bi-relational dynamics that bring our wicked problems and (re)solutions to collective attention; perhaps in a way that provides some resilience, humour, empathy and sensible melancholy as we face them together. I have little doubt that artists, like the teacher of dance interviewed in Chapter 11, can facilitate much more powerful and extensive onto-epistemological developments through their work than I can ever hope to do through academic prose. I would also hope to see synthetic explorations of bi-relational development and wicked problems that lead to fruitful interpenetrations and syntheses between the arts and the sciences in the perennial quest for their (re)solutions.

There is also a need for more explicit bi-relational or dialectical contributions to the processes of design and production, particularly in relation to the wicked socio-ecological problems of our time. In Chapter 2, I noted the emergence of design thinking as an increasingly popular paradigm in Western education and have been struck by its attempts to grapple with wicked problems in ways that move into and beyond formal logic and linear and analytical styles. Bi-relational approaches such as BirD can reunite analysis and synthesis, user and producer, tacit and explicit in the everyday process of design. A bi-relational approach to design would complement recent attempts to reconnect analysis and synthesis, subjective and objective, convergent and divergent, quantitative and qualitative and reductive and holistic in the process of design (e.g. Beckman and Barry, 2007). It would also encourage designers to further broaden the range of dyads that they recognise and reconcile in the process of design. Neglect of these dyadic dimensions can have far-reaching consequences. For example, a focus on design for quantity may reduce financial costs but may have devastating environmental costs. Bi-relational approaches to design and marketing can reveal and anticipate some of the wicked problems with which material products are linked such as pollution (e.g. non-degradable plastics) and substance abuse (e.g. alcohol-fuelled violence). The existence of implicitly bi-relational approaches to design warrants further, more explicit bi-relational explorations of design-thinking models and their contexts of application.

Perhaps the future development of bi-relational dynamics that I have the most personal interest in concerns the relationship between science and religion and its

278 Applications

primary dyads (e.g. matter/spirit, faith/reason, hope/despair). As I argued in Chapter 9, these more primary dyads must be brought to the surface and better differentiated to facilitate an otherwise misdirected and mutually destructive exchange. I have both experienced and spent years observing the experiences of others on both 'sides' of this conflict. I have experienced, observed and may even have unintentionally contributed to some injuries in this particular 'war'. The reconciliation of opposites is especially significant in the post-September 11 age of the 'new fundamentalism' and the 'new atheism', as they are expressed in wicked problems. We need scientists and theologians who pursue their respective fields with integrity and rigour, while being open to the co-creation of new and living metaphors to communicate their discoveries and creations. There is something bi-relationally poignant in our century about Einstein's claim in the last century that 'religion without science is blind and science without religion is lame'.

Finally, I hope to see closer attention to bi-relational and dialectical dynamics in formal education. As a school and tertiary educator with over twenty years' experience, I am still struck by the binary oppositions and pendulum swings that structure everything from classroom pedagogies to national curricula: transmissive versus discovery-based pedagogies, constructivist versus behaviourist approaches to learning, intrinsic versus extrinsic approaches to motivation, integrated versus compartmentalised curriculum, authoritarian versus authoritative behavior management and inclusive versus segregated classrooms – each contested as if one size fits all for all time. It is no use teaching about critical thinking if we teach it as an exclusive faculty of the left. It is no use teaching about values and responsibilities if we teach them as an exclusive domain of the right. We need a bi-relational language and new context-appropriate metaphors to (re)solve the wicked problems that arise in everyday classrooms and society writ large.

Final reflections

Though an author is only part of the sum of meaning, I hope that this book contributes to further reflection and action on the claim that we can better understand each other, the universe and ourselves by reconciling the opposites that reside in our most wicked problems. As I observed at the outset of this book, and affirm here at the end, the study of opposites illuminates the meaning of zero, one, two, three and infinity in relation to life's wicked problems and ultimate questions. I began this book by posing the direction and object of development as an existential riddle:

What becomes one
Which then becomes two
Which then becomes something
That is often thought of
And may well be fought of

Conclusion and final reflections 279

As Zero
Or One
Or Two
Or Three
Or even by some
As In-fin-ity?

I hope that a way of knowing has emerged throughout the interim pages that gives meaning and context to the following solution:

'What' can be Zero, One, Two and Three
For each helps to make sense of In-fin-ity

Inasmuch as a work in progress can have a conclusion, my conclusion is that the ultimate reconciliation of opposites is not 'both/and' in contradistinction to 'either/or': it is 'both/and/either/or' in relation and in context. The latter set of relations better equips us to recognise and (re)solve the wicked problems we face. Life *is* a wicked problem in a wonderful and terrible way. The particular problems of our individual lives and milieus have the same confounding structures as humanity's most ultimate questions. The structure of *two* offers an entry into these questions.

As Thacker (2011) writes, when all is said and done 'it would appear that two paths are left open – materialism or idealism, nihilism or mysticism, the hard facts and the great beyond, "it is what it is" and "there is something more ..."' (p. 18). My sense, which admittedly may appear to others as *non*sense, is that these 'two paths' are so deeply entangled with each other in life as we know it, that they need to be 'left open' to live at all. In human consciousness, as in human history, it is our ability to walk these separate paths to their convergence, to figure–ground shift these two realities, to separate them, combine them and to collapse them that lets us experience life. I have tried to express this most perplexing claim through BirD's avian acronym and its visual metaphors and applications in the broader belief that we may find ourselves in the wicked problems we face.

Finally, while I hope to have used both feet to navigate the terrain of writing a book, I am conscious of the inevitability of developing a limp in the very act of writing – especially academic book writing. In the arrangement of those most common life dyads – theory/practice, analysis/synthesis, abstract/concrete and reflection/experience – the very act of book writing tends to privilege the first constituents. As in most of life's dances, one foot must lead a step or turn, and a book is only a step in a dance. So now, in this space and at this time, I take Wordsworth's (2014) counsel from 'The Tables Turned':

UP! up! my Friend, and quit your books;
Or surely you'll grow double

References

ABC. (2013). Vote Compass project. Retrieved from http://www.abc.net.au/votecompass/

Beckman, S. L., and Barry, M. (2007). Innovation as a learning process: Embedding design thinking. *California Management Review*, 50(1), 24–56.

Hofstede, G. (1980). *Culture's consequences*. Beverly Hills, CA: Sage.

Thacker, E. (2011). Darklife: Negation, nothingness, and the will-to-life in Schopenhauer. *Parrhesia*, 12, 12–27.

Wordsworth, W. (2014). The tables turned: An evening scene on the same subject. (Original work published 1798.) Retrieved from http://www.bartleby.com/145/ww134.html

Index

9/11 events 193
50 Great Myths of Modern Psychology 62

Aboriginal Human Resource
    Council 190
abstract/concrete dyad 106–8, 279
accommodation (Piaget) 85, 88
adaptation (Piaget) 84, 88
Ahriman (spirit of evil) 64
Ahura Mazda (spirit of goodness) 64
analysis/synthesis dyad 27, 66, 100,
    279
Androgyny 39
anopthalma (absent or dysfunctional
    eye) 57
apartheid (South Africa) 170
Apollonius 64
apples/oranges dyad 65, 66
a priori/a posteriori dyad 8, 15, 109, 187
archetype 41, 84, 107, 117, 118
Aristotle: binary logic 97; hierarchical
    dualisms 204; *Three* 130
art/science dyad 25, 176–9
assimilation (Piaget) 85, 88
Aufhebung (contradiction) 106, 132

Bacon, Francis 217
balance concept 108–11
Barad, Karen 12
Basseches, M. 235
Bernoulli principle 268–9
*Beyond Modernity and Tradition: A Third
    Way for Development* 222
bi-lateral symmetries (biology) 56–7,
    61–2

bi-relational development (BirD):
    archetypal regions 118–33;
    conclusions and final reflections
    278–9; definition 4–5; description
    10–12; development 58–9, 71; dyads
    and wicked problems in education
    172–81; dyad types 65; dynamics
    135–7; education 233–47;
    identification 137–8; illustrative dyadic
    relationships 46; individual/group
    developments 73; life narratives
    153–72; metaphors 145–9; multiplicity
    130; narrative explorations 250–74;
    onto-epistemology 58; positive/
    negative dyads 65, 68; summary 9,
    77–8; theoretical background 82–111;
    theory 101, 103–11, 116–44; wicked
    problems, representation of 138–40;
    wicked socio-cultural problems
    184–96; wicked socio-ecological
    problems 198–211; wicked socio-
    religious problems 214–28; *see also*
    dyads (origins and classification)
bi-relational dynamics (conceptual tool):
    BirD and representation of wicked
    problems 138–40; identification 137–8
binaries *see* binary oppositions
binary oppositions: analysis 205;
    colonialism 189; dualism 26; dyadic
    formulations 57–8, 71, 135; gender
    38–9; globalisation's 'inherent tensions'
    191; knowing and being 125; literature
    and literary criticism 40, 42–3; lives
    and society 8; myth 64; nature vs.
    nurture 202; order 110

bindu (*One* or *Zero*) 48
biosymmetry 56, 61–2
black/white dyad 192
Blake, William 41
Bohr, Niels 98
book summary: applications 17; illustrations 16–17; premises 14–15; theory 15–16
brightness illusion 145–6
Buddhism: noble truths 169; non-theistic 42; *see also* nirvana; Zen Buddhism
business 32

Camus, Albert 11, 120
Cartesian See-saw (CSS) 241–3, 245–6
cat/dog dyad 65
Cathedral of Notre Dame, Paris 49
cats and dogs 65–6
CERN 45–6
certainty/uncertainty dyad 186
change/stability dyad 163–5
Christianity: crucifixion 169; Pauline 41–2
chronemics (separation of past and future) 190
Cixious, Helen 38–9, 47
classification description 87–8
climate change 202
cognitive development 82–8, 107, 217
cognitive dissonance concept 87
cognitive operations 83, 87
cognitive-epistemic development 87, 90–2
Coleridge, Samuel Taylor 41
collapse (conflation, equivalence, entanglement) 126–31
collective/individual dyad 193
commitment (epistemological development): anticipation of 88–9; initial 89; multiple 89
complementary and alternative medicine (CAM) 25
connected/detached dyad 222
conservative/liberal dyad 77, 116, 171, 227, 243, 244
constructivism concept 147
continuous/dynamic dyad 107
contradiction 65, 69, 94
counterbalance 47, 60, 62, 179, 203, 208

creation (conception, origin, potentiation) 120–1
crisis and contradiction 94
cross (symbol) 48–9
Cultural Cognition Project 223
cultural dimensions theory 187
culture/structure dyad 186
Culture's Consequences 186
Cusa, Nicholas 7
cybergogy 33
cyclic/linear dyad 204

Dangerous Minds (film) 243
Dawkins, Richard 219–21
de Man, Paul 40, 47
décalage (uneven development) 86
decentration (co-ordination of multiple variables) 88
deconstruction process (binary oppositions) 39–40
design thinking 31, 277
despair/hope dyad 193
dexterity development 134
dialectical problems 234
dialogical speaking 246
Dialogic Imagination 106
dichotomy 28, 45, 106, 123, 160, 253
different logics: dialectical problems 234
differentiation: dialectical problems 234; information 88
Dionysus 64
disequilibrium 87
dissonance 72, 81, 87, 94, 148, 172
domain-general/domain-specific dyads 75–6, 103
domain-specific dyads 243
double helix structure 48
dragon (symbol) 48
Drawing on the Right Side of the Brain 62
Duality in Mathematics and Physics 45
duality (*Two*) 26, 129–30
dyadic reflexivity 266
dyadic relationships development: activities: 244–7; rationale 238–9; resources 239–41
dyadic vocabulary improvement: activities 237–8; rationale 236; resources 236–7

dyads: affinities 77; bi-relational development 5–10, 20–1, 46, 65, 68, 212; origins and classification: 55–65, 70–8; types 65–9

ecocentrism term 202
EfS (Education for Sustainability) 211, 226
egalitarian/hierarchical dyad 185
Egyptian mythology 64
Einstein, Albert 278
Eliade, Mircia 63–4
empirical/phenomenological dyad 100
enantiodromia (tendency to change into opposites) 122, 162, 229
'environmental depression' concept 225
'environmental grief' concept 225
'environmental metaphysic' 225
environmental pollution 199
epistemic cognition 90
epistemological reflective model (ERM) 91
epistemological understanding 91
epistemology concept 147
equilibrium (equilibration, Piaget) 87, 88, 94
Escher, M. C. 11, 108
Everywhere and nowhere: Are binary oppositions real? (video) 241
explanada term 96

faith/doubt dyad 171–2
faith/reason dyad 218–22, 228, 278
feeling/thinking dyad 165–6
fixed/fluid dyad 86
fixed/growth mindset dyad (education) 37
Foundations of Dialectical Psychology 93
Fowler, James 13, 73–4, 80–2
freedom/control dyad 172
French Revolution, 1789 23
Freud, Sigmund 43, 81, 216
future/past dyad 166–7, 181

Garden of Eden 28
Gardner, Howard 261
general/specific dyad 107
Genesis (Bible) 43–4, 47
genetic epistemology 83, 88, 90

Giddens, Anthony 23
Globalisation: Culture and Education in the New Millenium 195
Globalisation and its Discontents 188
God: gender 42; nature 44
God and the New Atheism 215
Godel, Escher, Bach 11
'gogies' (teacher/learner relationships) 32–3
Goldilocks 21
good/evil dyad 76
Gopnik, A 61
Greenberg, David 192–3
Greene, Brian 128
Ground of Being (God) 43, 49
Grozni, Nicolai 11
Gruber, Howard 10
Guha, R. 203

happy/sad dyad 65
Haught, John 219–20, 227
Hegel, G. W. F. 106, 132, 189
Heraclitus 130, 163
Hesse, Hermann 64–5, 129–30
Hofstadter, Douglas 11, 81
Hofstede, Geert 185, 186–7, 192
holism 187
holistic/analytic dyad 186
Holly King (seasons) 64
hope/despair dyad 66, 161–3, 193, 278
hot/cold dyad 66
'human dilemmas' 22
human/non-human dyad 201–2

identity crisis (psychology) 29
'ill-structured problems' 4
Imaginative Literacy Program 234, 238
individual/collective dyad 185, 186
individual/social dyad 26
'industrial ecology' 206
Institute of Art and Ideas (IAI) 244
integration: dialectical problems 234
Integrative Medicine 25
intelligence concept 93
interaction (development) 84
internal/external dyad 222
International Journal of Social Inquiry 185
intrinsic/extrinsic dyad (education) 37

284 Index

Investigative Education Research Group (IERG) 244
Is there a God? 214–16, 216–22, 222–8
isolating/integrating dyad 27
isomorphic dyad 65–9

Jeans, James 227
Jelinski, D. E. 59–61
Jesus 49
Jewish law 28
Jung, C. G. 6, 20, 43, 47, 63, 130, 132

Korean airlines (plane crashes) 192–3

Latour, Bruno 193–4
Lawrence, D. H. 41
Lebenswelt (everyday world) 80
left/right dyad 63, 77, 108, 120, 134
Lewis, C. S. 41
light/dark dyad 154–8
linear/cyclic dyad 86, 103–6
literal/symbolic dyad 173–4
local/global dyad 184–5, 193
long term/short term dyad 186
Lovejoy, A. O. 13, 55–6

Magolda, Baxter 91
mainstream/holistic dyad 25
male/female dyad 38, 43, 135
mandala (symbol) 47
'market fundamentalism' 188
masculine/feminine dyad 42, 77, 146, 186
Mathews, F. 222, 223–4, 227–8
matter/spirit dyad 66, 135, 198, 227, 228, 278
mechanistic/holistic dyad 27
men and women (dyad) 66
mental/physical dyad 223
mercy/justice dyad 180–1
mind/body dyad 167–9
moksha (Hinduism) 44, 132
monoism (*One*) 56, 58
'mono-tango' dance 219
monocultural/multicultural dyad 185
'Mother Nature' 60
multiplicity: early 88; infinity 130–1; late 88
Mysterium Conjunctionis 43
myth/reality dyad 194

Nakata, Martin 190
nature/culture dyad 116, 193, 198, 199–200, 200–1, 204, 227
nature/nurture dyad 35–7, 56, 76, 135
negation (*Zero*) 127–8
neo-atheism 81
neurotheology 216
New Scientist 45
Nietzsche, Friedrich 43, 64, 81, 127, 130, 132, 226
Nihilism Inc: Environmental Destruction and the Metaphysics of Sustainability 211
nirvana (Buddhism) 44
Nothing: From Absolute Zero to Cosmic Oblivion... 45
number theory (*collapse*) 126

Oak King (seasons) 64
Oh the Places that You'll Go 237
onto-epistemological development: binary oppositions 42; BirD 58; knowing and being 12–13; knowledge 76, 201; *to* or *from* religion?: beyond faith? 216–17; beyond reason? 217–18; bi-relational approach to socio-religious dyads 218–22
opposition/paradox dyad 58
order/chaos dyad 76, 110
organic/mechanistic dyad 204
orthogonal dyad 65–9
ouroboros (symbol) 48

paradigm concept 147
'parent dyads' 77
particular/general dyad 100
peace/conflict dyad 194
Pearson, Noel 35, 47
'pedagogies of hope' 225
pedagogy 33–5
pentagram (*Baphomet*) symbol 49
permissive/authoritarian dyad (education) 37
Perry, William 88–9, 90–2
phenomenology 62, 91
Piaget, Jean 72–5, 81, 82–8, 90, 93–4, 97, 122
Plato 132
'playful reversals' 42

pleasure/pain dyad 66, 169–70
polarisation (gay marriage) 135
population pressure 199
positive, negative and neutral dyads 65, 68
postformal development 83, 132
Prickles and Goo (video) 243
privacy/publicity dyad 27
pro-dyadic region (emergence, differentiation, formation, accommodation) 121–3
pro-dyadic region (intersection, opposition, dichotomy) 123–5
psychological/sociological dyad 26
public/private dyad 184, 204

quality/quantity dyad 67
quantitative/qualitative dyad 22, 26, 209, 277

rabbit and duck illusion 147–8
radicalisation (religious violence) 135
realist/relatavist dyad 92
reality/representation dyad 171
reductive/holistic dyad 100
reflection/experience dyad 279
reflective judgement model (RJM) 90–1
Reich, K. H. 13, 73–5, 80–1, 96–100, 234
'reintegration' concept 206
relational and contextual reasoning (RCR) 74, 96–9, 234
relational knowing 88
relative/absolute dyad 65, 76, 184
Religion Explained: The Evolutionary Origins of Religious Thought 217
resolve (epistemological development) 89
riddle-solving 7
Riegel and Basseches' dialectical thinking: Riegel's dialectical psychology 93–5; Riegel's dialectical thinking 95–6
Rod of Asclepius 48
Ross-Holst, C. 184, 195

sacred/profane dyad 42
sadness/happiness dyad 158–61

St Andrew's cross 48
St Peter's cross 48
saltire (x-shaped) 48
Satanism 49
satori (Zen Buddhism) 44
Schopenhauer 111, 127–8, 211
science concept 209–10
science/religion dyad 65, 66, 68
self/other dyad 76, 170–1, 186
separate/connected dyad 180
sequential/discontinuous dyad 86
Seuss, Dr 41, 237
Shakespeare, William 41
Singer, J. 39, 42, 47
single/multiple dyad 107
sociocognitive conflict 72
species extinction 199
spiritual/material dyad 222
Sri Yanta (symbol) 47
stability/flux dyad 94
stage: development 235; knowledge organisation 85
Stages of Faith: The Psychology of Human Development... 73
Stages of Thought: The Coevolution of Religious Thought and Science 75
Steppenwolf 64
Stewart, Ian 45
Stiglitz, J. 188
strabismus (eye co-ordination) 57
strict dualism 88
strong dyad 65–9
structure ('systemic properties of an event') 85
Studies of Polarity 106
subjective/objective dyad 66, 105, 109, 111, 116, 135, 186, 193–4, 223
sublation (mutually beneficial transformation) 189
sustainability: education for socio-ecology 207–11; environmental conservation 135; *see also* World Commission on Environment and Sustainability
symmetrical/asymmetrical dyads 108–11
synthesis (*Three*) 130
Systematic Theology 43

286 Index

Tackling Wicked Problems through the Transdisciplinary Imagination 4
Tao Te Ching 47
teaching/learning dyad 173–5
technocentrism term 202
technology/ecology dyad 227
Thacker, E. 279
The Authoritarian Biologist and the Arrogance of Anti-Humanism 203
The Blind Men and the Elephant (poem) 243
The First Three Minutes 226
The Great Divorce 41
The Marriage of Heaven and Hell 41
The Myth of Sisyphus 11
The New Yorker 61
The Opposite 237
The Paradoxes of Legal Science 28
The Political Psychology of Faith Development Theory 107
The Psychology of Religion: An Empirical Approach 74
The Revolt against Dualism 13, 55
theory/practice dyad 179–80, 279
tight/loose cultures dyad 186
Tillich, Paul 42–3, 49, 82, 221
time: dyads 191; trans-positional development 132–3
traditional/alternative dyad 25
traditional/progressive dyad 185
trans-positions: dyads expansion 200; knowing and being 191–2; re-entry, re-commitment, re-iteration 131–3; time 132–3
'transcendence' concept 206
triads (transitional dyads) 65, 68–9
trialism (*Three*) 56
Turtle Feet 11
Tzu, Lao 7, 82

unity (*One*) 128–9
unity/diversity dyad 184, 186, 193–4
up/down dyad 120

Venn diagrams 243–4, 244–5
village/cosmos dyad 186, 194
Vote Compass project 243

wave/particle dyad 21, 46, 48, 98
weak dyad 66, 69
Weinberg, S. 226
Western/indigenous dyad 186
'Which Way is Up'? 10
'wicked problem' 4
wicked problems and the recognition of opposites: bi-relational development 10–12; book summary 14–17; caveats 13–14; dyads and dyadic relationships 5–10; illustrative dyadic relationships 20–1, 46–50; illustrative dyads and dyadic relationships 22–44; introduction 1–5; onto–epistemological development 12–13
winged serpent (symbol) 48
Word Study Fun: Like and Opposite Meanings 237
Wordsworth, William 279
'work/life' balance 110
World Bank 188
World Commission on Environment and Sustainability (Brundtland Report, 1987) 207

yin–yang symbol (Chinese) 47

Zen Buddhism 11, 42, 44, 132
Zoroastrianism 64